Imbalance of Powers

IMBALANCE OF POWERS

Constitutional Interpretation and the Making of American Foreign Policy

GORDON SILVERSTEIN

New York Oxford
OXFORD UNIVERSITY PRESS
1997

Oxford University Press

Oxford New York
Athens Auckland Bangkok Bogotá Bombay
Buenos Aires Calcutta Cape Town Dar es Salaam
Delhi Florence Hong Kong Istanbul Karachi
Kuala Lumpur Madras Madrid Melbourne
Mexico City Nairobi Paris Singapore
Taipei Tokyo Toronto

and associated companies in
Berlin Ibadan

Published by Oxford University Press, Inc.
198 Madison Avenue, New York, New York 10016

Library of Congress Cataloging-in-Publication Data

Silverstein, Gordon
Imbalance of powers :
constitutional interpretation and the making of American foreign policy /
Gordon Silverstein.
p. cm. Includes bibliographical references and index.
ISBN 0-19-510476-5—ISBN 0-19-510477-3 (pbk.)
1. United States—Foreign relations—Law and legislation.
2. United States—Constitutional law—Interpretation and construction.
3. Executive power—United States.
4. United States. Congress—Powers and duties.
5. Separation of powers—United States.
I. Title.
KF4651.S72 1996 342.73′0412—dc20 [347.302412] 95-46428

1 3 5 7 9 8 6 4 2
Printed in the United States of America
on acid-free paper

For

Judith N. Shklar
scholar, teacher, mentor, friend

and for

Marilyn Cooper Silverstein and Josef Silverstein
the most important teachers in my life

Contents

Acknowledgments

The path to this book has been a story of continuing education, and it is a testimonial to all those from whom I have learned—family, teachers, students, friends and colleagues.

My interest in American political culture and constitutional interpretation goes back to a young age when I lived with my family in Southeast Asia: Living in Malaysia and Singapore during the Vietnam war gave me a different perspective on America and American politics. The more I learned about other countries and about the way the United States was perceived abroad, the more I wanted to know about American political culture. As an undergraduate at Cornell University, I tackled some of my questions in the classroom and the libraries, and some of them beyond the campus, as editor in chief of the *Cornell Daily Sun*. After graduation I spent three years as a journalist with the *Wall Street Journal* in New York and Hong Kong, and with the *San Francisco Chronicle*. On my lunch hour one day in New York I was browsing in a bookstore and stumbled on Samuel P. Huntington's *American Politics: The Promise of Disharmony*, which rekindled the deeper questions that had been gnawing at me since those years in Southeast Asia. I felt Huntington had exposed the soul of American political culture, though I found myself disagreeing strongly with his prescriptions. I decided to go back to school to study American politics, and particularly the role of law in the shaping of American political culture.

As a graduate student at Harvard University, I learned a great deal from a number of extraordinarily dedicated scholar/teachers who belied the myth of a faculty unconcerned about its teaching. It gives me the greatest pleasure to acknowledge the intellectual stimulation that Judith Shklar selflessly offered for a number of years. First as her teaching fellow, and later as her advisee, I was treated to a frequent seminar in the joys and value of teaching and scholarship. My work cuts across a number of academic lines, but Judith Shklar was eager to embrace it and work with me as I pulled together an often unwieldy package. Her encouragement was a beacon and the ultimate reward. Her premature death less than a year after chairing my dissertation defense was a devastating blow both to me and to the legions of graduate students for whom she served as a role model, mentor, and friend. That no future students will be able to repeat my experience as her student is a truly great loss, but I can only hope that those of us who have been blessed by the chance to learn with and from Judith Shklar will try to repay their debt by carrying on her mission, her dedication, her commitment, and her fearless pursuit of knowledge.

I owe a great debt as well to the other members of my dissertation committee—Samuel Huntington, Richard Neustadt, and H. W. Perry. It was Huntington's book on American politics that helped convince me to go to graduate school, and though he may well disagree with my conclusions, he was a model advisor who challenged me to back up my claims and question my preconceptions, all the while offering an open mind and an example of genuine intellectual curiosity. I was extraordinarily lucky in having Richard Neustadt as a third member of my committee and his insights on American politics and the American presidency were always sharp and thought provoking. His comments and questions were invaluable, as was his own scholarly writing. The final member of my committee, H. W. Perry, was a devoted advisor and role-model who contributed to my education in a host of different ways, not least by proving that good scholarship is the product of good teaching—that teaching is a wonderful way to test new ideas, and to maintain an active, vibrant, and relevant research agenda.

Beyond my committee, I was fortunate to have had extensive opportunities to learn from James Q. Wilson, whose intellectual integrity and commitment to excellence continue to be a source of inspiration. I am indebted as well to Paul Peterson, Stanley Hoffmann, Harvey C. Mansfield Jr., Joseph Nye, Mark Peterson, Morris Fiorina, Paul Pierson, and Harry Hirsch for their insights, inspiration and examples. It is also true, as Richard Rosecrance told me many years ago, that graduate students learn as much from each other as they do from the faculty, and my fellow graduate students both within the Department of Government and elsewhere made the tough months tolerable, and the fun months more so. Matt Dickinson, Deborah Spar, Sara Monoson, Charlie Johnson, and Yves and Cecile Balkanski, were there from the start, making a difference in classes and beyond.

Some of the chapters in this book started out as part of my dissertation, but the project has evolved far beyond the original vision. I am indebted to many people for their help in moving me past that first effort. I am particularly grateful to Paul Peterson, who showed confidence in me, providing an opportunity to turn some of these ideas into published work. I am also indebted to Loch Johnson and James Lindsay, two reviewers for Oxford University Press whose careful, detailed and very thorough reviews of the book have no doubt made it a stronger effort then it ever could have been without them. I am indebted as well to Louis Fisher, whose comments and suggestions over the years have always been welcome, and whose advice has been particularly welcome on this project. The errors that remain are mine alone.

I would like to thank the members of the Government Department at Dartmouth College who have provided a warm and collegial intellectual environment in which to research, write and teach. The completion of this manuscript was greatly facilitated by the generous support of the Walter Burke Research Initiation Award at Dartmouth, and by Peter Sisitsky, who served as a Research Assistant under the auspices of the Dartmouth Presidential Scholars' Program. My thanks as well to Lee Bollinger, David Lindgren, and Michael Grunwald.

I am indebted as well to Benjamin F. Bailar and Duane Windsor for giving me the opportunity to teach at Rice University, a marvelous institution where I served as Assistant Professor of Administrative Science and of Political Science in the Jesse H. Jones School of Administration. Among my colleagues and friends at Rice, I am particularly indebted to Doug and Kala Schuler, Eric Heineman, Graeme Rankine, Rick Wilson, Bill Ciminelli, Suzana Ramos, David Kilgore, Bill Leeman, and Connie Burke.

The heart and soul of each institution with which I have been affiliated is and always will be the undergraduates. As students and friends many of them have contributed indirectly to this book. Teaching has provided me with insights into my work and my self, and I am indebted to more students than I can name. Beyond the classroom, Harvard and Rice both have residential college systems for their undergraduates, and I was fortunate to be asked by Woody and Hanna Hastings to serve as a Resident Tutor for North House at Harvard and by the students of Lovett College to serve as a Resident Associate at Rice. At each I was warmly welcomed into the heart of the university and into the lives of a number of undergraduates. The students at North House and at Lovett College made my time there a real pleasure, and a few made a very special difference and I will always value their friendship.

I also have had the good fortune to receive unique support from friends in my former profession. The continued employment offered to me by the *San Francisco Chronicle* made my graduate training possible and provided a welcome respite from campus for a number of summers. I am particularly indebted to the *Chronicle*'s Executive Business Editor, Peter Sinton, and above all to the Assistant Managing Editor, Jack Briebart, for their friendship and support.

My greatest debt, however, is to the most significant teachers in my life, Marilyn Cooper Silverstein and Josef Silverstein, who along with my brother Frank have stood by me, supported me, and expanded my horizons. To them I owe my deepest thanks.

I

Introduction

Introduction

Responding to the growing power of a perceived "Imperial Presidency"[1] at the end of the Vietnam War and in the aftermath of Watergate, a majority in Congress tried to follow the constitutional blueprint to rebalance the separation of powers by passing a number of laws that were designed to assert legislative authority in foreign policy. These laws, covering war and emergency powers, trade and foreign aid, weapons sales, arms control, and intelligence issues, were hailed by some as proof that the system worked, and denounced by others as proof that the separation of powers no longer was suitable for a modern superpower. For better or worse, the reforms were designed with the *stated* goal of increasing congressional power in foreign policy. Looking back at this wide-ranging effort, critics and advocates of the reforms all would agree that with few exceptions these measures failed to achieve their *stated* goals. Rather than realigning the balance of power, tipping the scales back toward congressional control, these measures actually seem to have aggravated the problems they ostensibly were designed to solve. Why?

These efforts failed to achieve their stated objectives because 1) they were built on a misconceived new constitutional interpretation of the separation of powers in foreign affairs that evolved after the Second World War; 2) they sought to solve a political and constitutional problem with a statutory, legalistic approach that ultimately backfired; and 3) because legislators and presidents each pursued strategies that undermined their own political and policy objectives.

If the only cost of this failure were the continued dominance of foreign policy by the executive branch, it would be of little interest. But the cost is far higher. The emergence of a new constitutional interpretation in foreign policy has damaged the executive branch as well as Congress; it has profoundly damaged American foreign policy; and it has come home, altering the balance of power in American domestic policy as well as the constitutional interpretation that governs that policy.

A close study of the Supreme Court's role in the constitutional interpretation of foreign policy cases makes this final effect particularly clear. Because the Constitution is a unitary document that makes no provision for treating the powers of government differently in foreign and domestic affairs, a shift in constitutional interpretation in foreign policy ultimately serves as a precedent for creating a pattern for a similar shift in constitutional interpretation in domestic affairs. The shift of power from one branch to the other in the foreign arena provides a precedent for a similar shift of power in the domestic arena. This approach differs from that of the handful of studies that have examined judicial doctrine in American foreign policy.[2] Though excellent works, all were written by legal scholars and each of these has focused on law, emphasizing legal and statutory solutions to what were seen as legal and statutory problems. This book takes a different approach, arguing that a full understanding of the role constitutional interpretation plays in American foreign policy requires an understanding of the complex political and structural relationship of all three branches, and tries to demonstrate that the legal and statutory problems can only be understood, and corrected, within that broader context.

An executive prerogative interpretation in foreign policy is entrenched in constitutional interpretation and has been reinforced by failed statutes aimed at reasserting congressional influence. The executive prerogative interpretation may well have a destructive impact on the institutions of government and on America's foreign and domestic policy. But these events happened for many pragmatic reasons: the emergence of nuclear weapons and the belief that these weapons had to be controlled by a single authority able to make immediate decisions; the increasing dependence of the U.S. economy on world trade; and the long history of the Cold War. And they came about because many presidents and legislators focused on short-term policy objectives, ignoring the long-term impact their tradeoffs would have.

Some saw the emergence of an energized Republican majority in both houses of the 104th Congress in 1995 as an extraordinary opportunity for the reassertion of congressional prerogatives at home and abroad. But among the very first proposals this new majority offered were constitutional amendments to delegate line-item veto power to the President and to force a balanced budget, limiting legislative discretion. And, on 5 January 1995—the very first day of the 104th Congress—Senate Majority Leader Robert Dole proposed the formal repeal of the War Powers Resolution of 1973, replacing it with what he called the Peace Powers Act of 1995, a bill that would "untie the President's hands in using American forces to defend American interests," but which would, at the same time, restrict "the use of American forces and funds in United Nations peacekeeping."[3] Meanwhile, in the House of Representatives, Illinois Republican Henry Hyde's proposed amendment to repeal the War Powers Resolution[4] led Newt Gingrich, the new Republican Speaker of the House, to take the floor and offer an impassioned plea for repeal. Speaker Gingrich noted that he was rising "for what some Members might find an unusual moment, an appeal to the House to, at least on paper, increase the power of President Clinton."[5]

In the end, Hyde's amendment failed in the House, but it was a close vote (201-217). Nevertheless, the 1995 debate about the repeal of the War Powers Resolution found two of the most powerful members of the legislative branch—the Speaker of the House and the Majority Leader of the United States Senate—arguing forcefully to increase the power of the president.

Six months later the Senate voted to end the United States' participation in the international arms embargo on Bosnia—and the House overwhelmingly agreed to the same language a few days later. Though a direct rebuff to President Clinton, who lobbied hard to defeat the measure, the final language that emerged included two provisions that would undermine the legislators' stated objectives—the final measure provided Clinton with a 12-week grace period after the withdrawal of United Nations' troops before the embargo would be lifted, making it less likely that the Bosnians would request that withdrawal, since it might leave them exposed and under-armed for three months. More importantly, the legislators built in a provision that would allow the president to trigger an unlimited number of 30-day extensions of the embargo if he certified that those extensions were needed to assure the safe withdrawal of U.N. troops.[6]

On 13 December 1995, with American troops on the ground in Bosnia, and thousands more preparing to head into the Bosnian war zone, legislators took to the floor of both houses of Congress to condemn President Clinton's decision to send troops. Only a few were willing to challenge the president's right to do so. In the end the Senate rejected a bid to cut off funds for the deployment by a 22–77 margin. In the House, the vote was far closer (210–218). But once that resolution failed, the Senate passed a resolution supporting the troops and a limited mission in Bosnia. The House, on the other hand, passed a resolution that explicitly separated the troops from their commander, pledging to support the soldiers, but explicitly withholding any support for Clinton's policy and the mission itself.

The votes sent mixed messages, but among the messages sent, according to Georgia Democrat Sam Nunn, was a clear signal that President Clinton "will be viewed by most in Congress as assuming the full responsibility for the fate of the United States military mission in Bosnia."[7] Republican Senator William Cohen argued that long before the December vote the die was cast and legislators had once again evaded their responsibilities. "The fact is," Cohen told the Senate, "Congress has yielded its powers to the Executive over the years." Reviewing the recent history of congressional action concerning the use of military force, Cohen concluded that "Congress has chosen not to claim the power of deciding when to deploy American forces. . . . [W]e are where we are because we were not willing to risk the consequences of action. We have deferred, we have debated, we have waited, we have talked, and we have let the president take us to where we are today."[8]

Is it possible to alter this trend, and what advantages would such a change offer for Congress, for the president and for the nation?

A new pattern in foreign policy is possible, one that is flexible enough to respond to growing international interdependence and the need for quick and decisive action. This new relationship between the branches would require a different approach to constitutional interpretation than the one that has shaped American foreign policy since World War II. In essence this is a call to return to a political, institutional solution and away from the legalistic, statutory solutions that were popular in the 1970s and 1980s.[9] This book will show that a change needs to be made, that it can be made, and that failing to do so will have consequences far beyond a simple academic interest in a nicely balanced Newtonian system of government—consequences for American constitutional interpretation, American foreign and domestic policy, and the continued vitality of American political institutions.

The Courts, Constitutional Interpretation, and Foreign Policy

The Constitution and constitutional arguments are frequently used weapons in political contests, called upon to secure support and in efforts to block policy choices. Constitutional interpretation is not a function of the judiciary alone—all three branches interpret the Constitution, and that interpretation is woven into every piece of legislation. To understand why American foreign policy looks the way it does requires an understanding of how constitutional interpretation, in all three branches of government, shapes and constrains the policy process. If we want to understand American foreign policy we must understand how each branch interprets the Constitution and uses that interpretation to gain and secure power.

Before attempting to explain why the leaders of the first Republican-controlled Congress in forty years would move quickly to delegate constitutional power to the Executive and to "untie the president's hands" in the use of American military force and before trying to understand how legislation designed to shift power to the legislative branch in the 1970s and 1980s wound up building power in the executive branch, it is necessary to understand the evolution of constitutional interpretation in foreign policy. While the courts have had the least visible role in foreign policy, judicial decisions (particularly those of the Supreme Court) have shaped the way those in the other branches of the government understand the Constitution, and have shaped the national debate over constitutional interpretation in every area, including foreign policy. These judicial interventions include well-publicized decisions such as the Court's 1952 decision that forced President Truman to reverse his order nationalizing the steel mills during the Korean War, but there have been many others, each building on the other, and together building an ever more solid foundation for the claim that in foreign policy the president is allotted extraordinary discretion and even prerogative authority.

Congress and the executive engage in the foreign policy debate, and use constitutional interpretation to gain and block power and affect particular policies. With their evolved authority as arbiters of the battle between the branches, the decisions the Supreme Court Justices hand down set important precedents for future legal cases as well as constraining policy options and shaping future executive–legislative disputes. A close examination of the evolution of the judicial doctrine reveals it to be surprisingly consistent and coherent.

We often forget that in the United States there are two types of separation of powers: A *vertical* separation of powers (state vs. national powers) as well as the now more familiar *horizontal* separation of powers (executive-legislative-judicial). Prior to World War II, the *vertical* separation of powers dominated the Court's docket. Concern for national power in general (the power of the executive and legislative branches, acting together), not the division of that power *within* the national government, was the focus of the Court's doctrine in domestic and foreign policy cases alike.

Chief Justice John Marshall saw no constitutional distinction between foreign and domestic policy. If Congress had the power to enact laws that were necessary and proper to carry out its enumerated powers, then it had that power whether or not the subject was foreign policy. If Marshall was right, however, and if the Constitution was to be read the same at home and abroad, then expansive national power in foreign policy would mean expansive national power in domestic policy, threatening state autonomy.

Alarmed by this interpretation, a number of justices in those early years struggled to develop a doctrine that would allow the Constitution to be read differently in foreign and domestic policy. As Chapter 1 concludes, the oft-cited touchstone case in foreign policy, *United States v. Curtiss-Wright Export Corp.* (1936), is powerfully misunderstood. *Curtiss-Wright*, so often cited as the Court's definitive statement about executive prerogative in foreign policy, is nothing of the kind. Instead it is part of a long series of cases where the Court struggled, and failed, to find a doctrine that would legitimate a strong national government in foreign policy while maintaining a weak, decentralized government in domestic affairs. This doctrinal struggle, which failed in each of its incarnations, must be understood if we are to understand the Court's traditional interpretation of the Constitution in foreign affairs, and if we are to understand the way in which the Court signaled the political branches about how the Constitution was to be interpreted in foreign policy in the 1970s and 1980s when many legislators sought to reassert congressional authority.

Congress, the Executive, and the Traditional Interpretation

Despite the regular pendulum swings in power between Congress and the executive branch and despite the occasional intervention of the Supreme Court, certain fundamental assumptions about the Constitution and foreign policy developed early and were steadily maintained by all three branches, at least until the First World War. All three branches shared the traditional interpretation that the specific restrictions in the Constitution were inviolable: Congress had a legitimate role to play should it choose to assert that role in any and all areas including foreign policy; and though foreign policy might be treated more loosely, it nonetheless was governed by the same Constitution as was domestic policy.

On those occasions when the president felt necessity dictated policy that was constitutionally suspect, there was no attempt to avoid the problem by reinterpreting the Constitution. Jefferson, for example, reluctantly agreed to abide by congressional wishes and forgo a constitutional amendment he thought necessary to legitimate the Louisiana Purchase, writing that he hoped he wasn't setting a bad precedent.[10] Lincoln delayed the recall of Congress and exercised extensive emergency powers, some of which clearly exceeded the president's constitutional mandate. But when Lincoln went to Congress in July of 1861 it was not to argue that his actions were above or beyond the Constitution, but rather to seek *post-hoc* approval or rejection from legislators in Congress, acknowledging that it was their constitutional prerogative to do so. "In full view of his great responsibility," Lincoln told Congress, the chief executive "has, so far, done what he has deemed his duty. You will now, according to your own judgment, perform yours."[11]

Even Theodore Roosevelt, who insisted that the president "was a steward of the people bound actively and affirmatively to do all he could for the people, and not to content himself with the negative merit of keeping his talents undamaged in a napkin," acknowledged that the executive power was limited "by specific restrictions and prohibitions appearing in the Constitution or imposed by the Congress under its Constitutional powers."[12] Though presidents such as Adams, Jefferson, Jackson, Polk, Lincoln, and Theodore Roosevelt all pressed Executive power to its constitutional limits and sometimes beyond, they did not seek to legitimate that action by offering an alternative interpretation of the Constitution. The second chapter will outline what might be called the Executive branch's traditional interpretation of the Constitution in foreign policy, and demonstrate that even the most activist presidents before the Second World War subscribed to at least the rudimentary precepts of that interpretation.

A New Interpretation: Executive Prerogative in Foreign Policy

The development of nuclear weapons at the end of the Second World War and the prolonged Cold War in which the United States led an international coalition of countries in a bipolar struggle combined to give the executive ever greater authority for two reasons: Nuclear weapons meant that there might be no time for deliberation, and ultimate responsibility for these weapons had to rest on one person; and the prolonged Cold War allowed the executive to accrue extraordinary power by arguing that the United States was engaged in a national emergency, even though that emergency—and the legislation that supported it—lasted more than forty years.

These developments contributed to the emergence of a new interpretation of the Constitution regarding foreign affairs. This executive prerogative interpretation held that in foreign affairs the president alone had final authority, and when the national security was imperiled (a judgment left to the executive) the president was legitimately entitled to override constitutional constraints to preserve and protect that security.

Arthur M. Schlesinger Jr.'s *The Imperial Presidency*[13] chronicled the evolution of prerogative claims in the executive branch. Moving beyond Schlesinger, this book argues that the executive prerogative interpretation is the product of all three branches of government—the judicial no less than the executive branch. Schlesinger's work called for the assertion of legislative power. But when that assertion came in the 1970s and 1980s, not only did it fail to achieve its stated objectives, but in fact it made the imbalance of powers even worse. This result cannot be understood without a careful consideration of the interrelationship of constitutional interpretation in all three branches and a careful examination of the incentives that drive individuals in all three branches.

Chapter 3 will detail the development of the executive prerogative interpretation as well as the Congressional role in accepting, supporting, and even encouraging this development, arguing that the executive prerogative interpretation grew in two streams—a rhetorical stream starting with Truman, and a statutory stream initiated by President Eisenhower. Though in the end Truman was willing to be constrained by the bounds of the traditional interpretation, he argued forcefully for a new interpretation of executive power in foreign policy, whether it was in defense of his order to seize American steel mills during the Korean War, or his conviction that the existence of the Cold War and nuclear weapons mandated extensive centralization of power in the White House. As Truman put it in his final state of the union address in 1953, the president "also has to lead the whole free world in overcoming the communist menace—and all this under the shadow of the atomic bomb." Eisenhower laid the statutory foundation for the executive prerogative interpretation, going to Congress for open-ended delegations of foreign policy power. These delegations in the Middle East and Taiwan (then called Formosa), designed to provide the President with negotiating strength, were formal delegations of power. Chapter 3 concludes with a look at the convergence of these rhetorical and statutory streams during the Kennedy administration, when the Bay of Pigs invasion and the Cuban Missile Crisis demonstrated to Kennedy the need to move more and more foreign policy authority into the White House. His efforts to do so were not opposed in Congress and, in fact, were lent powerful legitimacy by congressional passage of a broad statement of support for executive authority just before the Missile Crisis. By this point, firm precedents had accumulated: The executive branch had articulated and defended an executive prerogative interpretation, which had been incorporated into statutes passed by Congress. Any future Court battles between the branches over foreign policy would be influenced and constrained by these precedents.

Chapter 4 turns to the blossoming of the prerogative interpretation under Presidents Johnson and Nixon. Johnson continued to expand both streams, using the statutory stream to legitimate his claim to executive prerogative through congressional delegations such as the Gulf of Tonkin Resolution; and the rhetorical track established by Truman and Kennedy to argue that congressional authorization was merely supplementary and incidental, since the executive possessed prerogative powers in foreign affairs and could act autonomously.

Under President Nixon, the prerogative interpretation rose to new heights, both in its articulation and its execution. If, Nixon argued, the president is constitutionally able to act with few constitutional constraints in foreign affairs, it is because this is necessary to assure national security. If, therefore, a threat to national security happens to arise at home, the President has the constitutional right, if not obligation, to act with similar broad discretion at home as he has abroad, since the objective is one that concerns foreign affairs.

Nixon's use of the prerogative interpretation demonstrated—just as Chief Justice John Marshall had argued so long before—that one could not isolate foreign policy (and foreign policy powers) from domestic affairs. The argument, however, had come full circle. Whereas once the need to limit the government at home constrained the president's ability to act in foreign affairs, now, the president's need to act freely abroad was said to justify similar prerogative powers at home.

The executive prerogative interpretation was now fairly clear: In foreign affairs the president alone had final authority, and when the national security was imperiled (a judgment left to the executive) the president was legitimately entitled to override constitutional constraints to preserve and protect that security.

Lending Legitimacy to the Executive Prerogative Interpretation: Prerogative Power in Court

If *Curtiss-Wright* definitively resolved anything, it was that the *national government*—the president *and* Congress, acting together—faced few constitutional constraints in foreign policy. What remained an open question was what the courts would do when the branches of government clashed—when the president took action that contradicted the will of Congress, or when the president acted in an area of uncharted waters, where legislators had not made their will clear.

Chapter 5 examines the Court's doctrine in foreign policy cases from *United States v. Curtiss-Wright* (1936) through the Pentagon papers case of 1971. Conventional wisdom holds that *Curtiss* and *Youngstown Sheet and Tube Co. v. Sawyer* (the steel seizure case) in 1952 represent the polar extremes of the Court's doctrine in foreign policy. But this interpretation is based on a fundamental misreading of *Curtiss-Wright.* The Court's doctrine was consistent in both of these cases. It wasn't until much later, in the Pentagon papers case and other cases in the 1970s, 1980s and 1990s, that the Court's doctrine shifted, and a second paradigm began to emerge.

Reading *Curtiss-Wright* and the steel case as opposites has led to flawed prescriptions and misunderstood signals from the Court to the elected branches of government. By extending the analysis from the 1950s into the mid-1990s, Chapter 5 will demonstrate that a very different interpretation better explains the evidence and leads to a very different set of prescriptions for all three branches.

Though we tend to see the Pentagon papers case as a powerful statement against the executive and in favor of a free press,[14] a careful reading shows that it actually is a powerful signal from the Court that it would tolerate significant delegations of power from Congress to the executive in foreign affairs. The justices ruled against the executive branch because Congress explicitly denied it the precise powers the president claimed to have by prerogative. However, even some of the Court's staunchest civil libertarians went out of their way to note that absent a clear and explicit statement from Congress denying these powers to the executive, the Court might well have been sympathetic to the prerogative claims advanced by the Nixon administration.

What happened between the steel seizure case and the Pentagon papers case? In the steel case, Justice Jackson developed a template of three categories to evaluate any executive claims to power in foreign affairs: cases where the president acts in concert with Congress (and executive power is at its zenith); cases where the president "takes measures incompatible with the expressed or implied will of Congress" (where presidential claims are constitutionally weakest); and cases that fall in what Jackson termed a "zone of twilight" where the president and Congress may be said to have concurrent powers.[15]

Chapter 5 argues that the Court continued to apply its steel seizure template, but began to soften the barriers between the categories, gradually accepting the notion that the executive branch would be given the benefit of the doubt. By 1980, Justice Rehnquist made clear what had been happening. Though the concepts behind the steel case's categories remained valid, Rehnquist argued, the clear divisions between them were not. Rehnquist wrote that in foreign affairs most executive action falls "not neatly in one of three pigeonholes, but rather at some point along a spectrum running from explicit congressional authorization to explicit congressional prohibition."[16]

In the steel case, the Court had made clear the importance of congressional signals and congressional delegation. What changed was the degree to which the Court would insist on explicit congressional limits on executive powers. These murky boundaries allowed the Court to support delegations of power, but demand ever more specific restraints on the exercise of that power: It was easier for the executive to exercise power and ever more difficult for Congress to restrain that exercise. This development, combined with the pragmatic needs of the time and Congress' political incentives to give the president discretion in foreign policy, lent legitimacy to the emerging executive claim to prerogative powers in foreign policy.

The Legislative Response: Legal Solutions to Political Problems

The institutional structure of the Constitution is a delicate balancing of mechanical wheels and gears all predicated on a particular understanding of human nature. As James Madison noted in his *Federalist* 51, this was a government that would use its own fatal flaws to guarantee its survival. Institutions were built to compete with each other: "By so contriving the interior structure of the government as that its several constituent parts may, by their mutual relations, be the means of keeping each other in their proper place," the founders built a system where competition and constraint were assured.[17]

If Madison was right, it would seem that an assertive Congress could and would rise up, challenge the president, and defeat the emergence of a novel constitutional interpretation that could erode the separation of powers and remove a critical component of the system of checks and balances that applies to foreign and domestic policy alike.

Indeed, members of Congress did rise to assert their authority and reclaim their institution's place in the foreign policy process in a series of extraordinary pieces of legislation passed in the 1970s and 1980s. The first of these, the War Powers Resolution of 1973, served as the model for many other attempts at congressional reassertion in the 1970s and 1980s. Because the War Powers Resolution was the model for these reforms, the flaws built into that resolution appeared over and over again in the others. Chapter 6 examines the process and ideas that produced this flawed effort which is important if we are to understand why the other bills not only failed to achieve their stated objectives, but actually made the imbalance of powers worse. In intelligence oversight and emergency powers as well as in defense spending, arms control, foreign assistance and foreign trade, the War Powers model was extended and expanded with different results that will be explored in Chapter 7.

A close examination of these measures reveals a common pattern: In each case, the initial proposal was a strong one, defining powers clearly and constraining executive prerogative. But Congress is not a unitary body, and each house is a collection of a large number of individuals, each with different political agendas and different beliefs about the Constitution and its proper interpretation in foreign policy. While there was a surge of support for reform legislation that would constrain the executive in foreign affairs right before and after Watergate, that legislative momentum was not enough to force narrow, constraining laws through Congress. Not only was it difficult to achieve a majority in each house, but it was even harder to secure the two-thirds majority in each house that would be needed if the executive vetoed these bills. As with any piece of controversial legislation, a compromise was sought and reached, but in almost every one of these cases, the compromise ended up adopting broader language, or moving the constraining language from the law itself into a non-binding preamble or statement of purpose. The legislation left large loopholes, or adopted the executive's language to secure passage. While Congress as a whole had not endorsed the executive prerogative interpretation, enough members had, and they forced these legislative compromises through.

If this were the full story, one would be tempted simply to classify these laws as less effective than their sponsors had hoped. But these laws often did more than merely fail to achieve their ends—often they resulted in more power for the executive and in greater legitimacy for the executive prerogative interpretation of the Constitution.

To strike a balance between constraint and efficiency, the legislation often formally delegated power to the president, but Congress tried to counterbalance that formal delegation with a congressional ability to recall or repeal the executive's decision through legislative vetoes.

Legislative vetoes have always operated under a constitutional cloud, and in the early 1980s, the Supreme Court ruled that the legislative veto in an immigration case was unconstitutional.[18] Without the legislative veto, the statutes that sought to balance delegation of power with congressional oversight wound up delegating broad, formal powers to the president, while the oversight mechanism was dropped. Thus, the laws designed to redress the perceived imbalance of power favoring the president became laws that in fact exacerbated that imbalance.

It is a mistake to try and treat foreign policy as a single entity—different policy areas generate different levels of interest within Congress and the public at large. Similarly, legislative tools are more appropriate and useful in some areas than they are in others. Although Congress retains the means to control foreign policy through the appropriations process, the degree of influence Congress exercises varies widely across these different areas.[19] In some areas legislators traded statutory control for significant influence over day-to-day policy outcomes. But there is a critical distinction to be made here—*influence* over a particular policy outcome is not the same as control. That distinction is even more pronounced when the potential for judicial review by the courts is considered. In terms of influencing day-to-day policy decisions in some areas of foreign affairs, alternative or indirect means of influence such as procedural requirements, public pressure, and the influence of anticipated reactions[20] or consultation, hearings, oversight and floor statements, among others[21] can have important policy results. But these methods carry little weight if and when a foreign policy dispute winds up in court. In court, statutes matter, and if statutes delegate discretion to the executive, or if they simply fail to circumscribe executive discretion, then the executive tends to win. More simply put, alternative means of influencing foreign policy may allow legislators to win foreign policy battles, but they also enable the executive to win the war.

In trade, as in a few other areas, using alternatives to statutes surely has allowed legislators to "limit, modify or veto Executive actions" and thereby shape policy. But the fact that legislators can influence foreign policy "not *despite* delegation but *through* it,"[22] does not diminish the constitutional importance of a formal delegation of power, or even the failure to explicitly circumscribe a formal delegation of power. The delegation of power in statutes—even when counterbalanced by strong, non-statutory means of influence over day-to-day foreign policy—matters because presidents can and have used these as legal and constitutional precedents in confrontations over foreign *and* domestic policy. Ultimately, a series of statutes that delegate power and discretion to the executive have a cumulative effect on the constitutional interpretation of foreign policy powers, and a series of such delegations can begin to add up to a broad abdication of both constitutional and practical control, particularly when foreign policy disputes end up in court. Finally, a series of delegations of power to the executive can add up to a precedent that can and has been imported in the Court's doctrine in domestic policy—the subject of Chapter 8.

Why the Courts Won't Save Congress Overseas—or at Home

Many in Congress expected the Court to do what Congress could not, or would not, do—to assert and protect legislative prerogatives in foreign policy. Far from protecting legislative prerogatives, the justices increasingly have contributed to their degradation. Congress has the authority to intervene and claim power in foreign affairs, but to do so the Court has insisted ever more stringently in recent years that legislators have to be explicit, they have to make their claims clear in the law and not just in the legislative history. While presidents continued to veto legislation and attach clear statements about constitutional interpretation to those veto messages, Congress continued to compromise the legislative language. The Court then read that language strictly, becoming increasingly receptive to claims of executive discretion if not outright prerogative. The Court, far from saving Congress from itself as many legislators hoped and expected, made the imbalance of powers more pronounced as the precedents set by the legislature and the Court came to shape the distribution of power.

In recent years, the justices have lowered the barriers to executive discretion in foreign policy in three important ways. First, the Court has been extremely tolerant of congressional delegations of power and discretion to the executive. Second, the Court has been extremely tolerant of executive action in the absence of congressional action or in the face of congressional silence. Finally, the justices recently have gone one step further: Where once the Court's default position seemed to be a presumption in favor of congressional prerogatives, now the Court has subtly turned the default presumption to one that assumes congressional acquiescence in the absence of explicit and narrowly drawn statutes that would *deny* discretion to the executive.[23] This change in the Court's default doctrine is apparent in domestic and foreign policy alike[24]—legislative decisions in one realm have been used to support judicial opinions in the other realm.

In many instances in foreign policy legislators consciously choose to implicitly and explicitly delegate to the executive. But because the Court is unwilling fully to divorce foreign and domestic policy, the implicit and explicit delegations in foreign policy have been used by the justices to support their default presumption of the same sort of implicit delegations in domestic legislation as well.

The Court can only rule on what it is given, and if it is given legislation that legitimates executive prerogative in foreign policy, no one should be surprised that the Court will not rescue congressional prerogatives. The statutory route to the reassertion of congressional power in foreign policy was a mistake. It was the wrong solution—it was a legal solution to a political problem. But more than that, by putting the issue into law, and into the courts, Congress has made any future effort to reassert power in foreign policy even more difficult.

Incentives to Rebalance Power?

Why does Congress delegate its own powers? Madison argued that the problem would be to constrain the power-hungry—he argued that ambition would counter ambition, and that human passions would be sufficient to assure that each branch of the government would protect its own powers.[25] And yet in foreign policy many in Congress seem determined to shed power, to cede control to the executive. Was Madison wrong?

Madison wasn't wrong—but he may not have fully anticipated the distinction modern legislators would draw between assertions of power through legislation (formal power) and assertions of power through alternative or informal means. There is clear evidence of the growth of informal congressional influence in foreign policy.[26] But that doesn't tell us why legislators would continue to delegate *formal* power even while trying to increase the level and volume of informal influence.[27] Chapter 9 will explore the incentives that might drive individual legislators to agree to and even embrace these formal delegations of power.

Legislators are capable of asserting their prerogatives, but very reluctant to do so both to avoid blame and because individual legislators, for various reasons, have decided that their time and effort are better invested elsewhere. Those who advocate an executive-centered foreign policy certainly would welcome this response.[28] But is it the best response for the American system and for American foreign policy? If not, and if legislators won't save congressional prerogatives, should another branch of the government intervene to bring Congress back into the process?

Counterintuitively, one of the strongest arguments for bringing Congress back in may well be that it would be in the *executive's* own political interest to refuse to take full power (and therefore full responsibility) to set *and* execute risky or potentially costly foreign policy decisions. This proposition ultimately hinges on the same set of questions asked above about Congress: Does the president have the proper incentives to voluntarily surrender power, and force Congress to take a measure of responsibility in foreign policy? Would the self-interest of the executive drive the president to share power with Congress? The rest of Chapter 9 will try to demonstrate that the president has precisely that incentive and that it has been a profound error for presidents since World War Two to assert and act on a prerogative reading of the Constitution. By *re*-interpreting the traditional interpretation of the Constitution in foreign policy as laid out in Chapters 1 and 2, the president actually will be able to conserve power, build a better reputation (a crucial source of power)[29], and insulate the administration from some of the more hazardous risks of prerogative power (and exclusive responsibility) in foreign affairs.

Could it be in the president's best interest to reject the huge delegations of sole responsibility that come with both the assertion of prerogative power by the president *and* with the delegation of power and discretion from Congress? Theodore Lowi argues that "at a minimum, a *rational* President would veto congressional enactments delegating powers so broad and so vague that expectations cannot be met."[30] Would this have made sense over the past 45 years? The answer might be yes, qualified by the pressure of the emergency environment within which the elected branches and the Court operated. But if it was a qualified yes before, now, in the wake of the end of the Cold War, it is even more convincingly so.

*   *   *

It is, of course, entirely plausible that Presidents and their supporters in Congress since World War Two have been right in arguing that modern demands require a stronger executive in foreign policy. Perhaps the Constitution should formally treat foreign and domestic affairs differently. Or perhaps the Constitution itself simply has outlived its utility.[31] If that view is correct, the Constitution should be amended after a thorough national debate. But that is not the route that has been taken. Instead, the executive has asserted prerogative power in foreign affairs while legislators in Congress, both intentionally and accidentally, have legitimated it. Now the courts are reinforcing that legitimation, and writing prerogative assertions into American law and constitutional interpretation abroad—and at home.

The end of the Cold War presents an opportunity to correct the imbalance of powers, and this book argues that Americans should seize upon it. Above all, though, this book tries to demonstrate the importance of studying *both* the legal and political process—and the ways in which they influence each other—and it tries to demonstrate that an understanding of American foreign policy requires an understanding of the way in which constitutional interpretation shapes and constrains its construction.

II

Constitutional Interpretation and Foreign Policy: The Traditional Interpretation

1

The Traditional Interpretation in Court

It is, emphatically, the province and duty of the judicial department, to say what the law is. Those who apply the rule to particular cases, must of necessity expound and interpret that rule.

—Chief Justice John Marshall

The Constitution establishes the parameters of power within which the federal government functions. It defines the institutions of government and the process by which government is to function. But the Constitution is not a strict blueprint. It is a broad document that has evolved with time. Its evolution has been driven by all three branches of the federal government, but the system has come to rely on the judiciary, and the Supreme Court in particular, for the final resolution of questions of constitutional interpretation. The Court works with laws passed by Congress, actions taken by the president, and with constitutional interpretations made by people in both elected branches, all of which provide a powerful set of constraints on the constitutional interpretation that emerges from the Court. Nevertheless, the Court has an often decisive word on constitutional interpretation, and legislators and presidents are aware of that reality—their actions are shaped with the Court in mind, and often are justified and defended by reference to judicial precedent.

To understand the impact of constitutional interpretation in foreign policy requires a clear understanding of the role played by the judiciary. The Courts are responsible for the constitutional context within which the other branches operate, and the Supreme Court will judge the interpretation offered by the other branches, either giving it the sanction of constitutional legitimacy and establishing that law or action as a precedent for future officials, or striking it down and sending it back to the political system for alternative solutions. Before tackling the evolution of constitutional interpretation in the executive and legislative branches, it is necessary to understand the constitutional context within which that interpretation has evolved, and to do so requires an understanding of the judicial doctrine in foreign policy. A close examination of the evolution of the judicial doctrine reveals a surprisingly consistent and coherent doctrine.

From the beginning, the Court has maintained that one of its primary obligations in foreign and domestic policy disputes is to police the separation of powers. Even Justice Frankfurter, no great fan of judicial interference in the political system, argued that the Court was duty-bound to police the separation of powers:

> No doubt a government with distributed authority, subject to be challenged in the courts of law . . . labors under restrictions from which other governments are free. It has not been our tradition to envy such governments. In any event our government was designed to have such restrictions. The price was deemed not too high in view of the safeguards which these restrictions afford.[1]

We often forget that in the United States there are two types of separation of powers: a *vertical* separation of powers (state vs. national powers) as well as the now more familiar *horizontal* separation of powers (executive-legislative-judicial). This double division, Madison wrote, provided a "double security" for the rights of the people: "The different governments will control each other, at the same time that each will be controlled by itself."[2]

For the greater part of American history, those concerned with constitutional interpretation, including presidents, Supreme Court justices, and representatives, all focused on the *vertical* separation of powers. That focus shifted after World War Two to a greater interest in the *horizontal* separation within the national government. Nevertheless, Frankfurter's statement applies equally well to both the vertical and the horizontal separation of powers.

Is foreign policy different? The Court repeatedly has endorsed statements such as Justice Frankfurter's that "broad as the power in the National Government to regulate foreign affairs must necessarily be, it is not without limitation. The restrictions confining Congress in the exercise of any of the powers expressly delegated to it in the Constitution apply with equal vigor when that body seeks to regulate relations with other nations."[3] While the Court never has accepted the idea that foreign policy is free of all constitutional constraint, it has struggled to find a way to enforce those constraints without imperiling the nation. As the Court argued in 1963, "While the Constitution protects against invasions of individual rights, it is not a suicide pact."[4] And yet, should the justices accept the notion that foreign policy is unconstrained by the Constitution, they may well ignore their duty and legitimate laws that would "sanction the subversion of one of those liberties . . . which makes the defense of the Nation worthwhile."[5]

The Court has accepted foreign policy cases, and it has ruled against the government even when claims of dire necessity and national security have been advanced. It is true that judicial intervention in foreign policy cases has been infrequent and that the Court is reluctant to accept them, but when the judicial doctrine in foreign policy over the past 200 years is examined, it becomes clear that the doctrine that has emerged is both coherent and consistent. It is a doctrine the president and Congress profitably can study in the continuing effort to develop and execute effective American foreign policy, as well as in the continuing struggle between the branches to control that policy.

As in any case, when the Court confronts a case touching on foreign policy the justices have three options. They can strike down the disputed exercise of power; they can legitimate and justify it; or they can refuse to rule on the case by invoking the political-question doctrine or by invoking other judicial requirements such as standing or 'ripeness.'

Should the justices choose to strike down the disputed policy, they generally will do so on one of two grounds: either the government as a whole has exceeded the power granted to it by the Constitution, and the policy in some sense violates constitutionally protected individual rights; or the policy, though substantively constitutional, was enacted or executed improperly. In the latter case the Court is exercising its role as a guardian of the Constitution's institutional structure.

Should the justices choose to sanction a constitutionally suspect exercise of power, they can do so by following one of at least three possible routes of constitutional interpretation: 1) the justices can legitimate the policy through a broad reading of the Constitution; 2) they can offer a pragmatic justification for a narrow exception to their own constitutional doctrine; or 3) they can argue that the Constitution treats foreign and domestic affairs differently, and what would be prohibited at home is permissible in the execution of foreign policy.

What are the costs of these options? If the justices choose to base their justification on a broad reading of the Constitution, they take the risk that this reading will return to haunt them later. Since the American judicial system relies heavily on *stare decisis*, where the case law is built upon precedent, broad readings in foreign policy cases can become precedents for equally broad readings in domestic policy cases drawing on the same constitutional phrases. As Justice Jackson warned in *Korematsu v. United States*, the 1944 Japanese-American internment case,

> once a judicial opinion rationalizes such an order to show that it conforms to the Constitution, or rather rationalizes the Constitution to show that the Constitution sanctions such an order, the Court for all time has validated the principle [and it] then lies about like a loaded weapon ready for the hand of any authority that can bring forward a plausible claim of an urgent need. Every repetition imbeds that principle more deeply in our law and thinking and expands it to new purposes.[6]

Should the Court choose to make a narrow and pragmatic exception to its doctrine, it risks weakening the edifice of predictable law uniformly applied. As Hamilton noted in the *Federalist Papers*, the Court has no independent power, ultimately depending "upon the aid of the executive arm even for the efficacy of its judgments."[7] Haphazard exceptions to established doctrine, or pragmatic exceptions that are other than clearly and absolutely unavoidable will damage the Court's delicate legitimacy. Justices understand the delicacy of their task and generally are loathe to jeopardize the Court's legitimacy.

Finally, the Court can try to have it both ways, strictly policing the system at home and allowing greater latitude when the power is exercised in pursuit of foreign policy. Here the trouble is in crafting a doctrine to separate foreign and domestic policy under the Constitution, when the Constitution itself does not make those distinctions.

Through more than two centuries of constitutional interpretation, Supreme Court justices have flirted with the options of avoiding foreign policy cases, of finding narrow, pragmatic exceptions, and of attempting to read the Constitution differently in foreign and domestic affairs. But these efforts consistently have been rejected by the Court's majority.

The Court's doctrine in foreign policy cases can be divided into three coherent periods. Before the world wars, the Court applied a traditional interpretation focusing on what the *national government* (the executive and legislative branches) *acting together* could do in pursuit of foreign policy. In the second period, from World War Two until the 1950s, the Court confronted the emerging executive prerogative interpretation, and generally gave the executive great latitude except where there was clear congressional opposition. The third period started in the 1970s, when the Court increasingly came to accept executive claims and insisted on ever more explicit, ever more clearly worded statutes from Congress before the justices would block presidential interpretations of foreign policy powers.

The Traditional Interpretation

The first period (addressed in this chapter) was one where, in concert with the other branches of the national government, the Court developed what might be called a traditional interpretation of the Constitution in foreign policy cases. Here the main concern was the power of the national government, as a whole, versus claims of individual rights or claims of the usurpation of powers not explicitly delegated to the national government, or reserved to the states. There seemed to be consensus that specific restrictions in the Constitution were inviolable in foreign and domestic policy and a clear conviction that Congress had a legitimate role to play should the legislators choose to assert that role. Though foreign policy might merit a slightly looser treatment, there was a clear and consistent conviction that the Constitution governed foreign and domestic policy alike.

In foreign and domestic policy cases, the Court struggled to maintain the balance of energy and stability in government with what Madison called the "inviolable attention due to liberty and the republican form."[8] As Hamilton argued, energy in government often is associated with an active chief executive,[9] but stability was to come from a predictable and consistent legislature. And to balance these against republican forms and preserve liberty, the government of the United States was divided and then divided again. Though individuals would surrender power to the state, the power they surrendered was first "divided between two distinct governments, and then the portion allotted to each subdivided among distinct and separate departments."[10] In other words, the system first was divided by the *vertical* separation of powers (national vs. state), and then subdivided by the *horizontal* separation of powers (legislative vs. executive vs. judicial).

Prior to the Second World War, the vertical separation of powers dominated the Court's docket. It was a concern for national power in general, and not the division of that power within the national government, that was the focus of the Court's doctrine in domestic and foreign policy cases alike. The power to conduct foreign affairs clearly was delegated to the national government, but the contentious question was, if the Constitution makes no distinction between foreign and domestic powers, then could the powers claimed by the national government for the administration of foreign policy be used to increase its power in domestic affairs as well? Since that seemed a logical conclusion, the Court was faced with four options: 1) read the Constitution as a unitary document that provided for strong government in foreign *and* domestic affairs alike; 2) read the Constitution as a unitary document that provided for weak, decentralized government in foreign *and* domestic affairs alike; 3) try to find a way to read the Constitution differently in foreign and domestic affairs—finding authority for a strong central government in foreign policy but maintaining a weak and decentralized government for domestic policy; or 4) find a way simply to avoid foreign policy questions altogether. Each of these, with the exception of the third option, was consistent with the traditional interpretation, though each represented a distinctly different vision of that interpretation.

Chief Justice John Marshall saw no constitutional distinction between foreign and domestic policy: If Congress had the power to enact laws that were necessary and proper to carry out its enumerated powers, then it had that power whether or not the subject was foreign policy. If Marshall was right, however, and if the Constitution was to be read the same at home and abroad, than an expansive foreign affairs power might well jeopardize individual state autonomy and provide a way to expand the constitutionally limited role of the national government at home.

Alarmed by this interpretation, a number of justices in these early years struggled to develop a doctrine that would allow the Constitution to be read differently in foreign and domestic policy. But the struggle here had nothing to do with executive powers or prerogatives. Rather it focused on the vertical distribution of power between the state governments and the national government. It is in this context that the Court's traditional interpretation emerged and must be understood, and in this context that the presidents of this period also developed and adhered to their own version of the traditional interpretation of the Constitution in foreign policy (see Chapter Two).

Most students of the Constitution and foreign policy tend to start their analysis with the widely read and even more widely misunderstood case of *United States v. Curtiss-Wright Export Corp.*[11] This case, dealing with an arms-trade embargo in South America, turned on the question of whether or not Congress *and* the president, *acting together*, had the authority to cut off the arms trade between American arms firms and the belligerent nations. In the course of attempting to devise a coherent and convincing way to read the Constitution differently in foreign and domestic affairs, the majority opinion authored by Justice George Sutherland made some comments about the division of authority between the executive and legislative branches. But the case itself was merely another in a long line of cases that turned on the *vertical* separation of powers and another effort to work around the logical implications of a unitary reading of the Constitution in foreign and domestic policy, a unitary reading that started with Chief Justice John Marshall. *Curtiss-Wright* was another effort to find a way to have a strong, central government for foreign policy and yet retain a weak and decentralized government at home. Like other similar efforts, it fell apart. But it is remembered, cited, and revered as a precedent for the prerogative powers of the president in foreign policy. It is used as ammunition in modern debates, including the 1987 Senate hearings on the Iran-Contra affair.[12] This misinterpretation is far easier to understand if the case is read and understood in the context of the long history of cases dealing with foreign policy and the implications those cases held for the separation of powers. This chapter will attempt to put the *Curtiss-Wright* case in that context and to demonstrate that far from a turning point in constitutional interpretation, and the dawn of the prerogative view, it was instead a logical part of a coherent string of cases that produced a clear, coherent, and predictable doctrine in the constitutional interpretation of foreign policy cases.

The Courts and Foreign Policy before Curtiss-Wright

The first question Supreme Court justices might ask in any foreign policy case is whether or not the government as a whole has the constitutional authority to exercise the power it claims. Does the Constitution explicitly prohibit the government from executing its policy? This line of questioning touches on the Constitution's structural guarantees, including the vertical separation of powers, and its guarantees of individual rights including due process claims. Once the Court is convinced that the power asserted is within the realm of what the Constitution allows the *United*

States to do, the Court must next consider the process itself—whether the action taken was properly enacted and executed. This includes claims that the horizontal separation of powers has been violated. Even some of the Court's most ardent advocates of judicial deference to the political branches in foreign affairs consistently have maintained that though the government as a whole might have a particular power, that does not mean the executive branch can exercise that power on the authority of the president alone. Similarly, in those cases where the executive asserts powers against the explicit or implicit will of Congress, the Court has overturned executive orders even when doing so would, in the words of Justice White, "do substantial damage to public interests."[13]

The Court's traditional foreign policy doctrine focused primarily on the broad question of what the national government, acting as a whole, could and could not do in foreign policy. The horizontal separation of powers questions that are more familiar today were rare. As early as 1803, in *Marbury v. Madison*,[14] the Court had flirted with the notion of executive prerogative. In *Marbury*, Chief Justice John Marshall had suggested that those acting under presidential instructions might not be held liable for illegal actions. But the Chief Justice closed this door rather firmly just one year later, in a case called *Little v. Barreme*. Marshall was explicit in the *Little* case: no person, not even the president in his capacity as the nation's military leader, was above the law, and the law was made by Congress. Marshall made it clear that the executive powers delegated to the president by the Constitution were not unlimited, not even in foreign affairs. Even in his capacity as commander in chief, Marshall held, the president could not authorize a military officer to perform illegal acts.[15]

Little v. Barreme arose in December 1799 when a Danish ship was captured by two U.S. frigates acting on orders from the Secretary of the Navy on behalf of President John Adams. While a law passed by Congress authorized the seizure of American ships suspected of sailing to French ports, the orders under which Captain George Little acted instructed him to seize "vessels or cargoes [that] are apparently, as well as really, American" and "bound to, or from, French ports."[16] Captain Little seized the Danish ship *Flying Fish*, which was sailing "from, not to, a French port."[17]

It was clear to the Circuit Court and the Supreme Court that this violated the law, but the question was whether the ship captain was to be held liable for this illegal action. Captain Little argued that he had merely followed the orders of the president, and thus was immune from legal responsibility. But Chief Justice Marshall wrote that even in his capacity as commander in chief, the president could not authorize a military officer to perform illegal acts. Only Congress can make laws, Marshall argued, and regardless of the fact that the president may have ordered his subordinate officer to perform an illegal act, that act was still illegal, and the officer performing that act was responsible for his behavior. Not even a military officer, Marshall wrote, could use the "instruction of the executive" as an excuse for performing an illegal act.[18]

Marshall wrote that in those areas where Congress had failed to act "it is by no means clear that the President [might] have empowered the officers" to seize the ships as he instructed them to do. But in this case "the legislature seem to have prescribed that the manner in which this law shall be carried into execution" and did not authorize the executive order.[19] Thus, though the president's order may well have been reasonable[20] and even far more likely to achieve the ends many in Congress may have desired, it was illegal: And any officer who acted under illegal instructions was responsible for his actions. "[T]he instructions cannot change the nature of the transaction, or legalize an act which without those instructions would have been a plain trespass,"[21] Marshall concluded.

This extreme version of the doctrine that the orders of a superior officer are not a defense for violations of law was an important cornerstone for the American doctrine that no person, not even the highest officer of the land, is above the law.[22] In addition, it was a foundation for the Court's commitment to police the separation of powers and maintain the Constitution's institutional structure even in foreign affairs—even when the nation's security might be at stake.

Little v. Barreme was not typical of the foreign policy cases that formed the Court's traditional doctrine. Far more common were questions about the scope and limits of the power of the national government, acting as a whole, in foreign policy. These cases dealt with the question of national powers: Did the government of the United States have the constitutional authority to do what had been done? Although Chief Justice John Marshall confronted few judicial questions that dealt explicitly with foreign policy, he ruled on many that decided the proper scope of national powers. And while Marshall advocated a broad reading of the Constitution, he acknowledged that there were actions the Constitution prohibited altogether—that there were things that Congress and the president, separately or together, were powerless to change. "Should Congress," he wrote,

> in the execution of its powers, adopt measures which are prohibited by the Constitution; or should Congress, under the pretext of executing its powers, pass laws for the accomplishment of objects not entrusted to the government; it would become the painful duty of this tribunal . . . to say that such an act was not the law of the land.[23]

For Marshall, the Constitution was to be read as a unitary document that does not recognize a legal distinction between foreign and domestic affairs. But to say that there are actions the Constitution prohibits the national government from doing is one thing; it is quite another to determine just what is prohibited and why. A narrow reading of the Constitution creates a highly constricted and inefficient system, poorly equipped to deal with other sovereign nations let alone to confront unexpected emergencies. But reading the Constitution broadly to provide flexibility and adaptability in foreign affairs has obvious implications for domestic politics. A broad reading overseas creates a strong, central government equipped for efficient foreign affairs, but such a reading also creates a strong, central government in domestic politics, and it was that sort of government that the founders endeavored to undermine with the Constitution's limited powers, checks and balances and the prohibitions of the Bill of Rights.

Justifying Foreign Policy: A Broad Reading of the Constitution

The Constitution contains a number of specific enumerated powers that have been delegated to the national government. In addition, the states are forbidden to exercise a number of powers, primarily those having to do with foreign affairs and interstate commerce. While the Constitution designates the president as commander in chief of the armed forces, it gives Congress alone the power to "raise and support Armies," to "provide and maintain a Navy" and "to declare War." Similarly, while the president has the power to make treaties, such treaties must be approved by two-thirds of the Senate. Beyond these specifics the Congress is authorized to "make all laws which shall be necessary and proper for carrying into Execution" the enumerated powers, while the loosely defined "executive power" is vested in the president.[24]

From its earliest cases, the Court has argued that the Constitution cannot detail the scope and limits of every possible exercise of power. As Chief Justice John Marshall put it in *McCulloch v. Maryland* in 1819, "A Constitution, to contain an accurate detail of all the subdivisions of which its great powers will admit, and of all the means by which they may be carried into execution, would partake of the prolixity of a legal code, and could scarcely be embraced by the human mind."[25]

The Court plays a major role in determining what is "necessary and proper" for executing the powers that are delegated to the government. Marshall acknowledged that the question "respecting the extent of the powers actually granted, is perpetually arising, and will probably continue to arise, as long as our system shall exist."[26] All of the powers of the government are limited, Marshall acknowledged, and those limits "are not to be transcended." But when it comes to national powers, "the government of the Union, though limited in its powers, is supreme within its sphere of action." As between the nation and the states, later cases would make it abundantly clear that foreign affairs are national affairs. Foreign policy was a national issue for Marshall; his doctrine made no distinction between national and foreign policy.

In *McCulloch v. Maryland*, Marshall picked up Alexander Hamilton's arguments in the *Federalist Papers* that the Constitution contained both enumerated powers and certain implied powers necessary to execute the enumerated powers. "A government, intrusted with such ample powers . . . must also be intrusted with ample means for their execution,"[27] Marshall wrote. If, for example, the government has authority to control the "sword and the purse, [and] all the external relations" the government must have the powers necessary to execute that authority. "Is that construction of the Constitution to be preferred, which would render these operations difficult, hazardous and expensive?"[28] Marshall asked.

As Edward Corwin wrote in 1913, "In a word, it was upon the most impregnable foundations, both historical and logical, that Marshall rested his doctrine of national supremacy."[29] The problem with justifying broad foreign policy powers through a broad reading of the Constitution is that this broad reading is equally applicable in domestic politics. If Congress has the power to enact laws that are necessary and proper to carry out its enumerated powers, it has that power whether or not the subject is foreign policy.

Marshall's national supremacy doctrine in foreign policy cases was equally influential in cases touching on state powers and federalism. An ideal example of the overlap came in 1832 when Marshall held that the State of Georgia had no power to enforce its legislation on the lands of the Cherokee nation within the borders of Georgia.[30] While Marshall conceded that the Native American nations were not exactly foreign sovereignties, they were to be considered "as distinct, independent political communities, retaining their original natural rights, as the undisputed possessors of the soil. . . . The Constitution, by declaring treaties already made, as well as those to be made, to be the supreme law of the land, has adopted and sanctioned the previous treaties with the Indian nations and consequently admits their rank among those powers who are capable of making treaties." And those powers unequivocally were national powers. "The whole intercourse between the United States and this nation, is, by our Constitution and laws, vested in the government of the United States."[31]

To achieve an efficient and effective foreign policy and yet maintain a commitment to the Constitution, it is perfectly reasonable to argue that the Constitution is to be construed broadly. As Marshall argued in *McCulloch*, "Let the end be legitimate, let it be within the scope of the Constitution, and all means which are appropriate, which are plainly adapted to that end, which are not prohibited, but consistent with the letter and spirit of the Constitution, are constitutional."[32] Marshall made no distinction between foreign and domestic authority. In fact, Marshall was constructing a broad reading of national power explicitly to deal with domestic events rather than foreign affairs.

Marshall's ruling in the Cherokee cases, though never enforced, was a clear signal that the Court's doctrine in foreign policy cases could have powerful implications for state power and for federalism. In short, the message was that the Court's doctrine was built on a broad reading of the Constitution and of national powers. Because the Constitution vested broad powers to make foreign policy possible, and excluded the states from foreign policy control, this could well be a way to build central power in general. Since the Court's doctrine made no distinction between foreign and domestic affairs, strong central power in one policy area could, and likely would, foster strong central power in the other. This concern was confirmed in 1919 when Justice Oliver Wendell Holmes extended the logic of a broad reading of the Constitution in foreign policy to enable the national government to regulate hunting restrictions in Missouri.

Missouri tested the Court's broad reading of foreign policy powers when it fought national legislation that would have banned the hunting of endangered migratory birds. Arguing that such legislation was a violation of the state's right to exercise its authority within its own borders, Missouri challenged the legislation in lower federal courts, and won.[33] Unwilling to concede, advocates of the restrictions turned to the broad power that clearly was delegated to the government in foreign policy to achieve what seemed impossible to achieve in a purely domestic context. If national legislation was unconstitutional, then the answer might lie in an international treaty. The treaty power clearly is a national power, and states were obliged to respect and enforce legitimate international treaties. After the national government signed a treaty with Canada concerning the protection of the birds—which migrated between the United States and Canada—Missouri was forced to return to court to challenge what was seen as an attempt to circumvent the Constitution.

Justice Holmes' opinion for the Court in *Missouri v. Holland*[34] added to the emerging foreign policy doctrine the argument that the Constitution is a flexible document, capable of responding to the growth and evolution of the United States. Constitutional interpretation, Holmes suggested, had to do so as well. "We must consider what this country has become in deciding what [the Tenth] Amendment has reserved."[35]

"No doubt," Holmes wrote, "the great body of private relations usually fall within the control of the States, but a treaty may override [a State's] power."[36] In the end, Holmes held that the treaty was a legitimate effort to confront a problem with legitimate international implications and, "the treaty in question does not contravene any prohibitory words to be found in the Constitution."[37]

Justifying Foreign Policy: Variations of the Traditional Interpretation

Marshall and Holmes clearly read the Constitution as a unitary document that provided for strong government in foreign *and* domestic affairs alike, though acknowledging that there were things the Constitution prohibited and its substantive guarantees would not allow. The opposite position—to read the Constitution as a unitary document that provided for weak, decentralized government in foreign *and* domestic affairs alike—never gained any serious support since it was clear that one of the primary motives behind abandoning the Articles of Confederation had been the need for a better, more efficient, and more effective national foreign policy. But the broad reading of the Constitution necessary for a strong foreign policy directly contradicted the objectives of limited government that seem to rest at the heart of the Madisonian Constitution. That problem led some on the Court to flirt with a position that seemed out of line with the traditional interpretation, an effort to find the authority for setting up a strong central government for foreign policy while keeping it weak and decentralized for domestic policy. A number of justices engaged in this enterprise, but it never came to displace the traditional interpretation established by Marshall and reinforced by Holmes.

The alternative effort followed two tracks: 1) an attempt to develop a coherent doctrine that would actually find constitutional support for the argument that the Constitution was meant to be read differently in foreign and domestic policy;[38] and 2) an attempt to develop a coherent view of the Constitution as a document that delegates restricted powers to the central government, but would sanction pragmatic exceptions where circumstances might warrant.

One notable example of the pragmatic exception doctrine arose in *Durand v. Hollins*, an obscure case from 1860 that has been elevated to the status of a significant precedent for advocates of executive prerogative in foreign affairs. In 1860 Supreme Court Justice Samuel Nelson, on circuit, was asked to rule on an American citizen's claim that the sacking of Greytown, Nicaragua, by the United States was an unconstitutional exercise of war powers by the president without the approval of Congress and that therefore the United States should compensate him for the destruction of his property in Greytown. Justice Nelson used Marshall's arguments about executive prerogative in *Marbury v. Madison* to argue that there were pragmatic reasons why the judiciary should give the president wide latitude in the conduct of international affairs. Justice Nelson ignored the fact that Marshall had trimmed his own view of Executive prerogative in the case of *Little v. Barreme* just one year after *Marbury*.[39] Nelson argued that "the interposition of the President abroad, for the protection of the citizen, must necessarily rest in his discretion; and it is quite clear that, in all cases where a public act or order rests in executive discretion neither he nor his authorized agent is personally civilly responsible for the consequences."[40]

President Franklin Pierce had offered no pragmatic justification for the otherwise unconstitutional act of sacking Greytown, but Justice Nelson constructed one for him. After outlining the pragmatic argument the executive branch had failed to make, Nelson had little trouble in overlooking the technical violation of the separation of powers that, absent Nelson's analysis, may well have failed Constitutional scrutiny.

While *Durand* has been cited as a precedent for executive prerogative in foreign policy, Michael Glennon has pointed out that Nelson was not sanctioning a claim of executive prerogative, but merely endorsing the view that when Congress is silent, as it was in this matter, the president had broad powers to use force to protect American lives and property.[41]

The historical dispute centers on whether or not those lives and property were in danger.[42]

Durand serves as an example of the pragmatic exception doctrine, and it raises two real problems: It is highly subjective, and there is no logical way to limit pragmatic exceptions to the foreign policy realm alone. As with the Marshall-Holmes approach, what is legitimate in foreign policy inevitably spills over to domestic affairs as well.

Not surprisingly, the Civil War provided a number of cases where the Court was asked to accept pragmatic justifications for constitutionally suspect policies. These exceptions frustrated a number of jurists who considered them unconstitutional. They tried to articulate a doctrine that would construe the Constitution differently in foreign and domestic affairs. Though this effort failed to unseat the traditional interpretation in the era before the world wars, it proved to be influential in later periods.

In the Civil War era, Supreme Court Justice Stephen Field provided important precedents for this approach. Unwilling to allow the emergency needs of the sovereign nation to destroy the constitutional constraints placed on the domestic government, Field authored a blistering dissent in the 1870 *Legal Tender* cases, condemning the use of pragmatic arguments about national sovereignty to justify the expansion of federal power in the domestic sphere. But, writing for the majority 19 years later in an immigration case known as the Chinese exclusion case (1889), Field argued that the rationale he had condemned at home was perfectly acceptable in foreign policy cases. In the *Legal Tender* cases Field insisted on a narrow reading of the Constitution. But in the foreign policy case, he argued for a broad interpretation of the Constitution, insisting that in their relations with foreign governments, the United States was vested with all the authority of *any* sovereign nation, regardless of the paucity of constitutional instructions regarding foreign affairs powers.

The *Legal tender* cases were a number of cases that challenged the authority of Congress to make treasury notes legal tender for debts contracted during and after the Civil War. If the Court had overturned these statutes it would have thrown American commerce into total disarray. Nevertheless, the majority opinion noted that serious as the consequences might be, those consequences "must be accepted, *if* there is a clear incompatibility between the Constitution and the legal tender acts."[43]

The majority held that when the national government is confronted by revolution it may take a fairly utilitarian approach to the idea of non-enumerated, implied, or inherent powers. "No single power is the ultimate end for which the Constitution was adopted. It may, in a very proper sense, be treated as a means for the accomplishment of a subordinate object, but that object is itself a means designed for an ulterior purpose." The majority opinion continued, "It is impossible to know what those non-enumerated powers are, and what is their nature and extent, without considering the purposes they were intended to serve. . . . [the Constitution] certainly was intended to confer upon the government the power of self-preservation."[44]

Concurring with the majority, Justice Bradley focused on the concept of sovereignty, arguing that the United States was vested with certain general powers that are part of sovereign authority. "The Constitution," he wrote, "established a government, and not a league, compact or partnership. . . . As a government it was invested with all the attributes of sovereignty."[45]

In a dissent joined by Justice Field and Justice Nathan Clifford, Chief Justice Salmon Chase directly confronted the sovereignty issue. Chase, speaking for the three dissenting justices, wholly rejected the doctrine "advanced for the first time, we believe, in this court, by the present majority," that the legislature has any powers "which grow out of the aggregate of powers conferred upon the government, or out of the sovereignty instituted by it."[46]

In his separate dissent, Justice Field rejected arguments of necessity or utility. "The utility of a measure is not the subject of judicial cognizance, nor, as already intimated, the test of its constitutionality."[47]

Field's dissent suggested that there were no inherent powers in the national government; the fact that a power that was not expressly forbidden to the national government was not sufficient warrant to tolerate such behavior. That notion, he wrote, "would change the whole character of our government." The true doctrine, he added, "is the exact reverse, that if a power is not in terms granted, and is not necessary and proper for the exercise of a power thus granted, it does not exist."[48] Were it any other way, Field argued, "our government would be, not what it was intended to be, one of limited, but one of unlimited powers."[49]

Less than 20 years later, in *Chae Chan Ping v. United States* (1889), Field argued that the government had all the powers of any sovereign nation when it came to dealing with foreigners and resident aliens. This case, also known as the Chinese exclusion case, arose when the United States altered treaty terms with China. Where once a Chinese laborer could come and go from the United States, under the new terms Chinese immigrants and resident aliens were prohibited from entry, and Chae Chan Ping, who left the U.S. under the old treaty, was refused admission when he returned after the terms of the treaty had been altered.

Justice Field's opinion differed distinctly from what he had written in the *Legal Tender* cases. There, he had argued eloquently that the government could do only that which the Constitution allowed, refusing to accept the idea that the government could do anything except what was specifically forbidden. Sovereign powers were subordinate to the Constitution, "restricted in their exercise only by the Constitution itself and considerations of public policy and justice which control, more or less, the conduct of all civilized nations."[50] But, suddenly, in the Chinese exclusion case, Field argued that there were foreign affairs powers inherent in sovereignty. "Jurisdiction over its own territory to that extent is an incident of every independent nation," Field argued. "It is part of its independence."[51]

In foreign affairs, Field embraced the exact doctrines he had so eloquently urged the Court to reject in the domestic *Legal Tender* cases. Although he did not spell out an explicit distinction between foreign and domestic affairs, neither did he overrule or even refer to his earlier position. The only way he could do this was by adopting the view that the Constitution was to be read differently when foreign affairs were involved. The majority, however, was consistent, accepting a broad reading of the Constitution at home (in the *Legal Tender* cases) and in foreign policy (in the Chinese exclusion case) where Field wrote the majority opinion. The most logical route to arrive at the conclusions Field arrived at in these cases would be to argue for a separate reading of the Constitution in foreign affairs—a position that is difficult to maintain since foreign and domestic affairs do not divide neatly. In addition, since the Constitution makes no explicit distinction between its applicability in the two spheres, adjudicating disputes over questions that are both foreign and domestic would be an exceedingly difficult task. That difficulty was well illustrated at the end of the Spanish-American War.

When America took possession of Puerto Rico and the Philippines after the Spanish-American War, the Supreme Court confronted a series of challenges known as the insular cases. Since the Constitution makes no provision for colonial rule, the Court was confronted with the need to develop a doctrine to deal with America's emerging role as a colonial and world power. But the insular cases were particularly tricky since it was unclear whether these lands were to be treated as domestic territories or as sovereign foreign nations. The Court had three options. First, the justices could force the government to treat these areas just as they would treat traditional territories in the continental United States (i.e., plan ultimately to incorporate them into the United States). Alternatively, they could force the United States to treat these areas as sovereign nations. Or the Court could, and in fact did, follow a third course, and devise a justification for distinguishing these colonial territories such that they were neither part of the United States nor independent sovereign entities. In this way the government would be left free of constitutional constraints in administering life—and tariffs—on these island possessions. While the Constitution generally can support a narrow and restricted reading or a flexible interpretation, it offers no textual basis for supporting both at the same time.

Eight cases reached the Supreme Court in 1901, and they all revolved around the fundamental question of the constitutional status of these new possessions: Were they part of the United States? Could the United States constitutionally acquire colonies? And, once their status was established, how would they be treated by tariff and trade laws? The key cases generally concerned tariff laws: For purposes of tariffs, were the insular possessions foreign or domestic? This focus on tariffs obscured the implications of the insular cases for the Court's emerging doctrine on foreign policy. Though the issue was tariffs, the implications for constitutional law in foreign policy cases were far broader. To resolve the insular cases—which consumed thousands of pages—the justices developed a tortured, complicated, and confusing doctrine that seemed to embrace the idea that the Constitution could be read differently in foreign and domestic affairs, but made equally clear how difficult it was to sustain such a reading without actually altering or amending the Constitution.

Ultimately the Court moved away from the effort to construct a fully coherent doctrine that would justify the constitutional separation of foreign and domestic policy, but the insular cases hinted that the Court was sympathetic to the argument that the national government should be granted more latitude in foreign affairs than in domestic affairs. The problem was that, in the eyes of most of the justices, sympathy aside, this view was incompatible with the Constitution itself.

Removing the Courts from Foreign Policy: The Political Question Doctrine

The insular cases proved to some that the Court really had no incentive to involve itself in foreign policy disputes. The confusing decisions damaged the Court's credibility. But if the traditional interpretation was incapable of dealing with modern exigencies and if the Court was unwilling or unable to construct a doctrine that would treat the two areas differently, then the only other option might be simply to get out of the way and leave all foreign policy cases to the political branches.

By declaring a question to be political in nature, some on the Court tried to argue that some issues are beyond judicial competence, or that the Constitution leaves some issues to be resolved by the elected branches of the government. The political question doctrine "would have it that although in general, in a proper case, the courts will examine the actions of government for conformity to constitutional authorizations and limitations, some constitutional requirements are entrusted exclusively and finally to the political branches of government for 'self-monitoring.' "[52]

From time to time the Court has flirted with the idea that all cases touching on foreign policy pose inherently political questions. Nearly two decades before *Curtiss-Wright*, the Court was asked to consider the recognition power in the case of *Oetjen v. Central Leather Co.* In that case, a 1917 challenge to the legitimacy of a Mexican government decree, the Court ruled that the power of recognition was and had always been considered a power of the political branches of the national government, and not subject to judicial review. In *Oetjen* the Court offered a standing invitation to future jurists to leave any and all foreign policy questions to the political branches. Writing for the majority, Justice Clarke said, "The conduct of the foreign relations of our government is committed by the Constitution to the Executive and Legislative—'the political'—Departments of the Government, and the propriety of what may be done in the exercise of this political power is not subject to judicial inquiry or decision."[53]

Despite the oft-stated conviction that foreign policy cases may be the prototypical political questions, few justices have been willing to accept *Oetjen*'s invitation to rule that all foreign policy cases inherently are beyond the reach of the Court. While acknowledging the appeal of such an argument, in the post- world war era the Court usually has reached a decision on these cases, often upholding the action on purely pragmatic grounds,[54] or on the ground that foreign policy powers are derived not from the Constitution but rather from national sovereignty.[55] The political question doctrine would assert that there are governmental actions that are unconstrained even by the most explicit of constitutional guarantees, and that is a doctrine that has found some rhetorical favor, but almost no actual support on the Court, particularly in the period before the Second World War.

A Turning Point in Foreign Policy Doctrine: Curtiss-Wright

Oetjen, handed down 19 years before *Curtiss-Wright*, was a clear invitation to remove the courts from foreign policy disputes, leaving their resolution strictly to the political process. Justice George Sutherland flatly refused this invitation in his opinion for the Court in *Curtiss-Wright*, since he was unwilling to rule that all foreign policy cases were non-justiciable. After all, the political question doctrine removes the Court from the process, and leaves the final determination of constitutional controversies to the other branches. Had Sutherland turned to the political question doctrine in *Curtiss-Wright*, he would have surrendered what he viewed as a critically important decision about the Constitution to the other branches, and *Curtiss-Wright* was not a case Sutherland wanted resolved elsewhere. On the contrary, Sutherland used *Curtiss-Wright* as a vehicle to try to resolve "the key problem facing conservatives who were also ardent nationalists and who somehow wanted strong national powers in foreign affairs but protection for certain states' rights in domestic affairs."[56] Sutherland returned to the third option, desperately trying to craft an intellectually sound interpretation of the Constitution that would allow the Court to support broad, strong, central power in foreign affairs, while preserving the constraints on domestic power that he and his brethren felt lay at the heart of the Constitution: Sutherland tried to create a constitutional justification for a strong, centralized government in foreign affairs without sacrificing individual rights or limited government at home.

For Sutherland, it was critical to distinguish foreign from domestic policy. Just a few months before *Curtiss-Wright*, Sutherland had written an opinion for the Court in *Carter v. Carter Coal Co.* (1936), in which he "denied the existence of any unenumerated, 'inherent' federal powers in domestic matters"; the question of inherent power over external affairs, he wrote, "is a wholly different matter which it is not necessary now to consider."[57]

Sutherland wanted to use the courts to make sure the national government would be empowered to pursue an active foreign policy as unfettered by the states and individuals as possible. Removing the courts from foreign policy altogether would not achieve Sutherland's goal, nor would it have been consistent with his political and legal convictions. In his 1919 book, *Constitutional Powers and World Affairs*, and his 1936 opinion in *Curtiss-Wright*, Sutherland argued that all powers were subordinated to the Constitution. But where the Constitution was silent, as it largely was in foreign affairs, the government had great discretion, "The primary concern of the States is with individual and local affairs. The primary concern of the Nation is with the interrelations of the states, and their several peoples, and of the sovereign whole with the world outside. Any unwarranted encroachment upon the former or any captious restriction of the latter must be alike avoided, if the symmetry of the great governmental structure designed by the founders is to be preserved".[58]

The political-question formulation of *Oetjen* would have precluded judicial intervention to protect what Sutherland saw as an essential national prerogative. For Sutherland, it emphatically was the Court's duty to maintain the separation of domestic and foreign affairs, thereby protecting national unity and power abroad, as well as local control and popular sovereignty at home.

Reflecting on the lessons of America's belated entry into the First World War, Sutherland argued that America should and could retain the promise of its written Constitution without sacrificing its ability to perform necessary international duties. "The limitations of the Constitution are not bonds which fetter the people," Sutherland argued, "they are restraints imposed by the people themselves upon the government which they have created as an instrumentality through which they rule in order that their creature may never forget that it has a creator."[59] Nevertheless, Sutherland warned, "any rule of construction which would result in curtailing or preventing action on the part of the national government in the enlarged field of world responsibility which we are entering, might prove highly injurious or embarrassing" and cannot be supported.[60] Substantive constitutional constraints on America's international role, Sutherland argued, could be devastating: "The question which does arise is startlingly simple and direct: May the power be exercised by governmental agency at all? A negative answer to this question in any given case, it will be seen, might be of the most serious consequence". . . .[61]

Sutherland noted in his 1919 book that there were really three options: 1) abandon the Constitution as out of date and inadequate to deal with modern dilemmas; 2) stick with the Constitution strictly interpreted and abandon the world role; or 3) argue, as he did, that the Constitution could be seen differently when applied to domestic as opposed to foreign policy.

Sutherland did not invent his solution out of thin air; quite the contrary. An astute student of law, Sutherland well understood that the Supreme Court had from the beginning struggled with the dilemma of a constitutional federation of states confronting a world of various types of government. In his book and in his *Curtiss-Wright* opinion, Sutherland reviewed the case history and began to see a clear line separating the way in which the Constitution affected domestic and foreign policy.

To justify his reading of the Constitution, Sutherland first had to show that in foreign affairs the national government was supreme and had the broadest possible latitude. It was equally important, however, to construct a theory that would not suggest that the national government had similar "inherent" or "extra-constitutional" powers in domestic affairs, but rather would show that foreign affairs powers were derived from different sources than those given to the government in the domestic realm.

Sutherland was convinced that his theory, though never before laid out in one piece, was a logical and consistent extension of Supreme Court doctrine. He was quite right to find that the Court consistently had found the Constitution to be less restrictive in foreign as compared with domestic policy. But Sutherland based his opinion not on the pragmatic rationale stream of the third option, which had come to be the most common approach, but rather he focused on the notion that national sovereignty created a separate set of powers for the national government, and thus produced two sets of rules—one set applicable to the domestic sphere, and another applicable to the foreign policy sphere.

Sutherland argued that the power to conduct foreign relations never was a state power, but rather was a power inherent in *national* sovereignty. The power to control foreign affairs passed from England to the federal government of the United States. Since it was not a state power, it could not be delegated or restricted by the states through the Constitution. It was, in some sense, "extra-constitutional." He argued that the government's authority in domestic affairs stemmed from the powers enumerated in the Constitution and those that were necessary and proper to execute the enumerated powers. Whereas domestic authority was carved "from the general mass of legislative powers then possessed by the states," authority in foreign affairs was always completely within the purview of the national government. "Since the states severally never possessed international powers, such powers could not have been carved from the mass of state powers but obviously were transmitted to the United States from some other source."[62] Sutherland argued that the national government's authority in foreign affairs did not require "affirmative grants" of power from the Constitution because they were derived from a source outside of the Constitution.[63]

Arguing that the states never were independent nations, and therefore never possessed international sovereignty, Sutherland concluded that in foreign affairs, the national government had, from the moment it declared its independence from England, been a collective state. If the individual states never had sovereignty or international standing, it was not theirs to give, or delegate, to the national government. Thus, foreign affairs powers were not delegated powers, but were inherent powers, powers that any nation enjoyed and that were beyond the reach of the states or the Tenth Amendment. Naturally, if these powers stemmed from a different source, they could and should be treated differently by the courts, or anyone trying to interpret the Constitution.

> Where the powers claimed for the general government are to be subtracted from the mass of original state powers, *that is, where they relate to domestic and internal affairs*, the claim must be justified by the express grants of the Constitution, or by the implications arising therefrom; but where the powers claimed are among those originally acquired and always exclusively held by the nation, *that is, where they relate to external affairs*, the claim is justified unless the powers are prohibited by the Constitution, or unless [they are] contrary to the fundamental principles upon which it was established.[64]

Note well his last line: The claim is justified unless the powers are specifically prohibited by the Constitution, or unless those powers "are contrary to the fundamental principles upon which" the Constitution was established. Even for George Sutherland, the Constitution was not silent or invalid in foreign policy. Where the Constitution spoke, it was to be obeyed: no act of the government, whether in foreign or domestic policy, could contradict an explicit constitutional prohibition. Where the Constitution spoke, the traditional interpretation would hold.

While many jurists and scholars have rejected Sutherland's history and reasoning, the decision itself "remains authoritative doctrine"[65] and the foundation for a number of seminal cases on the constitutionality of various foreign policies.[66]

A critical problem Sutherland left unanswered, however, was the lack of a definition of "national government." To say that the federal government is supreme in foreign policy is one thing, but it is quite another to say that the president, acting alone, has that power, or that the president, acting against Congress, has that power.

The vagueness in Sutherland's position did not pose a problem in *Curtiss-Wright*. The case concerned an allegedly unconstitutional delegation of power by the Congress to the president. Both political branches were in agreement. While it would still have been possible for the Court to have ruled this an unconstitutional delegation of power, the statute benefited from the presumption in favor of foreign policy that functions when the two political branches cooperate with each other.[67]

Sutherland's opinion suggested that so long as the effect of a particular policy was wholly external, there was precious little the Constitution prohibited the national government from doing so long as the national government acted in unison or at least without dissension. Sutherland's suggestion, however, left a second serious problem: Even in Sutherland's time, the very idea that anything could be "entirely external to the United States" had become a fantasy. *Curtiss-Wright* itself involved an American corporation, American stockholders and American employees who were directly affected by the policy in question and by the Court's ruling.

Sutherland had written *Curtiss-Wright* with the hope of developing a doctrine that might allow the United States to play an aggressive and significant world role without giving up its checks and balances at home or its reliance on decentralized, local government. He wanted big, central and efficient government for foreign affairs and small, local and responsive government at home. His objective was intellectually noble, but fundamentally flawed. While his brethren would grow to accept the notion that there were legitimate distinctions to be made between domestic and foreign affairs in the postwar world, there could be no complete divorce, at least not if the Court were to apply the words and spirit of the Constitution.

Sutherland was a leading proponent of the concept that in America, politics could stop at the water's edge, a popular slogan that "encapsulated the hope that diplomacy could be separated from domestic politics." But, as the Cold War, Korea, and Vietnam would demonstrate, "Diplomacy could not be separated from domestic politics: An emergency abroad could not be stopped at the water's edge" and the Court could not draw a simple and hard line between the two.[68]

While many point to cases such as *Durand* and *Curtiss-Wright* as the foundations for executive prerogative powers in foreign policy, theirs is a fundamentally flawed reading that ignores the context in which these cases were decided, as well as the substance of the decisions themselves. This interpretation looks even more forced and inappropriate when one studies the presidents of the period. Though some were far more active than others, they all shared a general commitment to the Constitution's division of powers among the branches of the national government. The presidents shared with the justices an overriding concern *not* with the *horizontal* separation of powers between the branches of the national government, but rather with the questions of what powers the *national* government as a whole had.

Chapter 2 provides a close look at the presidents of this period and their own constitutional interpretation in foreign policy, and reveals a clear set of norms that can be called a traditional interpretation of presidential power in foreign policy. It is not the foundation for prerogative powers some might like to believe.

At the dawn of the Second World War, the Supreme Court was still unable to fix a clear line on foreign policy powers. The war and its aftermath swamped the Court in this respect, and attention began to shift from the quickly receding question of the vertical separation of powers to the more contentious issue of the claims by individuals against the government as a whole as well as the horizontal separation of powers. Chapter 5 will examine this development, arguing that the Court built on the doctrine developed before the war, and sent clear signals to Congress and the president—signals of what the national government as a whole could and could not do, as well as signals of what each branch could do in foreign policy.

2

The Executive and the Traditional Interpretation

Presidents obviously understand the value of wrapping themselves in the flag, and when it comes to foreign policy they understand as well the value of wrapping themselves in the Constitution. Constitutional justifications can help a president win political debates, and they certainly will help in any court battle. But constitutional interpretation is more than a cynical tool: How presidents conceive of the office powerfully shapes the measures they take. Similarly, since presidents have become primary sources of legislation, their interpretation of the Constitution and the place of foreign policy in the constitutional structure of government can set the terms of debate in Congress and the courts. If the other branches come to accept the executive branch's interpretation of the Constitution, that change influences present and future legislation in a system that is built on precedent; the nature and effectiveness of the separation of powers is affected as well.

Despite the regular pendulum swings in power between Congress and the executive branch, and the occasional intervention of the Supreme Court, certain fundamental assumptions about the Constitution and foreign policy developed early and were steadily maintained by all three branches, at least until the First World War. All seemed to share a traditional interpretation that the specific restrictions in the Constitution were inviolable; that Congress had a legitimate role to play should it choose to assert that role in any and all policy areas including foreign policy; and that though foreign policy might be treated more loosely, it nonetheless was governed by the Constitution. When the Constitution was perceived to be an unacceptable constraint, some made exceptions to the rules, but never challenged the rules themselves; they broke the rules, and defended their actions not as an alternate reading of the Constitution, but rather as a temporary exception under particular conditions. After the Second World War, practical needs combined with political choices to produce a new interpretation of the Constitution. The exceptions became the rule, and a prerogative interpretation of the Constitution emerged from the executive branch, acquiesced to by Congress, and given constitutional support by the Supreme Court.

Those who find precedents for the prerogative interpretation scattered among the activist presidents before the 1940s aren't exactly right. The actions they took seem to support the claim, but only if the president's actions are divorced from the presidential rhetoric behind those actions. A close look at these presidents reveals that they too subscribed to the traditional interpretation. Something very different happened in the post-war era when the prerogative claims were made—no longer were these advocated as exceptions to generally accepted norms, now the norms themselves were challenged and rejected.

There has been a change. But if that change merely reflects a pragmatic adaptation of the Constitution to changing needs and circumstances, then that change may well be in keeping with the constitutional scheme as laid out in the *Federalist Papers.* But if the change has undermined the constitutional scheme, if the change has disrupted the assumptions underlying the Constitution, then it needs to be confronted and understood.

* * *

At the dawn of the American republic there were two primary conceptions of the office of the president. Alexander Hamilton argued that the president had to be energetic and that his constitutional power naturally had to match his role. While Hamilton argued that the president would be limited by the specific prohibitions of the Constitution it was, as Theodore Roosevelt put it, "not only his right but his duty to do anything that the needs of the Nation demanded unless such action was forbidden by the Constitution or by the laws."[1]

The competing view was the Madisonian-Jeffersonian conception. This school argued that the president had been delegated specific powers and had the authority to execute those responsibilities. In the end, however, it was the job of the legislature to legislate and the job of the executive to execute. As William Howard Taft put it, "the president can exercise no power which cannot be fairly and reasonably traced to some specific grant of power or justly implied and included within such express grant as proper and necessary to its exercise. Such specific grant must be either in the Federal Constitution or in an act of Congress passed in pursuance thereof."[2]

In their competition, these conceptions have shaped the contours of the office of the president from the earliest battle between Hamilton and Madison (writing at Jefferson's insistence) over neutrality during the Washington administration, down to recent debates about war powers, intelligence gathering, and arms control treaties. Though it is safe to say that the Hamiltonian conception has dominated, Madisonian arguments have lingered and continue to offer a legitimate tool to challenge overly ambitious presidents. But regardless of where they fell on the Madison-Hamilton spectrum, presidents before the world wars all subscribed to certain absolute limits they agreed were imposed by the Constitution, and tended to accept the idea that though they might exercise a host of strategies to persuade or bully Congress into submission, in the end—should Congress care to—the legislature had a legitimate constitutional role in foreign as well as in domestic affairs. Some exceeded or avoided what they perceived to be constitutional constraints, but they in no way argued for prerogative rights.

The Traditional Interpretation and the Madisonian Presidents

Thomas Jefferson certainly should have embodied the Madisonian-Jeffersonian conception of the Chief Executive. No one understood the argument better, and no one—save Madison perhaps—could better articulate it. Nevertheless, by the end of his term Jefferson had presided over a near doubling of American territory through the constitutionally suspect Louisiana Purchase, ordered American naval units to attack the forces of the Barbary states without benefit of congressional authorization, and presided over a draconian attack on American civil liberties to support and defend a terribly unpopular embargo designed to keep America out of war with Britain and France.

President Jefferson had the welcome advantage of a strong majority in Congress, giving him greater latitude to take constitutionally suspect actions. Jefferson's actions would later be construed as precedents for future presidents to exploit and upon which to build even more expansive interpretations of presidential power.[3] But Jefferson did not attempt to legitimate his actions by reinterpreting the Constitution. In fact, he acted with the explicit understanding that his actions contravened the Constitution. He felt his actions were unavoidable in these instances, but made no effort to justify them by cloaking them in a prerogative interpretation of the Constitution.

In 1801, Jefferson decided that the constant harassment of American shipping by the Mediterranean Barbary states and their increasing demands for tribute payments no longer were tolerable. Not only that, but he maintained that the Barbary states actually had declared war on the United States. In an attempt to resolve the dispute through negotiation if possible, and force if necessary, Jefferson authorized the dispatch of an American naval detachment to the Mediterranean. In his annual message to Congress in December of 1801, Jefferson only announced that the squadron had responded to an attack, not that it had been ordered to prepare to attack. In his report, Jefferson emphasized that the squadron's actions had been constrained by a scrupulous respect for congressional war powers' prerogatives. "Unauthorized by the Constitution, without the sanction of Congress, to go beyond the line of defence," Jefferson told Congress,[4] the squadron had merely disarmed the attacking ships, remaining within their strict constitutional limits.[5] While this fit in well with Jefferson's attempt to govern vigorously behind a veil of anti-government theory,[6] Jefferson also used the occasion to call for legislation that would authorize the president to order offensive as well as defensive military action in similar incidents in the future. Three months after the president delivered his message, Congress passed an act authorizing the action the president already had taken against Tripoli.

The Barbary case appears to create a precedent for a prerogative interpretation of the Constitution only if we ignore Jefferson's arguments and his own understanding of his actions. Jefferson acted beyond the Constitution—and acknowledged that fact. Jefferson then went to Congress for *post facto* authorization, never making any executive-prerogative claims. In seeking formal delegation of new powers from Congress, he acknowledged that these powers were not his under the Constitution, and that only Congress could provide the executive with the power he sought.

Just as the Barbary incident later was construed to be a precedent in war powers, the Louisiana Purchase later was construed as a powerful precedent in constitutional interpretation, not just of the treaty power but of how presidents might reconcile constitutional scruples with perceived national needs.

Jefferson had long believed that the republic could only survive if it continued to be an agricultural nation. To do that it had to expand, increasing the amount of farmland to balance the growing cities. When presented with the sudden opportunity to get an enormous tract of land, Jefferson saw vital domestic and international advantages and was willing to act despite his own conviction that the Constitution did not authorize the national government, let alone the president, to acquire new territory for the United States. In outlining the agreement to his cabinet in July 1803, Jefferson told them that though he would submit the agreement to both houses of Congress (the Senate to approve the treaty and the House for needed appropriations), Congress "will be obliged to ask from the people an amendment to the Constitution authorizing their receiving the province into the Union."[7] By 18 August, however, Jefferson had been convinced that the delicacy of the negotiation might fall apart if he opened the door to a constitutional debate over Louisiana. As a result, he reluctantly agreed that the treaty should pass with as little discussion of the constitutional difficulty as possible. It would be "prudent," Jefferson wrote to Thomas Paine, "to say nothing on that subject, but to do *sub-silentio* what shall be found necessary."[8]

Some of Jefferson's advisors produced a set of constitutional justifications for the Louisiana purchase that hinged on loose readings of the Constitution. Albert Gallatin, Jefferson's secretary of the treasury, argued that the United States possessed all the powers of any sovereign nation, including "the power enjoyed by every other nation of extending their territory by treaties."[9] It would only be natural, Gallatin argued, to read the "several provisions which authorize the several branches of government to make war, to make treaties, and to govern the territory of the Union" as delegating the power of acquiring territory to the United States.[10]

It was precisely this sort of broad construction that most concerned Jefferson: He understood the precedent it would set. "Our peculiar security," he had written, "is in the possession of a written Constitution. Let us not make it a blank paper by construction."[11] Jefferson rejected the notion of stretching or manipulating the Constitution to arrive at a desired result. Jefferson was not arguing for a weak executive, or a weak nation. Rather, he was arguing that the constitutional flaws or inadequacies had to be corrected through proper channels, not simply interpreted away.

Jefferson's confidence in the American people and in the system of government was strong enough, he wrote, that he was sure "the good sense of our country will correct the evil of construction when it shall produce ill effects."[12] As Henry Adams noted, the evils Jefferson foresaw as a possible outcome of his decision on Louisiana were but remote possibilities; "in the hands of true republicans the Constitution, even though violated, was on the whole safe; the precedent, though alarming, was exceptional."[13] The Barbary incident and the Louisiana Purchase established important precedents for the president as commander in chief and for treaty-powers, but in neither case did Jefferson attempt to argue that these were his powers exclusively—in each case Congress played a decisive role either before or after the action. The action itself provided a precedent for future actions, as Arthur Schlesinger has well documented, but in neither case did Jefferson provide a precedent for the assertion of a constitutional prerogative power.

The economic embargo imposed in Jefferson's second term was a third landmark of extraordinary power, but again it was done with the full cooperation of Congress, and Jefferson never argued that these measures were within the president's exclusive authority. The Fourth Embargo Act of 1808 posed the greatest problems for Jefferson, for it wasn't until then that virtually all trade, both international and coastal, was prohibited. Before the Fourth Act, the coastal trade—shipping goods between the states themselves along the Eastern seaboard—had been legal. Not surprisingly, shippers had discovered that they could set out with a cargo bound for New York, and somehow end up needing to "dump" their cargo at sea, or put in for repairs in Canada or Newfoundland, where they would "jettison" that cargo. These loopholes were closed by the Fourth Act, but to make these prohibitions stick with a resistant public required an extraordinary exercise of power.

Jefferson exercised extraordinary and often oppressive power,[14] but always with congressional support, and was, in fact, enforcing laws passed by Congress. Jefferson often disingenuously argued that he was *merely* enforcing the congressional will, but actually Congress only agreed under extreme pressure. Nevertheless, he did have congressional and statutory authority, so opponents could not argue that the president had violated the separation of powers. Instead opponents would have to argue that the national government, as a whole, did not have the constitutional authority to pass and enforce the embargo.

Despite the examples he left behind, Jefferson never argued that the power to pursue constitutionally suspect policies was his alone. In each case he went to Congress either after the fact (as with the Barbary case) or during the event (Louisiana) or to secure advance support, legitimacy and authorization (as with the Embargo). Gerhard Casper has argued that Jefferson considered himself an agent of the people, "and it was that agency relationship—rather than a false confidence in Hamiltonian 'sound judgment'—that afforded Jefferson the hope of 'indemnity,' of an ultimate vindication for legal trespasses." Jefferson, Casper concludes, "interpreted that agency relationship according to the written 'instructions' of the Constitution," though there were times, as in Louisiana, when he stretched the agency relationship into more of a guardian's relationship.[15] Though Jefferson certainly can be cited as a source of support for a broad interpretation of the powers of the *national government*, acting as a *whole*, it is quite incorrect to cite Jefferson and the Barbary, Louisiana, and Embargo cases as support for a broad reading of executive prerogative in foreign or in domestic affairs.

* * *

Jefferson was not the only strict-constructionist president responsible for important precedents that would later be used to develop and legitimate an Executive prerogative interpretation of the Constitution. James K. Polk nearly doubled the size of the United States during his administration by adding Texas, the Southwest, California, and Oregon. But these gains came at some considerable cost not only in lives and treasure, but also in precedents for the exercise of extensive executive power—precedents that sharply contrasted with Polk's frequently aired strict reading of the Constitution.

It would be reasonable to argue that Polk's commitment to strict construction applied only to domestic affairs,[16] for in foreign policy Polk set some extraordinary precedents and contributed mightily to the extension of executive power. But like Jefferson, Polk made no attempt to articulate a distinction between foreign and domestic policy in his constitutional interpretation. In fact, he set important precedents, with the support of Congress, though this support often came after the fact, and required a good deal of persuasion.

The annexation of Texas was all but complete before Polk took office in March 1845. Though President Tyler had been rebuffed when he tried to secure support for a treaty on the Texas question, he had come up with what he argued was a perfectly legitimate alternative to annexation by treaty. Tyler argued that a joint resolution of Congress (requiring a simple majority rather than the two-thirds of the Senate required for a treaty) would be sufficient.[17] Three days before Polk took office, Tyler signed the joint resolution and dispatched a representative to Texas to conclude the annexation negotiations. Late in Polk's term, Senator Tappan of Ohio claimed that Polk had met with reluctant senators before the inauguration to urge them to vote for the joint resolution. Though in his diary Polk denied having done this, he acknowledged "having had conversations with Senator Haywood and other Senators on the subject in which he had urged Congress to act positively before it adjourned."[18] Both Tyler and Polk were clearly seeking to circumvent the constitutional constraint of the two-thirds requirement for treaties, but neither tried to assert anything resembling a prerogative interpretation. Both sought legislative approval for their policy.

The war powers question was the next to arise. As soon as Texas agreed to the annexation, Polk ordered the army to move south from the Nueces River to the Rio Grande, even though Mexico insisted that the Nueces, and not the Rio Grande, was the legitimate border. On 9 May 1846 Polk told his cabinet that he would go to Congress on the following Tuesday (12 May) to seek a declaration of war against Mexico. Within hours of the cabinet meeting, however, Polk learned that the American forces he had dispatched to the disputed Rio Grande border had been attacked on the northern bank of the Rio Grande and that, in the words of General Zachary Taylor (who was commanding the American forces at the River), "Hostilities may now be considered as commenced."[19]

With war already underway, Polk asked Congress "to recognize the existence of the war, and to place at the disposition of the Executive the means of prosecuting the war with vigor, and thus hastening the restoration of peace."[20] By overwhelming majorities, the House and Senate passed Polk's resolution declaring that a state of war existed with Mexico.

One soon-to-be powerful voice denounced the president's action. Congressman Abraham Lincoln was appalled, particularly by the prerogative arguments made by others, including his own law partner, William Herndon, to defend Polk's actions.[21] If to prevent or repel invasion, Lincoln wrote to Herndon, the president may "invade the territory of another country," who was to judge this necessity? If "the President is to be the sole judge," this was a blatant violation of the Constitution. "Allow the President to invade a neighboring nation, whenever he shall deem it necessary for such purpose," Lincoln wrote, "and you allow him to make war at pleasure. Study to see if you can fix any limit to his power in this respect, after you have given him so much as you propose."[22]

That Polk ordered the troops to take a controversial position that he knew would inflame the Mexicans is hard to deny; that he anticipated hostilities and possibly war is similarly well supported by the documents that are available. Polk placed the troops into a disputed area and had every reason to expect them to be attacked. When they were, he could argue that they were responding to an attack on American territory, and thus there was no need for a declaration of war. But Polk *did* go to Congress to ask for legislative support and for the statutory authority "to call into the public service a large body of volunteers"[23] to fight the war.

As had President Jefferson, Polk established important precedents for future claims of executive prerogative in foreign affairs. Also like Jefferson, Polk actively secured *post facto* congressional support for his actions. Though Polk argued that he had intended to secure authorization for the Mexican war before hostilities occurred, that is not what happened, and it added to the precedent set by Jefferson in the Barbary case. The precedent, that constitutional violations could be legitimated after the fact by Congress, was an important one for Polk's contemporary critic, Abraham Lincoln. The Mexican War precedents were explicitly cited by the Supreme Court in 1863 when the Justices sanctioned a number of Lincoln's constitutionally suspect policies that had received *post facto* authorization from Congress.[24] But Polk never articulated or defended a prerogative interpretation of the Constitution itself, and kept within the loose confines of the traditional interpretation.

The Traditional Interpretation and the Hamiltonian Presidents

While there were a number of strict constructionist presidents before the Second World War, there were many who interpreted their role in a more Hamiltonian fashion. They understood the Constitution to limit certain actions and forbid others, but beyond these specific restrictions they argued that the President had broad authority and was expected to exercise it vigorously.[25]

Of all the presidents, Madisonian and Hamiltonian alike, none faced a more fundamental challenge to the nation than did Abraham Lincoln. Though Lincoln stretched, pushed, bent and even violated the Constitution, Lincoln's interpretation of it can nonetheless be viewed as a traditional one. Though his constitutionally questionable actions were almost exclusively concerned with domestic affairs, it is appropriate to consider him here because his actions often are invoked as defense for, and justification of, the executive prerogative interpretation for foreign policy. Even under the trial of a civil war, however, Lincoln did not articulate or defend an executive prerogative interpretation of the Constitution. His strategy varied from using the *post facto* authorization that Jefferson and Polk used all the way to openly admitting that he had indeed exercised powers that were, perhaps, beyond those constitutionally delegated to the president. But, he was quick to note, even if he were to concede that these powers were not assigned to the president, they were powers that were constitutionally assigned to Congress. He may have overstepped the powers of the executive, but he was not authorizing action prohibited to the *national* government, an important distinction in the era governed by the traditional interpretation of foreign policy powers. Furthermore, his securing of *post facto* authorization would legitimate even these most questionable actions. He would argue that the violations were necessary, but he did not argue that they were within the scope of legitimate presidential prerogative. It is one thing to argue that necessity requires a violation of the Constitution; it is altogether different to argue that the Constitution itself permits temporary suspension in time of emergency. In Lincoln's case, he argued that *if* he violated the Constitution, he did so because he saw no alternative and *not* because he found *constitutionally* sanctioned prerogative powers within the Constitution itself.

When Lincoln finally addressed Congress in a special message in July 1861, he argued that he had never exceeded the powers of the government as a whole, and that he had acted in the confidence that Congress would ratify and legitimate his exercise of congressional and/or national powers. He addressed a number of measures he had taken, including the call-up of a 75,000-strong militia and the proclamation "for closing the ports of the insurrectionary districts by proceedings in the nature of Blockade." These measures, Lincoln argued, were "believed to be strictly legal."[26]

On the question of the power to suspend the writ of *habeas corpus*, Lincoln's message to Congress was particularly tortured. First Lincoln developed an extensive defense based on his contention that the Constitution never meant that the Union should fail because one law must be enforced. "[A]re all the laws, but one to go unexecuted," Lincoln asked, "and the government itself go to pieces, lest that one be violated? Even in such a case, would not the official oath be broken, if the government should be overthrown, when it was believed that disregarding the single law, would tend to preserve it?"[27] Here Lincoln seemed to be preparing an alternative to the traditional interpretation of the Constitution, but suddenly he stepped back. After making the case for the violation of an explicit Constitutional provision, Lincoln denied that there was any violation at all. "It was not believed," Lincoln wrote, "that any law was violated. The [*habeas corpus*] provision of the Constitution . . . is equivalent to a provision—is a provision—that such privilege may be suspended when, in cases of rebellion, or invasion, the public safety does require it."[28] Lincoln then proceeded to refute the claim that *only* Congress could suspend the writ, arguing that "the Constitution itself, is silent as to which, or who, is to exercise the power." To further bolster his position, Lincoln added that the provision for the suspension of the writ "was plainly made for a dangerous emergency, [and] it cannot be believed the framers of the instrument intended, that in every case, the danger should run its course, until Congress could be called together; the very assembling of which might be prevented, as was intended in this case, by the rebellion."[29]

On the question of the draft, Lincoln explicitly conceded that he may indeed have exceeded the constitutional powers of the presidency, but he never claimed that he had the constitutional authority to override the Constitution itself. His measures to expand the regular Army and Navy, he argued, "whether strictly legal or not, were ventured upon, under what appeared to be a popular demand, and a public necessity; trusting, then as now, that Congress would readily ratify them."[30] Lincoln again demonstrated a belief in, if not a firm commitment to, the idea that Congress alone had the power to *legitimate* these actions, though necessity might require that he perform them in the absence of congressional approval. Lincoln seemed to be developing a distinction between an extraordinary exercise of emergency power and the legitimate exercise of constitutional authority. While he acknowledged that only Congress could legitimate an expansion of the regular Army, Lincoln noted a few months later that the Court too had a legitimate right to review his decision on the draft. As he wrote in a letter to New York Governor Horatio Seymour in 1863, "I do not object to abide a decision of the United States Supreme Court . . . on the constitutionality of the draft law. In fact, I should be willing to facilitate the obtaining of it; but I can not consent to lose the time while it is being obtained. . . . My purpose is to be, in my action, just and constitutional; and yet practical, in performing the important duty, with which I am charged, of maintaining the unity, and the free principles of our common country."[31]

Clearly, Lincoln was willing to do what he believed was necessary, but he did not argue that necessary action was transformed into legitimate action by the word of a single man.

Lincoln's position on the Emancipation Proclamation was another example of his skillful expansion of executive powers within the traditional interpretation. Lincoln argued that the government had no power to free slaves in peacetime. But, as a measure designed to further American war aims, he believed he could constitutionally order slaves freed as a military measure under his authority as commander in chief. Lincoln argued that the Constitution gave extensive powers to the commander in chief in time of war and, just as the military commander might seize property from a belligerent and dispose of it to aid the cause, so too might the military commander seize and free the slaves in disputed territories. As he noted in a letter to Salmon Chase in 1863, Lincoln could only free slaves in military zones. "The original proclamation has no constitutional or legal justification, except as a military measure." To free the slaves in uncontested areas, Lincoln argued, would be an unconstitutional exercise of arbitrary power. Without the argument of military necessity, he asked, would he not be "without any argument, except the one that I think the measure politically expedient, and morally right? Would I not thus give up all footing upon Constitution or law? Would I not thus be in the boundless field of absolutism? Could this pass unnoticed, or unresisted? . . . Would it not lose us the elections, and with them, the very cause we seek to advocate?[32] Relying on the argument that the commander in chief enjoyed certain war powers was both handy and effective, since it allowed

Lincoln to remain within the contours of what he understood to be a legitimate and traditional reading of the Constitution.

In his path-breaking work, *The Imperial Presidency*, Arthur M. Schlesinger Jr. argues that there are circumstances under which the executive might be justified in exercising extraconstitutional power. He notes, however, the critical distinction between actions justified by appeals to necessity, and actions justified by assertions of "routine or inherent presidential power."[33] By focusing on Lincoln's constitutional interpretation rather than on his actions, it is possible to advance an alternative argument; that there is a clear and important distinction between the exercise of prerogative powers under the guise of legitimate constitutional authority, and the exercise of power under the conditions Schlesinger outlines, but without any attempt to assert for these exercises of necessary power the cloak of constitutional legitimacy. Lincoln appears to have understood this distinction well, as did Jefferson, Polk, Wilson, and both Roosevelts. The distinction is an important one because the exercise of *extraordinary* emergency power—power that is not described or legitimated by the Constitution itself, but is inherently under a cloud of illegitimacy—is far less likely to be folded into the accepted interpretation of the Constitution than is the uncontested assertion of constitutional prerogative.

Lincoln's *actions* certainly exceeded what one might have expected from an adherent to the traditional interpretation, but his rhetoric was that of one who believed in it. He lived in an extraordinary time, but he was able to see the nation through its greatest challenge without reinterpreting the Constitution in part because of his own skills, and in part because the powers he asserted often were new, and therefore represented less of a direct contradiction with established precedents or established powers of Congress or the court. It was, as Clinton Rossiter put it, "new, untapped power" but "Congress gave him nothing but unenthusiastic acquiescence. . . ."[34]

Though many later presidents would misread Lincoln's actions as a precedent for a reinterpretation of the Constitution, one perceptively recognized the important distinctions. In his reflections on his time in office, William Howard Taft conceded that Lincoln, "with the stress of the greatest civil war in modern times felt called upon to do things, the constitutionality of which was seriously questioned." But, "Lincoln always pointed out the source of the authority which in his opinion justified his acts, and there was always a strong ground for maintaining the view which he took."[35] On the issue of *habeas corpus*, Taft argued that Lincoln had gained the subsequent approval of Congress and that the Supreme Court had sustained that statute. Taft praised as well Lincoln's justification of the Emancipation Proclamation as a necessary military act carried out under his constitutional authority as Commander in Chief. What truly distinguished Lincoln, in Taft's view, was that he "never claimed that whatever authority in government was not expressly denied to him he could exercise."[36]

Theodore Roosevelt: Energy in the Executive

Although Lincoln's commitments and theory seem to fit within the traditional interpretation, his actions—like those of Jefferson and Polk—set important precedents for presidents facing potential emergencies. Theodore Roosevelt, who consciously set out to expand the powers of the presidency, used the actions taken by Jefferson, Polk, and Lincoln as support for his actions. No president, he wrote in his autobiography "ought to content himself with the negative merit of keeping his talents undamaged in a napkin."[37]

Although Roosevelt did spell out a far more wide ranging view of the powers of the presidency than had his predecessors, a close examination reveals a skilled politician who articulated a bold view of the presidency but functioned within the parameters of the traditional interpretation. Roosevelt's rhetoric was, in the end, considerably bolder than were his actions, but even his rhetoric reveals a deep-seated commitment to the fundamental tenets of the traditional interpretation. Roosevelt ultimately bullied, cajoled, and built public pressure to gain congressional approval for his policies, without asserting a prerogative interpretation of Executive power.

In his reflections on his time in the White House, Roosevelt echoed Hamilton's insistence on the need for "energy" in the executive, but each of these assertions was followed quickly by a caveat that the president should do all he could to meet national needs "unless such action was forbidden by the Constitution or by the laws." While the first part of the caveat—unless forbidden by the Constitution—was compatible with an executive prerogative interpretation, the second part was not, for it endorsed the idea that Congress (which makes the laws) has the legitimate authority to block the president. If forbidden "by the laws," even the active, energetic "steward" of the people said he would be forced to relent. This commitment turns up again when Roosevelt emphasized that he "did not usurp power" as president, but did "greatly broaden the use of Executive power." Roosevelt was proud of the fact that he had "acted for the common well-being of all our people, whenever and in whatever manner was necessary," but again he added the caveat that he did so "unless prevented by direct constitutional or legislative prohibition."[38] Were these caveats merely an attempt by Roosevelt to adjust his own historical position? Perhaps. But the fact that he felt it appropriate or useful or necessary to articulate these caveats suggests that he was unwilling to advocate a different interpretation of the Constitution. At least formally, he was interested in being seen as a subscriber to the traditional interpretation.

There is some confusion about Theodore Roosevelt largely because he tends to be viewed from a modern perspective rather than in the constitutional context of his own time. When we look back at Roosevelt's active use of power and expansion of presidential power in particular, we see it from the perspective of the struggle for power *within* the national government, in other words, the struggle between the executive, legislative, and judicial branches of the national government. But in his era, as for most of the history of American constitutional development before the world wars, the real battle was between advocates of a strong nation versus those who feared central power, struggled to retain checks on it, and advocated the continuation of decentralized authority.

Though Roosevelt may have signaled the start of a shift to the struggle *within* the national government, that shift would have to wait until the Second World War. Roosevelt's efforts focused on the then more familiar struggle to assert national authority in the face of claims for state autonomy. Roosevelt argued that there were inherent rights in the nation itself, and maintained that this interpretation was grounded in the words and writing of James Wilson, one of the founding fathers.[39]

Wilson provided the support for Roosevelt's belief that "an inherent power rested in the nation, outside of the enumerated powers conferred upon it by the Constitution, in all cases where the object involved was beyond the power of the several States and was a power ordinarily exercised by sovereign nations."[40] This does not, of course, mean that this national power is vested in the president. Quite the contrary, in Wilson's own words these powers belong to "the United States in Congress assembled."[41] For Roosevelt, the controversial and critical point was that the national government should not be limited to only those powers that were explicitly delegated by the Constitution.

When it came time to act, Roosevelt did not act alone. He readily admitted to using the tools of executive power to bully and cajole support from legislators. In discussing his efforts to secure Senate confirmation for controversial appointments, Roosevelt admitted that "where I could arouse public attention, I could force through the appointment in spite of the opposition of the Senators."[42]

In a case involving an executive commitment to an agreement to settle outstanding debt problems in the Dominican Republic, Roosevelt faced firm opposition in the Senate. Roosevelt maintained that he could enforce his policy preference during his own term in office but that he had no constitutional authority to commit the nation to that policy beyond his own administration. Facing strong Senate opposition to a negotiated treaty concerning the debts, Roosevelt executed an agreement before the Senate acted on it, arguing that the agreement itself was constitutional because "the Constitution did not forbid my doing what I did."[43] Roosevelt distinguished what he perceived to be needed action and legitimate law. "[I]t was far preferable that there should be action by Congress, so that we might be proceeding under a treaty which was the law of the land and not merely by a direction of the Chief Executive which would lapse when that particular Executive left office. I therefore did my best to get the Senate to ratify what I had done."[44]

The Santo Domingo treaty certainly provided a precedent for the use of executive agreements, but it was as much a result of Senate inaction as it was the result of presidential action. Roosevelt acted, but with uncharacteristic caution. The agreement called for certain payments to other nations, and Roosevelt arranged for those payments to be placed in escrow until the Senate acted. Roosevelt agreed that only the Senate could make his agreement into law: "In the event that the Senate rejected the protocol," he said, "the money would be returned to the Dominican Republic."[45]

* * *

Unsurprisingly, William Howard Taft took exception to Roosevelt's characterization of him as a pusillanimous pushover.[46] Taft, though far more of a traditionalist than was Roosevelt, could hardly be called an enemy of energy in the executive. Taft saw tremendous power in constitutional interpretation and even greater power in statutory interpretation. "In executing a statute of Congress," Taft wrote, "the president's course is as clear, or as doubtful, as the statute. In order that he or his subordinates shall enforce the statute, they must necessarily find out what it means, and on their interpretation of it enforce the law." Taft concluded, therefore, that "statutory construction is practically one of the greatest of Executive powers." Or, as Taft put it, "some one has said, 'Let me make the ballads of the country, and I care not who makes the laws.' One might also say, paraphrasing this, 'Let any one make the laws of the country, if I can construe them.' "[47]

Beyond statutory construction, Taft argued that one can be a strict constructionist with a traditional interpretation of the Constitution and yet still believe that the president derives power from the "take care" clause of the Constitution.[48] Citing Supreme court opinions, Taft wrote: "Nor are the laws of the execution of which the president is to take care, confined to express congressional statutes and provisions having force of law in treaties."[49] Taft suggested as well that in those areas where Congress failed to act, it would be within the president's legitimate authority to act on his own. Taft did believe, however, that there were limits to presidential autonomy. The president could "exercise no power which cannot be fairly and reasonably traced to some specific grant of power or justly implied and included within such express grant as proper and necessary to its exercise."[50] Here Taft was setting up his attack on the implications of Theodore Roosevelt's rhetoric—if not Roosevelt's actions—in favor of a far broader exercise of executive power.

Taft made a particular point of noting that in a very difficult coal strike situation in Pennsylvania, Roosevelt had discussed the exercise of executive powers beyond the Constitution, but in fact used his political skills and his clearly constitutional powers to bring the situation under control: What was *actually* done was the result of [Roosevelt's] activity, his power to influence public opinion and the effect of the prestige of his great office in bringing the parties to the controversy, the mine owners and the strikers, to a legal settlement by arbitration.[51]

Taft argued that Roosevelt and members of his cabinet had articulated a theory of the presidency that offered a fundamentally new interpretation of executive power. Taft recognized that Roosevelt had not, in fact, *acted* on this interpretation, but nevertheless, the rhetoric was on the table.

The traditional interpretation, which had survived in fact during Roosevelt's administration, revived in spirit during Taft's term. Despite their differences, both presidents agreed that when it came to foreign affairs, all power was vested exclusively in the *national* government. And even though Taft and Roosevelt had begun to hint at the shift from the question of the state-national (*vertical*) separation of powers to a focus on the division of power *within* the national government (*horizontal*), neither was yet at a point where they would explicitly focus on the separation of powers at the national level. It wouldn't be until the Second World War that the struggle to adapt a Constitution of limited powers to a world of unlimited force would finally and decisively shift the focus.

A Constitutional Scholar in the White House

Woodrow Wilson came to the presidency well versed in constitutional theory and had argued extensively in his writing for a stronger chief executive. Wilson maintained that the wall of separation between the legislative and executive branches had to be breached—that the procedures and forms growing out of the Constitution were outmoded, and had to be adapted to modern conditions. Wilson did not, however, argue that the Constitution itself was outmoded, nor that there needed to be a radical shift in constitutional interpretation. Instead, Wilson maintained that there was and should be a critical distinction between the forms and procedures growing from the Constitution and the principles embedded in the document.

Wilson was captivated by Charles Darwin, as were many intellectuals of his day, and he was eager to apply to the social sciences the conclusions Darwin drew from the natural sciences. For Wilson, Darwin's ideas had to replace the founders' paradigms that derived from Sir Isaac Newton's physical theories. When Wilson looked at the Constitution he rightly concluded that it was powerfully influenced by the mechanical theories of Newton: "If you pick up the *Federalist*," Wilson told one audience, "some parts of it read like a treatise on astronomy instead of a treatise on government. They speak of the centrifugal and the centripetal forces, and locate the president somewhere in a rotating system. The whole thing is a calculation of power and an adjustment of parts."[52] It was a cranking, clanking system and, according to Wilson, government must be seen "not as a machine, but a living thing. It is accountable to Darwin, not to Newton. No living thing can have its organs offset against each other as checks, and live. On the contrary, its life is dependent upon their quick cooperation, their ready response to the commands of instinct or intelligence, their amicable community of purpose.[53] Notice that this is not a plea for executive dominance, nor for a hierarchy of the branches of the national government, though that might be consistent with a Darwinian approach. The argument is for cooperation, for the division of tasks, and, in a sense, for applying theories of comparative advantage to the division of responsibility in government.

For Wilson, the president was meant to be as powerful and as influential as possible. To do this, Wilson argued, was quite feasible within the limits of the Constitution. The means were available and a skillful president could be a very powerful one. Wilson argued that the President had to use the tools of his office, particularly the party machinery and the President's ability to influence public opinion and bring it to bear against a recalcitrant legislature. Naturally, Congress was free to go head-to-head in any battle with the president—Wilson rejected the idea that the president could simply ignore Congress. If in a contest between them, however, the president were to win, that would merely suggest that the President had been more skillful than had the legislators. "If Congress be overborne by him, it will be from no lack of constitutional powers on its part, but only because the President has the nation behind him, and Congress has not."[54]

Wilson noted that there are both legitimate and illegitimate tools a president might use in his effort to persuade. Among the illegitimate tools Wilson discussed would be an attempt by the president to substitute his own orders for acts of Congress that he wants but cannot get. Such things, Wilson wrote, "are not only deeply immoral, they are destructive of the fundamental understandings of constitutional government and, therefore, of constitutional government itself."[55]

Wilson's argument for an aggressive presidency and for an assertive theory of executive leadership fit within the corners of the traditional interpretation. Wilson rejected the idea that the president was above the law, and accepted that ultimately the legislature had the final power to decide the fate of most presidential initiatives. Statutory restrictions were to be respected: In discussing the president's authority to seize a radio station at Sisconset, Massachusetts in 1914, Wilson's attorney general argued that the President had "the right and the duty to protect" American neutrality and, in so doing, he might order his subordinates to seize the station, but only "in the absence of any statutory restriction."[56] The legitimate authority of Congress to pass legislation prohibiting this seizure was acknowledged, and the president's power was seen as limited to an area where there was no statutory prohibition. Clearly this is a Hamiltonian view of the Constitution—a document of limits rather than a list of limited powers—but one that acknowledges a legitimate congressional role.

As a wartime president, Wilson exercised extraordinary powers, but they were derived from statutes, not extrapolated from vague constitutional phrases, nor sanctioned after the fact. Wilson went to Congress and persuaded the legislators to grant him extraordinarily open-ended delegations of power to wage and win the First World War. A good example of Wilson's approach to war powers is his address to Congress in 1917 requesting the authority to arm American merchant ships. He approached Congress, sought, fought for, and won an extraordinary delegation of power, and proceeded to exercise it to the hilt.[57] Wilson clearly established the notion that power went to the branch that sought it out,[58] but he did so within the parameters of the traditional interpretation.

War and the Rhetoric of Executive Prerogative

Like Wilson, President Franklin D. Roosevelt (FDR) secured broad powers and authority not from a loose construction of the Constitution, but from congressionally approved statutes.

Also, like Wilson, FDR entered office convinced that the Constitution was a document designed to change with the times and adapt to the needs of the country. The founders, FDR argued, had "successfully planned for such use of the Constitution as would fit it to a constantly expanding nation." And the fact that the Constitution established a framework that was still able to govern a nation that had grown from "less than four million" to "more than one hundred and thirty million people" was, Roosevelt concluded, "the best tribute to the vision of the Fathers."[59]

Though not ever to be confused with a strict constructionist, FDR nevertheless was firmly committed to following the Constitution's forms and respecting the separation of powers. His administration had sponsored the neutrality legislation of 1935, which was reauthorized in 1937. But as the war in Europe escalated, FDR became convinced that the legislation was actually aiding the Germans, rather than helping to maintain American neutrality. Before calling a special session of Congress in September 1939 to seek the repeal of the embargo provisions of the Neutrality Act, FDR had tried on a number of occasions to convince Congress to alter the Neutrality Act, only to be rebuffed by a nearly unanimous Republican minority and a fair number of Democrats. Rather than offer a prerogative or emergency-powers interpretation of the Constitution, FDR bitterly complained that Congress had effectively—and legitimately—tied his hands. He said that the opposition had "made a bet with this country that the president was wrong," arguing that legislators were gambling that the world situation would not worsen before they reconvened in January. "[I]f they are not right and we have another serious international crisis they have tied my hands, and *I have practically no power to make an American effort to prevent such a war from breaking out.*"[60]

The Neutrality Act doubtless did restrict the president, but he was not powerless under the Act. Before the special session FDR already had exercised extraordinary powers—powers granted to him by statute after he declared what he termed a limited national emergency on 8 September 1939. By issuing this declaration, FDR triggered a host of "emergency powers" legislation, most of which had been written during the First World War. As he explained in his special message to Congress in September 1939, he had declared the national emergency "solely to make wholly constitutional and legal certain obviously necessary measures" such as increasing the personnel of the Army, Navy, Marines and Coast Guard.[61]

The famous destroyers-for-bases swap often is raised as an example of FDR's assertion and exercise of extraconstitutional prerogative powers.[62] Through a carefully worded opinion of his attorney general, FDR argued that he had adequate statutory authority as well as constitutional power to trade 50 American destroyers to the British in exchange for land for bases in a number of Atlantic and Caribbean ports.

Attorney General Robert Jackson offered an extended defense of the legality and constitutionality of the trade, concluding that though one might rest the entire matter on the president's undefined powers as commander in chief, it was not necessary to do so. In fact, Jackson argued, "I think there is also ample statutory authority to support the acquisition of these bases." Citing "two enactments of Congress and a decision of the Supreme Court," Jackson argued that the president was authorized "to make such disposition of naval vessels as he finds necessary in the public interest."[63] Needless to say, the statutes are not eminently clear on these points. The law said the president had the power to dispose of "unfit" vessels, yet Britain was eager to take and activate these "unfit" vessels immediately. While the opinion (Acquisition of Naval and Air Bases in Exchange for Over-Age Destroyers) is a carefully worded effort to find legal sanction for a constitutionally questionable action, Roosevelt did choose to follow the forms of the traditional interpretation rather than argue that the president had legitimate extraconstitutional powers, or even that a loose construction of the Constitution was sufficient to legitimate his decision.

Shortly after the destroyer deal was completed, Britain's need for supplies and war material began to grow, and Roosevelt feared that Britain could not continue to hold off the Germans without additional aid from the United States—aid precluded by the Neutrality Act. But Roosevelt was determined to find a way to supply Britain without having to repeal the Neutrality Act. In a press conference in December 1940, Roosevelt unveiled a new approach. Rather than giving the materials to the British (unacceptable on both sides) or selling them, he would seek congressional authorization to "lend" supplies to them for the duration of the war. At the end of the war, the materials could be returned, if undamaged, or replaced. Thus there would be no cash exchanged, no donations made. In fact, Roosevelt argued, this program was purely a selfish way to get American defense production up and running in the event the United States was to be drawn into the war. Roosevelt laid his groundwork well, went to Congress at the end of 1940 and the start of 1941, and used "his every weapon of legislative leadership"[64] to win passage of a bill that delegated to the president extraordinarily broad powers to authorize the construction or manufacture of just about anything, and to transfer or lease those articles to any country whose defense the president decided was critical to the defense of the United States. As Edward Corwin remarked, "the act delegated to the President the power to fight wars by deputy."[65] Extraordinary as these powers may have been, FDR did not have to obtain them via autonomous assertion of constitutional prerogative.[66]

Still hampered by the restrictions of the Neutrality Act, FDR finally acted without statutory or constitutional support in September 1941 when he took to the airwaves to tell the American people that in order to defend themselves, American ships might have to stage preemptive strikes. Arguing that "the time for active defense is now,"[67] He announced that American ships and planes "will protect all merchant ships—not only American ships but ships of any flag—engaged in commerce in our *defensive waters.*"[68]

Despite the radical change this represented in American policy, FDR maintained that it was hardly unprecedented. He cited the actions of President John Adams, who ordered American ships to protect American commerce in the Caribbean and in South American waters, as well as the actions of President Jefferson, who ordered the navy to protect American shipping along the Barbary Coast in North Africa. But Jefferson was not under the strictures of a Neutrality Act, and went to Congress for open-ended authorization of his actions after the fact. FDR should have cited Jefferson's congressional authorization, not his deeds. FDR broke with his own pattern of behavior by resting his authority on executive precedent not on Congress. In a 7 September 1942 message to Congress, he said, "My obligation as President is historic; it is clear. It is inescapable."[69]

Perhaps the closest FDR came to developing a prerogative argument about executive authority came in 1942. With Americans fighting the war in earnest, FDR went to Congress to seek legislation that would authorize him to stabilize prices, particularly farm commodities. By April 1942 he had laid out a plan for national economic controls. On 7 September 1942 FDR told Congress that he could no longer wait for the legislators to act on his plan. The delay, he wrote, "has now reached the point of danger to our whole economy." He noted that he had, by executive authority, carried out those parts of the plan that "did not require congressional action."[70] But he said he wanted legislation to control farm prices, and that he had to have that authority by 1 October. So far, FDR played the issue much as he had played all the others discussed above—exercising political powers and skills to achieve congressional authorization and/or delegation of authority to the executive. Suddenly the message shifted. Should Congress fail to act by the first of October, FDR warned, he would have to act to guarantee that "the war effort is no longer imperiled by threat of economic chaos. In the event that the Congress should fail to act, and act adequately I shall accept the responsibility, and I will act." The president, he continued, "has the powers, under the Constitution and under congressional Acts, to take measures necessary to avert a disaster which would interfere with the winning of the war."[71]

FDR never had to act without congressional authorization. Congress soon began to debate price stabilization measures, which the president signed into law on the second of October. But FDR's grim words about presidential power in time of war were on record, offering an important precedent for future chief executives. In the midst of the Second World War, as in the midst of the Civil War, the president had asserted extraordinary powers, though in the end he didn't act on them. Later presidents, embroiled in less daunting emergency situations, not only asserted these powers but actively exercised and defended them, not as temporary aberrations, but as legitimate Constitutional powers.

* * *

From Washington to Franklin Roosevelt, the traditional interpretation of the president's constitutional powers withstood extraordinary challenges. But with the dawn of the prolonged emergency of the Cold War and the acknowledged need for speed and unity of control demanded by nuclear weapons, presidents after FDR, Democratic and Republican alike, turned to the scattered precedents and rhetorical assertions of executive prerogative to construct and implement an alternative interpretation of the Constitution. By the late 1980s that rhetoric and action—aided and abetted by Congress and the courts—would begin to harden into an accepted alternative reading of the Constitution with important implications for the separation of powers, for American constitutional interpretation, and for the making of American foreign policy.

III

A New Interpretation Evolves: Executive Prerogative in Foreign Policy

3

Congress, the Executive, and the Emergence of Prerogative Power in Foreign Policy

The Second World War profoundly altered the underlying constitutional interpretation that had governed foreign affairs before the war. The war ushered in an era in which the United States no longer was isolated nor insulated from the rest of the world. Where once the Constitution was understood to limit government at home *and* abroad, it was now believed by many that such limits abroad were dangerous, if not impossible. The Cold War and the existence of nuclear weapons created an atmosphere of permanent crisis, and the constitutional distinctions between foreign and domestic policy continued to grow. As they had for Jefferson, Lincoln, Wilson, and both Roosevelts, legislators surrendered more and more of their authority in foreign policy, and presidents made ever broader claims to *constitutionally based* prerogative powers in foreign policy. This contrasted with the earlier model of presidents taking emergency actions without claiming they had the constitutional authority to do so. The claim of constitutional legitimacy was new. No longer were extraordinary actions seen as extraordinary, nor were they seen to require legislative sanction. Increasingly, presidents claimed these powers even in the face of congressional opposition. Congressional opposition, however, would be a long time in coming. Not only did legislators fail for years to fight executive claims and encroachment, they encouraged it. Through the Truman, Eisenhower, and Kennedy administrations Congress acquiesced in the evolution of the executive prerogative reinterpretation of the Constitution, often thrusting power—and responsibility—for foreign affairs onto a president who was more than willing to take control.

The postwar presidents continued some of the patterns established by their predecessors who subscribed to the traditional interpretation. The difference at first was in the rhetoric—and only later in the actions taken. When President Harry S Truman sought extraordinary powers from Congress in domestic labor disputes, he argued that these powers were justified by foreign policy and national security reasons. Truman followed the traditional pattern by asking Congress to delegate power to him to deal with the labor issue, but he went beyond the traditional approach when he acted on his own, sending troops to Korea and Europe and seizing the nation's steel mills. Although Truman used traditional arguments to support his exercise of power in each of these instances, he also used the new argument that he was authorized to act by virtue of his power as chief executive and commander in chief.

President Dwight Eisenhower took a more traditional approach, going to Congress for prior approval of broad grants of power in foreign affairs, but he set important precedents for future presidents who would act without congressional participation, using congressional acquiescence during the Eisenhower years to legitimate their constitutional assertions of prerogative power. Eisenhower's pattern of behavior fit well with the traditional interpretation, but while he followed the traditional process, many in Congress had come to the conclusion that modern conditions required ever greater deference to the executive. This pattern continued during the Kennedy administration, though it would not fully flower until the Johnson and Nixon years, when the signals sent by congressional statutes and by the behavior of individual legislators in postwar years combined with the evolving rhetoric of prerogative from the White House to produce a full-blown prerogative interpretation of the Constitution in foreign policy. Presidents no longer justified the exercise of extraordinary powers by claiming they were emergency measures, but rather argued that these powers were theirs constitutionally.

Chapter 3 will address the early evolution of the prerogative interpretation under Truman, Eisenhower, and Kennedy, focusing on the growth of delegated power from Congress, and the growing conviction of many in Congress that the Constitution could and should be read as granting prerogative powers to the executive. Chapter Four will address the Johnson and Nixon years, during which the executive fully articulated and acted on the prerogative reinterpretation of the Constitution.

* * *

Whether or not it is useful or beneficial to grant broad discretion to the president in foreign affairs is not the subject of this chapter. Such discretion has been granted to the president in the years since the Second World War, and it has been done without a thorough or explicit national debate. With each explicit delegation and with each instance of allowing the president to assert his view of the Constitution without offering an alternative argument, legislators provided important precedents that later presidents would build on, and that legislators would find increasingly more difficult to overturn. Before the proper balance of powers in foreign affairs can be decided upon, it is necessary to understand where that balance rests and why. Therefore, an understanding of the evolution of the executive prerogative interpretation and the manifestations of that interpretation that prodded Congress to react, is essential.

Truman and the Rhetoric of a Prerogative Interpretation

When Harry S Truman took the oath of office in 1945, he inherited a world war, the research and testing that would lead to nuclear weapons, and the seeds of a future Cold War. He also inherited an administration that had little faith in him and a Congress that had long suppressed its claims and prerogatives in deference to national war aims.

In dealing with a crippling series of strikes against the nation's railroads and coal mines, in deploying troops to Europe under the NATO Treaty, in sending troops to fight the Korean War without a congressional declaration, and in ordering the seizure of the nation's steel mills, Truman's rhetoric of executive prerogative moved away from the temporary, emergency claims, or explicit defiance of accepted doctrines that his predecessors had employed, to a new constitutional rhetoric built on the broad mandate of Article II and on the commander in chief clause of the Constitution. Truman was very much a transitional figure—his rhetoric contributed to the development of a new interpretation of the Constitution in foreign policy, but his actions mostly reflected a continuing commitment to the traditional interpretation. In the end, though he would articulate a prerogative interpretation, at the same time he would ground his actions on a second line of reasoning consistent with the traditional interpretation.

In four cases, Truman asserted broad authority to interpret the Constitution. In each of these instances he voiced the rhetoric of presidential prerogative built on the executive's foreign affairs and military powers, but he didn't follow through fully with his assertions of independent power and authority. In one case Truman explicitly sought congressional approval for his action; in two cases he argued that treaty obligations and commitments agreed to in principle with the advice and consent of the United States Senate gave him the authority he needed; and in the fourth case—the steel seizure case—Truman claimed he could and would act under his own authority, but in the end, reluctantly abided by the Court's ruling that ordered him to reverse his decision.

* * *

Early in his term a series of coal strikes posed a direct challenge to Truman, and as they wore on, they began to threaten a host of industries that depended on coal. Asked if he could end the strike by using his war powers, Truman said he could not, since those were "all expired." But, when asked whether that applied to his "inherent powers" as chief executive, Truman replied that it did not, noting that it was "a fine line to be drawn" and that "we will cross that bridge when we come to it."[1]

The first step across that bridge came in May 1950, when a strike shut down the nation's rail system. Truman sought mediation, but when that failed, he cut off discussions and went to Congress with a radical legislative request. He asked that Congress delegate him the authority to seize those strike-bound industries that affect "the entire economy of the United States." In such situations the law would authorize the seizure of the industry with any profits earned being turned over to the United States Treasury. In addition, the requested legislation would provide injunctive relief to order union leaders not to interfere and provide that any workers refusing to return to their jobs (once they were working for the government) would be stripped of their seniority and subject to criminal penalties. In addition, the president asked Congress "immediately to authorize the President to draft into the armed forces of the United States all workers who are on strike against their Government."[2] Once drafted, of course, the workers would be subject to military court martial and punishment, and the government could order them to return to work. At precisely this point in Truman's speech to a joint session of Congress, he was handed a sheet of paper informing him that an agreement had been reached and the rail strike had been settled. Nevertheless, Truman completed his address and pushed his legislative proposal to provide emergency powers in the event that other vital industries were struck.

While this proposal raised a host of constitutional questions, the process Truman followed of seeking statutory authority from Congress well fit the pattern established by the traditional interpretation. While the case contributed to the development of a prerogative argument, it was not because of Truman's assertions, but rather because his supporters relied on a prerogative interpretation in advocating the bill.

Truman's proposed legislation flew through the House of Representatives, though not without some instructive debate. Most House members rallied to the president.[3] The Senate refused to pass the bill unamended, however, and insisted on dropping the authority to draft strikers into the army. Still, it is the tension between those who would either happily or reluctantly extend presidential power that is relevant here. As Wisconsin Republican Robert LaFollette warned in Senate debate, "There seems to be no indication that the legislative arm of the Government ever recovers the rights of the people once they are given to the Executive."[4]

LaFollette reluctantly agreed that extraordinary times might call for extraordinary powers, but many of his colleagues were more than eager to delegate power to the president. Wisconsin's other Republican Senator, Alexander Wiley, admitted that he was uncomfortable with this broad delegation, but that it was unavoidable: "There are those who would fear such legislation. A decade ago I would not have been in favor of it, because I could see no reason for it at that time. But in this tremendously challenging period . . . I would have available and ready for any eventuality every instrument which, with foresight, I could bring into being."[5]

Truman portrayed the labor situation as a crisis—the strike, he told Congress, "has now become a strike against the Government itself."[6] But he never claimed to have independent constitutional authority to act against the strikers. Instead he took the traditional approach of asking Congress for new legislation. It was the legislators themselves who began to articulate the prerogative argument built on the perception of dire emergency. With the strike settled, the urgency for delegated emergency powers abated, and the Senate passed a number of amendments to the strike control bill[7] and sent it back to the House, where it was sent to committee and quietly died. But the incident revealed that Congress was receptive to the notion that the Cold War crisis might well justify the formal delegation of extraordinary power to the president.

Going to War Without a Declaration

When North Korean forces crossed into South Korea in June 1950, President Truman ordered U.S. forces to give the South Korean troops "cover and support," and ordered the Seventh Fleet to "prevent any attack on Formosa." Both actions, Truman said, were a response to the United Nations Security Council's call to all members "to render every assistance to the United Nations in the execution of this Resolution," which directed the invading troops to withdraw to the 38th parallel.[8] This statement and the President's decision to dispatch troops without explicit congressional authorization, much less a declaration of war, sparked a heated debate in the Senate and the House over constitutional interpretation. As was the case with the emergency labor bill, few in either house actually voted against the policy but the rhetorical opposition was strong. Truman rested his independent action on two pillars. First, as argued by the Department of State, the administration claimed that "the President, as Commander in Chief of the Armed Forces of the United States, has full control over the use thereof."[9] In war powers, the administration argued, the president had plenary power to deploy troops in defense of American national interests. But Truman did not rest exclusively on executive powers. In addition to his claim to plenary power, Truman also pointed to the United Nations Charter, to which the Senate had given its advice and consent. While the Department of State was careful to note that "even before the ratification of the United Nations Charter, the President had used the Armed Forces of the United States without consulting the Congress,"[10] the ratification of the charter by the Senate fortified this authority and lent it additional constitutional legitimacy. Truman thus had defended his action with the rhetoric of presidential prerogative, but he had acted with the additional, more traditional support of a treaty obligation.[11]

Truman's argument, that the Senate's assent to the U.N. Charter mandated U.S. participation when the United Nations issued a request, faced two primary objections. First, the U.N. statement was vague and did not necessarily call for military action; and second, the implementing act passed by Congress regarding the United Nations *explicitly* stated that the United States would agree to commit troops only in line with a separate military agreement that would be "subject to the approval of the Congress by an appropriate act or joint resolution." Noting that "the Russians have prevented the conclusion of any such agreement," Senate Republican leader Robert Taft argued in 1951 that "Congress has therefore never acted. The President simply usurped authority in violation of the laws and the Constitution" when he sent troops to Korea to support the U.N. Resolution.[12]

Taft's was a lonely voice. Even Taft acknowledged that he was fully supportive of the general policy pursued by the president; it was the process by which it was achieved that bothered him.[13] Around him Senators and Representatives on both sides of the aisle were eager to rally around the president, and many echoed Illinois Democrat, Senator Paul H. Douglas, who maintained that "the power of Congress being limited to a declaration of war, the President can take steps to resist aggression" without congressional authorization.[14]

Why the giveaway? For Scott Lucas, the other Democratic Senator from Illinois, it was a combination of the extraordinary threat to American national security posed by international communism combined with what he perceived to be a long established precedent ceding this authority to the president.[15] Even Republican Senator Wayne Morse, who strongly rejected Truman's earlier appeal for emergency powers to deal with strikes in vital industries, applauded Truman's actions in Korea, saying that Truman had made clear that he was merely "carrying out his duties under Section 2 of Article 2 of the Constitution." Senator Morse added that, "Those of us who have studied constitutional law know that the so-called Commander in Chief powers . . . have yet to be defined fully in the decisions of the Supreme Court. In my opinion, they are very broad powers in times of emergency and national crisis."[16] The chairman of the Senate Foreign Relations Committee, Tom Connally, explained that he had privately told Truman that he had to act unilaterally, and that he had every right to do so. Going to Congress might be a costly mistake: "You might run into a long debate in Congress which would tie your hands completely. You have the right to do it as Commander-in-Chief and under the U.N. Charter."[17]

It is important to draw a distinction between what mattered at the time, and what may matter more now as precedent. While a number of reluctant senators hinged their support for Truman's deployment of troops on the U.N. resolutions, in effect they voted to endorse a broad interpretation of the commander in chief clause of the Constitution. They may have seen their action as a vote to support collective security, but they also were voting to approve a precedent-setting policy that later would be used as a foundation for broader claims of executive prerogative by other presidents.

Sending Troops to Europe

If Senator Taft had been disturbed by the president's assertion of constitutional authority to send troops to Korea, he was enraged a few months later when Truman ordered the deployment of American ground troops to Europe to support the NATO command. Again, as in the Korean case, Truman rested his authority on dual grounds. Under his constitutional authority as commander in chief, Truman argued, he had "the authority to send troops anywhere in the world, . . . [which] has been recognized repeatedly by the Congress and the courts."[18] The more traditional support for his action that Truman used was the North Atlantic Treaty, which had been ratified by the Senate. The treaty provided a firmer justification for Truman's authority to send the troops to Europe, but both arguments sparked a more thorough debate in Congress than had the Korean deployment, setting important precedents for the prerogative interpretation.

The administration argued that the president's prerogative powers as commander in chief were adequate without the support of the treaty. The treaty was important not for what it *granted* to the president, but rather for what it *failed to deny* to him. When the Senate debated the treaty, it proposed a reservation that would have limited the president's power to deploy troops. But that reservation was rejected. According to the administration, the fact that the proposed reservation failed demonstrated that the Senate concurred with the administration's interpretation of executive powers in foreign relations. This argument set an important precedent. By considering and rejecting explicit limits on the president's authority, the Senate had, according to one Senate Committee report, ratified the prerogative interpretation. "The legislative history of the ratification of this treaty," the Senate report argued, "*negatives* the thought that prior congressional authorization is necessary before troops can be sent to Europe."[19]

Under the traditional interpretation, the burden of demonstrating the legitimacy of extraordinary action rested with the president, whose powers were limited unless he could persuade Congress and the public to make an exception. In the early 1950s the burden was shifting to Congress. The president could act in foreign policy unless and until he was formally and clearly prohibited from doing so. Ultimately, the executive prerogative interpretation would hold that even explicit congressional prohibition might not be legitimate. Truman, however, was far from ready to make that leap. He still saw the situation as a political battle in which he planned to use every political weapon at his disposal, including the rhetoric of prerogative. In the end he acknowledged that it was a battle for public support. Truman said that if Congress wanted to do political battle over the troop deployments, he was ready to meet them on that field. "[I]f they want to go to the country with that, I'll go with them." And, he added, "I licked them once" before.[20]

Seizing—and Returning—the Steel Mills

A few months later, challenged by intransigent steel-mill owners who insisted that any pay increase be offset by a price hike beyond the recommendations of Truman's wage stabilization board, Truman's rhetoric took a new turn. With a strike looming, he faced a number of unpleasant alternatives. He could have invoked the Taft-Hartley Act to force a 90-day cooling-off period; he could have acted under Section 18 of the Selective Service Act of 1948, which authorized the seizure of critical defense industries under a complicated and drawn-out process; he could have gone to Congress for explicit seizure authority; or he could seize the mills by executive order.

Each option had its disadvantages. The Taft-Hartley act clearly was antilabor and Truman had argued that labor was being cooperative, while the owners were not. Therefore, to invoke Taft-Hartley would be to punish the wrong group. Truman was loathe to further offend organized labor in an election year. To invoke the Selective Service Act required a drawn-out and complicated series of steps that probably could not prevent the strike in time.[21] Going to Congress probably was a lost cause given executive-congressional relations on labor issues at the time. That left Truman with the option of seizing the mills by executive order.

From his earliest days as vice president through to 1951, Truman witnessed an expansive presidency and a generally compliant Congress and public. In a case where the United States was engaged in combat, albeit not a declared war, Truman was convinced that the public would rally to his side and denounce the steel owners for their unpatriotic defiance of the wage board. Furthermore, the claim to power he asserted was hardly new or foreign. He had bandied about the rhetoric in all three of the earlier cases, though in each the claim to executive authority was paired with a more traditional argument. With the steel case, however, Truman offered no secondary or alternative foundation for his claims. He rested his action solely on executive power and article 2 of the Constitution, particularly the commander in chief clause, the "take care" clause, and the general delegation of all executive powers to the president. "In my opinion," Truman argued in his memoirs, "the seizure was well within my constitutional powers, and I had acted accordingly."[22]

The Truman administration went to court to defend the seizure, arguing that though the Court had no authority to block it the president would abide by the Court's ruling.[23] The Court held that the seizure would withstand constitutional scrutiny only if Congress delegated that power to the president in formal legislation. Accordingly, Truman returned the mills and went to Congress seeking the authority he had claimed was inherent in the executive office. While he disagreed with the Court's ruling that the executive was without the power to seize the mills unilaterally, he argued that surely the president and Congress could do it together: "Whatever may have been the intention of the Court's majority in setting limits on the President's powers, there can be no question of their view that the Congress can enact legislation to avoid a crippling work stoppage in the steel industry."[24] This position was entirely in keeping with the traditional interpretation, but Congress refused to delegate him seizure powers.

In the end the steel owners got a bigger price increase than had been authorized by the wage board, and the unions won the right to a closed shop in the steel industry as well as wage and benefit concessions. The case itself, *Youngstown Sheet & Tube v. Sawyer* (discussed in detail in Chapter 5), is rightly viewed as a blow against executive power. But from the perspective of the White House since Truman never conceded the argument, his actions and rhetoric were available to be revived by later occupants of the Oval Office.

* * *

Unifying all four cases that arose during the Truman administration is the idea that Congress and the president working together can do almost anything in foreign affairs. In each case Truman acknowledged the overarching power of Congress and president together. As his term wore on, however, his rhetoric increasingly suggested that in the absence of congressional action, or even in the face of congressional opposition, there were times when the president could and must act alone. "A wise President," Truman later recalled, "will always work with Congress, but when Congress fails to act or is unable to act in a crisis, the President, under the Constitution, must use his powers to safeguard the nation."[25] Franklin Roosevelt employed the same argument in 1942 when he threatened to stabilize the price of farm commodities should Congress refuse to do so.[26] But Roosevelt did not have to act without congressional approval; Truman did, thereby bridging the gap between presidents who subscribed to the traditional interpretation, though they would violate its tenants when they felt it necessary, and those presidents who felt that their actions in no way overstepped their constitutional authority. The new interpretation held that no one—not the courts, not Congress—could stop the president from performing those actions that were legitimated by the prerogative powers of the chief executive and commander in chief. Truman, of course, did as the Court ordered him to do, but he never conceded that the Court had the final word on constitutional interpretation. He merely accepted the order as a prudent political choice.

What had happened, what had changed? Was it just Truman? Hardly. The same change was already well underway in Congress. The move from a traditional to an executive prerogative interpretation of the Constitution started with the Second World War, which was a total war, declared and engaged in from start to finish with the conviction that it could not end until one side had totally vanquished the other. The Second World War put the United States into a state of total commitment and total emergency. The emergency didn't end for over 40 years, even though the war ended in total victory. But the war also ended in an unprecedented scientific-military-political moment, the detonation of nuclear weapons over Japan. Truman understood the transformation this development had wrought on an office he considered to be "the most powerful office that has ever existed in the history of this great world of ours . . . Genghis Khan, Augustus Caesar, great Napoleon Bonaparte, or Louis XIV can't even compare with what the President of the United States himself is responsible for, when he makes a decision."[27] When the weapon had been unleashed, Truman and most in Congress assumed that its control had to be centralized in the presidency. This awesome power and responsibility added greatly to the president's responsibilities, power and autonomy. The president, Truman noted in his final State of the Union Message on 7 January 1953, "also has to lead the whole free world in overcoming the communist menace—and all this under the shadow of the atomic bomb."[28]

The presidential claim to exclusive power over the bomb was one of a list of arrogations of power that the minority leader, Robert Taft, addressed in a long discourse on the need for constructive criticism of American foreign policy. Noting that Truman had committed troops to the Korean conflict as well as to Europe without substantive consultation with Congress, Taft argued that the president now "claims the right without consultation with Congress to decide whether or not we should use the atomic bomb."[29] Taft's was a lonely voice. The Senate was persuaded that extraordinary times demanded extraordinary measures. And while Truman's political unpopularity, particularly on Capitol Hill, at the end of his administration led some senators to guard some measure of power, they were very willing to cede power to the certified war hero, and commanding general who took over as commander in chief in the midst of the Cold War, Dwight D. Eisenhower.

Eisenhower: Building Prerogative Power through Traditional Means

By the end of the Truman administration, the National Security Act of 1947 had profoundly reorganized the national security system, and the existence of nuclear weapons combined with the real and imagined dangers of the Cold War had convinced many in Congress that authority in foreign affairs needed to be centralized and even ceded to the executive. Their motives varied. Some subscribed to this view out of the patriotic conviction that a real emergency necessitated extraordinary delegation; others saw political advantage in insulating themselves from American foreign policy decisions and debacles. This change took root during the Eisenhower administration, and by the end of Eisenhower's eight years in office Congress had handed extraordinary power to the Executive to deploy troops and distribute foreign aid in Asia and in the Middle East. In the Eisenhower years, it was Congress more than the president that significantly contributed to the development and entrenchment of the executive prerogative interpretation.

* * *

Eisenhower went to Congress, taking the initiative to seek extraordinary delegations of power in a resolution supporting the administration's authority to deploy troops to defend Formosa (Taiwan) and the Pescadore islands and later in a similar resolution on the Middle East to support what came to be known as the Eisenhower Doctrine. In both cases Eisenhower employed the rhetoric of the traditional interpretation, repeatedly proclaiming—as he did in answering a reporter's question about sending troops to Indochina—that "[T]here is going to be no involvement of America in war unless it is a result of the constitutional process that is placed upon Congress to declare it."[30]

Eisenhower clearly had learned from Truman's experience with Korea that a president needed to lock in the support of Congress for any military action that offered the slightest risk of high casualties or prolonged combat.[31] Eisenhower generally adhered to the traditional interpretation in foreign policy, though his extensive use of the Central Intelligence Agency (CIA) and his deep opposition to the Bricker Amendment (a proposed constitutional amendment designed to constrain national treaty powers) indicate a more mixed perspective. Eisenhower expressed the need to maintain the constitutional balance of power and repeatedly acknowledged that Congress had certain prerogatives in foreign affairs, particularly in war powers. And, as had Truman, Eisenhower argued that with or without a commitment to constitutional prerogatives, the constitutional process made it impossible to sustain a foreign military adventure without the support of Congress. "After all," he told one reporter, "you can't carry on a war without Congress. They have to appropriate the money, provide the means, the laws and everything else."[32]

In 1954 some in the Eisenhower administration advocated military intervention on behalf of the French in Indochina, and "well placed persons in the Administration" including "the Vice-President, the Secretary of State, and the Chairman of the Joint Chiefs of Staff" were "instrumental in having drafted a presidential message to the Congress seeking authorization to enter the war."[33] But discussions with key senators, including Majority Leader Lyndon Johnson, indicated that the Senate wouldn't go along unless the intervention had the full support of America's allies, particularly Great Britain. When the British made it clear that they would not help support the French, the proposal died. Eisenhower refused to proceed without congressional support.

Eisenhower was more successful in his effort to gain congressional support and authorization to deploy troops and distribute foreign aid in Formosa and the Middle East. At one extreme, it is tempting to argue that this strategy stemmed from a commitment to the traditional interpretation. But statements made by Eisenhower's secretary of state, John Foster Dulles, in both cases suggest that in the administration's view the president had sufficient constitutional authority to do what he planned to do with or without Congress. The request for congressional support, Dulles testified, was designed to send a strong signal to foreign friends and foes of the unity and commitment of the government of the United States. In fact, a close look at these cases suggests that Eisenhower turned to Congress in these instances for three reasons: 1) to avoid Truman's Korean trap where the country and legislators supported the policy but, without a formal commitment to it, later felt free to attack Truman when the strategy bogged down; 2) to secure the international advantages of which Dulles spoke; and 3) because Eisenhower had learned an important lesson in his bruising but successful battle to defeat a constitutional amendment proposed by Ohio's Senator John Bricker that was designed to constrain the national treaty power. The Bricker battle taught Eisenhower that he had to articulate a national security justification to secure public support for broad executive discretion in foreign policy while maintaining congressional support, or at least congressional silence.

The Bricker Amendment: Federalism Confronts International Responsibility

Prior to the development of America's world role after the Spanish-American war and the First World War, the primary constitutional concern of Congress and the judiciary was with the battle between central authority and state autonomy. From John Marshall's day on, the Court sanctioned ever greater central control of American life, primarily through the commerce and necessary-and-proper clauses of the Constitution. When foreign affairs and the treaty power emerged in the early twentieth century as additional pillars on which to build central power over the states, many in Congress began to bridle. One response, as discussed in Chapter 1, was to try to separate foreign and domestic affairs. But if they could not be separated, and faced with a choice between strong central government at home *and* abroad versus weak central government at home *and* abroad, some in Congress began to favor strong central government. Following the Second World War, a number of politicians began to argue that American treaty commitments to international organizations such as NATO, and most especially the United Nations, represented perilous threats to national sovereignty in general and state sovereignty in particular. If the doctrine of *Missouri v. Holland* were extended, they argued, then international organizations such as the United Nations might well demand fundamental changes in state and local law concerning what had been considered strictly local issues, issues such as segregation, education, and labor laws. After all, Justice Holmes had argued in *Missouri v. Holland* that treaties might well override otherwise valid state laws where "a national interest . . . can be protected only by national action in concert with that of another power."[34]

Starting in the late 1940s, a number of influential people, including officers of the American Bar Association and a number of members of Congress, became convinced that the internationalist trend of the Roosevelt administration and its continuation under Truman and Secretary of State Dean Acheson posed a real threat to the autonomy of individual states. In response, a Republican Senator from Ohio named John Bricker introduced legislation designed to ensure that no treaty could be made that would legitimate otherwise unconstitutional laws. By 1953 Bricker had converted his proposed statute into a proposed constitutional amendment.[35]

The Bricker Amendment attempted to do two fundamental and not necessarily compatible things. First it was designed to prevent future decisions like the one in *Missouri v. Holland* that would allow treaties to override state laws. To quote the proposed amendment, "A treaty shall become effective as internal law in the United States only through legislation which would be valid in the absence of the treaty."[36] Second, the amendment would give Congress the power to regulate all executive agreements with foreign powers and international organizations. Thus, the amendment was designed to address two different problems posed by the two types of separation of powers, horizontal and vertical. Addressing the vertical separation, the amendment's sponsors primarily were concerned that international treaties and international organizations could dictate local policies in American states, cities, and towns. While this provision worried members of his administration, the president himself had proclaimed to be a staunch defender of states' rights,[37] and acknowledged that there was "undoubtedly an honest fear" in the United States that the treaty power might be used to "contravene or to supersede our Constitution . . . In order to reassure America's population on this score, I am ready to do anything, even if it requires some kind of language in the Constitution." But while he was willing to accept constitutional language to restrict the dilution of the vertical separation of powers, he was unalterably opposed to any language that would alter the separation of powers between the executive and legislative branch. When it came to any amendment that would "change or alter the traditional and constitutional balances of power among the three departments of Government . . . I won't compromise one single word."[38]

To defeat the Bricker Amendment, the administration argued that the complications of living in a world threatened by totalitarianism, communism, and nuclear weapons required far more flexibility and central authority in the executive branch. Eisenhower won the battle, but not without picking up significant scars. If nothing else, the experience convinced Eisenhower of the importance of congressional support, or at least tolerance, for his foreign policy initiatives. When he later decided to stake American policy on bold statements backed by the threat of military force, he was determined to do so within the confines of the traditional interpretation—that is, at least with the endorsement of Congress. He would not be trapped, as Truman had been trapped, by legislators who celebrated a policy but denounced its effect.

The Formosa and Mideast Resolutions: Precedents for Prerogative?

In 1955 and again in 1957, Eisenhower went to Congress to request authorization to employ armed force at his discretion in the Formosa Straits and in the Mideast, and to distribute up to $200 million in appropriated funds in the Mideast in any way he deemed appropriate. Though appearing to follow the blueprint of the traditional interpretation, these resolutions wound up delegating highly unconventional power to the president.

In late 1954, a shelling campaign against the disputed islands of Quemoy and Matsu in the Formosa straits led Eisenhower to sign a treaty with the Nationalists in which the United States pledged to defend Formosa (but not Quemoy and Matsu) in exchange for a Nationalist pledge not to attack mainland China. In January 1955, the crisis heated up again, with the Chinese on both sides predicting that war was imminent. As Beijing ordered attacks on a series of small islands just off their shore, Eisenhower decided to go to Congress for authorization to commit American troops to the defense of Formosa.

Eisenhower followed a similar route in the wake of the Suez Crisis of 1956. The administration feared that the British and French withdrawal from the Mideast would leave a vacuum. To fill that void, Eisenhower decided to go to Congress in January 1957 to seek authorization to use armed forces if needed as well as authorization to use up to $200 million from appropriated funds to support his policy in the Mideast.[39]

Eisenhower did not assert a prerogative power, nor did he deny that the power to declare war belonged exclusively to Congress. But, as Secretary Dulles and others pointed out in testimony about the Mideast Resolution, the urgency of the situation precluded a thorough constitutional debate about the separation of powers. The resolution, Dulles argued, was no more than a simple effort to send a clear signal. "[T]here are times and occasions when, irrespective of constitutional doubts, irrespective of just where the division of powers lies, it is vital that the President and the Congress should speak clearly with one voice."[40] As Senator Walter F. George, a Georgia Democrat, argued during the debate on the Formosa Resolution, disputes about the constitutional division of powers were mere quibbles. For George, the president had come to Congress for moral support in a time of need, and that was good enough.[41] During the Mideast debate, however, Senator J. William Fulbright said that debate was vital since an affirmative vote would set an important constitutional precedent representing, he felt, an unconstitutional delegation of legislative powers to the executive. "Exclusive powers are given to the President," Fulbright argued, "All that can be said is that the Congress is dragged in by the heels to share, not the power, but the responsibility for the consequences of the Executive's use or misuse of the power blindly put in his hands by the Congress."[42] The Mideast Resolution was, in the view of Senator Sam Ervin, "a delegation by Congress of its constitutional powers to the President."[43] Or, as Senator Wayne Morse had insisted during the Formosa debate, this was an unconstitutional delegation of power, an act that Congress could do "only in fact, not legally."[44] These senators recognized the precedents that would be created, precedents that would be available for future presidents and, perhaps more significantly, for future courts.[45]

But Senators Ervin and Fulbright, along with Morse and a few others, were the exceptions rather than the rule. And if there was at least some impassioned debate over the Mideast Resolution, with few exceptions, there had been hardly any dissent to the Formosa Resolution of 1955. The only consistent complaint about that resolution was that it was unnecessary since, in the view of many legislators, the president already had constitutional authority to do everything the resolution delegated to him. Representative Clement J. Zablocki said that as commander in chief the president "already possesses adequate powers to deploy military forces as necessary to safeguard the security and the interests of our Nation." Nevertheless, Zablocki continued, if the President felt he needed "the special encouragement of a congressional resolution to exercise such powers, I feel that this body ought to go along and comply with his request, I hope unanimously."[46]

Why was Congress willing to forgo its constitutional prerogatives and approve a bill for the Mideast that Georgia Senator Herman Talmadge called "an undated declaration of war—a blank check to be signed by Congress and handed to the Chief Executive to fill in the date and place as he sees fit"?[47] The explanation lies in large measure in the Cold War and in nuclear weapons, two of the mainstays of the executive prerogative argument articulated by Truman, developed and fortified by Congress, and aggressively defended by later presidents. Whether this historical context convinced legislators that "[T]here is no place for politics in foreign policy,"[48] or that the dangers of the time forced them to approve a doctrine because to do otherwise would present "a divided front before the Communist world,"[49] the Cold War overrode a great many constitutional qualms, clearing the way for passage of the two resolutions that delegated broad power to the Eisenhower administration and creating precedents for later, broader claims of executive prerogative.

John F. Kennedy, Congress, and Cuba

The next major opportunity for Congress to contribute to the expansion of executive power in foreign policy came shortly before it adjourned for the 1962 election campaign. Since the disastrous Bay of Pigs invasion, the Soviet Union and the United States had exchanged increasingly harshly worded threats about Cuba. The United States insisted that the

Monroe Doctrine still held, and that no foreign power would be permitted to establish a military beachhead in the Western Hemisphere. In September 1962, President Kennedy called on Congress to authorize him to call up reserve forces to "permit prompt and effective responses, as necessary, to challenges which may be presented in any part of the free world,"[50] to which Soviet Premier Kruschev responded that a U.S. attack on Cuba would lead to nuclear war. The initial bill Congress considered would have stated that "the President of the United States . . . possesses all necessary authority to prevent by whatever means may be necessary, including the use of arms"[51] the extension of Cuban control.

For some in the Senate, the language in the initial proposal was too close to the language they regretted had been inserted in the Mideast Resolution. Several senators, including Richard Russell and Wayne Morse, insisted that this sort of language constituted a predated declaration of war. For Russell, the answer was to use the language of the Formosa Resolution, where Congress had "authorized" the president to employ the armed forces that he deemed necessary. "Congress has gradually been lapsing into a secondary position but couldn't we accomplish the same purpose by authorizing the President to do these things instead of just stating that he has the authority to declare war, to engage in war?"[52] While Russell's proposal maintained that Congress possessed the power to declare war, his language then formally delegated that power to the chief executive. Such a delegation was unacceptable to Morse. In the end, Morse's language prevailed, and Congress merely stated "that the United States is determined to prevent by whatever means may be necessary, including the use of arms," the spread of the Cuban revolution. This statement of the intentions of the nation, with no explicit delegation of power, conveniently sidestepped the question of which branch of government had the constitutional authority to initiate a war. While Morse may have won the battle over semantics in the Cuban resolution, the full impact of that debate and bill must be measured in how it was interpreted by a majority of legislators and the executive branch.

Was the Kennedy administration seeking war powers? Asked in a news conference whether there was "any virtue in the Senate or the Congress passing the resolution saying you have that authority," Kennedy replied "No . . . I think it would be useful, if they desired to do so, for them to express their view," thereby welcoming the resolution more as a way for Congress to contribute to the executive's development and execution of foreign policy than for granting him any authority.[53] A few months earlier, Kennedy had declared that there was no responsibility "which is more powerful, which is more singularly held in the Executive, as opposed to so many other powers in the Constitution which are held between Congress and the Executive, than that which is involved in foreign policy."[54] The legislation did nothing to contradict this interpretation. Within a few days of passing the Cuban resolution, Congress broke for an election recess. A few days later the United States and the Soviet Union approached the brink of nuclear war over Cuba. While the legislators had stated their broad position in the resolution, that was about the extent of the congressional role in the one moment generally acknowledged to have been the closest the United States ever came to nuclear war. When Kennedy called congressional leaders to the White House during the crisis, it was to brief them, not to seek their advice and authorization. By 1962 it was clearly accepted that the president alone controlled the use of nuclear weapons, and that speed, efficiency, and subtlety required a unified, central control of war powers.

Kennedy's meeting with congressional leaders during the Cuban missile crisis was, according to Kennedy speech writer Theodore Sorensen, "the only sour note of the day." Sorenson said that the president was "adamant" about his position: He was acting by Executive Order, presidential proclamation and inherent powers, not under any resolution or act of the Congress. He had earlier rejected all suggestions of reconvening Congress or requesting a formal declaration of war, and he had summoned the leaders only when hard evidence and a fixed policy were ready.[55] Kennedy's conception of the presidency, particularly in foreign policy, was a bold and assertive one. He was convinced that the president "must be prepared to exercise the fullest powers of his Office—all that are specified and some that are not."[56] As he began his campaign in 1960, Kennedy insisted that the president must act decisively in foreign affairs, with or without congressional support. It is, Kennedy told a National Press Club audience, "the President alone who must make the major decisions of our foreign policy." This, he added, "*is what the Constitution wisely commands.*"[57] He cited the congressional resolution on Cuba as no more than an endorsement of "the authority entrusted to me by the Constitution."[58] Kennedy seemed to embrace the theory that the president had the power, the authority and, most importantly, the constitutional legitimacy to do as he had done with no need for congressional participation.

By 1962 the idea that the president had prerogative powers in foreign policy was well in place. It had been articulated by Truman and cautiously embraced by Eisenhower, but for Kennedy it seemed to have become an uncontroversial fact. The Cuban missile crisis was tailor-made to reinforce Kennedy's conviction that the president had to be free to set foreign policy. It was urgent, complicated, and placed the world in nuclear jeopardy; time, central control, and subtle diplomacy were crucial to its peaceful resolution. But one easily can argue that it was truly a unique experience, that alone in the postwar era, the missile crisis "*really* combined all those pressures of threat, secrecy and time that the foreign policy establishment had claimed as characteristic of decisions in the nuclear age."[59] Lessons were learned, and among those lessons, many walked away convinced that the prerogative interpretation was the right one.[60] According to Arthur

M. Schlesinger Jr., Kennedy's approach and interpretation of the constitutional powers of the presidency in foreign policy, "which should have been celebrated as an exception, was instead enshrined as a rule."[61] On Capitol Hill, the crisis confirmed the conviction that the United States had to make institutional adjustments in order to deal with a trend that had been developing since the Second World War.

4

Johnson, Nixon, and the Assertion of Executive Prerogative

With Lyndon Johnson and finally Richard Nixon, the prerogative interpretation reached a new level of acceptance. The prerogative claim was asserted more boldly, and the executive branch no longer offered, as Truman had, both a traditional and prerogative defense for the president's policies, but rather relied upon the prerogative interpretation alone. No longer was there an argument for exceptions or adjustments—rhetoric and action combined to assert that there was a different way to read the Constitution, particularly in foreign policy. This raised obvious problems for the administration of foreign policy, but as it became increasingly harder to isolate foreign policy from domestic policy, this new interpretation began to affect the domestic balance of power, paving the way for prerogative arguments at home as well as abroad.

After following the Eisenhower model, and securing congressional authorization to act in Vietnam under the Tonkin Gulf Resolution of 1964, President Lyndon Johnson then blazed a new trail. Unlike Eisenhower, Johnson claimed that congressional support was welcome—but not necessary. And, unlike Eisenhower, Johnson took action, deploying troops into battle asserting that he had the authority to do so under the Constitution, with or without the broad delegation of power he had received in 1964.

Richard Nixon brought the evolution of the new interpretation to its apex. Facing both domestic and international violence, Nixon argued that the constitutional distinction between foreign and domestic affairs no longer made sense. Foreign and domestic affairs were interdependent, and the less restrictive constitutional rules that were by then understood to govern foreign affairs must be applied at home when the nation's security was at stake. If the president could legitimately exercise prerogative powers in foreign affairs, the Nixon administration argued, then it could exercise those same powers at home when it was attempting to protect the national security.

This presumed, of course, that the Constitution did in fact authorize the president to exercise prerogative powers abroad. Between the Second World War and Nixon's re-election in 1972, the precedents for this presumption had been set. Congress had acquiesced to, and even delegated extraordinary powers to the president, while the Court signaled that it would not intervene unless individual rights of American citizens were threatened, or unless legislators in Congress asserted their own institutional authority.

Congress Joins Johnson in Securing the Prerogative Interpretation

The Johnson administration set a new high-water mark in congressional deference to the executive prerogative interpretation of the Constitution in foreign policy. It also instigated a congressional revolt against the policy manifestations of that interpretation that eventually would bring forth a host of legislative attempts to regain control of foreign policy in the 1970s.

In 1964, in less than three days of discussion and debate, the House passed the Tonkin Gulf Resolution without any opposition, and the Senate passed it with only two negative votes. This resolution stated that the United States was "prepared, as the President determines, to take all necessary steps, including the use of armed force, to assist"[1] Southeast Asian nations in defending their freedom. Representative Carl Albert spoke for many of his fellow legislators when he said that "The President has asked us as representatives of the American people for our support. It is now time for all of us to join together as a nation firmly united behind our Commander in Chief and to express our complete confidence in him and in his leadership."[2] Even those who recognized that the Tonkin Gulf Resolution might open the door to an extended struggle on the mainland of Asia argued that it had to be done because, as Senator George Aiken put it, the decision and responsibility for the decision rested "squarely with the President, under the authority delegated to him by the Congress over the years." While Aiken was apprehensive, he insisted that no one in Congress could justify opposing the president's exercise of power and use of an authority which had been "delegated to his office" by Congress.[3] And indeed, no one in the House, and only two senators—Wayne Morse of Oregon and Ernest Gruening of Alaska—were willing to vote against the resolution.

While Truman and Kennedy articulated an executive prerogative interpretation of the Constitution in foreign policy, Eisenhower and Johnson were a bit more ambivalent. Both were powerfully influenced by Truman's experience in Korea, and both were committed to the idea that if their administrations were to engage in a foreign military operation it would not be done unless Congress was on record in support of the policy to avoid any *post hoc* political attacks should the policy fail or bog down.

In explaining why he wanted a congressional resolution after the Tonkin Gulf incident, Johnson focused on Truman's experience in Korea and said that he had decided that "before we go in there to a more advanced state to involve ourselves more substantially, I want the Congress to go in with me."[4] Because Truman never sought a declaration of war, or even an explicit legislative approval of his actions in Korea, he was vulnerable in 1952 when the Republican Party platform charged that his administration "had plunged us into war in Korea without the consent of our citizens through their authorized representatives in Congress."[5] Having learned that lesson, Johnson later argued that the idea was "to keep [Congress] in place, and to keep them in agreement with what our action should be." If we expected them "to be there on the landing," Johnson added, "we ought to ask them to be there on the takeoff."[6] Johnson consistently insisted that he had more than adequate authority to conduct the war in Vietnam without the Tonkin Gulf Resolution, and yet it regularly was cited as a strong source of legitimacy for his policy. This is not necessarily contradictory. While Johnson seemed to propound and accept a prerogative interpretation of the Constitution in foreign policy, he acknowledged that even though he believed that presidents *may* act alone in foreign affairs, they are far stronger when they act in concert with Congress. Thus, while he subscribed to and defended the prerogative interpretation, Johnson was more than willing to employ the congressional support that had been offered—knowingly or not—in the Tonkin Gulf Resolution, to further bolster his political strength.

President Johnson wasn't the only elected official who saw the Tonkin Gulf Resolution as both unnecessary and powerfully meaningful. Many in Congress who had voted for the resolution did so on the supposition that its purpose was limited and defined though its language was open-ended. The speed with which the bill passed had a lot to do with this second apparent contradiction. One senator asked William Fulbright, who guided the resolution through the Senate, whether it would in any way "authorize or recommend or approve the landing of large American armies in Vietnam or in China?" Fulbright responded that "the language of the resolution would not prevent it. It would authorize whatever the Commander in Chief feels is necessary. It does not restrict the Executive from doing it." But, he noted, "there is nothing in the resolution as I read it that contemplates [that]. I agree with the Senator that is the last thing we would want to do."[7] But while this passage often is quoted by those who argue that Congress well understood what it was doing with the Tonkin Gulf Resolution, Fulbright explained a few years later that the reason so much had been accepted on faith was the urgency with which the resolution had been cloaked: "We were told this attack had taken place," Fulbright explained, and that it was "wholly unprovoked and very serious," and "we were asked to pass this quickly," and "I was told that it would be most unfortunate if there were any amendments allowed or any delay, because this would evidence a lack of confidence and unity within the Congress."[8]

Why were legislators willing to grant broad authority to the president? In part because of their confidence that the resolution essentially was a show of unity and not an authorization for extensive military operations; and in part because increasingly Congress had come to accept the idea that the president had to have broad discretionary power in foreign policy. As Senator Claiborne Pell argued in 1967, the "system of checks and balances which was very right in 1776 and the Constitution, which we consider a pretty sacred instrument, may not actually measure up to all the responsibilities we have today in this quick-moving world that we are in."[9]

The president was able to gain some additional legitimacy from the Tonkin Gulf Resolution while continuing to deny its necessity. In calling on Congress to approve the Tonkin Gulf Resolution, President Johnson asked "Congress, on its part to join in *affirming* the national determination" and recommended "a Resolution expressing the *support* of the Congress for all necessary action. . . ."[10] In the eyes of the president, the resolution would affirm his decision and support it, it would not *authorize* it, nor would it legitimate it, because such authorization was not necessary. As Johnson noted in 1967, "we did not think the resolution was necessary to do what we did and what we are doing. But we thought it was desirable."[11] Indeed it was, because with the resolution the administration was persuasively able to argue that it had defeated all possible objections. If the administration did, in fact, need congressional authorization then, even though the word was not used, any reading of the resolution clearly suggested that Congress had in fact provided that authorization. As Nicholas Katzenbach (then Undersecretary of State) argued, "If the President needed authority, I think he got that authority." If, on the other hand, one rejected the notion that he needed authority, then one could see in the resolution only what its words actually said—that Congress offered support and affirmation for the president's policy. If the president "did not need that authority," Katzenbach continued, "then I think he got the support and sense of Congress on this." When pressed as to his own interpretation, however, Katzenbach reflected the Johnson administration position that in fact the president "does have that authority" without the resolution.[12]

The administration was happy to see the resolution from both sides. Either way it won, since it never conceded that the president needed congressional authorization and since the bill technically only affirmed and supported, and yet for all practical purposes authorized the president to act. In that way, the administration's executive prerogative interpretation of the Constitution was bolstered without a confrontation. In Congress, legislators took positions along a full spectrum ranging from those in agreement with one Iowa Republican who argued that the resolution was no more than "an after-the-fact sense resolution endorsing action already taken by the President," that served above all "as an expression of unity in this emergency,"[13] to Wayne Morse, who insisted that Congress was "giving to the President what I honestly and sincerely believe is an unconstitutional power—that is, the power to make war without a declaration of war."[14]

The Tonkin Gulf Resolution was hardly without precedent. In fact, the Formosa, Mideast, and Cuba resolutions were viewed by a great number of legislators as critical precedents suggesting that Congress and the executive perhaps had struck on a new way to manage the war powers, a way that accepted far more prerogative power in the executive while maintaining a patina of a congressional role. As New York Senator Jacob Javits (who years later would be the prime sponsor of the War Powers Resolution of 1973) optimistically argued before the passage of the Mideast Resolution in 1957, this "is a new technique in American policy. It is not a declaration of war; nor are we waiting for a situation to arise when it would be the prerogative of Congress to declare war. It is advance notice that we will combat force with force. In that respect I think it is a new technique in meeting Communist techniques which present us with a new situation, and one which the Senate should adopt."[15]

The earlier resolutions served as the building blocks for the Tonkin Gulf Resolution, helping to convince reluctant legislators that it was uncontroversial and built on established principles. "There can be no doubt," Secretary of State Dean Rusk testified in 1964, "that these previous resolutions form a solid legal precedent for the action now proposed."[16] Many in Congress insisted that the resolution did not provide a new precedent, since the House and Senate had taken "action similar to that requested today in the Formosa and Middle East crises when requested by President Eisenhower and . . . in the Cuba crisis."[17] Every time a precedent is repeated it builds the authority and legitimacy of the disputed function, and while Congress retains the constitutional authority to revoke the precedent, to overturn the earlier authorization, it becomes increasingly hard to do so. As Senator Hickenloper observed, "Precedent is piling upon precedent until we finally accept it as a fact."[18] Or, as Senator Morse put it, while "a repetition of mistakes does not create a legal right in the President" it does make it politically more difficult to alter what rapidly comes to be seen as the status quo in the balance of powers.[19]

The prerogative interpretation was well in place in 1965 when President Johnson, arguing that American lives were in jeopardy, dispatched American marines to the Dominican Republic to intervene in a coup the administration contended was dominated by communist forces. Congressional criticism of the Dominican deployment focused on the president's justification for his orders, not on the lack of congressional participation. In part this was because most legislators accepted that it was the president's responsibility to intervene abroad to protect American lives. Some in Congress soon rejected the president's claim that lives were in jeopardy and that that was the primary objective of the American military presence. If the rationale was something else, they argued, then Congress had every reason to ask why it had played no part in a significant foreign policy and war-powers decision. The Dominican situation, which rapidly lost popular appeal at home, finally sparked some major newspapers as well as some mainstream legislators to take stock of the balance of powers between the president and Congress in foreign policy. As the *New York Times* suggested, "Congress' control of the warmaking power has been eroded almost to the point of invisibility." In trying to understand this abdication, the *Times* accepted the idea that such abdication was appropriate "insofar as the waging of thermonuclear war is concerned." But, when the subject was something less than nuclear war, "there has been an institutional failure on the part of Congress to develop the new procedures and tradition necessary to protect its role in the making of foreign policy in a new age of international political warfare."[20]

Johnson had both perfected and destroyed the very effective strategy developed by Eisenhower. Eisenhower had gone to Congress, secured broad powers and authority, and used that authority as a negotiation tool. Johnson went to Congress and easily won support for similar language, but instead of using the authority as a negotiating tool, Johnson implemented it. When legislators no longer were comfortable with the exercise of the authority they had granted him, Johnson held the resolution over their heads and exploited it as far as he could.

By 1968 it was clear that Lyndon Johnson, who had won office just four years earlier in the then-largest landslide in American political history, would face a terrific battle for re-election. Eugene McCarthy had done remarkably well in the New Hampshire primary (though Johnson did, in fact, win the primary, he did so with a far lower percentage than was expected from a sitting president), and Robert Kennedy clearly was a potentially formidable challenger. Johnson announced in March that he would not run for re-election. But as the war dragged on, many in Congress had begun to question the result of years of deference to the executive in foreign policy. The electoral pressure that had encouraged delegation in foreign policy and national security slowly was shifting, and the elected representatives began to respond to these changing incentives.[21] A strongly worded report from the Senate Foreign Relations Committee on national commitments to foreign powers signaled that there were influential senators who felt that the Senate had to act to regain its authority. But the report led nowhere. The resolution (Senate Resolution 151) didn't make it to the floor of the Senate in 1967 or 1968. It was withdrawn because it was feared that it might complicate Johnson's negotiating initiative with the North Vietnamese.

In 1969, Fulbright revived his effort to have the Senate pass a resolution on national commitments that would restore a measure of legislative control in foreign policy. In the intervening time Americans had begun to fear the loss of domestic tranquility: Watts, Newark, and Detroit had been torched in riots; protestors had descended on Washington and on Chicago, where the Democratic National Convention was rent by riots and tear gas in 1968; the war in Vietnam raged on. By 1969, with Richard Nixon in the White House, enough senators were sufficiently upset about the course of the war and of American foreign policy in general that they were willing to vote for Fulbright's sense of the Senate resolution, which, though it had no legal authority, was designed to send a message to the president and to an increasingly frustrated electorate. The committee argued that the "principal cause of the constitutional imbalance has been the circumstance of American involvement and responsibility in a violent and unstable world." These events paved the way for both Congress and the president to be "unmindful of constitutional requirements and proscriptions, the executive by its incursions upon congressional prerogative at moments when action seemed more important than the means of its initiation, the Congress by its uncritical and sometimes unconscious acquiescence in these incursions."[22] Fulbright succeeded in 1969 where he had failed in 1967 to gain Senate approval for his sense of the Senate resolution. As the Nixon years wore on, Fulbright brought more and more legislators to his point of view, but while a growing number in Congress began to believe that they had over-delegated and deferred, the administration took an increasingly insistent position that executive prerogative was now a constitutional norm. At the same time, in trade legislation and in other areas of foreign policy, Congress continued to delegate, defer to, and authorize executive discretion.[23]

During the Nixon years, Congress tried to regain authority in foreign policy, and yet the very circumstances Fulbright had recognized—the Cold War, America's growing world role, and the complications of nuclear technology—made it impossible to fully restore the congressional role.

Nixon vs. Congress: A Constitutional Debate over Executive Prerogative

Despite the emergence of a number of antiwar critics in the House and Senate, a majority of legislators in 1969 continued to argue that the president had the responsibility and constitutional authority to shape American foreign policy in questions of armed force as well as broader issues. Nixon extended that argument to maintain that in an era of national emergency, the executive had broad constitutional latitude at home as well. No longer would the executive merely claim to be bound by loose constitutional restrictions abroad, now the executive would assume broad constitutional authority abroad and claim that the loose international restrictions could be applied at home as well, where it was required for national security. Nixon's argument that foreign and domestic policy no longer could be logically separated went a step beyond the more traditional interpretation of the Constitution offered by Chief Justice John Marshall who had argued that the Constitution was to be read the same in foreign and domestic policy alike. In Marshall's era, domestic priorities would dictate the nature of the national government's latitude in foreign policy. Nixon took the argument in the opposite direction. In an interdependent world that Marshall could hardly have been expected to anticipate, Nixon argued that foreign policy needs and powers could, should, and would dictate domestic priorities and constitutional authority.

When Nixon entered office he faced an increasingly hostile Congress, but one that was unwilling to do more than pass sense of the Senate resolutions. Nixon saw little role for Congress—he was elected by the people and his administration would act with strength, independence, and vigor. In a campaign speech in 1968 he promised a revitalized presidency. "The next President must take an activist view of his office." As a candidate, Stanley Kutler wrote, Nixon "never mentioned Congress in his scheme of governance; he offered no recognition of shared power whatsoever."[24]

Nixon wasted little time in putting his executive prerogative in foreign affairs into practice. Early in his administration, Nixon invoked the prerogative interpretation to legitimate his decision to authorize "secret" bombing runs over Cambodia, and later to sanction his unilateral decision to send American ground troops into Cambodia without congressional authorization. By the end of his term, Nixon argued that foreign policy needs gave him the constitutional authority to order wiretaps on American citizens at home[25] and the constitutional authority to impound funds appropriated by Congress. In addition his administration ordered an extensive surveillance campaign conducted by the Central Intelligence Agency that targeted American citizens and focused on political activity at home as well as overseas. Ultimately, the exercise of executive prerogative at home drew a congressional response. With the exception of Cambodia, the congressional backlash to the president's expanding view of presidential power was generated by the exercise of that power at home, and it was this distinction that helps explain the contours of the flawed legislation passed by Congress more to punish Nixon than to regain control of foreign policy.

* * *

Senator Fulbright's proposal to pass the Senate resolution concerning national commitments to foreign powers resulted in a strongly worded report in 1967. But by the time the Senate was ready to vote on the bill, Lyndon Johnson had decided to forgo any attempt to win the Democratic nomination for re-election in 1968. Instead, he announced in March of that year that he would suspend the bombing in North Vietnam and devote his remaining months in office to seeking a peaceful settlement of the war. In deference to the president's peace initiative, Fulbright thought it best to defer action on his proposal, fearing that it might weaken the president's bargaining position at a crucial moment. But when negotiations failed, and Johnson was replaced by Nixon, Fulbright revived his proposal and brought it to the Senate floor in 1969 for a vote.

As it had in 1967, the proposal sparked a heated debate in 1969. The lone dissenter on the Senate Foreign Relations Committee, Wyoming Democrat Gale McGee, wrote a stinging dissent that touched on the key postwar developments that many argued made it impossible and unsafe for Congress to play a decisive role in foreign policy. McGee argued that the nation had to vest responsibility for foreign policy in one branch or the other. The debate, he noted on the Senate floor, focused on "whether in a nuclear age we have the wisest processes for protecting the national interest, whether we can repose authority in a different way."[26] But, "mindful as we all are of the risk involved in increasing executive power in the field of foreign affairs, there would appear to be no reasonable alternative to assuming those risks save at the price of confusion, delay, and even inaction through some series of yet unspecified procedures implied in the commitments resolution."[27] McGee argued that in the nuclear era the nation most needed to be able to focus responsibility, and it could best do so by accepting presidential control of foreign policy. In fact, he argued, Americans should embrace executive control of foreign policy as a means of maintaining responsibility in one identifiable source. McGee's was not a purely pragmatic argument. In his view the president's authority was built on solid constitutional grounds, and the president had sufficient prerogative powers in foreign affairs to control foreign policy anyway.

McGee's was decidedly a minority point of view. Since the legislation was not binding, it gave a number of senators a chance to express their concerns about the slow erosion of legislative power in foreign affairs, without actually limiting the president or altering the balance of power. For some, like North Carolina's Sam Ervin "the trend to Executive supremacy" was a "product of the Cold War and of recurrent and almost constant crisis in which the stakes are often the very survival of this country and the world." Senator Ervin argued that crisis had led to a perception that the United States could not afford adversarial democracy in foreign policy, but that somehow bipartisanship in foreign policy had "developed into a withdrawal of Congress from any significant role in the formulation of foreign policy."[28]

For Senator Church, the bipartisanship and the resulting deference to the executive in foreign policy were the result of a crisis mentality. In crisis, Church argued, "Congress, like the country, tends to unite behind the President." The United States, still new to its world role, was unable to distinguish between "genuine emergencies and situations that only seem to require urgent action." As a result, Church said, Congress had acted with undue haste, "assuming, quite wrongly, that it would somehow be unpatriotic to question the President's judgment in a moment of assumed emergency."[29]

Despite the ringing statements of Ervin, Church, and others, the Senate was in fact prepared only to pass a statement and not a law. While Church sounded a note of regret that the state of emergency may have been exploited by the executive branch, others strongly agreed with McGee, who argued that the emergency was and continued to be a very real threat; such a threat, in fact, that the American commitment to democratic institutions might well have to be tempered in the face of a threat of destruction from totalitarian states. Democracy is awkward in an age of crisis, McGee and others argued, and Senate interference in foreign policy was a luxury the country could ill afford. McGee felt the resolution might "complicate and make worse the problems of a democracy trying to live within its constitutional structures in an age of monolithic governments and monolithic decision-making in other parts of the world." It was an age in which Americans were "always reminded of the clumsiness of a democracy," and it was hardly a time for the Senate to interfere with presidential control of foreign policy.[30] The suggestion was clear: We were now in an age when Congress had to consider the very institutions and structures of government as fundamentally under attack, and therefore, the need for survival might well dictate many constitutional compromises that would be unacceptable in a safer era.

In the White House, the Senate resolution seems to have had little effect on the Nixon administration. In a letter to Senator Fulbright, the Nixon State Department echoed the remarks made by the Johnson administration in 1967. It argued that the Constitution, supported by "consistent practice," gave the president "the power to enter into many agreements and to initiate many actions that can be considered commitments to other countries." In addition, the State Department said, the president had sole authority to command the armed forces "whether they are within or outside the United States," and had full constitutional power to "send U.S. military forces abroad without specific Congressional approval."[31] The Nixon State Department concluded that informing and consulting Congress was all the Constitution required, and that was what the president intended to do.

Informing and consulting Congress was, in fact, less than the president intended to do. One month before the Foreign Relations Committee issued its report, Nixon authorized an extensive series of bombing runs over Cambodia. These runs, starting on 17 March 1969, were approved with hardly any congressional consultation. The only legislators who were aware of Nixon's decision were Richard Russell and John Stennis of the Senate Armed Services Committee. In his memoirs, Nixon said that "in order to preserve the secrecy of the bombing," they were the only ones informed. Secrecy was critical, Nixon argued, because it made it politically difficult for North Vietnam to protest the mission and, at the same time, it would help diffuse the "problem of domestic antiwar protest." Arguing that his administration was only two months old, Nixon noted that he "wanted to provoke as little public outcry as possible at the outset."[32]

Cambodia and the War Power

A year later, the public outcry Nixon hoped to avoid could be avoided no longer. After deciding to send American ground forces into Cambodia, again without congressional consultation or approval, Nixon faced a major round of protests culminating at Kent State University in Ohio, where four students were shot and killed at a protest march. For Nixon, there was no question about his constitutional authority to order the troops into Cambodia. As far as he was concerned, it "is the right of the President of the United States under the Constitution to protect the lives of American men."[33] He didn't even justify the troop mobilization by mention of the SEATO treaty, or of the Tonkin Gulf Resolution, which the administration claimed was unnecessary. And, though the administration argued that the Cambodian mission was necessary to protect American lives, it was not framed as an emergency that simply could not wait. "Nixon cited no emergency that denied time for congressional action, expressed no doubt about the perfect legality of his [action] . . . and showed no interest even in retrospective congressional ratification."[34] This was a full-blown prerogative argument. No longer did it rest on twin pillars of prerogative *and* statutory authority—the Cambodia mission was defended on prerogative grounds alone.

While Nixon showed little interest in the legal debate sparked by his decisions on Cambodia, the administration did assign the task of expounding a legal defense to then Assistant Attorney General William H. Rehnquist. Rehnquist argued that the president had sufficient constitutional authority on a number of grounds, most of which had surfaced in similar arguments during the Truman, Eisenhower, Kennedy, and Johnson administrations. Rehnquist relied first on the constitutional authority of the commander in chief. Under this authority, Rehnquist argued, the president had the power to deploy troops anywhere even if that might invite war. Second, Rehnquist argued, the president had the power to commit troops to conflict. Finally, the commander in chief had the power to determine how a war already in progress would be conducted.[35]

Rehnquist wasn't willing to rest his defense solely on his interpretation of the commander in chief clause. Instead he argued that there was strong evidence that what may once have been a gray area of law had, through long-standing executive assertion and congressional acquiescence, taken on the legitimacy of precedent. Rehnquist listed a series of cases where presidents had deployed troops. Congress, he noted, had acquiesced in some of these, had ratified others, and had remained silent in still others. While a single such act of deference did not create a constitutional precedent, Rehnquist argued, "a long continued practice on the part of the Executive, acquiesced in by the Congress, is itself some evidence of the existence of constitutional authority to support such a practice."[36] Finally, Rehnquist argued, there was an important difference between foreign and domestic policy, and what the Constitution might forbid in one policy area, it authorized in the other. In responding to the charge that Congress is not free to give a blank check to the president, Rehnquist insisted that "Whatever may be the answer to that abstract question in the domestic field, I think it is plain . . . that the principle of unlawful delegation of powers does not apply in the field of external affairs."[37]

Through Rehnquist, the Nixon administration asserted that Congress could delegate as much power as it saw fit to do in foreign affairs; that such delegations, combined with congressional acquiescence or even silence over a long period of time blossomed into constitutional authority for the executive; and that under the commander in chief clause, the president had almost unlimited authority to deploy American troops anywhere in the world. Later Nixon would extend the argument: The Constitution gave the president prerogative in foreign affairs, and if foreign affairs happened to require the exercise of power at home, then the Constitution, by logical extension, authorized that as well.

Nixon's address to the nation on 30 April 1970, explaining his actions in Cambodia brought a swift domestic reaction, both on college campuses and on Capitol Hill. On 4 May the student protest at Kent State resulted in four deaths. Days after a mass student march on Washington on 9 May, the Senate Foreign Relations Committee passed the Cooper-Church amendment by a vote of 9 to 1. This amendment, tied to a military appropriations bill, required the president to remove all U.S. forces from Cambodia before 30 June. On 24 June, the Senate followed the unanimous recommendation of the Foreign Relations Committee and voted to repeal the Tonkin Gulf Resolution. Nixon signed the bill, but stated at the time that it was "without binding force or effect," and that his signing "will not change the policies I have pursued."[38] Finally, on 30 June, the full Senate passed the Cooper-Church amendment. This run of events had little impact on the administration's constitutional interpretation of executive powers. The Nixon administration already had disavowed the utility or necessity of the Tonkin Gulf Resolution, and in his memoirs, Nixon's only comment on Cooper-Church was that it had a symbolic impact, but no real importance. "The symbolism of the timing was as serious as the action itself was meaningless,"[39] Nixon wrote, since the troops already had been withdrawn. In responding to the Cooper-Church Amendment, a press officer in the White House told reporters that the amendment itself was unconstitutional since "it sought to curtail the President's constitutional powers as Commander-in-Chief."[40]

Prerogative Comes Home: Wiretaps, Impoundment, and Executive Privilege

In his defense of the Nixon administration's decisions on Cambodia, Rehnquist argued that there was a clear constitutional distinction between foreign and domestic policy and that the Constitution presented fewer limits and constraints on executive action in the foreign field. The major contribution of the Nixon administration to the evolution of the prerogative interpretation of the Constitution was to take this analysis one step further than it had been taken before. Starting with the intense and often violent protests against the war in 1969 and 1970, the administration began to articulate its view that national security abroad could be fundamentally threatened by domestic dissent and sabotage, and that therefore the president's broader constitutional powers to deal with foreign affairs actually could be interpreted to bestow upon the executive similar unfettered powers to protect national security at home.

The evolution of the executive prerogative interpretation of the Constitution in foreign affairs had now come full circle. First the Constitution had been viewed as a unitary document that controlled foreign and domestic affairs alike under the strict limits developed in the domestic context. Soon that view gave way to the need to build a strong central government for foreign affairs without sacrificing the diffuse and weak central government that was so treasured at home. This gave rise to the belief in all three branches that the Constitution in fact could be read differently in foreign and domestic affairs, with the executive facing far fewer constitutional constraints when the policy in question was purely foreign. Now, under Nixon, the president was understood to have broader powers in foreign affairs to protect national security. But protecting national security was not something that could be limited to foreign lands. The Nixon administration argued that national survival was the first priority, and therefore if national survival (as defined by the executive) was threatened, then the executive had the constitutional authority to employ the powers that had aggregated to the executive in foreign policy, whether or not the object of that exercise of power happened to be located in the territorial United States. This conviction flowered in the period leading up to the Watergate hearings, as the administration became convinced that national survival depended on the achievement of a particular partisan result in American elections. But the constitutional interpretation on which it was based predated the break-in at the Watergate. Even after the Watergate revelations, Nixon argued that what he saw as aberrant errors of campaign enthusiasm in Watergate should not be used as an excuse for Congress to attempt to limit or restrict executive power.

In an address to the nation in August 1973, Nixon noted that in ordering domestic surveillance, he was doing no more nor less than had his predecessors "in a reasonable belief that in certain circumstances the Constitution permitted and sometimes even required such measures to protect the national security in the public interest." In Nixon's view the danger that now loomed was that the public would overly constrain the president. While he indicated that Watergate revealed instances "in which a zeal for security did go too far," he emphasized that "it is essential that such mistakes not be repeated. But it is also essential that we do not overreact to particular mistakes by tying the President's hands in a way that would risk sacrificing our security, and with it all our liberties."[41] Since the administration was convinced that the president had extensive prerogative powers in foreign affairs, it is logical that the administration would reason that territorial borders should make no difference if the object was national security. Well before Watergate, the Nixon administration steadfastly defended domestic surveillance and wiretapping without warrants. In a 1971 court case, the administration argued that the president, acting through the attorney general, "has the *inherent constitutional power*: (1) to authorize, without a judicial warrant, electronic surveillance in "national security" cases; and (2) to determine unilaterally whether a given situation is a matter within the concept of national security."[42] The district court judges hearing this case were disturbed by this argument for two reasons. First, the administration made no distinction between domestic and foreign affairs; and second, the administration had suggested that when it comes to national security, no one, no court, no body of government, could restrict the president.

While the Nixon administration did not rely on Court opinion or congressional statutes to support its claims to prerogative power in national security surveillance cases, Nixon's position on domestic wiretaps was not merely the invention of his own imagination. Congress had contributed to the confusion when, in 1968, it passed the Omnibus Crime Control and Safe Streets Act,[43] in which it authorized wiretaps in a number of circumstances. The bill contained an ambiguous section that could be read as a meaningless statement of fact, or as an explicit acknowledgement of executive prerogative in wiretapping. The section read: "Nothing contained in this [Act] shall limit the constitutional power of the President to take such measures as he deems necessary to protect the Nation against actual or potential attack or other hostile acts of a foreign power, to obtain foreign intelligence information deemed essential to the security of the United States, or to protect national security information against foreign intelligence activities."[44] Prior to the passage of this bill, the executive branch had engaged in domestic surveillance, but it had been a gray area, one in which presidents acted without congressional authorization or participation. While some in Congress argued that the bill merely stated that the status quo was to be preserved, many saw this bill as a congressional authorization for presidential wiretapping. The Nixon administration positively saw the bill as a confirmation of what it interpreted to be a constitutional prerogative power vested in the president.

In a 1971 case before the Supreme Court, the Nixon administration cited the Omnibus Crime Act not as a source of congressional authorization, but rather as evidence that even Congress acknowledged the executive branch's *inherent* constitutional authority to order wiretaps in national security cases. In "excepting national security surveillance from the [Omnibus Crime] Act's warrant requirement, Congress *recognized* the President's authority to conduct such surveillance without prior judicial approval."[45] The key word is *recognized*. The administration did not argue that Congress had authorized or approved a delegation of power (which would imply that the power was Congress' to delegate), but rather that Congress had merely recognized a constitutional reality and acknowledged that reality in the statute. The Court insisted that the statute "certainly confers no power," a claim with which the administration agreed. While the Court overruled the administration in this case, the opinion suggested that it was plausible that foreign policy needs might well legitimate domestic surveillance under the right circumstances.

The Nixon administration argued that the executive had certain constitutional rights that other branches had no authority to invade or constrain.[46] Among these, the president contended, was the right to refuse to spend money that had been appropriated by Congress and the right to withhold information, documents, and testimony from Congress and even from the judiciary when the president judged such information to be protected by executive privilege. While none of these claims directly grew from foreign policy cases, they illustrate the contours of the prerogative power interpretation, an interpretation that, under Nixon, imported foreign affairs justifications to legitimate the exercise of prerogative power at home.

The emerging commitment to the prerogative interpretation of the Constitution by the executive was powerfully evident in the battle between Congress and Nixon over the impoundment of appropriated funds. If any constitutional power exclusively belongs to Congress it must be the power to raise and appropriate funds.[47] Nevertheless, presidents from the beginning have taken it upon themselves to refuse to spend some of the money appropriated by Congress. While the Constitution does not mandate that the president spend what is appropriated, it does mandate that he execute the laws. Nixon argued that in impounding funds, he was doing just what "Jefferson did, and Jackson did, and Truman did."[48] Earlier presidents generally defended their action as a better means to the congressionally mandated end. While Nixon did what they did, he defended it quite differently. Nixon followed Lyndon Johnson's lead and argued that he had full *constitutional* authority to refuse to spend appropriated money. Johnson's Attorney General, Ramsey Clark, offered a formal legal opinion in 1967 defending the president's authority to impound funds, arguing that "an appropriation act does not constitute a mandate to spend." Appropriations, Clark argued, place "an upper and not a lower limit on expenditures." To this point, the opinion seems noncontroversial; after all, Congress appropriates funds to accomplish certain ends—if those ends can be accomplished for less money, that should be fine. The twist Clark threw in, and that the Nixon administration embraced, was the notion that the executive had to weigh many different considerations in deciding how much to spend—not only should the executive consider the specific objective of the appropriation, but the executive also had to weigh "such factors as the effect of the authorized expenditures on the national economy and their relation to other programs important to the national welfare"[49]—considerations that traditionally had been considered within the prerogative of the legislative branch. Building on Clark's argument, and rejecting William Rehnquist's advice in a 1969 memo that the president was only free to impound funds in foreign affairs and was "not at liberty to impound in the case of domestic affairs,"[50] Nixon argued, "The constitutional right for the President of the United States to impound funds . . . is absolutely clear."[51] Stanley Kutler concluded that, for Nixon, "[T]he exercise of impoundment also became part of his constitutional responsibility."[52]

Instead of accepting Rehnquist's foreign/domestic distinction, which would have allowed impoundment in foreign affairs only, Nixon relied instead on arguments such as Casper Weinberger's (then the Director of the Office of Management and Budget) that impoundment was a logical and legitimate exercise of discretion in an attempt to "reconcile conflicting congressional goals."[53] Although impoundment largely affected domestic issues, Nixon's rejection of Rehnquist's foreign/domestic distinction again hints at the notion that the Nixon administration was uncomfortable with it, and was inclined to see the two areas as interdependent. And if they were interdependent, then foreign policy needs justified the expansion of domestic executive powers.

While Watergate brought the issue of executive privilege to a head, it was not the first time Congress and the president had battled over the question of when and how a president might shield his administration from congressional and judicial probes. Nixon's claims were not wholly new; he just took them to a new level. As early as March 1971 Nixon admitted to one reporter that he had been wrong in his battles with Harry Truman over executive privilege when Nixon served on the House Un-American Activities Committee. "Looking back in retrospect," Nixon acknowledged, Truman had "properly insisted" on the prerogatives of his office.[54]

As the Watergate investigation heated up, the executive branch stood firm on the question of executive privilege. In a brief filed in *U.S. v. Nixon* (the Watergate tapes case), Nixon's attorney argued that "[T]he foundation for the President's assertion of executive privilege is the Constitution." Inherent in the executive power vested in the president by article 2 of the Constitution, the brief argued, "is executive privilege; in this case, more accurately described as presidential privilege. Unless this is so, the full panoply of power embodied in the executive power, would be, in reality, greatly diluted, a concept at odds with the intent of the Framers of the Constitution."[55] The Nixon administration's position on executive privilege was an important component in the developing doctrine of presidential prerogative. The administration position began to focus on the argument that Congress had only two ways to restrain or punish a president. One was to refuse him funds, and the other was to impeach him. Short of those, the administration in numerous instances made it clear that Congress had no power to compel testimony or cooperation from the executive branch. As Assistant Attorney General Henry E. Peterson told a House committee in 1974, answering certain questions would "be a violation of the Constitution . . . whether it be to the Congress or to anyone else."[56] Again, as with the national security surveillance at home and impoundment, the assertion of privilege wasn't new, but it was presented as a constitutional right rather than merely a *fait accompli*.

In the wiretapping case, Congress inadvertently provided legitimacy for what had been considered undefined constitutional territory at best; in the case of impoundment, the administration tried to elevate a questionable practice to a constitutional principle. But in the case of executive privilege, it was the Court that lent legitimacy to the executive's claims, claims that had been made in previous administrations, but never constitutionally resolved.

In *U.S. v. Nixon* the Court ordered Nixon to surrender his tapes, thus defeating his claim of executive privilege in that case. At the same time, however, the Court acknowledged for the first time that there was such a thing as executive privilege and that there was constitutional support for the sorts of claims Nixon had made, if not for the particular claims made in the Watergate tapes case. The Court ruled that while nowhere in the Constitution "is there any explicit reference to a privilege of confidentiality, yet to the extent this interest relates to the effective discharge of a President's powers, it is constitutionally based."[57] Nixon had lost his battle, but he had contributed to winning the war by establishing an important precedent for future chief executives.

The Nixon administration built on the precedents and trends established by Truman, Eisenhower, Kennedy, and Johnson, and Nixon brought to full bloom the prerogative interpretation that others had tentatively nurtured. Nixon's unique contribution was in the constitutional reunion of foreign and domestic policy, arguing that the president's powers in foreign affairs had to be applied at home when national security and survival were at stake. The distinction that had evolved for more than 100 years had come full circle, and now rather than having the domestic Constitution's constraints limit the government abroad, the executive's broad discretion to act in the national interest abroad was seen by the administration as a constitutional justification to apply that power, authority and prerogative at home.

* * *

One certainly would expect Congress to rise up and react to this radical shift. But while it was true that presidents had moved away from the traditional interpretation and toward the prerogative view, so had the majority of legislators. And as legislation increasingly delegated power to the executive, the Court, in its interpretation of that legislation, offered no resistance, and some assistance, to the growing acceptance of a prerogative interpretation of the Constitution. The Court's role in this process will be examined in Chapter 5. Only with a clear understanding of the deeply entrenched nature of the prerogative interpretation will it be possible to examine, evaluate, and understand the legislative reaction to this trend. This reaction was aimed *not* at the assertion of prerogative power abroad, but rather focused on what legislators perceived to be a radical claim by the executive to act at home in the ways Congress had tacitly and explicitly authorized the president to do abroad. This was the shift that sparked the response. Congress was unwilling to allow broad discretion abroad to authorize the president to expand his domestic authority. The fundamental objection was not to the now accepted notion that in foreign affairs the president had to be granted wider constitutional latitude than in domestic policy. Rather, legislators in Congress were determined to make sure that the president's assertion of prerogative power would not authorize and constitutionally legitimate his exercise of prerogative powers at home. Many in Congress may have sounded like they wanted to return to the traditional interpretation, but the legislation they passed was built on by then well-established and well-accepted norms of the prerogative interpretation. What Congress wanted to do was to return to the status quo before Nixon, not the status quo before the Second World War. Therefore, it should hardly be surprising that the legislation failed to turn the clock back to the traditional interpretation.

5

Lending Legitimacy to the Prerogative Interpretation: Prerogative Power in Court

When a number of legislators began to fight to restore the congressional role in foreign policy in the 1970s, their efforts generally failed to achieve their stated objectives. They failed to do so for a number of reasons, most prominently, perhaps, because their efforts were built on a misunderstanding of the Court's doctrine. To make matters worse, the doctrine these legislators misunderstood was itself shifting.

The Court's traditional doctrine in foreign policy cases focused on the power of the national government (the executive and legislative branches) as a whole, versus claims of individual rights or claims of the usurpation of powers not explicitly delegated to the national government, or reserved to the states. In the period following the Second World War, the Supreme Court added a second focus to its scrutiny of foreign policy cases. While the Court continued to be concerned about the power of the national government acting as a whole (particularly in cases concerning the government's power to infringe the individual rights of American citizens), the Court also began to focus on the horizontal separation of powers—the distribution of power between the executive and legislative branches.

Twenty years after the *Curtiss-Wright* case, the Supreme Court ordered President Harry S Truman to return the American steel mills he had seized on behalf of the nation by executive order in a case called *Youngstown Sheet and Tube v Sawyer* (1952) (the Steel Seizure Case). *Curtiss* and *Youngstown* often are cited as the polar extremes of the Court's doctrine in foreign policy cases. These cases are not two ends of a limited spectrum, but rather two coherent and consistent points on a continuum.

Curtiss-Wright was a case about what the national government (the president and Congress, acting together) could and could not do in foreign policy. *Youngstown*, on the other hand, was about the division and separation of power *within* the national government—what the president could and could not do in the absence of congressional consent, or in the face of congressional opposition. In *Youngstown*, the focus was on the horizontal separation of powers.

These two cases established the foundation for the Court's postwar doctrine that in foreign affairs the national government (the executive and legislative branches acting together), is limited only by explicit constitutional prohibitions, particularly those against infringing the individual rights of American citizens without the provision of at least minimal due process. But this broad power applies only when the national government acts as a unified whole. When the president acts alone, the Court will look to Congress. Where Congress is opposed, the justices will support Congress and protect what they perceive to be legislative prerogatives in foreign policy. The question of just what might constitute congressional opposition remained unclear in the wake of *Youngstown*.

This doctrine has remained intact. Where Congress expresses formal opposition to executive actions, the Court continues to support congressional prerogatives. What has changed, however, is how the Court interprets congressional silence and legislative ambiguity. And it is that change which many lawmakers failed to understand as they crafted legislative efforts to rebalance foreign policy powers in the 1970s and 1980s. Because of that misunderstanding, many of their efforts not only failed to achieve their stated objectives, but actually made the imbalance of powers worse.

Avoiding a Decision: Political Questions and Foreign Policy

The Second World War, the development of nuclear weapons, and the Cold War all had profound effects on the executive-legislative relationship. Suddenly, there were incentives to separate foreign and domestic policy, and to allow Congress to delegate broad discretion and power to the executive. The justices of the Supreme Court were not unmindful of these realities and pressures. The question was, could constitutional interpretation respond to the radical changes wrought by the historical developments in the first half of the twentieth century?

One way to do so would be to revive the political question doctrine Sutherland had rejected after the First World War. Treating foreign policy issues as "political questions" beyond the Court's reach would provide the justices with a way to maintain their commitment to a unitary Constitution that formally applied to foreign and domestic policy alike, and yet would allow them to give modern leaders the latitude many felt was necessary in a nuclear world. As legal scholar Alexander Bickel put it, the Court could use this doctrine to abstain when judicial judgments, constitutionally correct though they might be, could imperil the nation, when the justices "not so much fear that judicial judgment will be ignored, as that perhaps it should be, but won't."[1]

Justice William Brennan explicitly dismissed that option in a review of the political question doctrine in a 1962 domestic voting-rights case (*Baker v. Carr*). Citing *Oetjen v. Central Leather Co.* (1918),[2] Brennan rejected "sweeping statements to the effect that all questions touching foreign relations are political questions."[3]

Regardless of the pragmatic realities of the postwar world, a broad application of the political question doctrine in foreign policy couldn't be accepted, because to do so would force the Court to abdicate one or both of its most fundamental responsibilities: the maintenance of the absolute guarantees of a limited Constitution where the government (acting as a whole) is expressly prohibited from taking certain actions; and the policing of the separation of powers, both vertical and horizontal, where the Court is obliged not only to judge the constitutionality of the actions taken by the government, but where the justices are obliged as well to judge the constitutionality of the process by which those choices are made and actions are taken.

These two pillars of the judicial function are clearly reflected in the modern foreign policy doctrine that emerged in the wake of two world wars. The first pillar—the policing of the separation of powers—was the focus in *Youngstown*, and the second pillar—the absolute limits of government action—was the focus of *Curtiss-Wright.* Together, these two pillars support a single, coherent foreign policy doctrine. It was that doctrine, and the shifts in that doctrine, that the legislators of the 1970s failed to grasp fully. To understand where they may have gone wrong, where the doctrine stands today, and how it is likely to evolve in the future, it is important to examine both its development and the twin pillars on which it has been built.

A Doctrinal Pillar in Foreign Policy: Policing the Separation of Powers

The Constitution laid the foundation for a government of separate institutions sharing power,[4] but this structure was not to be a mere guideline. Madison and the other framers hoped they could construct a government that would be at once safe and energetic. "A dependence on the people is no doubt the primary control on the government," Madison wrote in *Federalist* 51, "but experience has taught mankind the necessity of auxiliary precautions."[5] Among those auxiliary precautions was the establishment of three branches of government that would share and compete for power—unable to combine into a tyrannical system, and yet able to work together to accomplish necessary ends. The Constitution assigned some powers exclusively to one branch or another, and others were left vague. Still other powers were explicitly denied to one or all of the branches. Congress has certain enumerated powers and the authority to pass laws necessary and proper to carry out those enumerated responsibilities. The structural foundation has created an often inefficient system, but as Justice Brandeis explained in *Myers v. United States* (1926), "The doctrine of the Separation of Powers was adopted by the convention of 1787, not to promote efficiency but to preclude the exercise of arbitrary power. The purpose was, not to avoid friction, but, by means of the inevitable friction incident to the distribution of the governmental powers among three departments, to save the people from autocracy."[6] As with any highly competitive and delicately balanced structure, the American constitutional system is not a machine that can run entirely by itself. The Court plays a vital role in maintaining the balance, occasionally insisting that efficiency give way to propriety. Although the Court will give the executive far greater latitude in foreign policy than it does in domestic policy, often being persuaded by the context of the situation and strong, pragmatic arguments offered by the executive,[7] the justices have been willing to rule that a number of foreign policy decisions were unconstitutional because they violated the separation of powers or because the process by which an otherwise constitutional policy was enacted or applied violated the constitutional guarantee of due process for individuals affected by the policy.

The first procedural consideration is whether or not a policy was enacted in the proper manner; in other words, was it enacted without violating the separation of powers? This question is far more troublesome in foreign policy than it is in domestic policy because the Constitution is considerably more vague when it comes to the enumeration of foreign policy powers. While the president is to be the commander in chief of the armed forces, Congress alone has the power to "raise and support Armies," to "provide and maintain a Navy" and "To declare War." Similarly, while the president has the power to make treaties, such treaties must be approved by two-thirds of the Senate. Beyond these specifics, Congress is authorized to "make all laws which shall be necessary and proper for carrying into Execution" the enumerated powers, while the nearly unenumerated "executive power" is vested in the president.[8]

The Constitution lists a number of specific substantive guarantees but it is primarily a structural blueprint for government.[9] As such it is mostly about means—how representatives will be elected, which institution will have what powers, how money is to be appropriated. Controversy over the means used to achieve otherwise constitutional ends provides most of the instances when the Court actually has intervened in foreign policy cases. As Justice Brennan noted in a dissent handed down in 1979, the question of which branch has what power is one the courts are uniquely—and exclusively—qualified to answer, whether the subject of that law is foreign or domestic policy: "The issue of decision-making authority must be resolved as a matter of constitutional law, not political discretion; accordingly, it falls within the competence of the courts."[10]

Unfortunately for the Court, its intervention often is sought at moments of national crisis. Nevertheless, as Justice Jackson noted in the steel seizure case, the suggestion "that we declare the existence of inherent powers *ex necessitate* to meet an emergency asks us to do what many think would be wise, although it is something the forefathers omitted. . . . [E]mergency powers are consistent with free government only when their control is lodged elsewhere than in the executive who exercises them. That is the safeguard that would be nullified by our adoption of the 'inherent powers' formula. Nothing in my experience convinces me that such risks are warranted by any real necessity, although such powers would, of course, be an executive convenience."[11]

Unlike domestic policy, the boundaries of institutional authority are vague and oblique in foreign policy. When can a president act alone, and when does he or she need congressional authority? When confronted by a foreign policy question, Justice Jackson argued in the steel seizure case, the Court should acknowledge three general categories: cases where the president "takes measures incompatible with the expressed or implied will of Congress"(*president against Congress*)[12]; cases that fall in what Jackson termed a "zone of twilight" where the president and Congress may be said to have concurrent powers (*where the president acts alone*); and cases where the president acts in concert with the Congress (*president and Congress together*)[13]. All three categories have spawned Supreme Court cases, and Jackson's schema is a logical way to approach these questions.

President Against Congress

The steel seizure case was arguably the most significant case in the category where the president takes measures against the will of Congress. An extended strike in the steel mills loomed when the Wage and Price Stabilization Board refused to approve the higher prices for steel that the mill owners insisted were needed to pay for wage increases the unions were demanding. Unwilling to alienate union workers (who constituted one of Truman's few reliable sources of political support) by invoking the Taft-Hartley Act, Truman ordered the steel mills seized, arguing that the American war effort in Korea, and therefore American national security, would otherwise be imperiled. The Supreme Court overturned Truman's seizure, arguing that the executive had no legislative support for his action, and that in fact Congress had formally and explicitly considered and rejected his claimed powers.

To varying degrees, Justices Jackson, Black, Frankfurter, Burton, and Clark all focused on the fact that Congress actually had taken action in this area, and specifically rejected proposals to delegate to Truman the seizure power he asserted in 1951. The explicit consideration, and rejection, of a 1946 law that would have allowed the type of seizure ordered by Truman was, for these justices, a clear indication that the president was acting against the explicit will of Congress. For Justice Black, who wrote the opinion of the Court, it was an additional factor while Justice

Douglas argued that this was a power only Congress could invoke since Congress alone could authorize the treasury to pay compensation for property seized by the national government.

For every justice in the majority in the steel case, there was no question but that the national government was constitutionally able to seize the nation's steel mills. But to say that the government could do it was in no way the same as saying that the president could do it. As Justice Frankfurter put it, "The fact that power exists in Government does not vest it in the President. The need for new legislation does not enact it. Nor does it repeal or amend existing law."[14] While it is an open question how the Court might have ruled had Congress never considered what might be done in similar situations, the facts in this case convinced Frankfurter and his brethren in the majority that Congress had considered and explicitly rejected a proposal to give the president the sort of seizure power Truman used in the Labor Management Relations Act of 1947.[15]

Whether or not Congress chose wisely or well, it had acted and it had authorized the president to deal with industrial conflict without the power to seize property. Absent congressional action, some of the justices such as Clark would have been willing to consider the context of the seizure, the gravity of the situation, and the pragmatic arguments of the executive branch. But, Clark argued, "I conclude that where Congress has laid down specific procedures to deal with the type of crisis confronting the President, he must follow those procedures in meeting the crisis."[16]

Jackson was convinced that the steel seizure required the highest level of scrutiny. In a case where the president was acting against the explicit or implied will of Congress, the president could prevail only if the Court were convinced that the "seizure of such strike-bound industries is within [the president's] domain and beyond control by Congress."[17] Congress had not left this field to the president, and seizure clearly was within the congressional domain. Therefore, in Jackson's opinion, Truman could not prevail. Clark and Jackson suggested in the steel case that had Congress left the field untended, the situation might have been different, but the fact that Congress acted was determinative.

When the President Acts Alone

When Congress passes a law that the president signs or executes, it is clear that the national government has acted, and as far as the Court is concerned, has acted legitimately. But what about when Congress ignores an issue the president feels is critical? What happens when the president or his agents execute a particular policy without any attempt to secure congressional support? The Court has confronted cases where it had to decide whether the president's executive powers, many derived not from constitutional text but rather built over time by precedent, are sufficient to legitimate his actions in the absence of congressional authority.

In this "zone of twilight," Jackson argued, the Court often has to place the action in its context. "In this area, any actual test of power is likely to depend on the imperatives of events and contemporary imponderables rather than on abstract theories of law."[18]

When will the Court sanction presidential action taken without congressional approval? The Court seems to have developed a fairly consistent doctrine that holds that so long as the president is pursuing his article 2 powers, and so long as his action is not constitutionally forbidden or exclusively delegated to Congress, the Court will allow the president latitude. Whether it is under his power to recognize foreign governments, to negotiate treaties, or to "conduct" foreign relations, the Court has given the president broad discretion in the zone of twilight. The only clear exceptions come when individual rights are jeopardized: at that point the Court will police foreign policy for compliance with the due process clause.

President and Congress Together

"When the President acts pursuant to an express or implied authorization of Congress," Justice Jackson wrote, "his authority is at its maximum, for it includes all that he possesses in his own right plus all that Congress can delegate." Here, Justice Jackson wrote, the president's powers are at their greatest, for "in these circumstances, and in these only, may he be said (for what it may be worth) to personify the federal sovereignty."[19]

The only time this category might produce a separation of powers question would be when it was asserted (as it was in *Curtiss*) that Congress had exceeded its ability to delegate power to the president. As Jackson put it, if the president's act "is held unconstitutional under these circumstances, it usually means that the Federal Government as an undivided whole lacks power."[20] Almost the only time this condition has been met in a Court case has been when an individual claims that the president and Congress, together, have violated his or her individual rights in pursuit of a foreign policy or national security objective. Cases challenging foreign policy over the question of the violation of individual rights have generated the second pillar of the Court's doctrine in foreign policy.

The Other Doctrinal Pillar: Limited Government, Foreign Policy, and Individual Rights

The Court's role in foreign policy reaches beyond policing the separation of powers. Even in cases where Congress and the president act together in foreign policy, the Court has found and enforced constitutional limits on that policy when it has violated explicit constitutional prohibitions or when it has unduly infringed on the individual liberties of American citizens. As Chief Justice Earl Warren wrote in a 1967 case, "It would indeed be ironic if, in the name of national defense, we would sanction the subversion of one of those liberties . . . which makes the defense of the

Nation worthwhile."[21] While the Court has made it clear that individual liberties may have to be curtailed in the interest of national security, the government almost always is required to provide due process. When the exercise of one of Congress' "enumerated powers clashes with those individual liberties protected by the Bill of Rights," Warren wrote, it is "our 'delicate and difficult task' to determine whether the resulting restriction on freedom can be tolerated."[22]

Individual rights pose a particularly difficult dilemma for the Court in foreign policy cases. The dilemma is nowhere more clearly articulated than it was during the Second World War, when Japanese Americans were imprisoned for the duration without the provision of individual due process. In *Korematsu v. United States* (1944), constitutionally protected individual rights appeared to be in direct conflict with the needs of national security as articulated by both political branches and the United States Army.

In essence, the Court had three broad options in dealing with the dilemmas posed by this case. 1) The Court could fit the case into the traditional approach to foreign policy cases articulated in *Curtiss-Wright*, arguing that the national government had nearly unlimited discretion to act in foreign policy. 2) The Court could attempt to avoid the dilemma of choosing between individual rights and the government's claims to national security needs by invoking the political question doctrine, or something like it, and allow the result without giving it explicit constitutional sanction. 3) The Court could rule the policy unconstitutional on individual-rights grounds. The Court has chosen option 3 on a number of occasions since *Korematsu*, exercising one of three variations. At times the justices have imposed a "*no exceptions*" variation, ruling that the national government cannot deprive citizens of their fundamental rights, regardless of the foreign-policy rationale. At other times, the Court has articulated a "*narrow application*" variation in cases where the justices have ruled that the national government can infringe individual rights by law, but only where the statute under review is specific, clearly tailored to particular and pragmatically justified ends, and applied as narrowly as possible. Or, finally, there have been instances where the Court has endorsed a "*minimal test*" variation, insisting only upon the provision of minimal levels of due process before sanctioning the government's policy. These three subcategories have dominated the Court's recent approach to individual rights cases in foreign policy. Each of the three broad opinions was clearly articulated in the Court's tragic decision during the Second World War that sanctioned the national government's order to intern in detention centers Americans of Japanese descent and resident aliens from Japan for the duration of the war.

Justice Hugo Black wrote the majority opinion, which gave constitutional sanction to the internment of Japanese Americans. Simply stated, Black held that the Court had the authority and the responsibility to test this policy against the Constitution, and having done so, he found no constitutional constraint to impede its execution.

Justice Robert Jackson's dissent outlined the second option. Jackson argued that the Court could not block this policy because it might well be necessary and yet, he said, the Court could not give constitutional sanction and legitimacy to a clearly unconstitutional policy. If the Court ruled the measure constitutional, Jackson wrote, "for all time [the Court] has validated the principle of racial discrimination"[23]; but, if it struck down the measure as an unconstitutional invasion of private rights, the Court might damage the war effort, and thereby open the way for the destruction of the American government itself and all civil liberties.

Jackson would have had the Court refuse to sanction what he agreed might be a pragmatically necessary subversion of constitutional liberties. "A military commander may overstep the bounds of constitutionality, and it is an incident. But if we review and approve," Jackson wrote, "that passing incident becomes the doctrine of the Constitution."[24]

Jackson's solution articulated what may be as close to a "pure" political question theory as the Court has ever come.[25] Jackson would have vacated the judicial order and left it to the military to do what it felt necessary, but without the help or interference of the judicial authorities.

Justice Francis Murphy articulated the third broad option in his dissent when he argued that the Court must review constitutional challenges and must void unconstitutional practices, particularly when the facts make it clear that there are constitutional alternatives to achieve the same ends. The Court's duty, Murphy suggested, was not changed by the fact that the policy in question touched on foreign affairs. Rather, the Court must follow its own constitutional mandate.

Arguing that the measure was an "obvious racial discrimination" with "no reasonable relation" to an impending, imminent, or immediate public danger, Murphy maintained that this policy was unconstitutional. "Under our system of law individual guilt is the sole basis for deprivation of rights. Any inconvenience that may have accompanied an attempt to conform to procedural due process, cannot be said to justify violations of constitutional rights of individuals."[26] While the political question doctrine might help the Court to avoid decisions that might jeopardize American security, applying this doctrine to all cases touching on foreign policy, Murphy argued, was an abandonment of the Court's constitutional mandate.

From time to time the Court has faced the same choices presented by *Korematsu*. But the Court has been increasingly skeptical of claims that constitutionally suspect policies are required for national survival. Far from invoking the political question doctrine to avoid these cases, in the post–Second World War era the Court has maintained that merely labeling a policy as necessary for defense or security is not enough. The 1952 steel seizure case is a good example of this trend. Or, as the Court held in 1934, "even the war power does not remove constitutional limitations safeguarding essential liberties."[27]

Though *Korematsu* laid out the Court's options for dealing with individual rights in foreign policy cases, the doctrine has evolved since then. To understand the Court's doctrine in individual rights cases it might help to break post-*Korematsu* cases into two groups—cases where the national government (president and Congress) have acted together, and where it is alleged that the law violates individual rights; and cases where the president, acting alone or against the will of Congress, is said to have violated an individual's rights in claiming that the violation is authorized by the executive's constitutional foreign policy responsibilities and powers.

The National Government Versus the Individual

It is extremely rare, but not unknown, for the Court to overrule the government because a law or policy in the foreign affairs realm violates the Constitution's substantive guarantees of individual rights. Though the Court has flirted with avoiding foreign policy cases, or developing a doctrine that treats foreign policy differently, there are limits, limits the Congress and president must consider in developing foreign policy and statutory delegations of power in foreign affairs.

An instructive illustration can be found in a set of cases from the late 1950s and 1960s that eventually produced a clear ruling from the Court that the government—even with both branches acting together—had no constitutional authority to strip an American of his or her citizenship.

In *Perez v. Brownell* (1958), the government sought to revoke Clemente Martinez Perez's citizenship after he voted in a Mexican election, violating the Nationality Act of 1940. Not unlike Sutherland in *Curtiss-Wright* and any number of other justices before and after, Justice Frankfurter acknowledged in his opinion for the Court that there were constitutional limits in foreign affairs,[28] but found that the policy in question did not exceed those limits. In this case, Justice Frankfurter wrote, there needed to be a rational relationship between the constitutional end sought and the means used. Here, withdrawal of citizenship had to be reasonably related to American foreign-relations objectives. Since there was such a relationship, he argued, the law was constitutional.

While Frankfurter acknowledged theoretical limitations, the dissents in the case argued that *Perez* raised a fundamental problem "and must be resolved upon fundamental considerations."[29] Chief Justice Warren argued that citizenship was beyond the reach of government control. Since the American system was one where "the citizens themselves are sovereign, citizenship is not subject to the general powers of their government."[30] Warren maintained that citizenship is *the* fundamental right: "Citizenship is man's basic right for it is nothing less than the right to have rights."[31] Finally, Warren rejected the utilitarian arguments. Rational means and ends are fine, but when it comes to a fundamental right, there is no constitutional way to avoid striking down a law that violates the very foundation of American government. "Whatever may be the scope of its powers to regulate the conduct and affairs of all persons within its jurisdiction, a government *of* the people cannot take away their citizenship simply because one branch of that government can be said to have a conceivably rational basis for wanting to do so."[32] The Court, Warren argued, could and should act to protect fundamental constitutional rights whether the policy in question was domestic or foreign. In concluding his dissent, Warren wrote that "the Court also has its duties, none of which demands more diligent performance than that of protecting the fundamental rights of individuals."[33]

While Warren argued that citizenship was the right undergirding all others, Justice Douglas (joined by Justice Black) argued a more textual case. "What the Constitution grants the Constitution can take away. But there is not a word in that document that covers expatriation."[34] Douglas took a position here that was directly at odds with the *Curtiss-Wright* decision, which maintained that in foreign policy the national government had broad discretion *except* where the Constitution explicitly prohibited such action.

Douglas and Black said that to argue that the power to strip Americans of their citizenship "is found in the power of Congress to regulate foreign affairs" is to open a Pandora's box of potential abuse. If voting abroad could justify the loss of citizenship, they argued, then there was no reason why Congress couldn't impose this penalty for far more dangerous offenses such as speaking out in favor of unpopular political doctrines, trading with those under a ban, or violation of passport restrictions. "To many people, any of those acts would seem much more heinous than the fairly innocent act of voting abroad. If casting a ballot abroad is sufficient to deprive an American of his citizenship, why could not like penalties be imposed on the citizen who expresses disagreement with his Nation's foreign policy in any of the ways enumerated?"[35]

Frankfurter's utilitarian argument and inclination to defer to the political branches held sway in *Perez*, but it was a very short-lived victory. Although it would take the Court ten years to explicitly overturn *Perez*, it took only minutes before the Court formally undercut its own opinion. On the same day in March 1958 that the Court handed down its decision in *Perez*, the Justices also decided the case of *Trop v. Dulles*, a second expatriation case challenging the same Nationality Act of 1940. While the Court distinguished *Trop* from *Perez*, it was clear that the Justices were powerfully split, and unwilling to give Congress free reign to strip Americans of their citizenship whether or not there was a rational foreign policy justification.

In *Trop v. Dulles*, a native-born American citizen was stripped of his citizenship as a result of his desertion during wartime. Albert Trop had been stationed in Morocco, where he escaped from a stockade only to return, voluntarily, a day later. He was convicted of desertion, sentenced to three years of hard labor, and given a dishonorable discharge. Years later, Trop applied for a passport. His application was denied because, under the Nationality Act of 1940, he had lost his citizenship as a result of his conviction for desertion in time of war.

Chief Justice Warren wrote the majority decision in *Trop.* After having dissented in *Perez,* Warren now had a chance to put his views on citizenship into law, although the Court was not yet willing to adopt Warren's views of the fundamental character of citizenship. As a result, Warren offered two rationales for restoring Trop's citizenship: 1) As Warren had argued in *Perez,* the government had no constitutional authority to strip citizens of their citizenship, and 2) even if it did have that power, as the Court had just held in *Perez,* then it could not do so in this particular case because such a punishment was a violation of the Constitution's Eighth Amendment protection against cruel and unusual punishment.

By offering two rationales, Warren was able to win over those on the Court who felt that *Perez* was correctly decided. Therefore, *Trop* was an important step toward eventually overturning *Perez.* Black and Douglas concurred in *Trop,* sticking by their dissent in *Perez.* One important swing vote was Justice Brennan, who supported the government in *Perez,* but joined Warren in *Trop.* Brennan argued that where a rational relationship could be shown, the government should be granted broad discretion in foreign affairs. For Brennan, the question was whether or not expatriation was a reasonable means to achieve a constitutional end: Was expatriation in this case "designed to further the ultimate congressional objective—the successful waging of war"?[36] He concluded that it was not, and therefore that it was unconstitutional.

While Frankfurter's opinion in *Perez* no doubt was somewhat circumscribed by *Trop,* it took almost ten years before the Court would explicitly overrule *Perez.* In 1967 it did just that in *Afroyim v. Rusk.* With Frankfurter gone, Hugo Black wrote the majority opinion overruling *Perez.* Largely adopting Earl Warren's views from the two earlier cases, Black argued that the Constitution did not grant the power to expatriate and that the Fourteenth Amendment implicitly denied the government the power or authority to strip a citizen of his or her citizenship. "The Constitution, of course, grants Congress no express power to strip people of their citizenship, whether in the exercise of the implied power to regulate foreign affairs or in the exercise of any specifically granted power,"[37] Black wrote. That the government could strip people of their citizenship was, for Black, a contradiction with the substantive meaning of the Constitution. "The very nature of our free government makes it completely incongruous to have a rule of law under which a group of citizens temporarily in office can deprive another group of citizens of their citizenship."[38]

The *Perez, Trop,* and *Afroyim* cases well illustrate the Court's willingness to consider and enforce absolute constitutional limits against foreign policy statutes, the "no exceptions" variation of the Court's individual rights' doctrine in foreign policy discussed above. The second, "narrow application" variation comprises cases where the Court has ruled that the national government can infringe individual rights by law, but only where the statute under review is specific, clearly tailored to particular and pragmatically justified ends, and applied as narrowly as possible. Justice Brennan's opinion in another citizenship case that was decided in 1962, five years before *Perez* was overruled by *Afroyim*, provides a good illustration of this second variation.

In the 1962 case of *Kennedy v. Mendoza-Martinez*, the government argued that the Nationality Act of 1940 authorized it to strip two native-born Americans of their citizenship because, the government alleged, they had fled to Mexico to avoid the draft. Ruling that the deprivation of citizenship without a hearing was a violation of the Fifth and Sixth Amendments' guarantees of procedural protection, the majority struck down the expatriation, arguing that even the war powers of Congress "are subject to the constitutional requirements of due process."[39] In his majority opinion, Justice Goldberg insisted that even in time of war, the national government had to respect constitutional protections. But while Goldberg focused on due process and procedural protection, Justices Douglas and Black argued that citizenship was a substantive right beyond the reach of the national government.

Justice Brennan, however, took a middle course, arguing that foreign affairs needs might well allow extraordinary infringement of individual liberties. Like many justices faced with such tough competing claims (individual rights vs. national security), Justice Brennan demanded that the government establish an airtight case proving that deprivation of a citizen's rights was unavoidable to achieve the end desired. While Justice Brennan insisted on the provision of due process, he would have allowed Congress to expatriate, but only where the power to expatriate "was intrinsically and peculiarly appropriate to the solution of serious problems inevitably implicating nationality."[40]

The citizenship cases demonstrated that although the Court was eager to defend rhetorically a wide range of constitutionally protected rights in the face of foreign policy justifications, the justices were extraordinarily reluctant to enforce those guarantees in specific cases. In the vast majority of cases, the *Curtiss-Wright* standard still applies. Unless specifically forbidden, the Constitution grants broad discretion to the national government, acting as a whole, where there is a plausible foreign policy justification. The only uniform exception seems to be that the government may not ignore the Constitution's requirement of due process, whether the justification rests on foreign or domestic policy considerations.

Revocation of citizenship was, for many on the Court, far more fundamental a violation of the Constitution than were other infringements of individual rights. In a series of Cold War cases hinging on travel and political affiliation with communist causes, the Court consistently insisted on due process, but was reluctant to elevate implied rights to the level of fundamental rights. Here the Court was far more likely to favor the "minimal test" variation of their individual rights' doctrine in foreign policy discussed above—where the Court rules that the national government can deprive individuals of their rights when national security is at stake, so long as the government provides at least a minimal level of due process for each individual affected by the policy.

Unlike the citizenship cases, individuals whose passports had been restricted or those who had been fired from their work in defense plants because of alleged ties to the Communist Party or movement found support on the Court, but only when the government had failed to provide them with a measure of due process in the denial of their rights. Travel and employment, the Court argued, are protected liberties, not fundamental rights, and therefore they can be balanced against national security needs if due process is provided.

In 1958 the Court affirmed its view that travel restrictions might be allowed, provided adequate due process was assured. In *Kent v. Dulles*, Justice Douglas argued that travel is a right that can be denied only if the individual involved is provided due process.

In 1964 the Court struck down a law that was used to revoke the passports of officials of the U.S. Communist Party. In the majority opinion in *Aptheker v. Secretary of State*, Justice Goldberg argued that even though the purpose of the legislation—the protection of national security—was valid, that purpose could not be pursued by unconstitutional means. In the end, Goldberg held, Congress could have achieved its ends with a less drastic infringement of individual rights. Again, the problem was not the substance so much as it was the process used.

In a 1967 case, *United States v. Robel*, the Court was asked to rule whether the secretary of defense was authorized to fire a shipyard worker who was associated with a Communist Party organization. While the Court was willing to allow the government to exclude some Communists and Communist sympathizers from critical defense production work, the Court ruled that this law was unconstitutional because it failed to distinguish between people associated with groups that were benign from those individuals who posed an active and actual threat to American security. "The statute quite literally establishes guilt by association alone, without any need to establish that an individual's association poses the threat feared by the Government in proscribing it."[41]

That some individuals might pose a threat to the nation was beyond dispute; that all individuals who associate with Communists pose this threat, the Court ruled, was an unconstitutional presumption whether or not such an exclusion was considered an exercise of congressional and presidential war powers. If the government had provided a reasonable measure of due process, the Court ruled, this law might have been constitutional. The mere assertion of a national security justification was not sufficient. As Chief Justice Earl Warren wrote, "It is precisely because [this] statute sweeps indiscriminately across all types of association with Communist-action groups, without regard to the quality and degree of membership, that it runs afoul of the First Amendment."[42] And though the Court was sympathetic to the argument that the Court had given broad deference to the exercise of war powers by Congress, "the phrase 'war power' cannot be invoked as a talismanic incantation to support any exercise of congressional power which can be brought within its ambit."[43]

The Court will tolerate violations of individual liberties when the justices are convinced that national security is actually imperiled, but even in foreign policy cases, the Court takes seriously the Fifth Amendment's requirement of due process. Though laws might infringe certain individual rights in pursuit of some greater foreign policy objective, with the glaring exception of *Korematsu*, the Court consistently has insisted that the government ensure that the individual is guaranteed due process.[44]

Time and again, justices from both ends of the legal-political spectrum have rejected the idea that the Constitution sanctions the unlimited exercise of power by the government in any field—foreign or domestic.[45] While the Constitution is far more vague about foreign policy than it is about domestic affairs, the Constitution's explicit prohibitions and guarantees (free speech, press, religion, and assembly, the right to due process and just compensation, the right to the equal protection of the laws, and so on) are not to be violated except in the most extreme emergencies, and for some justices, not even then.

Separation of Powers, Executive Prerogative, and Individual Rights

The Court has refused to allow the government as a whole to violate individual rights with impunity in foreign affairs, and has been willing to combine the two doctrinal pillars in order to protect against the violation of individual rights by one branch of the national government. Shortly before *Curtiss-Wright*, the Supreme Court was asked to allow the president a broad reading of a treaty that would allow him to extradite two American citizens to France for prosecution of crimes allegedly committed there. While the Court was perfectly willing to allow extradition, it would do so only if this power explicitly were exercised by the national government acting as a whole: "It cannot be doubted that the power to provide for extradition is a national power . . . But, albeit a national power, it is not confided to the executive in the absence of treaty or legislative provision."[46] In this case, *Valentine v. U.S. ex rel Neidecker* (1936), the Court found that not only did the treaty fail to provide for such extradition, but it contained a clause explicitly denying that such an extradition would be mandated by the treaty. Faced with the executive's broad construction of the treaty and the individual rights in jeopardy, the Court argued that when individual rights are involved in foreign policy decisions, only explicit treaty terms or statutes could be employed: "The Constitution creates no executive prerogative to dispose of the liberty of the individual. Proceeding against [the individual] must be authorized by law.

There is no executive discretion to surrender him to a foreign government, unless that discretion is granted by law. It necessarily follows that as the legal authority does not exist save as it is given by act of Congress or by the terms of a treaty, it is not enough that statute or treaty does not deny the power to surrender. It must be found that statute or treaty confers the power."[47]

While the Court's doctrine on individual liberties and foreign policy is one that allows greater latitude than do similar doctrines dealing with domestic policy, the Court has demanded clear and explicit authority from Congress. When individual rights are to be sacrificed, the Court has insisted that the sacrifice be required by law. As Justice Black suggested in striking down a military court conviction of a civilian in Hawaii after the Second World War, war might justify the infringement of individual rights, but the Court would act only if Congress explicitly mandated that restriction—the justices would not do it for them.[48]

The Court has insisted on due process protection even in national security cases. When national security is at stake, the Court will allow a broader delegation of authority to the executive, but when individual rights are in the balance, the Court will exercise a narrower and more restrictive scrutiny, and will overturn foreign policy decisions to protect individual rights. As Justice Brennan said in his concurrence in *Robel*, "The area of permissible indefiniteness narrows, however, when the regulation invokes criminal sanctions and potentially affects fundamental rights, as does [this statute] . . . This is because the numerous deficiencies connected with vague legislative directives . . . are far more serious when liberty and the exercise of fundamental rights are at stake."[49]

The Court is aware of the delicate nature of foreign affairs, and generally will attempt to strike a balance between individual rights and national security. The tacit agreement seems to be that the better is the government's argument favoring extraordinary deference, the more willing the Court is to agree. In other words, in foreign affairs the Court will be more pragmatic and less doctrinal than in other areas. If the government can make a convincing case for extraordinary deference, the Court will, from time to time, find in its own doctrine a means of justifying the necessary conclusion, or it may invoke the political question doctrine, excusing itself from ruling on a political question.

In Foreign Policy Cases, Individual Rights Are Important, but the Separation of Powers Is Essential

While the Court has made it clear that there are substantive guarantees that override foreign policy objectives,[50] it has made it equally clear that there is a different threshold in foreign policy. Provided there is adequate due process and a sufficient relationship between ends and means, the Court will tolerate greater infringements of individual liberties in foreign policy cases than it will in domestic policy cases.

Constitutional scholars can debate whether or not the Constitution protects travel or even citizenship as a fundamental right beyond the reach of elected government officials. It would seem incontrovertible, however, that freedom of the press is a fundamental and constitutionally protected right. Many observers see the Pentagon papers case (*New York Times Co. v. United States*)[51] as a great victory for a free press. The Court refused the administration's request to impose a prior restraint on the *New York Times*, allowing the newspaper to publish what the Nixon administration claimed would be highly damaging documents about the conduct of the war in Vietnam. Was it a victory for press freedom? Actually, a careful review of the case suggests that it was less a victory for a free press than it was an affirmation of the Court's commitment to police the separation of powers and maintain the structural guarantees of the Constitution. Though one justice saw it as a First Amendment case, in the end it was seen by the majority as a case of the president acting alone, or even acting against the express wish of Congress, not as a case where the government as a whole was blocked from acting because the policy would violate the substantive guarantee of freedom of the press.

The Pentagon papers case invited the Court to rule that the government had no power to infringe a substantive guarantee—the First Amendment—in pursuit of foreign policy objectives. Only Justice Black maintained that an injunction was absolutely prohibited by the Constitution. Though bothered by the concept of a prior restraint, the other justices held that what was unacceptable was a president imposing this restraint without benefit of law, or in contradiction to the expressed will of Congress. Black alone argued that the First Amendment would not allow prior restraint of the press, period. "To find that the President has 'inherent power' to halt the publication of news by resort to the courts would wipe out the First Amendment, and destroy the fundamental liberty and security of the very people the Government hopes to make 'secure.' "[52] The First Amendment, Black maintained, was designed to constrain and restrict the general powers of government, and if that was its effect here, then so be it.

The majority composed a series of separate opinions. Justices Brennan, Stewart, and White all argued, to varying degrees, that the First Amendment could be made to bow before national security claims, but only when the danger posed "must inevitably, directly, and immediately cause the occurrence of an event kindred to imperiling the safety of a transport already at sea."[53] Although that standard would leave exceptions, it was still a fairly strong endorsement of the argument that the Court can and will intervene in foreign affairs to assure protection for the Constitution's substantive guarantees.

The second position, developed to varying degrees by Justices Douglas and Marshall, was a separation of powers argument that fit in quite nicely with the *Curtiss-Wright* tradition. And it was Marshall—usually a reliable advocate for civil liberties—who focused on this argument above all. Marshall all but ignored the First Amendment argument. Instead he saw a division within the national government, which turned the question from "What can the government do, as a whole, acting together in foreign affairs?"; into the question of "What can the president do, on his own authority, in foreign affairs?"

Had Congress passed a prior restraint law that the president then tried to enforce, Marshall argued, this would be a very different case. In 1957, Marshall noted, Congress actually considered a law that would have made it illegal for any person "willfully to disclose without proper authorization, for any purpose whatever," secret or top secret information.[54] Had this statute passed, "the publication of the documents involved [in this case] would certainly have been a crime. Congress refused, however, to make it a crime."[55] Thus, the prior restraint requested by the executive branch was unconstitutional.

Although he joined in Black's concurrence, Justice Douglas filed his own opinion, ultimately resting his rationale on the substantive values and protection of the First Amendment. Unlike Black, Douglas was influenced by the lack of unanimity in the national government. There is, he wrote, "no statute barring the publication by the press of the material" in question.[56] Douglas seemed to be endorsing the "narrow application" variation discussed above, where the Court will allow the violation of individual rights when that violation is codified in a specific, narrow, and clearly articulated statute that provides adequate due process. For Douglas, absent a clear statute, the president could only restrict the publication if that authority stemmed from some inherent constitutional power. Since the conflict in Vietnam was not a declared war, "we need not decide what leveling effect the war power of Congress might have," Douglas wrote, suggesting that under a declaration of war the president might well be able to claim far greater constitutional latitude.[57] Thus, for Douglas, with no congressional authorization, and no way to apply war powers, the restriction was an unconstitutional infringement of the First Amendment. The foreign policy rationale notwithstanding, the government had no case.

* * *

The justices seem committed to the idea that there are, in the Constitution, substantive restraints on foreign policy that they will uphold. On the other hand, there are precious few instances when they have found it necessary to do so. While the Pentagon papers case was decided against the executive branch, it is clear that had Congress passed a law allowing for prior restraint to protect national security, the case quite easily could have gone the other way. In fact, in a similar situation in 1979 (*United States v. The Progressive Inc.*), a lower court did rule against a publisher when the *Progressive* magazine attempted to publish blueprints for the construction of a nuclear weapon. The key difference? Congress had passed a law authorizing a prior restraint in cases such as that of the *Pro-*

gressive. With the statute in hand, the presiding judge invoked the Supreme Court's familiar doctrine on substantive restraints in foreign policy, that the national government, acting as a whole, has extremely broad discretion in enacting and executing foreign policy.[58]

Unlike the *Pentagon Papers* case, where there was no legislative support for the executive and where, as Marshall argued, the executive seemed to be acting against the explicit wishes of Congress, in the *Progressive* case the government was acting as a whole, and the Court was asked to decide between the government's position that publication would have a direct and important effect on national security, versus the Constitution's guarantee of a free press in the First Amendment. With a statute in hand, a unified national government, and a plausible case establishing the potential for harm of the publication in question, the judge was willing to issue a preliminary injunction.

The Court as Agent of Constitutional Constraint in Foreign Policy

No president need fear that the Supreme Court will attempt to manage the day-to-day intricacies of foreign policy. Neither should any president forget that the Court can, has, and will involve itself in foreign policy when the executive significantly oversteps the constraints built into the Constitution. That such intervention is rare, and accompanied by difficult doctrinal contradictions, makes it no less significant.

As Alexander Hamilton put it in Federalist 78, the judiciary has "neither force nor will but merely judgment." But the "firmness of the judicial magistery" can indeed influence the choices made by both the legislature and the executive. When the officers of the political branches of the government see "that obstacles to the success or an iniquitous intention are to be expected from the scruples of the courts, [they] are in a manner compelled, by the very motives of the injustice they meditate, to qualify their attempts."[59]

In designing foreign policy, a president must consider the constitutionality of the executive branch's assertion of authority within the Constitution's institutional structure. Should a president decide to pursue a constitutionally questionable policy, the strategy chosen to override the constitutional constraints will be shaped in no small measure by considerations of what the Court will and will not tolerate, and the type of arguments that the Court is likely to find most persuasive. Similarly, when struggling with the dilemma of delegating the power needed to run a modern superpower and yet at the same time maintaining a check on the executive, legislators would be advised to pay close attention to the Court's doctrine in foreign policy. In July of 1991, a congressional conference committee opted to accept the president's language in a bill designed to improve congressional oversight of the intelligence agencies. In accepting that language, the conference report noted that the intelligence committees in both Houses rejected the president's interpretation of that language, but they wrote it into law anyway, confident that the Court ultimately would interpret the language as Congress understood it. But the Court's most recent cases in the foreign policy area (discussed in detail in Chapter 8) indicate clearly that the Court has continued to build on the clear and fairly consistent doctrine outlined above. That doctrine reads laws restricting foreign policy discretion narrowly, and reads laws delegating power to the executive rather broadly. While the Court continues to argue that it can and will intervene to police the separation of powers, increasingly the doctrine has moved to a position where a conflict between the branches needs to be ever more clearly focused.

That legislators in 1991 could believe that the Court ultimately would read broad language delegating authority to the president in a narrow and constricting fashion[60] is a clear indicator that they had not studied the Court's doctrine, and were relying on what they imagined the doctrine should hold, rather that on an understanding of where the doctrine stood after 200 years of slow but steady development. Recent cases continue to demonstrate that legislators still haven't realized what the Court's doctrine really suggests. The message is clear, but only if the cases and doctrine are closely examined; only if *Curtiss-Wright* and the steel seizure case are properly understood; and only if Congress can see the Court's distinctions between its doctrine in cases concerning the separation of powers versus cases concerning individual rights.

IV

Why Statutes Don't Work: Congress Strikes Back, and Makes It Worse

6

The Legislative Response: Legal Solutions to Political Problems

Facing the Cold War and the complexity of nuclear weapons after the Second World War, most in Congress were eager to centralize authority in foreign policy and delegate ever broader powers to the president. On intelligence questions, as on many issues of foreign policy, "Congress chose not to be involved and preferred to be uninformed."[1] But that conviction was shaken by a series of abuses that were disclosed in the 1970s. The continuing American involvement in Indochina, combined with electoral pressure and genuine outrage over domestic abuses of executive power, led many legislators to seek greater oversight.[2] Starting with the War Powers Resolution of 1973, Congress passed a host of legislation in an effort to assert a more active role in a number of foreign policy areas ranging from intelligence to defense spending, foreign aid, international trade, weapons sales, emergency powers, and arms control.[3] Though these policy areas have very different histories, and the measures designed to assert a congressional role in each can only be fully understood within the context of the particular policy area,[4] there are common traits in the different methods legislators have employed to try to increase congressional influence in each. But congressional influence is not the same as formal power or outright authority. As Richard Neustadt put it in the 1990 revision and expansion of his 1960 classic on presidential power, we should "keep in mind the distinction between two senses in which the word *power* is employed." One sense is when it is used "to refer to formal constitutional, statutory or customary authority" and the other is in the "sense of effective influence on the conduct of others." Neustadt suggests that the word *authority* might be substituted for power in the formal sense, while *influence* might be substituted for power in the more informal sense.[5]

Using Neustadt's distinction, we can see that legislators have had marked success in gaining a measure of influence, though often by sacrificing formal authority, in a number of policy areas—in some aspects of intelligence oversight,[6] in trade,[7] and in arms sales, and arms control.[8] But these measures of success have come through the development and implementation of alternative means of influence. These means of influence developed as *alternatives* to failed and flawed statutory efforts to increase legislative *authority* that preceded them. These alternatives included non-binding legislation, consultation, public appeals, hearings, floor statements, and lawsuits, among others.[9] They have had the effect of forcing the executive to consult, or at the very least preemptively to consider, congressional interests before implementing American foreign policy. The fact that they are *alternatives* to traditional legislation isn't terribly important if the objective is to increase congressional influence on day-to-day foreign policy. If, on the other hand, the objective is to increase congressional power in a struggle between the branches for the control of foreign policy, then the decision to exercise alternatives to legislation has far more significant ramifications, particularly when the Court is called upon to judge future disputes in that area, and in foreign policy in general.

The more effective alternatives have not replaced the flawed statutory efforts, but have been pursued simultaneously. Though this approach may allow Congress to enjoy some measure of influence in day-to-day foreign policy, it has real impact on court cases dealing with foreign policy. Chapter 8 will demonstrate that the Court pays little attention to anything but explicit assertions of power by Congress. Alternative measures that may influence day-to-day policy outcomes have little impact on judicial opinions, and therefore on the broader issue of the separation of powers in foreign policy. The Court is left with flawed statutes that set important precedents in foreign policy. But those same flawed statutes also set important precedents in the general category of separation of powers disputes—foreign *and* domestic. Because of this broad and overflowing impact, it is vital to understand when, how, and why legislators have written flawed statutes in the struggle over foreign-policy powers.

In the 1970s and 1980s, legislators (like the constituents they represented) increasingly turned to the courts to resolve political disputes.[10] Even when they exercised some of the political tools at their disposal, they did so only in a narrow range of policy areas, and they did so while at the same time passing poorly crafted statutes. To assure passage, those statutes had to be built on a series of compromises. Since they were designed to chip away at executive power, they were likely to face a veto, requiring even greater compromises to assure the votes to override the veto. There were a host of different compromises, but one thing almost all these legislative efforts to rebalance power lacked was any clear assertion of congressional prerogative. Legislators were fighting individual battles with occasional wins and losses, but the executive branch was fighting a war, and despite the occasional local setback, was winning the broader effort.

The effort to reassert the legislature's constitutional role in foreign policy grew from a number of sources, but the primary source was the war in Vietnam and a reaction to what many in Congress perceived to be the overreaching of the Johnson and Nixon administrations in the assertion of war powers. Starting in the early 1970s, with the successful effort to pass a war powers resolution over President Nixon's veto, the reformers in Congress moved on to build similar legislation in intelligence oversight, the administration of emergency powers, defense spending, weapon sales, arms control, and foreign trade. Each has followed the pattern set by what this book argues was the fundamentally flawed War Powers Resolution. Before examining those other efforts in the next chapter, this chapter will focus on the battle over the control of war powers.[11]

* * *

Passed over President Nixon's veto, the War Powers Resolution of 1973 was hailed as the high point of a congressional reassertion of authority in foreign affairs. The nation's elected representatives seemed to insist on their prerogatives, to reject clearly the then dominant executive interpretation, and insist on their constitutional right not only to share power in war, but to control the initiation of hostilities. But the resolution has not worked as its originators had hoped, and in fact has never been formally invoked. By 1988, Senator Thomas Eagleton, one of the bill's original sponsors, said "the Act in practice has been a total failure. It has in no way established a shared-power relationship in war-making."[12]

The interpretation of the effect of the War Powers Resolution divides across a broad spectrum. At one end are those who say it did in fact rebalance powers (for better or worse).[13] At the other end are those who contend that the resolution not only failed to rebalance powers, but actually ended up giving the president more power, by putting the congressional stamp of approval on executive prerogative powers. Between the two extremes, some argue that the resolution was merely a protest limited to its own context and time, with no net effect. There are those, including a number of noted legal scholars, who argue that the resolution itself was flawed and, as written, possibly counterproductive, and that the flaw lay in the drafting of the bill and the compromises that were made to get it passed.[14] This camp, which includes Eagleton, John Hart Ely, and Harold Hongju Koh, argues that an effective war powers measure is possible, one that will guarantee a congressional role in determining when and where the United States shall risk war. Finally, there are those who would prefer no bill at all. Some of those would simply entrust war powers to the executive, and others would repeal the bill and encourage Congress to do what Congress has found it nearly impossible to do—reassert its traditional political tools, including appropriations and oversight.[15]

The majority of legislators seem to be uncomfortable with strict constraints on the president in foreign relations, in part because they continue to subscribe to the executive prerogative interpretation and in part because of the electoral appeal of leaving the president with responsibility for war decisions.[16] These legislators are unwilling to repeal or revise the resolution despite frequent proposals from both ends of the spectrum to do so.

Since 1973, American armed forces have been introduced into hostilities or into situations where hostilities are imminent in a number of cases ranging from the rescue of the *Mayaguez* off Cambodia and the evacuation of Saigon, to the attempted rescue of American hostages in Iran, the operations in Grenada, the bombing of Libya, the deployment of troops to Lebanon, the reflagging of Kuwaiti oil tankers in the Persian Gulf, Operation Desert Storm in Kuwait and Iraq, the deployment of humanitarian aid to Somalia, and the deployment of troops to Haiti, among others[17]—and yet the War Powers Resolution has yet to be invoked.[18] Nevertheless, the resolution remains the law, and it serves as an important precedent for all three branches of government.

That it remains the law would seem at first glance little more than a curiosity. It is not. If one looks at the American system of government as a whole, it soon becomes apparent that while keeping an unused law on the books is a political convenience for Congress, it provides important rhetorical support for a president who wishes to propound a prerogative interpretation of executive power in foreign policy. Perhaps more important, it provides a profound legal precedent for the courts should a war powers case ever make it to the docket.

The resolution that finally won overwhelming approval in Congress provided a number of procedural means to constrain the president, but it also acknowledged that the president may unilaterally deploy American armed forces anywhere in the world for a period of time. There was a clear tradeoff—in exchange for granting the president explicit authority to deploy troops for a limited and specified amount of time, the resolution was designed to make it possible for Congress to revoke that authority by default. The bill had to reverse the traditional political burden: the Senate version would have narrowly defined specific instances when the president would be authorized to use force, but set a strict time limit on that use of force. At the end of that period, the president was legally bound to disengage and recall the troops. The only way the president could continue the military mission would be if Congress passed a bill specifically authorizing such an extension. Thus, if Congress did nothing, the troops had to be removed. For them to stay would require legislative action. The resolution delegated power to the president with one hand but constrained that delegation with the use of a legislative veto with the other.

Testifying before a House committee considering the resolution in 1970, former Attorney General Nicholas Katzenbach, who had argued that Johnson had full constitutional authority to conduct the war in Vietnam without a declaration of war from Congress, suggested that the proposed legislation actually delegated too much power to the president.

If any of the proposed bills were enacted, Katzenbach testified, "there is a real danger that the President's authority would be expanded rather than ordered, contrary to what I believe to be their purpose." Congress, he argued, realizes that it must provide for presidential response to emergencies, but "at the moment" the fact that the president has to "assert this authority without formal congressional sanction . . . has a moderating effect on his actions." If Congress recognizes his authority in a formal bill, Katzenbach continued, then the president has "an additional power in his hands. He can cite it to justify his acts over a fairly broad spectrum of factual situations."[19]

The response, one might argue, is that the bill's sponsors were trading the new authority in exchange for the statutory imposition of new constraints. Katzenbach argued that while the president would gain new authority from the bill, the fact that Congress cannot legislate changes in the Constitution meant that if the president continued to assert a constitutional authority that precluded a congressional role in his decision to use force, then the president would be "left free to use those provisions [in the law] which support his own interpretation and reject those which he believes are incorrect. Thus he will make political use of those provisions he likes and treat the others as inoperative."[20]

Each house passed its version of the War Powers Resolution in July of 1973 and sent it to a conference committee that was instructed to blend the two into a single bill. The final bill contained the Senate's definitions of when a president might introduce force, but instead of being part of the legally binding, operative language, the definitions were inserted into the purpose and policy section, where they have no binding force. "The Senate bill disappeared in conference," Eagleton said on the Senate floor during the debate on the vote to override Nixon's veto. What emerged from committee, Eagleton charged, was "pious, nonoperative, non-binding, nonenforceable language." According to Eagleton, the final bill stated "that the President can send us to war wherever and whenever he wants to."[21] Senator Goldwater, one of the leading conservative opponents of the whole project to reassert congressional authority in war powers agreed, but unlike Eagleton, Goldwater applauded the result. The language in the conference report, he said, "puts into the law language that is not contained in the Constitution, but only assumed to be there because of the delegation of Commander-in-Chief powers to the President."[22]

With the Senate's definitions of when the president could use force relegated to the non-binding section of the law, the binding part of the law retained broad authorization language from the House version, and the two sides split the difference on the time limit, with the final bill providing for 60 days of action and an additional extension of 30 days for a total of 90 days in which the president could use military force on his own authority.

Looking back, the bill appears to have favored executive power, but at the time, President Nixon argued that it unconstitutionally usurped executive power and vetoed the measure. Why then did the bill pass? Nixon was opposed, conservative members of both parties and both Houses were opposed, and even some of the president's most determined critics who were committed to reasserting congressional control and limiting the president, were opposed. The bill passed in part because the vote was taken just days after Nixon fired Watergate special prosecutor Archibald Cox and others in the "Saturday Night Massacre."[23] It also passed because it was an historic opportunity to send a message to the public and the president, and because many members from Jacob Javits down to first term representatives felt that while the bill was less than perfect, it was all that was possible at the time, since it needed support from two-thirds of each house. The reformers saw the bill as a start. As Congressman DuPont argued, even if the bill doesn't "go far enough in securing powers for the Congress . . . surely this bill and the rules that it sets down are better than nothing at all. Nothing at all is what we have today."[24]

For those in the middle, the bill surely seemed better than nothing, and theirs were important votes. But the key votes that made the override possible came from the liberal members who had so clearly and bitterly denounced the House version of the War Powers Resolution. While Eagleton urged a "no" vote, he realized that the bill represented a unique opportunity for Congress to defeat President Nixon. In the eight attempts to override Nixon's vetoes during that session of Congress, not one had succeeded. The Watergate investigation was reaching a peak, and the frustration in Congress was palpable. Eagleton claimed that when he asked Senator Gaylord Nelson, a member of the Conference Committee that accepted the looser House standards, why he had accepted the compromise, Nelson replied "Tom, I love the Constitution, but I hate Nixon more."[25] While that was a private, offhand comment, it was not unrepresentative.

Congressman Ron Dellums urged his colleagues not to fall victim to "symbolic politics," reminding them that "Richard Nixon is not going to be President forever," and that voting against Nixon at the cost of strengthening executive branch claims to unilateral authority in war powers was a poor bargain.[26] But New York Representative Bella Abzug spoke for many of the more liberal members that day when she said that the vote to override had little to do with war powers and everything to do with Nixon. "Today's vote, is a vote of no confidence in the President's use of power." While she had criticized the bill for giving the president too much power, Nixon claimed the bill unduly restrained him. Abzug said she hoped "that it will prove to be, in fact, limiting. . . . Until today, Congress has not been able to override any Presidential veto in this session. But today's vote comes at a time of revulsion of the people against the crimes and corruption in this administration. . . . This could be a turning point in the struggle to control an administration that has run amuck. It could accelerate the demand for the impeachment of the President. On that basis, I will vote to override the veto."[27]

The War Powers Resolution became law. Despite the complicated political imperatives that generated the votes needed to make this bill a law, as passed it would not reflect that debate. Its plain words and authorizations now were available for presidents to use in justifying and rationalizing their claims to power, and these same words were what the courts would have to interpret. The law as written would serve as a source of legal and historical precedent.

No Repeal, No Revision: No Use?

Since 1973, American troops have been introduced into hostilities or into situations where hostilities are imminent in a number of cases, and yet the War Powers Resolution has yet to be invoked. Despite its inactivity, the law remains on the books, spurring calls for the repeal or revision from both sides of the American political spectrum. On the opening day of the 104th Congress in January 1995, Senate Majority Leader Robert Dole proposed the formal repeal of the War Powers Resolution, to be replaced with what he called the Peace Powers Act of 1995—a bill that would "untie the President's hands in using American forces to defend American interests," but which would, at the same time, revisit the Bricker Amendment debate,[28] restricting "the use of American forces and funds in United Nations peacekeeping."[29]

In June 1995, Representative Henry Hyde, an Illinois Republican, offered an amendment to repeal the resolution.[30] Hyde's amendment failed on the floor (one of the few GOP-sponsored initiatives that suffered that fate in the early rush of proposals in 1995) despite an impassioned plea by the Republican Speaker of the House, Newt Gingrich, who noted that he was rising "for what some Members might find an unusual moment, an appeal to the House to, at least on paper, increase the power of President Clinton."[31]

Gingrich argued that it is quite correct to say that the House has "no role up front" in military engagements, "because in an age of instantaneous change . . . there are times and moments when you need what the Constitution called 'the Commander in Chief.' " Gingrich concluded that he wanted "to strengthen the current Democratic president because he is the President of the United States. And the President of the United States on a bipartisan basis deserves to be strengthened in foreign affairs and strengthened in national security. He does not deserve to be undermined and cluttered and weakened."[32]

For Gingrich, Hyde, and a number of others on both sides of the aisle in 1995, the War Powers Resolution was not just a bad idea, it was a dangerous idea. In their view it unduly constrained the president, giving aid and comfort to potential enemies who might hope that congressional inaction would restrict a president's military options.

Hyde's amendment would have repealed the 60-day time limit on executive deployment without congressional authorization. Hyde revisited the 1973 debate by arguing that Congress has, and always has had, the power to control war powers through appropriations. Taking it one step further, Hyde argued that not only was appropriations an appropriate route for Congress to take in influencing war powers, but that it was the only constitutional authority Congress had, now that declarations of war "are anachronistic." The appropriations power, Hyde argued, is "the inescapable function of Congress, and that, too, is constitutional, to provide the appropriations. Without the appropriations, [troops] cannot get a drink of water."[33]

For some members, Hyde's faith in the appropriations power was misplaced and demonstrated a poor understanding of history. Oregon Democrat Peter DeFazio argued:

> Certainly we have the powers of the purse, but once you have deployed troops, secretly, after consultation with one or more Members of Congress, if the opportunity arose and it was convenient for the President, once those troops are on the ground, under hostile fire, is this Congress going to stand up and repeal the funds immediately? No. Member after Member will come to the well and say, we must stand with the Commander in Chief, we must stand behind those troops, no matter how ill-intentioned the initial deployment. This Congress is not going to have any more guts to cut off the funds than it does to use the implementation of the act and to require that the President submit a report, which has not happened during my time in this Congress.[34]

Lee Hamilton echoed this sentiment, arguing that "the power of the purse is not equivalent to Congress sharing the critical threshold decision, up front, about whether to send troops at all." Hamilton acknowledged that the power of the purse was an important instrument, but maintained that "the power of the purse is usually, not always, but usually exercised after the fact, weeks after the fact, sometimes months after the fact."[35]

The problems with the use of appropriations as a tool are particularly difficult in the area of troop deployment. But the dispute over the power of the purse was not just a fight about the efficacy of a particular tool. Rather, it was also a debate about whether or not that power was the *only* constitutional tool available to Congress.

For Ohio Republican Rob Portman, who served in the White House Counsel's office in the Bush administration, the War Powers Resolution tipped the balance of power too far toward Congress, "by allowing Congress to override the President's constitutional authority by mere inaction. . . . In my mind, this is a taking. It is Congress taking authority away from the President to act as Commander-in-Chief."[36]

A few in Congress argued that the resolution needed to be repealed not just to delegate exclusive power to the president, but to deal the executive exclusive responsibility for foreign policy failure. The repeal of the War Powers Resolution, according to North Carolina Republican David Funderburk, "increases the President's responsibility" in this case for "explaining to the American people the reasons for expanding our role in

Bosnia." For Funderburk, and a number of others who took the floor that day, the War Powers Resolution was "clearly unconstitutional. At its heart is an attempt by the Congress to define the war powers of the President. The Congress has no such authority. The President's power comes solely from the Constitution of the United States not a temporary majority on Capitol Hill. Congress has the power to provide the President with an Army and a Navy and to declare war but it has no constitutional authority to deny the President his right to deploy and engage American forces in any action short of offensive war."[37]

For Lee Hamilton, abdication of power and responsibility lay at the heart of Hyde's amendment. "One of the mysterious attributes of this body is that we do not sometimes want the power that the Constitution gives us."[38]

Among the remarkable aspects of the debate was the rarity of any comments arguing that the flaw in the War Powers Resolution could be repaired by expanding the congressional role. Representatives Robert Torricelli and Hamilton both argued passionately that the War Powers Resolution had been and continued to be an important restraint on the executive. Hamilton argued that the resolution could be improved, while DeFazio and Dellums[39] argued that the flaw in the original resolution made it too weak.

In the end, Hyde's amendment failed, but it was a close vote (201–217). It was not the first effort to revise, reform, or repeal the War Powers Resolution, nor likely the last. But the debate over the Hyde repeal was remarkably similar to earlier debates.

Frustrated by the futility of the War Powers Resolution to achieve its objectives, in 1988 four top Democratic leaders in the Senate (Senators Robert Byrd, Sam Nunn, John Warner, and George Mitchell) proposed Senate Joint Resolution 323 in the 100th Congress, which focused on improving the consultation between the branches in war powers. While proposing the creation of a special group of House and Senate leaders with whom the president could consult in confidence, the bill would have deleted the legislative veto provisions of the War Powers Resolution. The leaders felt that the way to return power to Congress was to provide in the law a mechanism that would allow any member to bring suit in federal court to force the president to comply with the War Powers Resolution. The idea was to remove the constitutional question from political debate and turn it over to the judiciary.

As a final indication of the degree to which the new bill would gut the 1973 measure, the Byrd-Nunn-Warner-Mitchell amendments provided that the non-binding definition of circumstances when the president was authorized to dispatch troops without prior congressional approval would be dropped. This delineation already had been shifted from binding law in the original Senate version of the War Powers Resolution to a preambular preference statement in the final version of the bill that passed over Nixon's veto, but now even this sense of legislative intent was to be eliminated.[40]

It was clear that this amendment would have freed the president to act in any circumstances, while attempting to ensure that he would act with the advice, if not with the consent, of the leaders of Congress. For Eagleton, the Byrd-Nunn-Warner-Mitchell proposal was a "cure worse than the known disease." Eagleton said he would be inclined to simply repeal the law. "I might, for an instant, consider going back to the basic words of the Constitution," but, he added, he would only consider this for an instant since a repeal of the War Powers Resolution might well be construed by the Supreme Court "as legislative history supporting the President's unilateral right to wage war however and whenever he liked."[41]

If repealing the bill sent an unacceptable message to the president and to the courts, and if the Byrd-Nunn-Warner-Mitchell approach was an unacceptable set of concessions to the executive, why couldn't Congress muster the will to pass a stronger bill in 1988 or 1995? In 1988, Eagleton concluded that "Congress really didn't want to be in on the decision-making process as to when, how, and where we go to war."[42] The Congress, it can be argued, was "hiding behind the law,"[43] unwilling to revise or repeal because, in fact, a number of legislators actually were pleased with the way the law had provided them with political advantages. It gave them a law to point to as a symbol of power, and yet allowed them to defer to the president on war powers questions that might carry a heavy political price tag.

When legislators confronted the question of how to react to President Clinton's decision to send 20,000 troops to Bosnia, Oregon Senator Mark Hatfield sadly noted that the War Powers Resolution "was intended to force Congress to take action, to participate in the decision. Unfortunately, Congress has found ways to avoid taking action . . . in recent years, we have voted on nonbinding resolutions, in some cases, and we have allowed troops to be deployed in the Persian Gulf, Somalia, Rwanda, and Haiti, without authorizing legislation. We are about to do so again today." Reflecting on this history, Hatfield noted, "I have a feeling that there is a reluctance over the last few years, since we passed the War Powers Act, for Congress to stand up and take responsibility. It is much easier to criticize the president, whether Republican or Democrat, than to assume a partnership role, as provided under the War Powers Act."[44]

Constitutional Interpretation: Executive Spin on the War Powers Resolution

The fact that it hasn't been tested doesn't necessarily mean that the War Powers Resolution hasn't had any impact. Its very existence has influenced executive behavior. Presidents from Ford through Bush have had to explicitly state that they did not accept the strictures of the War Powers Resolution. Each time they deployed troops, they filed reports with Congress that were consistent with the Act's requirements, stating meanwhile that these reports in no way constituted acceptance of the War

Power Resolution or its constitutionality. Unlike Congress, which with the exception of the hearings in 1988 generally left the war powers issue dormant, the executive continued to define a constitutional role and a constitutional interpretation of war powers that built on the executive prerogative interpretation. As a staff report for the House in 1982 concluded, the executive branch started issuing legal opinions as early as 1974 limiting the application of the resolution.[45]

The executive has continued to fill a vacuum of power described by legal scholar Alexander Bickel in 1971. Bickel argues that unless Congress acts, "it tacitly invites the President in the nature of the dynamics of our institutions to step in and act on his own authority."[46] But similarly, one could argue that merely acting is not enough. Constitutional interpretation is an ongoing enterprise, and if Congress is unwilling to continue to define and apply its laws, then it leaves that function to the other branches. And, since the courts are reluctant to intervene in foreign policy generally and in war powers especially, congressional silence opens up the field to the president. It was, one should recall, precisely the executive's independent interpretation of the Constitution in the early 1970s that led many in Congress to support a war powers resolution in the first place. Reacting to President Nixon's veto message in 1973, Congressman Robert Leggett argued that it was reminiscent of the "pseudo-constitutional arguments we have been hearing from the President's lawyers on the subject of executive privilege, where everything the President favors is automatically judged 'constitutional' and everything he opposes is 'unconstitutional'."[47] Since executive interpretations of the War Powers Resolution hadn't formally been challenged in Congress, they swiftly began to develop and solidify. Some no doubt welcomed the default of power back to the executive, and others simply hoped that when needed, the resolution would be effective. But most in Congress simply ignored the resolution. The result, as Senator William Cohen concluded in 1990, was that "the War Powers Act is not working because, first, the President does not recognize the constitutionality; and second, the Congress itself does not recognize its viability. . . . [W]e have passed a bill that has been put into law over the objection of a President, and we have ignored it."[48]

Kuwait and Iraq: A Return to Executive Prerogative?

When Iraq invaded Kuwait in 1990 and President Bush responded with the deployment of troops to the Persian Gulf, Congress avoided any discussion of the War Powers implications until October. But even then there was no majority inclination to start the clock of the War Powers Resolution. Instead, Congress passed generally worded resolutions of support for the president. However, when Congress reconvened in January 1991, over 500,000 troops were deployed in the Middle East, and any claim that those troops did not face imminent hostilities was untenable. Congress had to take a stand, and it was hard to see how they might do so without invoking the War Powers Resolution. In fact, they found a way. They authorized the use of force and did so explicitly outside the context of the War Powers Resolution. By doing so without amending or repealing the Act, they again added to the legal and legislative precedents that presidents since the Second World War have been able to use to establish the foundations of an executive prerogative interpretation of the Constitution in foreign policy.

1991: A Return to Executive Prerogative?

In the years between 1973 and 1990, American presidents deployed troops for fairly short periods of time which, under the loose language of the House version of the War Powers Resolution, were indeed within the president's newly legitimated authority. Most engagements, from *Mayaguez* through the attempt to rescue American hostages in Iran, from the bombing of Libya to the operation in Grenada, lasted less than 60 days, and came with little or no warning. In longer operations, such as the reflagging of Kuwaiti tankers, Congress passed specific legislation outside the parameters of the War Powers Resolution Act, to authorize the president's policy. While one can argue that the existence of the time limits in the War Powers Resolution may well have influenced the choice of these operations and conceivably dissuaded presidents from using force in more extended operations, the fact remains that there were few times when Congress had a chance to debate in advance the deployment of American armed forces. One very significant exception to this trend was the 1990–1991 deployment of American armed forces to the Persian Gulf.

The initial deployment, in August 1990, was designed, in the president's view, as a defensive force to protect the borders of Saudi Arabia. At that point American policy was to join the United Nations in the application of diplomatic and economic sanctions while containing Iraqi forces. In notifying Congress of his decisions, Bush said "I do not believe involvement in hostilities is imminent."[49] But on 8 November, Bush decided to escalate dramatically the number of troops in the Persian Gulf. "These forces," he wrote to Speaker Tom Foley, "include a heavy U.S. Army Corps and a marine expeditionary force with an additional brigade. In addition, three aircraft carriers, a battleship, appropriate escort ships, a naval amphibious landing group, and a squadron of maritime pre-positioning ships will join other naval units in the area."[50] Despite the changed face of the deployment, Bush continued to insist that the mission's objectives remained the same as in August. The forces were in no danger of imminent hostilities in August, and, he added, "My view on these matters has not changed."[51]

The Persian Gulf buildup took more than five months, providing Congress with ample time to develop legislation and to build political coalitions. Two different approaches were offered. One, sponsored by Senator Mark Hatfield, authorized the president "for a period of 90 days . . .

to deploy United States Armed Forces" in the Persian Gulf. This bill was phrased to be in accord with the War Powers Resolution, and authorized the use of force only to defend the territorial integrity of Saudi Arabia or to enforce United Nations Security Council's resolutions.[52] The bill, Hatfield argued, would give the president broad and firm support from Congress. Ninety days would give the president full congressional authority to cover the period of time in which Congress would be in recess, and in January Congress could consider a change in its authorization, if needed. In the House, Representative Dante Fascell introduced a bill that supported "the deployment by the President of United States Armed Forces to the Persian Gulf"[53] with no time limit. The House resolution noted that to date the president's actions had been consistent with the War Powers Resolution, but that in no way was the House formally invoking that law. Hatfield's bill failed; Fascell's passed.

In urging his colleagues to invoke the War Powers Resolution while fully supporting the president's military decisions, Hatfield argued that his bill was "a vehicle for this body to accept its responsibility."[54] In arguing against the bill, Senator Sam Nunn maintained that it was impractical and faced certain veto. He noted that one key problem "is that the President obviously is not going to trigger [the War Powers Resolution], this President or any other President." And since he was convinced that Congress could not "muster two-thirds vote . . . to do that" it wasn't worth trying.[55] Hatfield responded that the War Powers Resolution, despite its flaws, was the law of the land, and Congress had an obligation to at least try to perform its duties under that law, regardless of the president's likely response. "There is no way that we can excuse ourselves from inaction merely because, well, the President might veto it, or parts are not operative down the line."[56] But the Senate was unwilling to use the resolution, or even to try to use it. Instead, Congress embraced the approach suggested by Congressman Fascell, who argued that Congress could neither afford to invoke the resolution, nor to remain silent. In part, one can attribute this sense that Congress for once could not afford to silently allow the president to take full responsibility in the exercise of war powers to the existence of the law itself. But the pressure only forced many in Congress to speak, not necessarily to take on a full share of responsibility. The House bill was written to signal "full support with what the President has done," Fascell said, and did so "in an affirmative sense rather than in a negative or indirect sense or doing so by not saying anything."[57] California Representative Robert Lagomarsino noted that the bill was important because it clearly showed "beyond a doubt" that Congress "is fully supporting the President, his actions and his objectives [and that] there will be no internal dissension regarding the war powers issue."[58]

For a few representatives, such as Wisconsin's Les AuCoin, the bill's failure to address the War Powers Resolution was unacceptable: "The War Powers Act was passed for a reason. But what we have here is an evasion of the responsibilities of the War Powers Act."[59] It would seem AuCoin was right, leaving two questions: Why the evasion, and what impact might it have on constitutional interpretation in foreign policy?

Those questions were more sharply focused in January 1991, when the House and Senate engaged in marathon debates over proposals to authorize the use of force days before a January 15 deadline imposed by the United Nations for Iraq to withdraw from Kuwait. The debate was conducted on the highest plane and revisited the war powers debate in some measure. But it took place just hours before President Bush's strict deadline, when nearly 500,000 American troops were amassed in the Middle East. As a few legislators noted in January, Congress had explicitly provided for the reconvening of both houses when it adjourned in October,[60] but rather than reconvene, Congress allowed the buildup to proceed without debate until January. The debate took place between 4 January and 12 January. This, Senator Slade Gorton and others insisted, made full deliberation impossible. Congress should have been recalled in December, he said, when "the debate could have been conducted at length, and at some distance in time from the key date of January 15, 1991."[61]

In January, few were willing to tie the president's hands at such a late date. The competing proposals that were debated each offered the president the support of Congress, with one urging the continued application of economic and diplomatic pressure, and the other explicitly authorizing the use of force at the president's sole discretion. Few wanted to invoke the War Powers Resolution explicitly. The solution, according to Senator John Warner (who co-sponsored the final bill) was a law that would create an alternative to the War Powers Resolution . In urging support for his bill, Warner assured his colleagues hours before they voted to authorize the use of force in the Persian Gulf, that the section of the bill describing a reporting procedure the president would follow to keep Congress informed of his decisions was "wholly unrelated to the War Powers Act." If signed by the president, Senator Warner declared, this resolution "will become new, precedent-setting law. . . . [T]he form of the determination required by this section is to be decided by the President. The President may decide if the determination is to be in writing, oral, or both."[62]

Faced with more than five months of prior notice, Congress refused to invoke the War Powers Resolution, and instead passed a bill that explicitly bypassed it. While Warner and others insisted that the Persian Gulf authorization had no effect at all on the balance of war powers between Congress and the president, the parallel approach his bill created added support to the re-emerging belief in executive prerogative in war powers. As Massachusetts Senator John Kerry noted, President Bush certainly had not indicated any degree of acceptance of congressional prerogative in war powers. On the contrary, while saying that he welcomed congressional support, Bush consistently insisted that his authority as commander in chief and the further support of the United Nations resolutions generated sufficient constitutional authority to use the troops as he saw fit in the Persian Gulf. "President Bush did not approach the Congress to say I have a difficult decision to make, this is why I believe it is right, and I hope you will support me," Senator Kerry noted. "Instead, he made the decision to deploy American forces, defended his right to do so, and suggested that those of us who criticized this decision were endangering the troops he had sent."[63]

The War Powers Resolution: What Sort of Precedent?

What impact has the congressional decision on Kuwait, and by extension, what impact has the full history of the War Powers Resolution in Congress, had on constitutional interpretation in foreign policy and the evolution of the executive prerogative interpretation of the Constitution? As Congressman Ted Weiss of New York noted in the closing moments of debate on the Persian Gulf resolution in 1991, President Bush, "like President Reagan before him, claims to be a strict interpreter of the 'original intent' of the Framers of the Constitution. It is odd that President Bush supports the original intent of the Founders when the Constitution is vague, yet opposes the Framers' intent when it is crystal clear, as on the issue of congressional war powers."[64]

The War Powers Resolution remains the law, giving, as Senator Eagleton charged, congressional sanction to executive autonomy in the use of force, at least for a period of 60–90 days. This matters in three ways: 1) It provides a legislative precedent that future legislators will be less willing to reverse. 2) It may well eliminate a strong argument within the executive branch against unilateral use of force. No longer, the argument would go, will the president have to explain why he exceeded his constitutional authority, now he needs only point to the War Powers Resolution and argue that he has full legislative, and therefore constitutional, authority to act. 3) It may well provide a judicial precedent should the courts ever take the opportunity to decide a war powers case.

The War Powers Resolution ironically provides another support for executive claims to prerogative powers in foreign policy. As a minority report opposing the original War Powers Resolution argued in 1973, passing laws "cannot give Congress foresight or wisdom, and will not force an uncooperative President to be more forthcoming. In fact, it may achieve just the opposite effect. A President faced with a possible congressional veto of his actions might be tempted to circumvent Congress . . . [it] might well encourage a President to be less than candid when setting forth the circumstances and justifications for his actions."[65] These views seem somewhat prophetic with the perspective of more than 20 years and the experience of the Iran-Contra affair behind us. If Congress wanted to define and limit the president's powers explicitly, it could have done so, but the compromise approach didn't do that. In the end, Congress might well have been better able to achieve its ends through the use of traditional tools and political negotiation. That way, if a case wound up in court, the justices would have to interpret the Constitution rather than the statute. But the statute is law, and that is were the Court is likely to begin and, probably, to end its analysis as well.

7

The Legislative Response: Building Foreign Policy on the War Powers Model

The War Powers Resolution was a flawed model upon which Congress built other statutory efforts to reassert foreign policy power in a number of areas. This chapter will explore the results of extending and expanding the war powers model to those areas, including intelligence oversight, emergency powers, defense spending, arms control, foreign assistance, and foreign trade.

To say that legislators built flawed statutes based on the war powers model is not to say that Congress was and is without influence in foreign policy. But there is an important distinction to be made between statutory control and non-statutory influence, or in Neustadt's terms, between authority and influence.[1] When the Court is asked to intervene in foreign policy and separation of powers cases, formal, statutory language holds the greatest power while non-statutory, informal avenues of influence are the least persuasive. This tendency has solidified in the Rhenquist court and, as Chapter 8 will show, the Court has continued to raise the standard of statutory language that it requires before it will restrain the executive in foreign policy.

It is a mistake to try and treat foreign policy as a single entity. Different policy areas generate different levels of interest within Congress and among the public at large. Similarly, legislative tools are more appropriate and useful in some areas than they are in others. The degree of influence Congress may have varies across these different areas.[2] Although foreign policy can be divided into any number of analytic categories, Ripley and Lindsay argue that Samuel Huntington's categories of crisis policy, strategic policy, and structural policy continue to serve quite well.[3] Crisis policy responds to the belief that the United States faces an urgent threat, often including the possibility of armed conflict. Strategic policy is more common, encompassing the choices made in foreign policy on a daily basis. Structural policy concerns choices about what to spend, which governments should be aided, and with which resources. While crisis policy least resembles the sort of policy legislators are used to developing at home, structural policy most closely follows that pattern.

As a number of scholars have shown,[4] Congress has been least successful in influencing crisis policy. Legislators enjoy the most success in influencing foreign policy falling into the structural category. There is a critical distinction to be made here—*influence* over a particular policy outcome is not the same as *control*. That distinction is even more pronounced when considering the potential for judicial review by the courts. In terms of influencing day-to-day policy decisions in some areas of foreign affairs, appropriations[5] as well as alternative or indirect means of influence, such as procedural requirements, public pressure, and the influence of anticipated reactions,[6] consultations, hearings, oversight, and floor statements, among others[7] can have important policy results. But these methods carry little importance if and when a foreign policy dispute winds up in court. In court, statutes matter, and if statutes delegate discretion to the executive, or if they simply fail to circumscribe executive discretion, then the executive tends to win. More simply put, alternative means of influencing foreign policy may allow legislators to win foreign policy battles, but they help the executive to win the war.

Congressional efforts have been most effective in structural policy, where the question turns on appropriations and the use of resources, and the decision-making process "most closely resembles decision making on domestic, distributive policies."[8] Conversely, congressional efforts have been least successful in controlling crisis policy, with influence over strategic policy falling somewhere in between. Congress has had some success in influencing trade policy, foreign aid, and defense spending, but in these areas as well as in emergency powers, intelligence, and war powers, success generally hinged on informal means of influence. Any statutory efforts by Congress generally took the form of delegation to the executive coupled with new constraints. When these initial bills drew opposition from the White House and from significant blocs within Congress itself, the compromise that was reached generally maintained the delegation of discretion, while watering down or even eliminating the constraints. "Even when Congress succeeds in legislating foreign policy," James Lindsay writes, "the results may be less than meet the eye. In passing legislation Congress typically delegates tremendous power to the executive branch. Such discretion is justified on the grounds that the president needs flexibility when conducting foreign affairs. But discretion gives the president the opportunity to subvert the intent of Congress."[9] In trade, as in a few other areas, using alternatives to statutes surely has allowed legislators to "limit, modify or veto Executive actions" and thereby shape policy. But the fact that legislators can influence foreign policy "not *despite* delegation but *through* it,"[10] does not diminish the constitutional importance of a formal delegation of power, or diminish the failure to explicitly circumscribe a formal delegation of power. The delegation of power in statutes—even when counterbalanced by the appropriations power as well as by strong, non-statutory means of influence over day-to-day foreign policy—matters because presidents can and have used them as legal and constitutional precedents in confrontations over foreign *and* domestic policy in all three policy areas (crisis, strategic, and structural). Ultimately, a series of statutes that delegate power and discretion to the executive have a cumulative effect on constitutional interpretation of foreign policy powers, and a series of such delegations can begin to add up to legislators' broad abdication of both constitutional and practical control, particularly when foreign policy disputes end up in court. Finally, a series of delegations of power to the executive can add up to a precedent that can and has been imported into the Court's doctrine in domestic policy—a result that will be explored in Chapter 8.

Legislative efforts to share control over foreign policy have followed the pattern set by the War Powers Resolution. Before turning to examine why legislators have and may continue to follow this pattern, it is important to show where and how this pattern has been replicated in intelligence oversight, emergency powers, weapons sales, arms control, and trade policy.

Congress and Intelligence Oversight: Limited Success, or Limited Failure?

Despite the congressional override of Nixon's veto of the War Powers Resolution, one area where the executive continued to maintain nearly unchallenged control was in the supervision of the U.S. intelligence system, which covers a broad spectrum of tasks, agencies, and bureaucratic links. Since the 1970s, Gregory Treverton argues, "the role of Congress in intelligence matters has increased dramatically, and the intelligence community has become like the rest of the government."[11] After 1975, another study concludes, there was a new environment for intelligence. "The balance of power shifted as the pendulum swung from a permissive presidential dominance of the intelligence function to a more politicized system in which Congress and the mass media became major actors and inhibiting factors."[12] But these general statements must be qualified in two ways. First, the role of Congress in the oversight of intelligence activities has not increased in all areas of intelligence. The big exception has been in the oversight of covert operations. This, Treverton agrees, remains the "focal point of conflict between the two branches. . . . There, in the nature of both constitutional and political reality, the conflict cannot be resolved, for it runs to the heart of foreign policy: balancing the responsibility of Congress with the primacy of the President."[13] Second, this control has come largely through alternative means. Among others, legislators successfully exercised leverage through the control of authorizations, their power of confirmation of appointees, and general oversight and reporting requirements. The House and Senate intelligence committees have shifted "from lawmaking to oversight, a long-term and institution-wide trend."[14] Though some "knowledgeable observers continue to question the steadiness and staying power of legislative oversight, and some have discounted its effectiveness all together," Loch Johnson concludes that the "evidence indicates that Congress is nevertheless now an actor in the conduct of strategic intelligence policy."[15] Another study argues that despite the growth of alternative sources of influence, "throughout the entire 1947–89 period, congressional overseers tended frequently to defer to executive leadership even though the Congress has significant powers of its own in this area."[16]

Watergate, the War Powers Resolution, and Nixon's resignation had little impact on the supervision and administration of the U.S. intelligence system. In 1975, for example, at the height of the Church Committee investigation into the American intelligence system,[17] Deputy Assistant Attorney General Kevin T. Maroney testified that the Ford administration continued to subscribe to the view that the president had "unilateral constitutional authority to use electronic surveillance . . . to protect important security interests."[18] Many in Congress were sympathetic with the administration's interpretation of the Constitution in intelligence matters, but their confidence had been powerfully shaken by Seymour Hersh's December 1974 *New York Times* exposé of an extensive program of domestic surveillance and domestic covert actions conducted by the CIA within the territorial United States and directed at allegedly subversive American citizens. The stories set off a fresh alarm on Capitol Hill that produced quick calls for legislation to limit the CIA. Congress hurriedly passed the Hughes-Ryan Amendment, requiring the president to authorize all covert activities and to report these activities to appropriate committees in Congress. This dramatic measure had two important, though perhaps unintended, consequences: 1) The intelligence agencies and the administration were distressed by the requirement for disclosure, since this meant revealing secret activities to six different committees and their staffs. The requirement offered a foundation for the charge that Congress had gone too far, because the intelligence community had to be unleashed to be effective.[19] 2) It provided for the first time some measure of explicit congressional authorization for covert action on the part of the executive and lent some measure of legitimacy to executive claims to the autonomous power to order covert action.

The National Security Act of 1947, which established the CIA, contained an ambiguous phrase that the executive branch long had interpreted as congressional sanction for covert activities.[20] Hughes-Ryan explicitly required the president to authorize and report covert actions. By requiring presidential authorization and reports, Congress implicitly sanctioned executive control of covert activities. In 1976, the Church Committee (formed in January 1975 to investigate alleged CIA abuses), found that the Hughes-Ryan provision requiring the president to make a "timely report" did "provide support for the position that Congress has authorized the CIA to conduct covert action or, more specifically, activities that are not intended solely for intelligence gathering."[21] Just as the War Powers Resolution formally ceded what had been the contested authority to initiate military action, so Hughes-Ryan formally authorized what had been a shaky assertion of power in intelligence affairs.

One of the only recommendations the Church Committee made that resulted in a law was the consolidation of congressional oversight into two permanent oversight committees. The committee's other central recommendation, that Congress write full and explicit charters for the CIA and the other intelligence agencies to replace the outdated and vague National Security Act of 1947, never won legislative approval.

The main lesson in Hughes-Ryan was that legislation designed to constrain often inadvertently can delegate more power than its sponsors may imagine, and that therefore legislators need to approach any statutory charters with caution. As Senator Philip Hart warned his colleagues, future crises no doubt would "once again place intense pressures on officials in the Department of Justice to stretch any authority we provide to its limits. For these reasons we must be extremely careful not to build too much flexibility and discretion into a system of preventative intelligence which can be used against domestic dissidents.[22] It was a valuable warning, but a difficult one to enforce. As time slowly dampened the shock caused by Hersh's revelations in the *New York Times* and the Church Committee's interim report on assassinations, and as world events gave credence to arguments that a modern superpower could not afford to constrain unduly its own security apparatus, many in Congress moved closer to accepting the argument that constitutional fidelity might have to give way to practical necessity when it came to foreign intelligence.

Senator John Tower, who served on the Church Committee, noted in 1981 that many in Congress finally were coming to the conclusion that to restore what he saw as the "traditional balance between Congress and the President in the formulation and implementation of foreign policy" would require that "much of the legislation of the past decade should be repealed or amended."[23] By 1980 support for comprehensive charter revision had waned, and advocates for reform "were fewer and more deeply ideological in their rhetoric" and "had lost much of their audience in Congress."[24] While Tower applauded the trend, others such as Congressman Ted Weiss were dismayed: "I remember when I arrived here nearly four years ago, that Congress was awash with efforts to try to get our intelligence agencies under control, to make them more accountable. That has been totally reversed. All of this year and last, what we have been hearing is that we cannot fetter the intelligence agencies."[25] Pleased or dismayed, both sides seemed to agree that the trend had reversed, and that Congress was returning to a position where legislators accepted the idea that the executive needed broad latitude and autonomy concerning the intelligence services.

1980: Charter Revision Gives Way to Oversight Guidelines

The reversal of the post-Watergate trend toward ever greater assertion of congressional authority was evident as early as 1978, when Democratic Senator Walter Huddleston finally introduced the long anticipated charter for the intelligence agencies. Huddleston's bill, the National Intelligence Reorganization and Reform Act of 1978, was an enormous undertaking that ran to over 200 pages of highly specific rules and regulations. The charter reform ran into opposition from both ends of the political spectrum, with liberals criticizing it for granting too much autonomy to the intelligence agencies, and conservatives for granting too little. The charter died in 1978 and, when it was reintroduced in 1979, it was again the victim of waning interest. Congress was disinterested in such sweeping reform, and the Carter administration implemented certain executive orders that put in place many of the reforms the charter would have legislated. Finally, in 1980, those interested in pursuing legislative reform of the intelligence system conceded that they simply didn't have the support they needed. The broad consensus required for charter reform no longer existed.

Instead of a comprehensive charter revision, the Senate approved the Intelligence Oversight Act of 1980, a very brief bill designed to formalize a procedure for the administration to report to Congress on the activities, particularly the covert ones, engaged in by American intelligence agencies.[26] The law required prior notice to the intelligence committees, but it provided a few important loopholes. First, it allowed the president, at his discretion, to inform only eight people in Congress: the chairmen and ranking minority members of the intelligence committees in both houses, the speaker and minority leader of the House, and the majority and minority leaders in the Senate. The bill further undercut the prior notice requirement by noting that in those instances, which were not defined, when the president chose to withhold prior notice, he would report "in a timely fashion" to the committees on those operations. The bill also made it clear that Congress was not attempting to legislate an active role in the initiation of covert action, stating that the prior notice provisions of the bill were designed to provide Congress with information and a chance to comment, not a chance to veto those decisions. The bill did "not require approval of the Select Committees as a condition precedent to the initiation of any such anticipated intelligence activity."[27]

The bill succeeded for two reasons. First, the Carter administration did not oppose it. Second, it avoided the tough constitutional questions of which branch had what powers in the intelligence field. The bill allowed the president to determine when prior notice might be withdrawn, and the bill started with an explicit notation that the oversight law was only applicable "to the extent consistent with all applicable authorities and duties, including those conferred by the Constitution upon the Executive and legislative branches."[28] The bill made no attempt to lay out what those authorities and duties might be, as a comprehensive charter would have to have done. Many in Congress and the administration argued that this provision made sure the bill didn't upset the status quo. But from the perspective of developing a constitutional interpretation of foreign policy powers, the bill's acceptance of undefined instances when the president might withhold prior notice at his discretion gave congressional sanction to the executive branch's claim to prerogative powers. Senator Huddleston, the primary author of the comprehensive charter revisions, said that the 1980 act left this dispute unresolved, but in fact the passage of the act fortified what he described as the executive branch's argument that "the President's 'constitutional authorities and duties' might permit a withholding of prior notice through the exercise of the President's constitutional authority."[29] Despite concerns, Huddleston and other supporters of charter reform favored the 1980 bill as a step in the right direction. While it did offer support for presidential claims of prerogative authority, it also reversed the reigning assumption about oversight. Before the 1980 bill, the assumption was that Congress would be told only those things about which it asked. The 1980 act in effect reversed this burden, and now the assumption would be that the executive branch would tell Congress everything, except a few select things. On balance, it was argued, Congress gained.[30] In terms of day-to-day oversight and administration of the intelligence community, this clearly seems to be true. But the formal acceptance of an executive prerogative to withhold information added to the growing *constitutional* case for the prerogative interpretation.

The 1980 Act, just like Hughes-Ryan before it and not unlike the War Powers Resolution, provided a statutory requirement for reporting, but in so doing, it also provided congressional authorization for the executive to conduct covert activities through the intelligence agencies. Perhaps more significantly, it provided legislative authorization for conducting such activities, under certain specified conditions, without informing Congress in advance. So once again, Congress' attempt to control the executive's actions in foreign policy only provided fresh and unprecedented explicit authorization for executive prerogative. Congressman Ted Weiss worried that while legislators were attempting to tighten control and improve the oversight of intelligence agencies, they were "really opening up more and more loopholes and making it even more difficult to get accountability from [the administration]."[31]

The system, improved though it was by the 1980 bill, was entirely predicated on an assumption that the executive branch would cooperate with Congress, and fulfill its half of the bargain. Without sanctions or penalties, it was plausible that an administration convinced that Congress was blocking or impeding intelligence activities believed to be vital to American security might use the loopholes to evade the oversight process. And should an administration choose to do so, the oversight legislation itself detailed an arguable constitutional defense for that action. That is precisely what happened in 1986, when the Reagan White House developed a secret plan to resupply the Contras fighting in Nicaragua using money raised by surreptitious arms sales to the government of Iran, which would, in exchange, intercede to help free American hostages in the Middle East.[32]

The Iran-Contra Affair and Executive Prerogative

On 3 November 1986 *Al-Shiraa*, a newspaper in Lebanon, revealed that the United States had been selling arms to Iran in the hope that the government of the Ayatollah Khomeini would intervene to help win the release of American hostages being held in Lebanon. They had been doing so despite the Reagan administration's frequent statements that the United States was steadfastly oposed to selling arms to the government of Iran. By the end of November, the story took a new turn: The money that was generated by the arms sales to Iran was being channeled to the Contra forces fighting in Nicaragua, despite an explicit congressional prohibition against such assistance.

The fundamental question of constitutional authority, which Congress carefully had avoided in the years after the Church Committee issued its final report in 1976, became the pivotal question during hearings on the Iran-Contra affair held in the summer of 1987. While Congress had spent the intervening years struggling with the constitutional question, writing legislation that specifically avoided the issue, the Ford, Carter, and Reagan administrations continued to assert claims to executive prerogative in foreign affairs and to argue that their prerogatives extended to autonomy in administering the intelligence services. Their claims were supported by past practice and constitutional argument. One of the earliest clear statements that relies on prerogative power as the constitutional support for executive autonomy in the execution of covert activities came in 1962, when the Office of Legislative Counsel in the Department of Justice produced a memo that constructed a legal defense for the Kennedy administration's operation at the Bay of Pigs. The Justice Department argued that the operation in Cuba was undertaken "without express statutory authorization" but that actions ordered were "within the constitutional powers of the President."[33] The memo focused on the Cold War, arguing that if, as the courts had ruled, the power to wage war is the power to wage war successfully, then surely the president's constitutional duty "to conduct foreign relations should be deemed to be the power to conduct foreign relations successfully, *by any means necessary* to combat the measures taken by the Communist bloc."[34] This argument was firmly developed in the Johnson and Nixon administrations and powerfully revived by the Reagan Administration. The Ford and Carter administrations subscribed to the argument as well, though both were far more willing to negotiate oversight guidelines with Congress. These guidelines, however, were not hard and fast regulations that might carry criminal penalties and provide constitutional precedents.

As Carter's term ended in 1980–1981, Congress passed the Intelligence Oversight Act, discussed above, that was the remnant of the 1978 charter revision. The 1980 act passed in large measure due to the cooperation of the Carter administration,[35] and generally was conceded to be a codification of rules the Carter and Ford administrations had put into place under executive orders.[36] Carter's executive order specifically prohibited many clandestine activities and set up strict rules for others. But in December 1981, the Carter and Ford orders were replaced by dramatically different ones issued by President Reagan.[37] The Reagan orders held that the intelligence community was to use every means available to gather intelligence, except those that were specifically and explicitly prohibited. The agencies, the order read, should use "all means *consistent* with applicable United States law and this Order."[38]

The National Security Council staff began to struggle with the dilemma of finding a way to continue support for the Contras despite the Boland Amendments, a series of statutory restrictions sponsored in the House by Massachusetts Democrat Edward Boland, against the use of American government funds to aid in the overthrow of the government of Nicaragua. (Versions of these amendments were attached to different appropriations bills between 1982 and 1986.)[39] In finding a way around those restrictions, the staff had on its side Reagan's executive order, the Intelligence Oversight Act of 1980, and an ever-lengthening history of congressional deference to the executive in foreign policy. In the Iran-Contra hearings, the congressional committees discovered how difficult it was to rebut executive claims when the applicable legislation explicitly avoided detailing a congressional interpretation of these contested authorities and at the same time provided implicit and even explicit congressional authorization for autonomous behavior by the executive in foreign affairs and in the execution of covert activities in particular.

When the House and Senate Select Committees called administration figures in to testify about their roles in the Iran-Contra affair, the question of constitutional and legal authority was a frequent and important topic of discussion. Both Admiral John Poindexter and Lieutenant Colonel Oliver North relied heavily on explicit executive prerogative arguments to defend their actions. In their view, the president had full constitutional power to authorize their actions whether or not those actions conflicted with statutory rules imposed by Congress. In an exchange with North, Senator George Mitchell revived a debate over the inherent conflict between the requirements of secrecy and efficiency if a nation is to support an effective intelligence system, and the requirements of open government mandated by the Constitution.

Covert action is secret by definition, and yet the American system is predicated on an informed electorate—or at the very least an informed government—making public decisions. But an effective intelligence service that is expected to engage in covert activities cannot be judged in a public forum, at least not prior to taking the action it plans to take.[40] North consistently maintained that his actions, in executing the orders of the president, were constitutionally valid because the president was vested with the constitutional power to control foreign policy. "Since the founding of the Republic, [the president] has always held that he could send his agents . . . within the framework of the constitutional authority as the head of state and the commander-in-chief." These claims have "widely been held to be within his presidential purview."[41] North then extended his argument to say that the president constitutionally could conduct covert actions with unappropriated funds. He maintained that this was constitutionally legitimate because the president was a nationally elected leader who ultimately had to subject himself to public judgment, and therefore his actions were consistent with a democratic system. Senator Mitchell noted the inherent contradiction posed by covert action: How, Mitchell asked, could the president be judged when the judges—the public—were unaware of the president's actions? If the president could use unappropriated funds to pursue covert actions, Mitchell asked North, to whom would the President be accountable?

> *North:* To the American people . . . that elected him, Senator . . . . my point is that the President is the highest official in the land . . . answerable to the American people and ultimately under the Constitution answerable to the people through a variety of means. Reelection; they can vote him out of office. They chose not to do so.
>
> *Mitchell:* But of course, if, by definition, covert action is secret and he doesn't tell them about it, there's no way the American people can know about it to be able to vote him out of office on that basis, is there?[42]

While the Iran-Contra investigation took on the appearance of a inquest into past wrongs, it was not a judicial proceeding. Rather, it was supposed to be an attempt to gather information needed by Congress to write more effective intelligence oversight laws. The Iran-Contra committee confronted the same choices that the Church committee had considered in 1976. Faced with the fact that "the operation of an extensive and necessarily secret intelligence system places severe strains on the nation's constitutional government,"[43] Congress really only had three options. One option would be for Congress to ban covert activities (a position that had a number of advocates in Washington[44] but few in Congress or in the administration). Second, Congress could acknowledge that such activities are an inevitable necessity for a superpower in the twentieth century, and that they must be left to the executive branch. This was the position taken by the minority report attached to the congressional report on the Iran-Contra affair. To work, the minority argued, intelligence services have to be autonomous and secret. Since secrecy is antithetical to the constitutional norms under which Congress investigates, debates, and legislates, then the executive branch is far more suited to administering agencies that need "secrecy, efficiency, dispatch, and the acceptance by one person, the President, of political responsibility for the result." If the country is to have "an effective foreign policy, this basic framework must be preserved."[45] This option assumes that pragmatic need trumps constitutional legitimacy. But it also assumes that pragmatic exceptions are no more than that. In fact, as this book tries to demonstrate, pragmatic exceptions create precedents that profoundly influence constitutional interpretation. The third option, and the one recommended by the majorities on the Church and Iran-Contra committees, was the development and implementation of far stricter and clearer statutory guidelines to govern the administration of the intelligence agencies.

The Iran-Contra experience produced a host of proposed legislative reforms, but like the charter reform proposed by the Church Committee, they largely failed to attract enough political support to get off the ground. Frustrated by the inability to pass legislation that would effectively block any possibility of a repeat of the Iran-Contra affair, New York's Senator Daniel Patrick Moynihan turned to one of the strongest of congressional powers, the power of the purse[46] and proposed an amendment to the State Department's appropriation bill that would have made it a crime for anyone in the government to solicit "funds or material assistance by any foreign government . . . for the purpose of furthering an activity or activities the assistance of which is prohibited by law."[47] While this might seem a straightforward attempt to punish the violation of American law, the Bush Administration vigorously fought the amendment. According to Deputy Secretary of State Lawrence Eagleburger, Moynihan's amendment was "an impermissible intrusion on the President's constitutional prerogatives."[48]

For Senator Jesse Helms, this amendment clearly was unconstitutional, since it went "to the heart of the President's powers under the Constitution. . . . [It is] a direct, explicit, and conscious attack on the separation of powers. . . . [Under the Separation of Powers doctrine] the President is and must continue to be relatively free to do what he thinks is best in the area of foreign policy."[49]

The Bush administration's advocacy of prerogative power in foreign policy went well beyond the Moynihan bill. In May 1990, while a new effort to codify the reporting requirements of the intelligence agencies to Congress was working its way through the Senate and House, a senior attorney in the Department of Justice and the legal advisor to the counsel to the president wrote that "the Framers placed a general foreign policy power in the hands of the Executive, subject to specific but limited congressional checks." That constitutional foreign affairs power, they argued, includes both explicit powers and "a discretionary power, sometimes termed the 'prerogative,' which includes both a broad authority to meet national exigencies by acting for the public good and a residual power that encompasses all authority not expressly delegated to the other branches of government."[50]

Despite Moynihan's failed effort, the Iran-Contra experience continued to inspire congressional efforts to write more explicit statutes to prevent something like it from happening again. These congressional efforts have followed the 1980 pattern, focusing on tightening rules without addressing the underlying constitutional conflict. The pattern was reinforced in 1990 when the Intelligence Authorization Act for 1991 emerged with a number of provisions that directly addressed concerns raised by the Iran-Contra committees.

The 1991 Authorization bill required advance written "findings" from the president for all covert actions, though when prior notice was impossible, it could be provided "in no event more than forty-eight hours after the decision is made."[51] In addition, the bill limited the government's authority to use third parties in covert actions, and mandated that "no funds appropriated for any . . . entity of the United States Government, may be expended . . . for any covert action . . . unless and until a presidential finding . . . has been signed or otherwise issued."[52]

Despite the lack of any attempt to define constitutional powers, President Bush vetoed the measure because, in his view, it unconstitutionally infringed on the President's authority, particularly in its requirement that the president provide written notice within 48 hours of any decision to use covert means. In a letter to the intelligence committees in August 1990, Bush noted that he intended to provide advance notice to Congress of nearly all covert actions. "In those rare instances where prior notice is not provided, I anticipate that notice will be provided within a few days. . . . [A]ny withholding beyond this period will be based upon my assertion of authorities granted this office by the Constitution."[53]

By insisting on the time limit provision it seemed legislators were, in a small way, finally insisting on their own prerogatives. But following the Bush veto, Congress and the administration struck a compromise that "accepted Bush's promise of 'within a few days' as the best way to proceed when prior notice is not possible." The compromise, explicitly recognized that "the President may assert a constitutional basis for further delay and agrees to disagree with him if he does so."[54] As Representative Les Aspin put it in 1980, by agreeing to disagree and leaving vague the constitutional authority to refuse notification to Congress on covert actions, Congress left a "statutory possibility that the Administration can, in effect, just waive the whole thing."[55]

By writing vague language into the law in 1980 and again in 1991, Congress may well have contributed to the further establishment of the prerogative interpretation. In the 1991 conference report, the legislators noted that "Neither [intelligence] committee has ever accepted this assertion" of presidential prerogative in determining whether or not to provide notification of covert actions. But, the conferees added, the ultimate determination of the constitutional question "is the exclusive province of the judicial branch."[56]

The problem, of course, is that the judiciary will look to the statute books for guidance. In foreign policy, the Court is loathe to interfere in cases where it can be argued that a contested action has the support of both political branches. And, in recent cases, the Court has developed a tradition of reading foreign policy statutes strictly. Should the statute fail to address a specific dispute between the branches, the Court increasingly has come to the default assumption of an implicit delegation of power. If that trend continues, then the conferees' confidence that the Court ultimately will rescue the legislative branch's constitutional prerogatives seems sadly misplaced.

Others have documented the degree to which legislators have been able to prevail on specific issues in foreign policy.[57] These accounts generally view the process as a set of individual battles. But many of these battles were won with crucial compromises that buttress and legitimate the constitutional claims of executive prerogative. Legislators prevailed on specific issues and policy decisions, by delegating formal authority and prevailing on the specific question through constitutionally questionable legislative vetoes and non-legislative means, including reporting provisions, oversight hearings, and political agreements.[58] The pattern was established in the War Powers Resolution, but was expanded and fortified in a consistent stream running through foreign policy legislation spanning the spectrum from intelligence reforms to emergency powers, from defense spending to arms control and foreign aid.

Sometimes, as in the case of intelligence reform, the fortification of the executive prerogative interpretation came as the result of Congress' failure to challenge executive interpretations. In other cases, such as in the reform of emergency powers legislation, the executive prerogative interpretation was fortified by the explicit delegation of formal power to the executive.

Emergency Powers: Congress Denies Power with One Hand, Delegates with the Other

Most Members of Congress accept the proposition that emergencies, particularly in foreign affairs, are inevitable and that they usually require central authority and dispatch, two qualities Congress often lacks.[59] The prolonged Cold War, combined with frequent, more limited emergencies, allowed powers that had been designed for temporary use to become part of the executive's day-to-day exercise of power. By the early 1970s, some in Congress were saying that the crisis mentality had led to an ill considered expansion of executive power.[60]

While emergency power may be needed, some reformers argued, it needed to be structured and controlled by Congress. As former Attorney General Ramsey Clark testified to a Senate committee in 1973, it was "through crises, more than any other time or way, [that] the Congress has abandoned its duties to the President."[61] Clark took a dim view of the expansion of executive power, but another former Attorney General, Nicholas Katzenbach, argued that there were advantages as well as disadvantages to the expansion of executive power, which had occured because Congress had made it possible. "There is no question in my mind [that] the role of Congress has tended, over many years, to give way to increasing Executive power—sometimes because of claims as to constitutional prerogative, more often as the result of congressional delegation."[62]

Unlike the debates over intelligence and war powers, which quickly took on a partisan flavor, the debates on the need to review emergency powers were bipartisan efforts from the beginning. For instance, Democrat Frank Church and Republican Charles Mathias, co-chairs of the Senate's Special Committee on National Emergencies and Delegated Emergency Powers, noted that the effort to pass the National Emergencies Act[63] could only be understood "within the context of congressional efforts to reclaim prerogatives abandoned to the Executive." In this effort, they wrote, Congress had "enacted a War Powers Act, defeated major weapons proposals, investigated the intelligence community, and moved to impeach a President."[64] The National Emergencies Act, and a later bill amending the 1917 Trading With the Enemy Act, had bipartisan support and executive support. In the end, however, the bills failed to achieve the objectives set for them by their original sponsors. Like the War Powers Resolution, these bills may well have inadvertently ended up leaving the executive with greater legitimacy for prerogative claims.

The various committees that investigated the emergency powers delegations discovered literally hundreds of laws that delegated extraordinary powers to the executive in times of war and whenever the president might declare the nation to be in a state of emergency. Such a declaration is not a constitutional requirement. The concept was born in the First World War and increasingly used in various pieces of legislation designed to delegate broad power to the chief executive. Although the concept of national emergencies was something the Constitution never mentioned, it was quickly woven into the American political fabric. The political reformers of the 1970s were determined to change the pattern, but they faced a fundamental dilemma. While Congress certainly could have moved to revoke any and all "emergency" power authorizations to the president, the realities of the post–world war world seemed to foreclose that possibility. Thus, Congress had somehow to balance the need for flexibility and quick response on the part of the president with the need for accountability and democratic control. Congress had to make sure that the power it must delegate to the president would not be abused. To do so, the original legislation set out to define what constituted an emergency, to establish a way for Congress to terminate extraordinary powers once the president had chosen to invoke them, and to attempt to reassert some measure of congressional power in emergencies.

The emergency power legislation followed the pattern of the War Powers Resolution in a number of ways. Original, narrow definitions were dropped, as was the attempt to reverse the political burden and force the president to win political support for the extension of emergency powers. When the National Emergencies Act finally reached the House and Senate, narrow definitions of an emergency were gone, and it seemed to reflect a clear executive perspective. The final bill gave the president full discretion to define any situation as an emergency. The only provision it made for Congress to terminate emergencies was through a constitutionally suspect legislative veto.[65] While the final bill terminated hundreds of laws delegating power to the president in an emergency, the president's unilateral decision to declare an emergency still provided extraordinary powers.

In the original emergencies bill, once the president had declared an emergency he would have had six months to act. If at the end of six months Congress had failed to extend the emergency declaration, that declaration would automatically terminate. In the final bill, the president could continue to act until Congress voted to stop him.

When the National Emergencies Act reached the floor of the House of Representatives it drew opposition from only five members, all of whom had actively opposed the War Powers Resolution before Nixon's veto.[66] They felt that the bill as it emerged from committee might well be worse than nothing. For Representative Elizabeth Holtzman, the whole point of the bill was to reverse the burden of granting emergency powers to the president, but the bill Congress was about to pass put the burden right back on the legislature: "Congress has the burden of stopping a presidential impropriety instead of giving the President the burden of affirmatively demonstrating that an emergency really exists."[67]

After the Supreme Court ruled legislative vetoes unconstitutional in *INS v. Chadha* in 1983, Congress amended a number of statutes, including the National Emergencies Act.[68] In some cases, as Louis Fisher points out, legislative vetoes were replaced by the need for a joint resolution of *approval.* This was done in a number of domestic policy statutes, most prominently in executive reorganization and in the District of Columbia Home Rule Act.[69] But in foreign policy areas, including the national emergencies act and foreign assistance legislation, Congress replaced the legislative veto with a requirement for a joint resolution of *disapproval*—in essence putting the burden on Congress to stop unacceptable legislation.

While the National Emergencies Act may have started as an effort to rebalance the separation of powers in foreign policy, it ended up as little more than a useful housecleaning. It established a better and more coherent procedure, but it did little to reassert formal congressional authority in foreign policy. In fact, it may have contributed to the diminution of that authority.[70]

When the National Emergencies Act was passed, Congress intentionally left intact a number of provisions, the most prominent of which was the Trading with the Enemy Act of 1917 (TWEA). This was done because it was felt that the 1917 act was too thoroughly woven into government operations to be revised as part of the broader package of reforms, and it was agreed that it would be tackled separately. In 1977 Congress quickly developed and passed, with executive branch cooperation, the International Economic Emergency Powers Act (IEEPA), a measure designed to delegate power to the executive to restrict trade and currency transactions, as well as other international economic measures, as tools to confront international crises. The main objective was to separate wartime powers from powers exercised outside of war situations, a distinction that TWEA had failed to make. The primary problem was that over time, the executive had come to use the TWEA as a means of exercising central authority over international economic regulation, and a host of regulations were built on the national emergency declared by President Truman at the time of the Korean War.

Like the National Emergencies Act and the War Powers Resolution before that, the new IEEPA was developed to check unbridled executive power, but by the time it became law, it avoided any real constitutional assertions of power. It contained no hard definitions of emergencies, no penalty for failure to consult with Congress, and the burden remained on Congress to revoke an emergency, rather than on the president to demonstrate its necessity.[71] In the end, the House International Relations Committee concluded that it was best to look to the future, rather than to try to battle the administration over myriad laws and regulations that were built on the TWEA. In its report to the House, the Committee reported that its members had decided that "to revise current uses, and to improve policies and procedures that will govern future uses, in a single bill would be difficult and divisive. . . . By 'grand-fathering' existing uses of these powers, without either endorsing or disclaiming them, H.R. 7738 adheres to the committee's decision to try to assure improved future uses rather than remedy possible past abuses."[72] The grandfathering of current uses was a very significant concession, and while Congress made no formal endorsement of the executive use of these powers, the absence of a contrary position in fact offered a source of legitimacy that the courts might adopt should there be any legal challenges to the future use of emergency powers by the executive.[73]

The IEEPA Applied: The Iran Hostage Agreement

The IEEPA was not a confrontational bill. It "was drafted in full consultation with the Administration and in several respects uses language proposed by the Administration."[74] When President Carter developed a response to the seizure of American hostages in Iran in 1979, the IEEPA was exercised for the first time, and "Carter made every effort to adhere to the letter and spirit of the new statutory framework when he declared the Iranian emergency."[75] The Carter administration found the IEEPA to be a useful and practical tool in its efforts in Iran. It was one of the statutory foundations of the order to seize and freeze Iranian assets and, later, to arrange for their return via an international arbitration board. Carter's former counsel, Lloyd Cutler, testified that the administration had found "IEEPA adequate, useful and extremely effective in dealing with the strange set of problems caused by the seizure of the hostages."[76]

In taking this testimony, the committee focused on whether or not the IEEPA had overly restricted the executive—certainly not on discovering the degree to which Congress had achieved its stated goal of restoring legislative control of foreign policy. Representative Bingham, a sponsor of IEEPA, was relieved to "infer from [Cutler's] statement that at least in this very difficult situation you do not feel that the President's hands were in any way tied, that he had sufficient powers and flexibility within the statutory framework set forth by Congress to deal effectively with this problem."[77] IEEPA was not the only authority cited by the administration when it took action. The administration relied on what a former Deputy Secretary of the Treasury called "a three-cornered stool" constructed from the IEEPA, the sweeping Hostage Act of 1868, and the general assertion of "the constitutional power that the President has to conduct foreign affairs."[78] Although the administration argued that the IEEPA provided adequate authority, it was complimented by the 1868 Hostage Act which gave the president broad and undefined powers to obtain the release of American hostages. Representative Jonathan Bingham argued that the 1868 act authorized the president to use "such means not amounting to acts of war as he may think necessary and proper."[79] The two statutes plus the general claims to executive prerogative in foreign affairs amounted to a strong foundation of power.

Far from restraining or limiting the president, the IEEPA was perceived by the administration, and later by the courts,[80] as a source of additional power. Instead of forcing the president to seek congressional support, The IEEPA added to the arsenal of powers available to a president whenever, at his own discretion, he chose to declare a national emergency.[81]

One question that remained a troubling problem for the reform of emergency power legislation was the lack of a clear and agreed upon understanding of just what exactly constituted a national emergency. As with the War Powers Resolution, the effort to clearly define this term failed in the face of objections that such definitions inevitably became unduly restrictive when unanticipated circumstances arise. On the other hand, the lack of a clear statutory definition made it far more difficult to expect the Court to define what Congress explicitly had refused to define. The lack of clear definitions and narrowly defined terms provided great flexibility, but also undermined the objective of constraining the executive.

* * *

In war powers, intelligence oversight, and emergency powers, Congress followed a fairly consistent pattern throughout the 1970s and 1980s. There was a clear conviction that Congress could and should assert its authority in foreign affairs. To do so, in each case, legislators faced three basic options: Congress could simply take over the policy, passing narrow and limited laws on each policy question and actively using the power of the purse to enforce those decisions; or Congress could simply accept the changed nature of international affairs and explicitly delegate broad powers to the executive. Since these extreme positions were unacceptable, legislators sought a way to delegate the power they felt appropriate while still keeping a voice, if not a veto, in foreign affairs. In each of the three areas discussed above, legislators struck on the legislative veto as a way to delegate power while retaining control.[82]

Of course, war powers, intelligence, and emergency powers do not cover the full range of policy that comprises America's foreign relations. Congress has been far more effective in broadening its role in such foreign policy areas as defense appropriations, foreign aid, weapons procurement, arms control, and trade policy.[83] From the 1970s on, legislators have played an increasingly more significant role in many foreign policy areas, by using negotiations over appropriations and alternatives to legislation.[84] These strategies have allowed Congress to increase its role without fundamentally challenging the executive prerogative interpretation. Indeed, Congress has backed down from most direct constitutional confrontations, and while each executive since Nixon has continued to assert and defend the executive's interpretation of the Constitution in these areas, legislators have muted their claims, leaving it to legislative history and the courts for final resolution.

Congress has been most successful in gaining power and influence in weapons sales and foreign aid, and to a lesser degree, in influencing the direction of arms control efforts. These areas share important characteristics they do not share with the war powers, intelligence oversight, or emergency powers cases. Comparing these groups suggests that where Congress has clear constitutional authority (appropriations, the power to raise and support armies); where Congress has available the necessary tools to achieve its legislative objectives, and where the proper incentives exist to insure congressional oversight and follow-through, then Congress can indeed significantly increase the degree of influence it has in the day-to-day shape of American foreign policy. But as Neustadt noted, influence is not the same as formal authority or control.[85] In a cooperative environment influence is enough. In a confrontational atmosphere, and more particularly, in a litigious atmosphere where both political branches turn to the courts for resolution, definitive control can matter. When these disputes reach the courts, implied delegations take on far greater weight than they might in the give and take of political negotiation.

Alternative means of influencing foreign policy can and have been effective, but they do have their limits. Congress has the power of the purse, an effective tool if properly used.[86] But if the legislators restrict themselves to controlling marginal spending and do not intervene in the policy-planning stage, their influence is limited. Even when Congress asserts an oversight role through appropriations or other congressional tools, those activities alone, without a formal assertion of constitutional authority, do not necessarily go very far to counter the assertion of constitutional authority that consistently has emerged from the White House since the Second World War. In other words, absent a constitutional assertion, the increased congressional role relies on the cooperation of the executive branch. Should the executive decide to suspend or end that cooperation, legislators have little formal support for their claims. Should the case go to court, the executive can point to most of the reform legislation of the 1970s and 1980s as actually enhancing executive over legislative claims.

A review of weapons sales, arms control, and foreign trade legislation illustrates that while Congress has gained significant influence in these areas, it has been through the alternative means discussed above and not through the assertion of formal constitutional authority. Where there has been a more formal effort, that effort most often has followed the pattern set by the War Powers Resolution—a pattern followed in the statutes that sought to assert congressional power in intelligence oversight and the management of emergency powers. Together, these statutory efforts have contributed significantly to the asserted legitimacy of the executive prerogative interpretation.

Congress and Weapons Sales

One area in which legislators have been able to increase the day-to-day role of Congress has been in decisions on the sales of arms abroad. In the 1970s some in Congress began to argue that the existing practice of broad delegation to the executive in arms sales was a mistake, and that realization was linked to a fundamental shift in attitude. Previously most in Congress had viewed arms sales as no more than a item of trade—these were products the United States made efficiently, and the price of these products at home could be lowered through economies of scale. Arms sales helped the balance of trade, helped domestic employment, and lowered the cost of items in the American arsenal. But in the reform atmosphere of the 1970s, some in Congress began to take the position that arms sales were a tool that could be used diplomatically, particularly as part of an overall policy on arms control. The effort to assert a congressional role in arms sales fit in quite well with the general trend toward greater legislative activity in diplomacy in general.[87]

The Senate Foreign Relations Committee argued in 1976 that a bill it was reporting to the Senate recognized the "evolving United States security interests and the danger to world peace from runaway arms sales." The new law, the committee report argued, "shifts the policy emphasis from expanding arms exports to strengthening controls, especially congressional controls."[88] In its report the committee noted that its members agreed that the existing policy regarding arms sales was an ad hoc one that had developed "through its own momentum." It was, the report noted, "an anachronism of an era when Congress chose to leave major foreign policy matters to the President . . . [The] lack of a coherent policy on arms sales is not the fault of the Executive Branch alone. Congress bears a measure of the responsibility as well because of its failure to give more effective policy guidance and to exercise proper oversight on arms sales matters."[89] The bill reported to the Senate contained a number of strong provisions, one tying human rights policies to arms export sales; another that blocked any further military assistance to Angola; and several that would make military sales more public. The strongest provisions hinged on congressional vetoes, once again following the pattern set by the War Powers Resolution. The veto provisions allowed Congress to intervene in a case-by-case review of arms sales, and it was these vetoes as well as a general separation of powers argument that formed the core of President Ford's objections to the bill. Ford vetoed the measure, arguing that Congress was exceeding its constitutional mandate.

In his veto message, Ford focused on the congressional vetoes which, he said, "violate the constitutional separation of Executive and legislative powers . . . [This] frustration of the ability of the Executive to make operational decisions violates the President's constitutional authority to conduct our relations with other nations."[90]

But Ford objected to more than just the legal device in question. The prospect of congressional involvement in case-by-case decisions particularly bothered him: "Congress cannot itself participate in the Executive functions of deciding whether to enter into a lawful contract or issue a lawful license, either directly or through the disapproval procedures contemplated in this bill."[91]

Unlike war powers or intelligence policy, arms sales and foreign military aid often are seen as discrete and separate cases. While this actually is a false perception, since the overall arms sales/assistance policy is an integral part of foreign policy in general, it contributes to the conviction that Congress could and should be more intimately involved in details in this policy area. Here is an area involving the raising of revenue and the expenditure of capital, an area where many in Congress argue that their branch has significant and perhaps even exclusive constitutional authority.[92] As Senator Alan Cranston argued in defending the propriety of inserting human rights provisions in an arms sales bill, legislative intervention was justified because "these are tax dollars to the tune of over $4,500,000,000 that Congress is being asked to approve in security assistance."[93]

Despite Ford's veto, the legislation that ultimately emerged from compromise negotiations retained some modified prior notice provisions and some limited congressional veto provisions. Significantly, the threshold costs of individual sales needed to trigger the provisions were raised substantially. In the years since this bill passed, Congress no doubt has had a significant impact on arms-sales policy, despite the fact that since 1974

Congress rarely has voted to deny or postpone any announced sale. The *potential* to change administration commitments no doubt has had a chilling effect in some cases, for better or worse, and Congress has had a greater role in this area than it has had in war powers.

Unlike war powers, most defense issues are debated and spending allocated in advance, without the pressure of imminent hostility overhanging the decision. Unlike the war powers debate, "with regard to arms sales no Administration, however unhappy, has officially denied the legitimacy of Congress's actions."[94] In part this is due to the clear constitutional mandate that Congress shall regulate foreign commerce, and in part it is because Congress has the skills and tools needed for effective oversight of individual sales of weapons and the provision of particular packages of military aid to individual foreign governments. Finally, Congress has domestic incentives to keep active in this area, from those employed by military producers and by a very vocal and active minority of constituents with a well-organized lobbying effort tied to arms sales. Though arms sales may not have great salience in the general population, among active and supportive constituents it can carry profound weight.[95] Even where a representative's constituents show little if any interest, arms sales are the sort of issue where legislators are likely to worry about the retrospective judgment voters may have.[96] Many legislators may sincerely believe that a wrong vote on arms sales could have a powerful backlash electorally sometime down the road when a sudden reversal of a regional balance of power may focus attention on that vote. Whether or not this is true, the belief that it is true can affect their voting decisions.[97] Finally, with the prime focus of much of the arms-sales debate hinging on the Middle East, the already well-developed lobbying network in this policy area has been intimately involved in the weapons-sales debates, and has heightened constituent pressure on representatives to maintain an active role in the oversight of arms sales. But arms sales and military assistance are only part of the foreign policy story, and in terms of congressional efforts to reassert control in foreign affairs, possibly the most successful story. The story was quite different in arms control policy, another area in which Congress attempted to reassert itself in the 1970s and 1980s.

Congress and Arms Control

Weapon sales are related to arms control, but have the advantage of greater constituent interest and a direct link both to congressional appropriations power and to the Constitution's delegation of the power to regulate foreign commerce to Congress. In terms of increasing its role in broader arms-control issues, particularly in international arms-control treaties, Congress lacked the institutional tools and faced fewer constituent pressures than it did regarding weapons sales. And treaties have less salience in Congress as a whole since they are subject to the approval of just the Senate and not the House. There is quite a strong and vocal number of political organizers and lobbyists focused on arms-control issues, and the constitutional mandate—though limited to the Senate—is clear and unequivocal.[98] Treaties, however, ultimately are executed by the executive, and an executive determined to interpret a treaty differently than the Senate would has a number of powerful tools available to support his or her interpretation. When a conflict over treaty interpretation actually occurred in 1987 (in a dispute over the Anti-Ballistic Missile Treaty), the Senate reacted strongly and publicly, attaching restrictive language that attacked the president's constitutional interpretation to a defense appropriations act.[99] But when President Reagan vetoed that bill, the Senate agreed to accept informal executive assurances about the interpretation of the treaty without imposing formal statutory language. The Senate achieved its objectives in the particular dispute, but the president succeeded in keeping a congressional assertion of constitutional authority out of the statute books.

President Reagan's 1987 broad reinterpretation of the Anti-Ballistic Missile Treaty sparked extensive hearings in the Senate.[100] A number of senators with fairly conservative credentials on defense issues were outraged by the executive's claim, as they saw it, that a treaty that had been approved was still subject to executive reinterpretation that could directly contradict the senators' explicit understanding of the treaty when they voted for that measure. Senators were particularly upset that while the administration, and the State Department in particular,[101] said that the treaty forbade any development of new defensive weapons systems, Reagan asserted that the final words of the treaty itself, as well as the negotiation record, indicated sufficient ambiguity on that point to allow the development of the Strategic Defense Initiative (SDI). Even many of the senators who supported the research effort on SDI were distraught over the president's assertion that regardless of an explicit understanding between the branches when the treaty was ratified, it ultimately was subject to executive reinterpretation. Senator Sam Nunn of Georgia argued that the position taken by the State Department's legal advisor, Abraham Sofaer, "sends a clear message to the Senate: You cannot rely on our representations as to the meaning of a treaty." This realization, Nunn continued, suggested "adverse consequences" that extended "far beyond the ABM treaty."[102] Nunn argued that the Senate now would have to "incorporate into its resolution of consent to any treaty an amendment or understanding for every explanation given by an executive branch witness that we deemed important, lest it be disavowed . . . after ratification."[103]

The problem for the Senate was how to deal with this dispute. The only options really were to issue a Sense of the Senate Resolution or to attempt to force compliance with the Senate interpretation through legislation. If legislation was selected, then the question was whether to attach the law to appropriations statutes or to debate the ABM reinterpretation as a separate measure. Recognizing the political advantages of using the legislature's strongest weapon, the power of the purse, the solution arrived at by Senators Nunn and Levin was to attach an amendment to the National Defense Authorization Act for Fiscal Years 1988 and 1989. The Levin-Nunn amendment essentially denied funds for the development or testing of anti-ballistic missile systems *unless* the president submitted a report to Congress that detailed the system or components the president planned to develop or test. Congress then would have to pass a joint resolution authorizing the expenditure of funds for the new system or components. This approach reversed the burden. The president could not proceed unless authorized to do so by Congress and the result of non-action would be the disapproval of the president's plan.

The Levin-Nunn proposal severely split Congress, almost completely on partisan lines. The floor debate reflected the continuing dispute within the legislative branch over the constitutional role Congress should play in foreign policy. Senator Pete Wilson argued that Levin-Nunn was unconstitutional because it sought "to usurp the authority of the President of the United States, assigned to him exclusively by the Constitution, for the conduct of foreign policy."[104] Senator Dan Quayle was convinced that some in Congress were trying to take advantage of what they perceived to be an executive branch that was severely weakened by the then current investigation in the Iran-Contra affair: "At a time when the Executive branch has been weakened, I think it is natural that a coequal branch of Government, in this case the Congress, might in fact want to try to change a careful balance of power that our Founding Fathers instituted and be able to usurp some of that power from the Executive branch."[105] And, for Senator John Warner, the Levin-Nunn amendment would "permit an unacceptable intrusion by Congress into the President's jurisdiction to conduct our nation's foreign affairs."[106]

The Republicans argued that once the treaty was ratified, interpretation properly should be left to the executive branch. Senator Nunn and his colleagues rejected this proposition, noting that the appropriations bill actually authorized about $4.5 billion for SDI research. Nunn argued that under the Republican interpretation, the president could abrogate the ABM treaty at any time without congressional approval, and he noted that while the bill stopped testing or deployment, it offered an expedited procedure for altering that rule should the president choose to seek a change. Nunn even offered a way out. "If the Administration decides that this is a partnership," Nunn said, if they decide that this "government is not a government by King and [that] the Congress of the United States has something to say about this, if they take that attitude, and give us the proper assurances, there is no need to have anything in law."[107] If the administration were willing to cooperate, cooperation was possible. But, if the administration insisted on waging a technical, legal battle, then the Senate would compete on that level. Unlike the other areas discussed above, this weapons treaty was an instance when some in Congress actually would assert their constitutional prerogatives in law in response to similar assertions by the executive.

On 2 October 1987, the Senate approved the Defense Authorization bill, including the Levin-Nunn amendment, and the House approved similar language. The *Congressional Quarterly* even went so far as to predict that "Because a House Defense Authorization bill contains similar language, some version of those provisions almost certainly will emerge in the final bill to be worked out by a House-Senate conference."[108] But as the conference dragged on, and the Republican members of the House conference committee refused to sign any report that contained the treaty interpretation language,[109] it was clear that a compromise had to be reached or the defense appropriations might well be jeopardized.

A familiar compromise emerged. While those who favored a greater role for Congress (in this case, those who argued that the president could not unilaterally reinterpret treaties), won substantive concessions on their particular concerns in this particular case, the law itself made no mention of the congressional interpretation of the Constitution, and in no way added to congressional statutory authority in foreign affairs. The administration privately had assured Nunn and others early on that it would proceed with caution and in consultation, but the key point from the administration's perspective was to make sure that the law itself would not lend legitimacy to congressional assertion of power in foreign policy (in this case in treaty interpretation) or undercut the president's assertion of that power. The compromise required that the U.S. tests conform to the narrower, traditional interpretation of the treaty, "but in each case, the compromise limitation made no reference to the treaties. The White House had vowed to veto any bill enshrining the traditional reading of the ABM pact or the SALT II ceilings."[110]

The president emerged from the treaty battle with some powerful tools, including the fact that a significant minority in Congress accepted the idea of the executive's prerogative to interpret ratified treaties. In any confrontation between the executive and Congress in foreign policy, the executive can wield a number of significant tools, including appeals to the public and Congress on broad national security grounds, a tactic President Reagan employed to great advantage in 1981, when Congress threatened to veto the sale of AWACS planes to Saudi Arabia. President Reagan was able to turn a number of votes "by his ability to change the focus of the debate" making the vote a referendum on national security, and putting the focus on "presidential and national prestige."[111]

With a host of notable politicians from both parties endorsing Reagan's need to be able to fulfill his commitments to preserve national honor, enough members of Congress swung over and voted for the president's position. And if an inherent acceptance of the executive prerogative interpretation combined with appeals to national prestige and national security weren't enough to secure a victory for the executive in foreign policy generally, and arms control in particular, the president retained a final option of completely circumventing the Congress. Jimmy Carter threatened to do just that in 1979 when he said that if the Senate would not ratify the SALT agreement, he "might recast it as an executive agreement and seek its implementation by ordinary legislation. And, he added, if the legislation failed to secure a majority in each chamber, well, he would conclude SALT as an executive agreement based solely on his plenary powers as Commander in Chief."[112]

Given the presidential tools available, it is hardly surprising that many in Congress were quite pleased with the 1987 compromise on ABM testing and deployment. The ABM debate resulted in *particular* actions that conformed to congressional wishes, but the law continued to be ambiguous, and thus continued to lend credence to *general* executive claims to power in foreign affairs. Thus, one can conclude that legislators in Congress increased their role and influence in arms control specifically, and foreign policy in general, but in terms of setting any kind of precedent or developing any kind of a congressional interpretation of the Constitution that would guide the courts should they ever be called upon to settle a dispute between the elected branches, the ABM controversy did nothing to strengthen their claims.

Congress and Trade Policy

In war powers, emergency powers and intelligence oversight, one can argue that Congress has the constitutional authority to assert itself against the president but lacks both the technical ability to take charge and the necessary incentives to maintain the needed level of interest. These factors clearly are present, however, in the area of foreign trade regulation. Unlike weapons sales, foreign trade regulation lacks a clear military-security interest to interfere with a congressional prerogative interpretation, despite the fact that Americans increasingly have come to realize that foreign trade is a critical component in national security and foreign policy. Foreign trade, therefore, seems the best fit of any foreign policy area to the three requirements of asserting congressional prerogative: clear constitutional authority, the existence of applicable congressional tools to implement policy, and the incentive to maintain legislative interest in the control of policy. It is tempting to predict that if legislators can and will assert themselves in any foreign policy area, they would do so in foreign trade—but that prediction would be wrong.

The constitutional authority is clear. Article 1, section 8 of the Constitution says Congress "shall have power . . . to regulate commerce with foreign nations." The tools are much the same as those that Congress wields with great power and authority to regulate domestic commerce plus the additional tool of the constitutionally delegated power "to lay and collect . . . duties, imposts and excises".[113] As for incentives, foreign trade intimately and immediately affects most industries in the United States and has a direct impact on the prices paid by all consumers. Many lobbyists and all constituents, then, have a direct interest in foreign trade legislation, and increasingly constituents are coming to realize the impact these policies actually do have on their lives. Legislators have developed and imposed a number of procedural devices designed to "limit, modify or veto executive actions" and "through these procedures Congress can shape trade policy outcomes."[114] But overall, as I. M. Destler concludes, Congress "is likely to end up refining at the margins the mechanisms for indirect influence rather than taking direct control of specific product issues or specific bilateral trade relationships."[115] Congress certainly has been "more active and more visible on trade issues, asserting its priorities and imposing greater procedural constraints on the U.S. Trade Representative and other executive branch officials. . . . But the buck still stops with the president and the USTR. [And] this arrangement still appears to suit Congress very well."[116] Despite the changes at the margins, and the development of procedures designed to increase legislative influence, legislators have followed the patterns established in the other foreign policy areas, and have not, as one might expect, had disproportionately greater success in asserting their constitutional role in foreign trade.

Legislative assertiveness in foreign trade has been focused almost exclusively on those measures that most directly affect domestic industries. In other words, legislators have successfully divided foreign trade policy into two halves, trade rules that primarily concern domestic industry and protection, and rules that focus on foreign affairs.

The Trade Reform Act of 1973–1974 is an excellent example of this pattern. In urging its passage, Oregon Democrat Al Ullman, who shepherded the bill through the House Ways and Means Committee, insisted that the bill "most assuredly does not, however, give the President unfettered new power and authority." Rather, Ullman insisted, the bill delegated broad negotiation powers to the president "under strict statutory guidelines and more specific limitations than ever before. . . . [The bill] will constitute a return to this Congress of its rightful role in carrying out its constitutional responsibilities over tariffs and trade."[117] The Trade Reform Act actually delegated to the president the power to "enter into trade agreements with foreign countries for a period of five years, and to authorize the President to proclaim, subject to certain conditions and limitations, such modifications or continuance of any existing duty, such continuance of existing duty-free or excise treatment, or such additional duties *as he determines is required or appropriate* to carry out such trade agreements."[118] While the leadership supported the bill, others were appalled at what they saw as a huge delegation of power to the president. For Representative Charles Whalen, the trade bill was a reform bill only "in the sense that it confers unprecedented power upon the President to increase tariffs almost without limit."[119] The reform bill, Whalen suggested, delegated to the president the power to determine tariffs and trade policy, a delegation that never before had been considered seriously. And for one dissenting Democratic member of the House Ways and Means Committee, the bill "would make the President of the United States the foreign trade czar of this nation."[120] Representative James Burke argued in a dissent to the Ways and Means Committee's report to the House that this massive delegation of authority to the President constitutes a virtual abdication of congressional authority and interest in the foreign trade area."[121]

The House Ways and Means Committee acknowledged that the bill entailed a "substantial delegation of congressional authority,"[122] but insisted that this was balanced by the insertion of procedural reforms designed to increase congressional oversight. The Trade Reform Act was designed to delegate to President Nixon the necessary discretion to enter into international agreements to promote world trade liberalization.

The procedural improvement the committee hailed was, once again, a congressional veto provision, and this time it was to apply in a host of situations ranging from the power to disapprove the implementation of broad trade agreements on non-tariff barriers as well as executive-imposed retaliatory trade measures, to the disapproval of executive use of quotas or orderly marketing agreements. "In each of the first four titles of the bill," Representative Ullman told the House, "there is a provision for a veto procedure which I think is very important."[123]

While the legislative veto certainly offers an intriguing possibility of delegating broad authority while still retaining congressional control, it already was under a constitutional cloud even in 1973. As Representative Burke argued in his dissent to the Ways and Means Committee Report, "the very expression 'congressional veto power' indicates the extent to which constitutional arrangements have been turned upside down of late." Trade legislation, he argued, was not like treaty ratification, but rather was "a matter of original jurisdiction in the Congress. As such it was to be a central feature of congressional power."[124] Instead, Burke argued, Congress simply was delegating its responsibility to the president without even attempting to draw the admittedly hard lines on what the American negotiation team might offer or refuse.

But Burke and Whalen's concerns, though sincere and probably realistic, had to be put aside on this issue if Congress wanted to achieve its policy objective of lowering of trade barriers. To do that required negotiations. And negotiations, Representative Bingham reminded the House, require discretion and flexibility. Bingham noted that many in Congress felt strongly that "Congress should not delegate to any President, least of all the present incumbent [Nixon], such powers as are delegated to the President in this bill." But that position was unrealistic, Bingham argued. While he was "all for the Congress asserting its proper role in matters of foreign trade and foreign policy . . . [in this case] Congress cannot possibly do what we want the President to do: The Congress cannot negotiate trade agreements or negotiate for the reduction of nontariff barriers; this is something that only the Executive can do."[125] In the end, legislators delegated the broad power to the president, and pinned their hope for the reassertion of congressional authority in this aspect of foreign policy on the plethora of congressional veto provisions written into the law. Congress thus delegated broad authority by law, and indicated that it retained the final word in trade policy. But the law did not assert congressional power to set policy, only the power to check its abuse. Thus in trade as in weapons sales, arms control, emergency powers, and intelligence oversight, Congress ultimately won particular concessions, but agreed to leave its assertions of the power to control policy-making out of the language of the law. The broad delegations of power in the law, combined with the constant and consistent assertions of executive prerogative, helped solidify an executive prerogative interpretation of constitutional power in foreign affairs. Ultimately, it would be left to the Court to determine if the Congress had given away too much, or if the executive branch had taken more than its constitutional share.

* * *

In the War Powers Resolution, in intelligence oversight, in the National Emergencies Act, and in the International Economic Emergency Powers Act, Congress followed a consistent pattern. In each case Congress started from the assumption that presidential power had grown too large and that a statutory way to reassert the legislative role in foreign policy was needed. In each case, legislators started with a commitment to narrowly define when and how power would be delegated to the executive and in each case those definitions were significantly broadened in the final bill. In each case, Congress started with a commitment to reverse the burden. If the president were to act on his own authority, the burden would be on the administration to convince Congress of the propriety of the president's policy—should the administration fail to do so, inaction on the part of Congress would cancel the executive's policy. But those reversals of the burden were dropped. In the end, legislators inserted congressional veto provisions that created a far more viable system for them to challenge the exercise of presidential power in foreign policy, but in each case the legislators made it possible to sever the constitutionally questionable veto provisions from the rest of the legislation. These choices of course were designed to insure that the whole effort to restructure foreign relations powers would not crumble should one provision be ruled unconstitutional. But by making these provisions severable, what the legislators in fact did was to separate the delegation of power from the restraint on power. Should the veto provisions be revoked, what would be left would be broad and sweeping delegations of power to the president with no additional restraints. Such a situation might in fact create a legally more difficult situation for legislators determined to rein in presidential power. Before these bills were passed (with the exception of the emergency powers provisions), Congress could assert that these questions were open to conflicting constitutional interpretations. In other words, this was a gray area where congressional assertions and interpretations would at least be competitive with the executive's interpretation. The steel seizure case sent the signal to Congress that absent congressional assertions in law, the

Court would be inclined to accept presidential action in the gray area, and legislators took that instruction to heart. But the laws Congress passed may actually have made it harder for those who sincerely wanted to reassert congressional power to do so.

The story of the congressional attempt to reassert power is not, of course, the story of only one branch. While Congress was passing the legislation outlined above, the executive continued to assert prerogative powers and to insist that innovations such as the legislative veto were unconstitutional. The fully developed prerogative interpretation, outlined in Chapters 3 and 4, was strengthened by continued assertions made by the Reagan and Bush administrations and, to a lesser degree, by the Ford and Carter administrations. While the executive branch was able to win most of the battles over legislative language, even in those cases where the language was not fully in line with the executive perspective, the president consistently insisted in statements attached to the bills that while the president accepted the law, he rejected the provisions designed to reverse the burden or increase congressional authority. As President Ford noted in signing the National Emergencies Act in 1976, "I support the purposes of the enrolled bill. One of its provisions, however, would purport to permit the Congress to terminate a national emergency by a concurrent resolution. This feature of the bill is unconstitutional." Ford added that he considered the veto provision "as separable from the rest of the bill, and would therefore expect the other provisions relating to emergency powers to remain in force."[126] The executive, from Truman through Bush, consistently has used the approach of noting constitutional objections when signing legislation.[127] And while the Court has ruled that such objections in no way release the executive from executing the laws as written,[128] along with formal executive vetoes they contribute to the clear and consistent record of executive interpretations of the law and the Constitution.

Many legislators continue to believe that the courts will enforce congressional authority when they come to interpret these acts. One example, noted above, came in July 1991 when the House-Senate conferees on a bill to establish rules for covert action on the part of U.S. intelligence agencies noted in their report to Congress that while they had accepted the executive's language in their bill, that in no way indicated that they accepted the executive's interpretation of the language, nor did it signal a legislative acceptance of the broader claims to executive prerogative suggested by the language. The conference report insisted that the final determination of what the language meant would be left to the courts "because, they said, authoritative interpretation of the Constitution 'is the exclusive province of the judicial branch.' "[129] If the Court decides, as it has done in recent cases, to interpret broadly the delegation of power to the president in foreign policy, while insisting on clear and narrow limits on presidential power before it will restrain the executive,[130] then it is the legislative language and not the legislative history that will be determinative.[131] Executive claims, unhindered by the actual language of the laws, add to executive power, and build a strong precedent for future decisions in all three branches.

Congressional reluctance to engage the executive in constitutional debate, combined with the acceptance of the executive prerogative interpretation by a significant number of legislators, has undermined the objectives Congress set for the reform legislation of the 1970s and 1980s in foreign policy. Whether that is a good thing is unclear. What is clear, however, is that legislators have failed to achieve their stated objectives, and in some cases actually have exacerbated the problem they set out to solve—the imbalance of powers in foreign policy.

V

Political Solutions to a Political Problem: Incentives to Rebalance Power

8

Why the Courts Won't Save Congress Overseas—Or at Home

In over 200 years of developing a doctrine in foreign policy cases, the Supreme Court has made it clear that it will police the separation of powers in foreign as well as in domestic policy, but the doctrine is equally clear that where Congress fails to assert its prerogatives in law, the justices are inclined to authorize broader discretion for the executive. The failure to assert legislative authority is compounded when a majority of legislators agree to accept the executive's interpretation of disputed statutes—or, worse, where that same majority agrees to accept the executive's language in a bill with the hope or expectation that the courts ultimately will interpret the law as many legislators would prefer it understood. In a number of areas outlined in the previous chapter, legislators started with statutes designed to constrain or limit executive prerogative, but ultimately accepted legislation that was at best ambiguous and that at worst explicitly delegated discretion to the executive.

The 1990 legislative effort to revamp the intelligence system after the Iran-Contra debacle is a perfect example. The bill, though hardly a fundamental revision of the intelligence system, featured a requirement that the president report all covert actions in advance to Congress, except in a few circumstances when the president would be required to report within 48 hours. President Bush argued that this strict limit was an unconstitutional infringement of the executive's prerogative in foreign affairs and vetoed the bill. Without the political support to override the veto, the congressional conference committee reached a compromise with the administration, removing the statutory requirement in exchange for Bush's written assurance that prior notice of covert activities would be provided in all but a few "rare instances." Bush went on to note, however, that though he anticipated quick notice in most cases, "any withholding [of notice] beyond this period will be based upon my assertion of authorities granted this office by the Constitution."[1] The conference committee explicitly recognized that "the President may assert a constitutional basis for further delay and agrees to disagree with him if he does so." The committee report made clear that neither the House nor the Senate Intelligence Committee subscribed to the president's interpretation of the Constitution, but the letter of the law contained no such reservation. Instead, the committee report expressed confidence that the Court ultimately would interpret the law as Congress understood it rather than as the president understood it. Constitutional interpretation, the committee report noted, "is the exclusive province of the judicial branch."[2]

Many in Congress expected the Court to do what Congress could not, or would not, do—to assert and protect legislative prerogatives in foreign policy. Far from protecting legislative prerogatives, the Court increasingly has contributed to the degradation of those prerogatives. Congress has the authority to intervene and claim power in foreign affairs, but to do so the justices have insisted ever more stringently in recent years that legislators have to be explicit, making their claims clear in the law and not just in the legislative history. While presidents continued to veto legislation and attach clear statements about constitutional interpretation to those veto messages, legislators continued to compromise the legislative language. The Court then read that language strictly, turning increasingly receptive to claims of executive discretion if not outright prerogative. The Court, far from saving Congress from itself as many legislators hoped and expected, made the imbalance of powers more pronounced as the precedents set by the legislature and the Court came to shape the distribution of power.

In recent years the justices have lowered the barriers to executive discretion in foreign policy in three important ways. First, the Court has been extremely tolerant of congressional delegations of power and discretion to the executive. Second, the Court has been extremely tolerant of executive action in the absence of congressional action or in the face of congressional silence. Finally, the Court has recently gone one step further: Where once the Court's default position seemed to be a presumption in favor of congressional prerogatives, now the Court has subtly turned the default presumption to one that assumes congressional acquiescence in the absence of explicit and narrowly drawn statutes that would *deny* discretion to the executive.[3] This change in the Court's default doctrine is apparent in domestic and foreign policy alike.[4] Legislative decisions in one realm have been used to support judicial opinions in the other realm.

In many instances in foreign policy, legislators consciously choose to implicitly and explicitly delegate to the executive. But because the Court is unwilling fully to divorce foreign and domestic policy, the implicit and explicit delegations in foreign policy have been used by the justices to support their default presumption in domestic legislation as well.

Before turning to the impact foreign policy doctrine has had on domestic policy cases, it is important to understand how, when, and why the Court reversed its default presumption from one favoring legislative prerogative to one favoring executive prerogative.

The Resilient Appeal of the Political Question Doctrine

As happened at other important points in the evolution of the Court's doctrine of constitutional interpretation in foreign policy cases, the modern Court considered, flirted with, but finally rejected the option of simply leaving the two elected branches to struggle for control in foreign policy. One chance to revisit the political question doctrine in foreign policy was presented in 1979, when President Carter decided to recognize the People's Republic of China in Beijing as the official government of China. To do so, the United States had to abrogate a defense treaty with the Republic of China (Taiwan). Carter argued that abrogation was a necessary condition for normalizing American relations with the People's Republic of China. Arizona's Republican senator, Barry Goldwater, challenged the Carter decision in court, arguing that the Senate had a right to a role in treaty termination. The Court of Appeals for the District of Columbia Circuit held that Goldwater had standing to sue, but that the president had constitutional authority to terminate the treaty without Senate action. Unless there was a specific termination clause calling for a Senate role, the appeals court ruled, the president alone has the power to decide when a treaty has been or should be terminated because of changed circumstances. The Senate had made no attempt to reserve a role for itself in the termination of the treaty and had made no effort to assert that right since Carter's decision. In essence, the appeals court held that the Senate had the political weapons it needed to fight Carter's decision, but had chosen not to use them. The court would not do what the Senate was unwilling to do for itself.

When the decision was appealed to the Supreme Court, the justices were bitterly divided. The Supreme Court split, and ordered the suit dismissed, but the justices did not agree on why it should be dismissed. Justice Powell argued that the case was not "ripe"; that since the Senate had not acted, there was no actual case or dispute between the branches. Justices Rehnquist, Stewart, Burger, and Blackmun argued that the suit should be dismissed as a political question. Justice Brennan dissented, arguing that the case was both ripe and justiciable and that the president did indeed have the constitutional authority to do what he had done.[5]

Goldwater v. Carter illustrated the Court's two schools of thought on when it is appropriate to invoke the political question doctrine in foreign policy cases. The 1917 *Oetjen* view, expressed by Rhenquist in the *Goldwater* case, held that questions involving "the authority of the President in the conduct of our country's foreign relations" are inherently "political" and "therefore nonjusticiable."[6]

Justice Brennan argued the second school of thought. He agreed that the Court had no business reviewing the policy preferences of the political branches, but if "the antecedent question [of] whether a particular branch has been constitutionally designated as the repository of political decision-making power" arises, the questions "must be resolved as a matter of constitutional law, not political discretion; accordingly it falls within the competence of the Courts."[7] Therefore the Court must decide on procedural challenges to foreign policy questions. *Goldwater*, Brennan argued, was precisely the sort of case the Court was most qualified—and most obliged—to review.

Taking the middle ground, Justice Powell argued that the Court should not do the work of another branch. In a statement attached to the Supreme Court's order to dismiss *Goldwater*, Powell suggested that should the political branches actually directly confront each other over the issue, then the issues raised might well be appropriate for Supreme Court review. But here, Powell argued, the case was not yet ripe for decision because neither house of Congress had made any attempt to assert its own prerogative. "If the Congress chooses not to confront the President, it is not our task to do so."[8]

Goldwater concerned the judicial commitment to police the separation of powers—one of the two pillars supporting the Court's doctrine in foreign policy cases. The other pillar is a commitment to protect individual liberties. Here the Court continues to insist that the national government, Congress and the executive acting together, is restricted in foreign policy only by clear constitutional prohibitions such as the guarantee of individual liberties. Just as the Court refused to embrace the political question doctrine as a way to escape foreign policy separation of powers questions, so too has the Court continued to flirt with, and to reject, the political-question escape option in individual liberties issues.

In a case that traveled up and down the American judicial ladder, *Ramirez de Arellano v. Weinberger*, a U.S. citizen's property in Honduras was taken over by the U.S. for military training purposes. Claiming the government had expropriated his property, the owner (Temistocles Ramirez de Arellano) sued. The United States District Court for the District of Columbia ruled that the case raised a non-justiciable political question and should be dismissed. On appeal, a panel of the United States Court of Appeals for the D.C. Circuit reversed the lower court, ruling that Ramirez had a case and could sue the government. The case was then reheard by the full court of appeals (which included Judges Ruth Bader Ginsburg and Antonin Scalia, both of whom would later sit on the Supreme Court). The full court of appeals agreed that this was not a political question, but ruled that the case should be dismissed for other reasons. By the time the case reached the Supreme Court, the military had left the disputed property and the case was dismissed. Despite this tortured path, the case generated an extended discussion of the political question issue at the appeals court level—a discussion worth considering since it so clearly articulates both the temptation to use the political question doctrine, and the powerful argument against doing so.

In *Ramirez*, the appeals court explicitly rejected the idea that *Curtiss-Wright* could be interpreted as a precedent for using the political question doctrine to avoid all decisions touching on foreign policy. Scalia wrote the majority opinion when the case was heard by a panel of the court of appeals. In the opinion, Scalia explicitly rejected the lower court's argument that the case raised a political question. Indeed, Scalia noted that "because this case involves land in Central America, and because United States military activities in that region are currently the subject of national interest and debate, the issue is presented in a more politically charged context. That may make it, in a sense, a political case,"[9] but cases that arise in a political context, Scalia argued, do not necessarily raise nonjusticiable political questions.[10]

When the case was reheard by the full appeals court, Judge Malcolm Wilkey argued that those who would use the political question doctrine to avoid foreign policy challenges were misreading *Curtiss-Wright*. Wilkey argued that it was Surtherland's intent in *Curtiss-Wright* that cases raising foreign policy questions were justiciable, and should be decided by the courts. They most certainly were not to be left to the vagaries of the political system. Wilkey argued that it was the duty of the judiciary to rule on cases that assert the government has denied or trampled upon the fundamental rights of its citizens, regardless of whether or not the policy was in pursuit of foreign affairs objectives. "The Executive's power to conduct foreign relations free from the unwarranted supervision of the Judiciary cannot give the Executive carte blanche to trample the most fundamental liberty and property rights of this country's citizenry. The Executive's foreign relations prerogatives are subject to constitutional limitation; no agreement with a foreign country can confer upon the Executive Branch any power greater than those bounded by the Constitution."[11] Wilkey forcefully argued that applying the political question doctrine to all policies having an effect abroad, or with a potential impact on foreign relations "would mean that virtually anything done by United States officials to United States citizens on foreign soil is nonjusticiable. This is not the law."[12]

The continuing attempt to define and invoke the political question doctrine in foreign policy indicates the degree to which judges are uncomfortable with reviewing policy choices in foreign affairs. Despite their discomfort, however, when an actual case presents itself they usually are unable to walk away from what they perceive to be their responsibility to come to a decision, interpret the Constitution, and protect the Constitution's institutional structure and guarantees of individual liberties. Even Thomas Franck, who forcefully argues that the judiciary is too willing to abdicate hard decisions in foreign policy cases, agrees that the Court has been willing to intervene in these two areas.[13]

Separation of Powers: When Can Congress Count on the Court?

The Court has maintained its commitment to police the separation of powers in foreign policy from *Curtiss-Wright* to today, but the boundaries the justices will enforce have changed significantly. When there is a clear conflict between the branches, the modern Court has made it plain that such disputes, rare though they are, can have their day in court. As Justice Powell insisted in *Goldwater v. Carter*, the Court would not rule in disputes between the President and Congress "unless and until each branch has taken action asserting its constitutional authority."[14] Short of a direct conflict, the Court has continued to subscribe to Justice Jackson's three categories of executive action outlined in the steel seizure case. The difference is that the justices are increasingly less willing to see those categories as clear and distinct. For Jackson, a president's actions fell into one of three groups: the first, where the president and Congress act together; the second, where the president acts in the absence of congressional action; and the third, where Congress opposes the president's actions. Justice Rehnquist noted in 1980 that in foreign affairs most executive action falls "not neatly in one of three pigeonholes, but rather at some point along a spectrum running from explicit congressional authorization to explicit congressional prohibition."[15] Though the Court continues to identify three broad categories, the lack of clear lines of demarcation allows a broad gray area between the categories, and allows the justices to broaden one category or the other without renouncing the general doctrine.

In fact, the justices have shrunk one of the categories while expanding the other two. Where Congress opposes the president, the Court has come to the defense of legislative prerogatives, but only when Congress has met increasingly higher standards of explicit, formal, and clear legislative opposition to the executive's policy. In the other two categories, (where the president acts alone, without legislative opposition; and where the president and Congress act together through legislation or the delegation of power from Congress to the president, explicitly or implicitly) the Court has been willing to find implicit delegation of power from Congress to the president, interpreting anything short of clear, formal, and unambiguous opposition as tacit approval. Finally, where legislators have tried to delegate with one hand while constraining and limiting that delegation with the other (as they did with any number of legislative veto provisions), the Court has upheld the delegation while striking down the devices designed to limit or constrain those delegations. Finally, this broad change in what the Court requires of Congress before it will enforce legislative prerogatives has had a profound effect in domestic policy, where debates over statutory interpretation and legislative intent have begun to borrow precedents and doctrine from the foreign policy cases. Since the Court has never formally recognized a clear distinction between constitutional powers in foreign and domestic policy, this reversal of the Court's default assumptions about what constitutes explicit and implicit delegation in foreign policy also can be found in domestic policy cases.

Congress Versus the President

In *Goldwater v. Carter* Justice Powell argued that the judicial branch "should not decide issues affecting the allocation of power between the President and Congress until the political branches reach a constitutional impasse."[16] But, Powell argued, if "the president and the Congress had reached irreconcilable positions, the specter of the federal government brought to a halt because of the mutual intransigence of the president and the Congress would require this Court to provide a resolution pursuant to our duty to 'say what the law is.' "[17]

When President Reagan signed the Competition in Contracting Act into law in 1984, he did so only after claiming that certain provisions of the Act were unconstitutional and instructing the executive branch to ignore those provisions. The law gave the comptroller general a role in managing bidding for military projects designed to steer military contracts to American firms. A military contractor, Lear Siegler Inc., went to court after it lost a navy contract to a lower bid from a foreign firm, despite the fact that enforcement of the law as passed by Congress clearly would have resulted in Lear Siegler's winning the contract. The company sued, and the appeals court ruled that the president had no authority to determine which part of the law he would "faithfully execute," as required by Article 2 of the Constitution.[18]

"According to the government," Judge Fletcher wrote for the 9th Circuit, "these clauses empower the President . . . to declare a law unconstitutional and suspend its operation." That position, the court ruled, was "utterly at odds with the texture and plain language of the Constitution, and with nearly two centuries of judicial precedent."[19] The court ruled that when presented with a piece of legislation passed by both houses of Congress, "the President must either sign or veto a bill presented to him . . . [The Constitution does not empower the president to] excise or sever provisions of a bill with which he disagrees. . . . [Such] an incursion into Congress's essential legislative role cannot be tolerated."[20] The court soundly rejected the notion that the president had broad discretion or prerogative when Congress had spoken so formally, and so clearly.[21]

While legislators occasionally do win in court, the rising threshold for what the judiciary will accept as adequate congressional opposition has meant that the president usually wins.[22] Rather than view these cases as conflicts between the president and Congress, courts recently have been moving these cases into the category Justice Jackson identified as those where the president acts alone, without congressional opposition. Jackson interpreted this category to be one that encompasses powers not asserted by Congress—cases where Congress truly was silent—but the modern Court has extended the category to those cases where Congress is unclear, and even to those cases where despite a surface clarity, the congressional intent could conceivably be read more broadly than Congress might have planned.

When the President Acts Alone

When the Carter administration negotiated the release of American hostages in Teheran in 1981, part of the executive agreement (it was not submitted to the Senate for advice and consent) set up a process for the disposition of private claims against Iran. Arguing that this process constituted an unconstitutional taking of its property without just compensation and that the action was beyond the scope of the president's constitutional authority, a firm called American International Group filed suit seeking an injunction against the transfer of frozen Iranian assets.

While the president had clear authority to freeze foreign assets under the International Emergency Economic Powers Act (IEEPA), the appeals court ruled that the president had no express or implied grant of power from Congress in the IEEPA to suspend the claims of American nationals against Iran. Nevertheless, the court found that "there is a longstanding practice of settling private American claims against foreign governments through executive agreements."[23]

Here the court found support for an executive initiative in foreign policy not in the Constitution itself, nor in a particular act of Congress but in Congress' *lack of action*.[24] The court was quick to note that it "would be confronted with a very different case if Congress had enacted legislation, or even passed a resolution, indicating its displeasure with the Iranian agreements." Here, the court ruled, Congress had made no effort to foreclose the option chosen by the president; there was a pattern of previous behavior; and allowing this agreement to stand, the court stated, should *not* be read as "foreclosing or eroding any powers to block or amend claims settlements that *the Congress may one day choose to assert*."[25]

When the Supreme Court considered the Iranian agreement in 1981, Chief Justice Rehnquist's opinion for the Court argued that the president's actions had been constitutional. Even though they were not explicitly authorized by an act of Congress, the IEEPA and the Hostage Act, Rehnquist wrote, were clear indications of congressional acceptance of broad executive discretion in similar circumstances to those presented by the case. Rehnquist argued that the courts cannot expect Congress to "anticipate and legislate with regard to every possible action the President may find it necessary to take or every possible situation in which he might act."[26] Taken together with the evidence of other related delegations of power in the IEEPA and the Hostage Act, Rehnquist concluded that "Congress has *implicitly* approved the practice of claim settlement by executive agreement."[27]

Despite these rulings, a simple assertion of legislative authority may not be enough. Recent cases indicate that the courts increasingly are looking

to blend its foreign and domestic doctrines. In a growing number of domestic cases the Court has taken to citing foreign policy precedents.[34] In both domestic and foreign policy the Court is increasingly receptive to congressional delegation, and increasingly unwilling to do what Congress may well be unwilling to do for itself. That is, the Court may no longer be willing to protect congressional prerogatives when Congress itself is eager to shed those prerogatives, and the executive branch eager to adopt them.[35] By granting greater latitude to Congress to delegate power to the executive in foreign policy, and by altering the Court's long-standing assumptions about congressional prerogatives and the role and method of construing and applying what many call legislative intent, rather than a more mechanical strict interpretation of the statutory language itself, the Court has significantly contributed to the growth of executive power, executive discretion, and the legitimacy of the executive prerogative interpretation of the Constitution at home and abroad.

Recent separation of powers cases have revealed a Court far more ready and willing to cede discretion to the executive and, at the same time, to make it increasingly difficult for Congress to assert itself (that Congress has been far from eager to assert itself only compounds the problem). If this trend continues, the executive prerogative interpretation will become even more entrenched, long before a clear debate can be had on the merits.

Legislative Intent: Definition and Application at Home

The leading domestic case dealing with statutory interpretation, congressional delegation, and legislative intent, is a 1984 Environmental Protection Agency case called *Chevron v. Natural Resources Defense Council.*

Chevron concerned a challenge to an Environmental Protection Agency (EPA) interpretation of the Clean Air Act Amendments of 1977. These amendments included the requirement that states that had failed to reach certain levels of clean air would create a permit program to regulate "new or modified major stationary sources" of air pollution. The dispute in *Chevron* arose over the definition of a "stationary source." The stringent requirements appeared designed to apply to any significant source of pollution—any new machinery, or any old machinery that had been modified significantly—in any one particular site. The EPA, however, ruled that it would consider the pollution produced not by each piece of equipment, but rather the level of pollution produced by the plant as a whole. Under this definition, if the new or modified equipment did not raise the total amount of pollution created by the plant as a whole, then it could escape the more stringent requirements. This method of calculation was referred to as a "bubble concept" since the EPA essentially looked at each plant as if it were encased in a bubble, and judged the pollution level of the bubble as a whole.

When an environmental group challenged this executive agency's interpretation, the district court ruled that though Congress had never defined a "stationary source," the *purpose* of the legislation was to reduce pollution; the bubble concept was aimed at the maintenance of status quo pollution levels, so the court ruled that the EPA's interpretation was not a reasonable reading of the statute.

On appeal, however, the Supreme Court overturned the lower court's ruling. The higher court ruled that the legislative intent was unclear, that Congress had sent overlapping and mixed signals, the EPA's interpretation was a reasonable one, and therefore the Court ought to defer to the EPA's interpretation.

In *Chevron* the Court started by suggesting that the first question which must be asked is whether Congress "has directly spoken to the precise question" in dispute. "If the intent of Congress is clear that is the end of the matter; for the Court, as well as the agency, must give effect to the unambiguously expressed intent of Congress." When the justices believe that Congress is unclear, or has failed to address a specific problem, then the Court has the choice of imposing its own construction, or, if one exists, deferring to an administrative agency's interpretation. When that agency's interpretation "is based on a permissible construction of the statute,"[36] then the Court should defer to that reading.

But *Chevron* created even more deference to the executive branch. The Court would defer not only when legislative intent was ambiguous. Where Congress explicitly leaves "a gap for the agency to fill, there is an express delegation," and even where the delegation is implicit rather than explicit, the majority held that the Court must accept a "reasonable interpretation made by the administrator of an agency."[37]

This broad deference to executive interpretation appears even more dramatic when one considers the impact *Chevron* has had on Court doctrine, and how it has been interpreted by one of the Court's leading advocates of narrow readings of legislation—Justice Antonin Scalia.

In a 1989 lecture, later published as a law review article, Justice Scalia laid out a clear statement on statutory interpretation. While he endorsed the Court's traditional view about the interpretation of plain and clear congressional language in statutes, he endorsed the *Chevron* decision, arguing that in cases of statutory ambiguity, the Court was replacing its traditional commitment to a statute-by-statute evaluation with an "across-the-board presumption that, in the case of ambiguity, agency discretion is meant."[38] In other words, absent clear congressional language, the Court could and should presume that Congress meant to delegate broad discretion to the executive agency. Scalia would have had the Court go further still. He argued that "ambiguity" means more than simply the existence of two interpretations where neither the executive agency's interpretation nor the putative congressional interpretation are dominant. If *Chevron* "is to have any meaning, congressional intent must be regarded as "ambiguous" not just when no interpretation is even marginally better than any other, but rather when two or more reasonable, though not necessarily equally valid, interpretations exist."[39] This would appear to be a tremendous resource for executive discretion and the prerogative interpretation and a real setback for congressional attempts to delegate the authority needed in a modern bureaucratic state while, at the same time, preserving some measure of control for the legislative branch. Scalia recognizes this implication, but his response is that Congress is neither better nor worse off—legislators clearly are on notice that lack of precision will lead to executive discretion, and thus should they persist in writing less than precise legislation, the court is fully justified in assuming that they meant to delegate discretion to the executive branch.

Scalia seems sanguine about the implications of his reading of *Chevron*. If legislators are concerned, then the ruling should lead to more careful statute writing. If legislators are willing to accept broad agency discretion, as Scalia suggests he believes they are, then *Chevron* has no real effect. Scalia has argued that the Court announced (and should abide by) a decision rule in *Chevron*—to defer to the administrative agency as a default position.

At least with Scalia's interpretive rule, Congress stands a chance should the legislators care to clearly assert their prerogatives. A critical problem arises, however, with justices who do ***not*** subscribe to Scalia's textualism and yet accept the deference doctrine outlined in *Chevron*. Should that view dominate, then the executive prerogative view, once limited largely to foreign policy, may well begin to influence domestic doctrine as well.

Congress and the Delegation of Power to the Executive

Recall Justice Jackson's three categories of foreign policy cases laid out in *Youngstown*: 1) cases "when the President acts pursuant to an express or implied authorization of Congress"; 2) cases "when the President acts in absence of either a congressional grant or denial of authority"; and 3) cases "when the President takes measures incompatible with the expressed or implied will of Congress."[40] The third type of case addresses the broad question of the interpretation and application of legislative intent. *Chevron* is a clear indication that the Court's distinction between foreign and domestic policy doctrine is getting muddier.[41] What about the other two categories? They address the question of the delegation of power: Are there limits to what Congress may, constitutionally, authorize the president to do? And just what is sufficient to indicate an expressed or implied authorization?

The question of delegation of power has a long and fairly tortured history in American judicial doctrine. The concept of a "non-delegation" doctrine turned up 1892 when the Supreme Court ruled that Congress could delegate broad discretion to the president to set and regulate tariffs. The law was challenged as unconstitutionally delegating legislative power to the executive, but the Court ruled that the delegation was constitutional. "That Congress cannot delegate legislative power to the President," the Court ruled in *Field v. Clark*, "is a principle universally recognized as vital to the integrity and maintenance of the system of government ordained by the Constitution."[42] But the act in question, the justices continued, "is not inconsistent with that principle. It does not, in any real sense, invest the president with the power of legislation."[43] The pattern followed in *Field* would later be repeated in other cases concerning alleged undue delegations of power. First the Court acknowledges that there are absolute limits, and then it proceeds to rule that in the case at hand, there is no violation—that Congress can delegate the power it has chosen to delegate.[44]

Despite the rhetoric in *Field*, the Court was slow to enforce this doctrine. In 1928 Chief Justice William Howard Taft held that the non-delegation doctrine did not block Congress from getting help from the other branches of government. After stating that it would be "a breach of the National fundamental law if Congress gives up its legislative power and transfers it to the President," Taft noted that this was not to say that the three branches couldn't or shouldn't cooperate. Provided that Congress establishes, "by legislative act, an intelligible principle . . . which the person or body authorized" to exercise the delegated power is directed to observe, "such legislative action is not a forbidden delegation of legislative power."[45] In determining when the gray line between legitimate cooperation and undue delegation was crossed, Taft ruled, "the extent and character of that [delegation] must be fixed according to common sense and the inherent necessities of the governmental co-ordination."[46] Clearly, this is a broad standard that leaves tremendous room for judicial discretion.

When the Court actually struck down congressional legislation on the ground of undue delegation it was at the height of Franklin Roosevelt's battle with the Supreme Court. In two famous cases in 1935—*Schechter Poultry Corp. v. United States* and *Panama Refining Co. v. Ryan*—the Court overturned legislation that would have delegated broad discretion to the president and executive agencies to control prices and interstate commerce.

In *Panama*, only Justice Cardozo's dissent argued that the circumstances in which legislation was passed should matter to the Court, and that those circumstances had led to the election of a president (Franklin Roosevelt) who was chosen to respond to emergency needs. "The statute was framed in the shadow of a national disaster," Cardozo wrote. The voters understood that "a host of unforeseen contingencies would have to be faced from day to day, and faced with a fullness of understanding unattainable by any one except the man upon the scene. The President was chosen to meet the instant need."[47] The majority opinion rejected these pragmatic arguments, ruling that the legislation itself, and the circumstances in which it was passed, were irrelevant. Congress had delegated power beyond what the Constitution authorized. Chief Justice Hughes argued that "the Congress manifestly is not permitted to abdicate, or to transfer to others, the essential legislative functions with which it is thus vested."[48] Noting that the law (which delegated to the president the authority to control the amount of oil sold in interstate commerce) might even exceed congressional power to regulate interstate commerce, the Court argued that even if Congress had the power to set this sort of policy, it could not surrender that discretion to the executive.

Panama illustrated the problem with the application of the undue delegation doctrine. The Court consistently has refused to see the division between the three branches as absolute, and yet the justices consistently agree that there is *some* limit to the overlap of power—some point at which Congress, the executive and the courts cannot delegate their powers and responsibilities.

As the Court phrased it in a 1975 *per curium* decision in *Buckley v. Valeo* that struck down a number of provisions in a campaign finance reform package of legislation, "the Constitution by no means contemplates total separation of each of these three essential branches of government. . . . [The founders] saw that a hermetic sealing off of the three branches of government from one another would preclude the establishment of a Nation capable of governing itself effectively."[49]

Even in *Buckley* the Court failed to develop any sort of clear test to measure when the line separating the powers had been violated. *Panama*, *Schecter*, and *Buckley* all demonstrated how very difficult it would be to find any sort of neutral standards to apply—and indicated that questions of undue delegation might well turn on the individual impressions of individual justices. Naturally, the closer the Court moves to one end of the spectrum (*laissez-faire* tolerance of broad congressional delegation) or the other (rejection of all but the clearest, most carefully delineated delegations of power), the easier it is to discover a bright line between what is allowed and what is not.

When the Court reversed its position on economic regulation in 1937,[50] it largely abandoned all efforts to restrict the national government's role in economic regulation and to restrict the degree to which Congress could delegate power to the executive. The Court had long acknowledged that there was a distinct gray area between what it would allow Congress to delegate and what went beyond the pale. Assuming some minimal definitions and specificity, Congress was pretty much free to delegate significant measures of powers and discretion to the executive branch. After the unhappiness of the New Deal experience,[51] the Court simply no longer was interested in trying to develop, articulate, or apply any sort of clear set of standards in the murky middle ground between clearly unconstitutional delegation and the delegation that was absolutely necessary to ensure an effective exercise of the "substantive powers granted to the various branches by the Constitution."[52]

The undue-delegation doctrine rarely has been revisited since the 1930s. In a 1979 concurrence he filed in a case concerning an Occupational Safety and Health Administration ruling on exposure to benzene in the workplace, Justice Rehnquist argued that the case should have turned on the question of undue delegation, but despaired that the doctrine may well have been unfairly interred along with substantive due process in the 1930s. "We ought not to shy away from our judicial duty to invalidate unconstitutional delegations of legislative authority solely out of concern that we should thereby reinvigorate discredited constitutional doctrines of the pre–New Deal era. If the non-delegation doctrine has fallen into the same desuetude as have substantive due process and restrictive interpretations of the Commerce Clause, it is, as one writer has phrased it, 'a case of death by association.' "[53] Rehnquist argued that there are limits to what the Constitution will permit Congress to delegate. The non-delegation doctrine, Rehnquist wrote, serves three purposes: it ensures that "important choices of social policy are made by Congress, the branch of our Government most responsive to the popular will." Second, the doctrine requires that when Congress finds it necessary to delegate power, it must provide clear principles "to guide the exercise of the delegated discretion." Finally, it requires these clear standards so that "courts charged with reviewing the exercise of delegated legislative discretion will be able to test that exercise against ascertainable standards."[54] Rehnquist was right to note the perhaps unfair death of the undue delegation doctrine. But what he failed to point out was that the concept of undue delegation had come to be seen as a one-way street. While the Court *had* learned the New Deal's lesson about deference to legislative choices in economic regulation, it had failed to separate that from the notion that the Court also had a constitutional responsibility to ensure that Congress did not abdicate its own responsibilities in foreign and domestic policy alike. By the time the Court considered the *Chevron* case in 1984, the justices were willing to allow Congress to delegate broad, undefined powers to the executive. Further, the Court stated that it was inclined to read ambiguity as favoring executive discretion. This is quite a stretch from *Panama* and *Schechter*, where Congress was blocked because of the lack of constraints the legislators had placed on their delegation of power. No longer was the question 'Would Congress be forced to constrain and restrict its delegations of power?' Now the question was, 'Could Congress delegate *limited* powers at all?'. Could Congress delegate powers and yet retain some measure of control to prevent a limited delegation from being construed as tacit approval for an executive prerogative interpretation in domestic and foreign policy?

The Court Blocks Congressional Efforts to Delegate With One Hand, While Checking With the Other

At the same time that the Court has been increasingly willing to see Congress hand away its powers, or to allow ambiguity to be resolved by deferring to executive branch interpretations, the justices have built a hard line against the constitutional innovations Congress has developed to allow it to delegate power without losing control. The leading examples of the Court blocking legislative efforts to develop a means of delegating limited power came in the 1980s in *Immigration and Naturalization Service v. Chadha* (1983)—the case in which the Court struck down the legislative veto, a device Congress had inserted in over 200 laws in an attempt to delegate power without losing control—and in *Bowsher v. Synar* (1986), where the Supreme Court supported the District Court's ruling in *Synar v. United States* (1986), striking down the key provision of a congressional effort to force the national government to cut the federal deficit. With these cases, the Court effectively ruled that delegation of power to the executive branch was constitutional, but that any limits on that delegation, any devices designed to constrain that delegation of power, were unconstitutional.[55]

While the majority in *Chadha* acknowledged the demonstrable utility of the legislative veto, "the fact that a given law or procedure is efficient, convenient, and useful in facilitating functions of government, standing alone, will not save it if it is contrary to the Constitution."[56] In dissent, Justice White argued that if the Court insisted on allowing Congress to "delegate lawmaking power to independent and executive agencies, it is most difficult to understand Article I as forbidding Congress from also reserving a check on legislative power for itself."[57] Without the legislative veto, White wrote, "Congress is faced with a Hobson's choice: either to refrain from delegating the necessary authority, leaving itself with a hopeless task of writing laws with the requisite specificity to cover endless special circumstances across the entire policy landscape, or in the alternative, to abdicate its lawmaking function to the executive branch and independent agencies."[58] The majority rejected White's concerns, arguing that the system was not designed to be efficient or convenient. Once again, as the Court had done in *Buckley* and as it would do in *Bowsher*, the majority cited *Youngstown* as a leading authority on separation of powers questions. There was no effort in any of these citations to suggest that *Youngstown* was special or unique because it dealt with foreign policy. On the contrary, it was cited as an important precedent and leading case in the general area of separation of powers.[59] Citing *Youngstown*, the majority in *Chadha* noted that "there is no support in the Constitution or decisions of this Court for the proposition that the cumbersomeness and delays often encountered in complying with explicit constitutional standards may be avoided, either by the Congress or by the President."[60] But Justice White was doing more than merely defending the legislative veto on simple pragmatic grounds. He alone noted the historic context of the legislative veto, and the fact that it had been successfully employed during the national emergency of the Second World War when "the legislative veto offered the means by which Congress could confer additional authority while preserving its own constitutional role."[61] White argued that the legislative veto was not a tool for Congress to "aggrandize" power at the expense of the executive, as founders Madison and Hamilton feared, but rather was a means of defense, a way for Congress to preserve its power against the growing power of the executive branch. White urged his brethren to ask whether the legislative veto was "consistent with the *purposes* of Article I," and he argued that it was and is. Here White also turned to *Youngstown*, quoting its admonition that governing under the Constitution "does not and cannot conform to judicial definitions . . . based on isolated clauses or even single Articles torn from context."[62] White concluded his dissent with incredulity, arguing that the Court's ruling now made it possible for Congress to delegate all manner of legislative discretion to the executive branch and to administrative agencies, but forbidding Congress from reserving a veto "over the exercise of that legislative power."[63]

The lesson of *Chadha*, combined with the Court's experience with economic regulation and the undue delegation doctrine seems clear. Congress is free to delegate, and in fact the Court will find tacit delegation in congressional silence; but it cannot delegate power with any reservations. The innovation of the legislative veto, designed to allow Congress to delegate necessary discretion to the executive without losing control, was disallowed by the Supreme Court.

* * *

Justice White continued his attack on the Court's "distressingly formalistic view of separation of powers" when he dissented from *Bowsher v. Synar*, the Supreme Court's review of *Synar v. United States*, the case that challenged the constitutionality of the Gramm-Rudman-Hollings Budget Act. The Supreme Court largely accepted the lower court's ruling in this case, and since the appeals court ruling was joined by then Judge (later Justice) Scalia, it is worth a quick examination.

In *Synar v. United States*, Scalia joined a ruling by the Court of Appeals for the District of Columbia that struck down the Gramm-Rudman-Hollings budget-balancing amendment. This was a measure designed to force deficit reduction, largely by making it appear automatic. The automaticity also offered the advantage of allowing legislators and the president alike to avoid the political price normally exacted for stiff budget cutting. To make the system work, Gramm-Rudman vested important responsibilities in the comptroller general, who was an executive appointee, though he or she was subject to removal by Congress under a number of specific conditions. In *Synar* and in the Supreme Court case that followed (*Bowsher v. Synar*), it was argued that vesting this authority in the comptroller general was unconstitutional, not because it was undue delegation from Congress to an executive branch appointee, but rather because it was a case of Congress attempting to exercise executive power through an agent who was beholden to the legislative branch.

The appeals court ruled that the delegation doctrine had long been read to allow Congress almost unlimited discretion to delegate away its own powers, but that Congress could not trench upon the powers of the other branches. The judicial doctrine, the *per curiam* opinion continued, displayed "greater deference to Congress' power to delegate" motivated in part by concerns that Congress "could not [otherwise] perform its functions" in an increasingly complex society.[64]

Here, then, is a clear example of precisely the sort of result Justice White warned about in his *Chadha* dissent. When the *Synar* case reached the Supreme Court as *Bowsher v. Synar*, Justice White again argued that the Court was interfering with a plan worked out between the two elected branches designed to resolve a problem that had not been anticipated by the Constitution. The Court's rulings in *Chadha* and in *Bowsher v. Synar*, White argued, were a "bar to the attainment of governmental objectives through the means chosen by the Congress and the President in the legislative process established by the Constitution."[65]

* * *

The sum effect of the cases discussed above seems to be that legislators can delegate as much power as they want to; but they must do so with absolute specificity and care. Any ambiguity, any missing elements will be construed by the Court as implicit delegations of power to the administration. Beyond that, any innovation—any attempt to balance delegation and control—will be met by judicial rejection. Thus, if delegation of any sort is needed (as no doubt it is in a modern superpower), the Court will construe such delegation as almost an all-or-nothing proposition.

In 1987 the appeals court (following *Chadha*) provided an excellent example when it severed a legislative veto from a statute that delegated broad power to the executive. In *Beacon Products v. Reagan* (1986), an emergency embargo ordered by the president under authority granted by the National Emergencies Act (NEA) and the IEEPA prevented a Massachusetts manufacturer from trading with Nicaragua. Since the NEA had a legislative veto provision, the plaintiff argued that the law itself was unconstitutional, and that the president therefore lacked the necessary delegation of authority to impose the embargo. The court ruled that the veto provision, which was unconstitutional according to *Chadha*, could be severed from the legislation. Therefore, the broad delegation of power that was included in the law was valid, and the president had adequate authority and discretion to impose the embargo. In effect, the court ruled that Congress had constitutionally delegated extraordinary power to the executive, but the device that Congress had inserted to control and limit that power was unconstitutional. The delegation of power stood, and the control was ruled invalid.

* * *

The problem with broad delegation is multi-layered. By delegating broad authority, legislators implicitly support executive claims to discretion in foreign policy bordering on prerogative; by delegating broad authority, legislators also hurt their case in Court since the judiciary has made clear that judges will give great weight to any sort of delegation as an indication of broad congressional support for executive initiatives.[66] In addition, the courts have also made clear that long-standing practices acquiesced to, or at least not actively opposed by Congress, also constitute a signal of congressional support for executive discretion.

In domestic policy and foreign policy alike, there seems to be almost no limit to what the Court will allow Congress to delegate to the executive; and, at the same time, very strict limits on what remedies the Court will allow Congress to enact to preserve its role in the system when delegation and some measure of discretion are seen as indispensable. The separation of powers does not require strict, bright lines, but it does require consistency. The system would remain equally sound and coherent with a loose construction of the delegation doctrine or a strict construction of that doctrine. But to apply a loose reading when Congress delegates, and a strict reading when Congress tries to constrain or shape that delegation, may well skew the constitutional result, shifting the Constitution's balance of power.

It is clear that the Court is less and less willing to help Congress to help itself. And the trend in foreign policy has begun to be replicated in the Court's domestic doctrine. Will the loss of congressional prerogatives in domestic affairs also mirror the surrender of congressional prerogatives in foreign affairs? If it does, the combination may well strengthen the executive prerogative interpretation of the Constitution at home and abroad.

9

Incentives to Rebalance Power?

What incentives are there for legislators to reassert themselves? What incentives exist to encourage them to accept the Court's challenge and move the collective will of hundreds of individual representatives to clear the hurdles placed in their path? Though recent scholarship shows that many in Congress have traded the assertion of formal power for a growing informal role in setting and supervising American foreign policy,[1] this book has tried to demonstrate that the tradeoff of informal influence for formal authority is one with significant implications in any future confrontation between the executive and Congress—in foreign and domestic policy alike.

To preserve formal authority in domestic and foreign policy, legislators will have to assert and defend it, but do legislators have sufficient incentives to reassert a formal congressional role in foreign policy? If so, what are they and can they be activated? If not, is there an alternative? The last chapter argued that the courts aren't likely to save Congress until Congress tries to save itself. Will the legislators save themselves, and if not, is there any other alternative?

There may be another alternative. If Congress lacks the proper incentives to rebalance power, and if the Court won't do it, it is worth asking whether the executive has the incentive to bring Congress back in—whether it is in the executive's political interest to do so. If it is, why have presidents since the Second World War increasingly asserted and acted on a prerogative interpretation of the Constitution? One answer would be that the historical context (the cold war and the threat of nuclear destruction) required it; a second answer might be that presidents have failed properly to calculate the cost the prerogative interpretation exacts on their own political interests.

* * *

In the *Federalist Papers*, James Madison argued that the problem would be to constrain the power-hungry. He argued that ambition was a reality, and rather than fighting to restrain ambition, the system should be designed to exploit it. Ambition, he wrote, must be made to counteract ambition. And lest anyone fear the collapse of power into a single branch, Madison suggested that if the interests of the individual officeholder were connected with the institutional interests of that person's office, one need not fear the amalgamation of power, since human nature would take over and guarantee that each individual would fight to protect and expand the powers of the institution to which they belonged. And yet from the early 1970s through to 1995 there are a significant number of instances when legislators have delegated power to the executive, or traded informal influence for formal authority.[2]

Was Madison wrong?

James Q. Wilson has defined power as "the ability of one person to get another person to act in accordance with the first person's intentions."[3] In other words, power can be seen "as the production of intended effects."[4] This is far more than a simple box score of points scored for and against, where one merely tallies the points to determine a winner and loser. These definitions are about achieving one's objectives, not necessarily about "winning" each confrontation.[5] In the natural sciences it is relatively easy to "measure the power of objects in terms of their capacities to do certain sorts of things." But in social science, the subjects of the study are individuals, and individual subjects choose "the way in which to behave" and are "not *merely* caused so to behave."[6] Was the final version of a piece of legislation the executive version—or the legislative version? Each version was, no doubt, shaped by perception, expectation, and anticipation of the opponent's strengths, weaknesses, preferences, and requirements. Though the congressional version may have been enacted, it may well be far from the bill a majority of individual legislators would have preferred. The procedure under which the bill reached the floor, and the order in which a series of bills reached the floor can make a profound difference.[7] Similarly, when can we say that the game has ended? Tradeoffs can be made within a single bill, or they can be made across policy issues. For instance, one side may sacrifice on a trade bill to succeed on a farm bill. Tradeoffs can be made across periods of time. The executive may modify an arms sales agreement on one weapon system in trade for a bill that more formally structures the delegation of power to negotiate future arms sales agreements. When one side wins a short-term gain by sacrificing a long-term objective, one can effectively argue that both sides have "won." Such tradeoffs are far from unique to politics and similar tradeoffs are quite common in large industries—layoffs, product mergers, and even the abandonment of significant sectors of the market may incur short-term costs, but in the long term produce a stronger, wealthier corporation. Finally, one can win by losing—by shedding responsibility for a necessary, though painful, course of action, one might strengthen both individual political power and institutional power as well. We need to realize that there are varieties of power. As Richard Neustadt put it in the 1990 revision and expansion of his 1960 classic on presidential power, we should "keep in mind the distinction between two senses in which the word *power* is employed." One sense is when it is used "to refer to formal constitutional, statutory or customary authority" and the other is in the "sense of effective influence on the conduct of others." Neustadt suggests that the word *authority* might be substituted for power in the formal sense, while *influence* might be substituted for power in the more informal sense.[8]

It is then quite plausible to believe than many individual legislators in Congress could and would consciously delegate formal power, or authority, on specific issues to gain influence in a broad policy area. Conversely, it is equally plausible to imagine individual legislators being willing and even eager to delegate both authority and responsibility to the executive in an area of foreign policy in exchange for influence on a specific question, or broad influence without specific responsibility. Recent studies of Congress and foreign policy argue that legislators have gained influence without necessarily gaining control.[9] This could well be seen as a logical means to the ends Madison described.

In the struggle between the executive and legislative branches, the language of the legislation may well matter in the long run, when statutory and constitutional interpretation come into play, but in the short term, an exclusive focus on legislation "misses a good deal of what Congress does in foreign policy." Increasingly, legislators have turned to "non-legislative means to influence the substance of policy."[10] By using alternative means of influence—alternatives to formal authority[11]—these legislators have been able to play a growing role in day-to-day foreign policy formation. But in terms of formal authority (and formal authority does matter, particularly when disputes wind up in court)[12] legislators have continued to delegate power implicitly and explicitly.

Perhaps Madison wasn't wrong—but perhaps he did not fully anticipate the distinction modern legislators would draw between assertions of power through legislation (formal authority) and assertions of power through alternative or informal means. This suggests that we need to examine the "ambition" Madison described. While there is clear evidence of the growth of informal congressional influence in foreign policy, that growth doesn't tell us why legislators would continue to delegate *formal* power even while trying to increase the level and volume of their informal influence. Nor does it tell us why legislators might not be inclined to increase *both* formal and informal influence. What are the incentives that might drive individual legislators to agree to, even embrace, these formal delegations of authority? And is there any reason to believe these calculations and trade-offs might change? Is there any reason to believe that individual legislators—and not just party leaders[13]—might more closely follow Madison's prediction that each member of an institution would fight to maintain and expand that institution's formal authority as well as its informal influence?

* * *

Within Congress, each legislator must make a number of calculations in each voting decision. Among those calculations is a concern with popular opinion, but even this is more complicated than it appears, since many legislators are known to be concerned not only with the immediate reaction of attentive constituents, but also deeply concerned about the reaction of inattentive constituents at some point in the future.[14] A reasonable legislator may realize that power flows *away* from those who do unpopular or unsuccessful things; similarly, that same reasonable legislator may realize that his or her power and influence ultimately hinges on the continued approval of particular groups of people, whether those groups are voters at home, powerful interest groups, or his or her political party.[15] As the domestic implications of foreign policy decisions grow, the number and influence of these groups is likely to grow and to carry more influence with individual legislators.[16] A voting decision in foreign policy may well be determined not by which policy will most please attentive constituents, but rather it may be determined by which policy will least displease inattentive constituents. As Morris Fiorina has argued it is often the case that voters cast their vote "retrospectively," that is, their vote is based on their response to what the legislator *has* done, rather than on their evaluation of what the legislator is likely *to do* in the future.[17] If this is the case, there may well be instances when a wise legislator would willingly abdicate power in one area to avoid a loss of power in all areas (being turned out of office, for example).

Whether political support is retrospective or prospective, many students of Congress agree that the "electoral connection" is vital, if not deterministic.[18] Richard Fenno has long maintained that "of all the goals espoused by members of the House, three are basic. They are: re-election, influence within the House, and good public policy."[19] Others, agreeing with Fenno, have emphasized re-election above all, since they argue it would be impossible to achieve influence within the House or good public policy if one is thrown out of office.

The focus on re-election is far from a new discovery. Madison not only anticipated that an interest in re-election would motivate legislators, he celebrated the idea that this natural tendency would keep legislators from conspiring to abuse their collective power. As Madison put it in the *Federalist Papers*, "those ties which bind the representative to his constituents are strengthened by motives of a more selfish nature." All the securities against the abuse of power by members of the House of Representatives, Madison added, would be found insufficient without the restraint of frequent elections. "Before the sentiments impressed on their minds by the mode of their elevation can be effaced by the exercise of power, they will be compelled to anticipate the moment when their power is to cease, when their exercise of it is to be reviewed, and when they must descend to the level from which they were raised; there forever to remain unless a faithful discharge of their trust shall have established their title to a renewal of it."[20]

It is fair to dispute the hierarchy of incentives once a legislator wins a seat in Congress. Those from relatively safe districts might well be expected to take re-election more for granted. If that happened, their emphasis could well turn to internal power or good public policy.[21] Despite the stunningly high rate of re-election, however, study after study seems to show that legislators have little confidence in their electoral odds, and incumbents spend huge amounts of time and resources on re-election concerns. The 1994 midterm elections likely have fed that perception, despite the fact that despite the historic shift of power from Democrats to Republicans, the rate of return for incumbents was extraordinarily high.[22] It is, therefore, fair to assume that though it is not the only motivating influence, re-election is among the highest priorities for most legislators.

If it is true that re-election is a (if not the) key motivation for many in Congress, it is reasonable to ask how that incentive might influence choices to delegate power in general, and power in foreign policy in particular. There are two broad ways in which the electoral concern might influence the delegation of power: There are negative incentives that encourage delegation and positive incentives that encourage delegation. The dominant negative incentive is fear; fear of being blamed for policy gone awry. Here Fiorina's "retrospective voting" analysis has been bolstered by those who explicitly target what R. Kent Weaver calls "blame avoidance" as a critical incentive driving the delegation of power to the executive and the bureaucracy.[23] Positive incentives, on the other hand, include decisions to delegate because of a desire to claim credit for supporting the president in a time of national crisis, a conviction that the Constitution actually mandates executive prerogative in foreign policy, and the belief that delegation—combined with innovative means of constraint—will produce better policy.[24]

Congressional Delegation: The Negative Incentives

In foreign policy, being wrong can have the highest costs. No one wants to be responsible for the death of American forces at home or abroad, and no one wants to be seen as undermining American security or prosperity. Opposition to a president in foreign policy carries a potentially high price tag, and one has to wonder whether the potential reward for being right is sufficiently high to counterbalance the potential cost. Since the Second World War, the traditional ethic in foreign policy has been that politics should stop at the water's edge, a popular slogan that "encapsulated the hope that diplomacy could be separated from domestic politics."[25] No doubt that ethic has been violated, sometimes for purely partisan reasons, but often out of real conviction that the policy being pursued by the White House was poorly conceived, or simply wrong. The reward, then, would be better policy, possibly saving lives and treasure. Nevertheless, given a public and a Congress inclined to rally 'round the flag, such opposition might well carry significant electoral costs.[26] The legislator's party leaders might punish any public opposition; and the legislator's constituents might well vote the legislator out of office. Retrospectively, this decision could simply be a punishment; prospectively it could well be motivated by concern about future unanticipated crises.

A cautious legislator might well wish to simply avoid taking a clear position, or better yet, delegate the decision—and the responsibility for making it—to someone else. The key consideration is that the legislator not be held responsible, or be seen to have poor judgment. Though being right could well bring honor and credit to the legislator, being wrong is far more costly.[27] "Politicians must, therefore, be at least as interested in *avoiding blame* for (perceived or real) losses that they either imposed or acquiesced in as they are in 'claiming credit' for benefits they have granted."[28]

To have supported the president (and the troops in the field) in a losing cause is far less damaging to a political reputation than would be the case if one were the person responsible for deaths or abandonment of allies—both charges being quite familiar to legislative opponents of every American military action ranging from the War of 1812 through the world wars, the Korean War,[29] the Vietnam War, and the Persian Gulf War of 1991.[30] When President Bush finally faced a congressional vote on his decision to use force to compel Iraq to leave Kuwait, he was able to win the votes he needed for many reasons but, as one senator noted, the key ultimately was that 500,000 American troops were in place, and the president "suggested that those of us who criticized this decision were endangering the troops he had sent."[31]

Blame avoidance certainly is attractive, particularly in questions of war and peace, but what of other areas of foreign policy? Again it is worth recalling that many foreign policy questions seem to have less salience with individual voters than do domestic questions. If we accept the claim that the electoral motivation is critical, the lack of a direct electoral connection will certainly lower the potential benefits of a strong congressional role in foreign policy, and clearly raise the potential costs of being held responsible for failure, whether the issue is weapons sales, international trade, debt relief or arms control.[32] Blame avoidance, as a negative incentive, would seem to contribute significantly to a congressional motive to delegate power and discretion to the president in foreign policy.

Congress, Positive Incentives, and Alternative Tools of Oversight

If legislators are powerfully influenced by their own calculations of how their behavior will influence their electoral support, it is fair to ask what these calculations will drive the legislators to *do* as well as what it will drive them to *avoid*.

David Mayhew argues that there are three "kinds of electorally oriented activities congressmen engage in—advertising, credit claiming and position taking,"[33] all designed to further a legislator's electoral hopes. Obviously, foreign policy provides opportunities to engage in all three of these activities. But, are these activities compatible with the delegation of power and responsibility to the executive?

Certainly, position taking, advertising, and general statements of policy are quite compatible, particularly for a legislator happy to tie him or herself to a political party, or one eager to be portrayed as loyal to the presumed national interest. Where the legislator can tie these objectives to a general philosophy about the Constitution, or the need for bipartisan foreign policy, so much the better. But what about credit-claiming? Is it possible to claim credit when you have handed off responsibility to another branch of government?

Delegation may seem a perverse method of claiming credit, but particularly in time of war or emergency, it can be a source of credit if the representative later can point to a successful outcome and proudly claim "bipartisan" support for the president in a time of crisis.

Beyond the electoral activities Mayhew describes, others have suggested different positive incentives for delegation. Among these is the production of good policy.[34] Here again the argument would hinge on the notion that foreign policy is different from domestic policy—more complicated, more delicate and less subject to negotiation or the give-and-take of an open legislative system. Delegation therefore is the gallant decision to put policy ahead of politics. The idea is to produce the best policy possible, and since it is assumed that the centralized authority of the executive branch is equipped to produce better foreign policy, delegation can be defended as the most direct means to that end.[35]

Still others have argued that in a changing world it is unreasonable to look only at simple votes in Congress to determine whether legislators have in fact abdicated their authority. Here the argument is that delegation is far more complicated than it appears. While formal powers may be delegated, Congress may well be able to maintain an active role in foreign and domestic policy determination through less formal, and therefore less quantifiable, ways. Legislators therefore replace formal control with innovative alternative tools of oversight. The incentive to delegate formal power, in this case, again is to achieve better policy or claim credit for effective policy, not by abdicating all power to the executive, but by building it through non-legislative innovations.

Though their work focuses on domestic delegation in general, and on the delegation of authority in the appropriations process in particular, Kiewiet and McCubbins' "abdication hypothesis" about congressional delegation seems to apply equally well in foreign policy. It is possible, they argue, "to delegate authority to others and yet continue to achieve desired outcomes. Indeed, it is often the case that desired outcomes can be achieved *only* by delegating authority to others."[36] Their argument hinges on the assumptions of management science where "delegation is not necessarily a dirty word" and where the effectiveness of the manager in question, or the organization in question is "determined not by how much authority is delegated, but rather by how well it is delegated."[37]

McCubbins and Page suggest a two-part analysis of delegations in their work dealing with delegation to regulatory agencies in domestic affairs. They suggest examining the structural arrangements of the delegation itself as well as the management tools that have been built in. Congress, they argue, can control its delegations by three structural devices: 1) Limiting the scope of any delegation by defining objectives; 2) by spelling out "the legal tools or instruments" that the executive agency can use "to implement the act," and 3) by spelling out the "procedures required to use the instruments." On the management side, they suggest that legislators have the ability to exercise control over delegation through the use of rewards and sanctions with the administration, and that they have the ability to use their oversight authority to hold hearings and engage in active monitoring.

Building on the third facet, legislators have tried to develop a number of innovative tools to constrain delegations of power. Some, such as the legislative veto, have been trimmed by the Court. Others, particularly less formal norms about consultation, are hard to track, and harder to enforce. Eileen Burgin argues that there are a range of tools running from informal devices, such as the passage of nonbinding legislation and demands for increased consultation, to political strategies, such as appealing to the press and public for support and working with various concerned interest groups to pressure the executive. There are also the more formal tools of hearings about and even lawsuits against the president, and, ultimately, threats to cut budgets. Most of these tools are reactive. Congress clearly delegates the initiative in foreign policy, and uses the innovations and tools to control or limit that delegation after the fact. And this is an important part of the problem. By moving from a policy-setting role to the reactive role of reigning in policies that offend, legislators have abdicated ultimate control, even while they may have increased a measure of day-to-day influence. Ultimately, Congress still has the ability to stop various programs and policies through the power of the purse.[38] But it is far harder to alter fundamentally the direction of policy, and even harder still to participate in shaping policy from the beginning. Furthermore, appropriations often can be a very blunt tool. "Sure, we can cut off funding," Representative Lee Hamilton said during 1995 floor debate on the repeal of the War Powers Resolution, "but it is very difficult to cut off funding beforehand because you want to keep your options open. [And] it is very difficult to cut off funding after the fact because the troops are already in the field."[39] Appropriations can be an effective tool only when legislators have the proper incentives to use that tool, and in war powers they may have more disincentives rather than incentives to use it.

Do these alternative tools make a difference? They can, but ultimately they are tools, not incentives. The presence or lack of incentives will really drive the decision to delegate—as it will drive the decision about whether to enforce any constraints on that delegation. Legislators may well feel better about delegation because they attach formal constraints as well as maintain the belief that they can and will exercise informal constraints. But when the constraints fail, legislators seem unwilling or unable to repeal the delegation. Witness the support for the War Powers Resolution, and the lack of support for its repeal; or look again at the oversight of intelligence affairs discussed above.

In the intelligence case Congress started out with a limited delegation, carefully structured, with reporting mechanisms built in, and ended up with a broad and ill-defined delegation of power and discretion to the executive. It is important to distinguish between tools and the incentives to use those tools. While it is true that modern governance may be impossible without broad delegation, and that broad delegation is acceptable to legislators because of the evolution of informal constraints, that only tells us that legislators may well be delegating with the best of intentions, but it doesn't tell us if, or when, legislators actually will exercise those constraints. And it does not tell us anything about the impact these formal delegations may have on the broader issue of constitutional interpretation in foreign and domestic policy alike.

Do Alternative Tools (and Positive Incentives) Work?

Legislators have been most successful in gaining power and influence in those areas of foreign policy that lie clearly within the constitutional authority of Congress, where the problems at hand are reasonably responsive to the tools Congress has at its disposal, and where the issues at stake have real and direct connections to the legislators' electoral interests. These three factors are critical in driving the congressional choice to actively participate or to delegate power to the executive (or, where delegation is seen as vital as it often is in trade negotiations, the incentive actively to use informal constraints to limit the needed delegation). By contrast, in areas such as war powers, intelligence oversight, and emergency powers, discretion is far more likely to be delegated, and even where innovative tools to constrain that delegation are present, they are far less likely to be actively engaged.

In war and emergency powers as well as in intelligence oversight, one can argue that legislators have the constitutional authority, but lack both the technical ability to take charge and the necessary incentives to maintain the needed level of interest. All three factors clearly are present, however, in the area of foreign trade regulation. Therefore, it is tempting to predict that if legislators can and will assert themselves in any foreign policy area, they would do so in foreign trade. But while they have altered the process and certainly increased their informal influence,[40] they have not profoundly altered the balance of power in this area, and they continue to delegate both power and responsibility to the executive.[41]

Foreign trade intimately and immediately effects most industries in the United States as well as having a direct impact on the prices paid by all consumers. Many lobbyists and all constituents, then, have a direct interest in foreign trade legislation, and increasingly constituents are coming to realize the impact these policies actually do have on their lives.[42] Legislators have asserted themselves in foreign trade, but that assertion has been focused almost exclusively on those measures that most directly concern domestic industries. In other words, legislators have successfully divided foreign trade policy into two halves—trade rules that have an immediate, identifiable, and tangible impact on local industry and trade, and trade rules focusing on foreign issues that only indirectly involve local commerce. In trade reform in the 1950s as well as in the 1960s and again in 1974, "Congress granted the President significant power, acceding to the President-dominant foreign policy aspect of trade."[43] The pattern set in the 1960s and 1970s has changed in the 1990s, but not across the board.[44] The point is that even in trade, where electoral interests are comparatively high, legislators have demonstrated that they will limit their role to what they perceive to be directly linked to those interests. If trade becomes electorally more salient, the congressional role may well rise—but even then, it is likely to rise in the informal, rather than in the formal sense. What this tells us about prospects for legislators to defend congressional prerogatives across the board in foreign policy issues generally is that it isn't very promising. This problem is compounded by the underlying impact these decisions have on constitutional interpretation—building a stronger case for executive prerogative, and vesting more and more responsibility for foreign policy exclusively in the executive branch.

What matters is not the innovations, nor the alternative means of supervising legislative delegations to the executive. What matters is whether or not individual senators or representatives decide that a particular issue is worth their time and effort; that they believe Congress is able to influence the result; and finally, that they believe Congress has the constitutional mandate to take responsibility. Finally, they must weigh the negative incentive of blame avoidance against the positive incentives of claiming credit and improving American policy—or improving the American policy-making system through innovative approaches to delegation.

The reality is that there are only a very few areas where individual representatives have the personal and political incentives to fight for legislative control. In those areas, they are largely motivated by electoral concerns. Where those incentives are lacking and—as Kent Weaver has suggested in his study of domestic affairs [45]—where there is a powerful negative incentive to avoid responsibility for errors in policy areas that are unlikely to offer any positive impact on election chances, there are strong incentives to get out of the way. Supporting the president in a successful policy is fine; opposing the president on a successful policy is dangerous; and being even partially responsible for a failed policy is potentially suicidal, in terms of re-election. So why do it?

Who Should Help Congress, If Congress Won't Help Itself?

The key to effectiveness lies in activity. If legislators want to control their delegations of power to the president, they certainly can do so. But delegation, accompanied by constraints or not, will be construed broadly by the Court and thereby bolster the president's claims to executive prerogative. The only alternative seems to be to ask legislators to do the impossible—to participate actively in foreign policy, to challenge the executive's claims to prerogative power, and to delegate only the bare minimum of power, and then only with strict, formal, and explicit limits spelled out in the legislation. It may be asking legislators to act against their own incentives. Is the only option then to continue to bolster the executive prerogative interpretation of the Constitution in foreign policy, waiting for the day when the Supreme Court might revisit its view of the delegation doctrine?

Legislators are capable of asserting their prerogatives, but very reluctant to do so both to avoid blame and because individual legislators, for various reasons, have decided that their time and effort are better invested elsewhere. Those who advocate an executive-centered foreign policy certainly would welcome this response.[46] But is it the best response for the American system and for American foreign policy? If not, and if legislators won't save congressional prerogatives, should another branch of the government intervene to bring Congress back into the process?

There may be another alternative, one that relies on neither good will nor the fortunes of Supreme Court appointments. The answer may lie in returning to Madison's own arguments about human nature in *Federalist* 51, but looking not at the Court or the Congress, but rather by thinking about the incentives that drive the president.

* * *

There are two broad arguments for trying to encourage Congress to assert its institutional and constitutional prerogatives. First, the failure to do so will do real damage to the American political system. Having too powerful a president will undermine the delicate balance of the American system of "separate institutions sharing powers" in foreign and domestic policy alike.[47] And second, bringing Congress back in will produce better policy.

The institutional structure of the Constitution is a delicate balancing of mechanical wheels and gears all predicated on a particular understanding of human nature. As Madison noted in his *Federalist* 51, this was a government that would use its own fatal flaws to guarantee its survival. Institutions were built to compete with each other. "By so contriving the interior structure of the government as that its several constituent parts may, by their mutual relations, be the means of keeping each other in their proper place,"[48] the founders built a system where competition and constraint were supposed to be assured. In many policy areas this has worked out remarkably well. The question then is have we simply evolved away from this competitive model or outgrown it in foreign policy—or has the evolution to a system with broad delegation and executive prerogative actually damaged the underlying system?

A no less significant threat is that changes to the system made in foreign policy ultimately will come to influence the distribution of power in the domestic arena. This will happen because the Constitution, which establishes and shapes the institutions of government as well as the procedures for policymaking, makes no clear distinction between foreign and domestic powers. Precedents set in one sphere can and do influence constitutional decisions in the other sphere.[49] Given that the justices of the Supreme Court have demonstrated that they will give broad leeway to the political branches and are unlikely to force a redistribution of power, the slow evolution toward a constitutional acceptance of the executive prerogative interpretation in the formal distribution of power is subtly but surely restructuring the American system. It is one thing to restructure the American system through debate, discussion, and formal revision through constitutional amendment,[50] and quite another to do so through the default of a steady accretion of power from one branch to the other.

The other way in which congressional delegation in foreign policy might be seen as damaging (and therefore worth redressing) would be if the trend could be seen as damaging American foreign policy interests. Here one enters a highly subjective world. There are many who sincerely argue that Congress plays far too great a role in the management of American foreign policy. In part this may be a realistic assessment of the policy process, but in part it may also reflect the general approval of the foreign policy preferences of the administration in power and the disapproval of what is seen as the alternative policy perspective emerging from Congress.[51]

When Congress plays its constitutional role in the policy process and refuses to acquiesce in the executive prerogative interpretation of the Constitution, it helps assure broad participation in the policy process, making it more likely that a policy able to survive the process will be less subject to criticism and non-compliance after the fact. "The inclusion of other views or interests," Robert Pastor argues, "not only increases the prospects of avoiding mistakes and forging a better policy, but it also gives groups a stake in the policy's success."[52] Public discussion of policy proposals can invigorate the process and help presidents avoid the pitfalls that often come from a closed process with limited input from like-minded members of the Administration.[53]

This raises the interesting point that with prerogative power comes exclusive responsibility. Presidents who have articulated and acted under prerogative interpretations to assert exclusive and secretive control of foreign policy also have lived to see flaws or failures of that policy come back to haunt them as they were assigned exclusive blame for a process they closed to outside parties as well as to Congress. The most obvious example likely would be the Iran-Contra debacle of the Reagan administration, where everyone, including some of the president's closest and most trusted advisors, were excluded from the decision-making process.[54] Counterintuitively, one of the strongest arguments for congressional involvement beyond the general improvement in the policy itself, may well be that it would be in the executive's own political interest to refuse to take full power (and therefore full responsibility) to set *and* execute risky or potentially costly foreign policy decisions.

Is It in the President's Interest to Force Congress to Reassert Itself?

As the previous chapter demonstrated, it is increasingly less likely that the Court will force a rebalancing of powers in foreign policy. If Congress won't protect its own prerogatives, and if the Court won't save Congress, and if there is reason to believe that the system requires (and is aided by) an active Congress, then we are left with the seemingly strange proposition that perhaps it is the president who can and should rebalance power and force Congress to play a role most legislators—most of the time—don't want to play.

This proposition ultimately hinges on the same set of questions asked above about Congress: Does the president have the proper incentives to voluntarily surrender power and force Congress to take a measure of responsibility in foreign policy? Should self-interest drive the president to share power with Congress? The rest of this chapter will try to demonstrate that the president has precisely that incentive and that it has been a profound error for presidents since the Second World War to assert and act on a prerogative reading of the Constitution. By *re*-interpreting the traditional interpretation of the Constitution in foreign policy as laid out in the first two chapters, the president actually will be able to conserve power, build a better reputation, and insulate the administration from some of the more hazardous risks of prerogative power (and exclusive responsibility) in foreign affairs.

Executive Incentives

There is no shortage of studies of the presidency, but despite the volume, it is a literature that focuses on the question of "how" rather than "why". Though we know a great deal about *how* presidents have pursued their interests and policies—where they have moved wisely, and where they have misstepped—we know very little about why they have made various choices about how they use their time and power. One of the earliest efforts to look at the modern president's incentives is still one of the very few efforts to do so.[55] In 1960, Richard Neustadt took a different tack on the presidency: to study it from the president's perspective—what were the choices presidents faced; why did they make the choices they made; what considerations drove their decisions, and what considerations had they ignored? Neustadt argued that the key consideration was to conserve personal power. For a president to be effective, he argued, the president had to be concerned with personal resources. The objective ultimately was to build and then exercise power effectively. For Neustadt, power in this sense was understood as influence; power was defined as "effective influence on the conduct of others."[56] Neustadt's book essentially made the case that to be successful, presidents had to exercise their power *prospectively*, worrying not just about the immediate issue, be it a test of will with Congress, a single bill or treaty, or a particular budget item. Instead, presidents needed to concern themselves with the longer-range effect. One example Neustadt cited in 1990 was Richard Nixon's decision to impound funds appropriated by Congress in 1973. For many, this was an example of the imperial presidency at its height. Here a president seemingly invaded the prerogatives of Congress, in fact one of the few powers (spending and revenue decisions) that the Constitution seems to most clearly delegate to Congress. But Neustadt's interpretation hinged not on the immediate victory Nixon seemed to have registered, but rather at how that battle advanced or retarded executive power more generally. To see this as a presidential victory, Neustadt wrote, would be "to confuse the first bite of invoked authority with longer-run effects on power prospects." According to Neustadt, Nixon fouled his relations with Congress just before the Watergate scandal broke with full fury. At the moment he most needed to draw on his resources of influence, he had fully alienated Congress. The impoundments were challenged by "a batch of lawsuits brought by congressmen, which overturned his more adventurous impoundments. He invited a restrictive statute that eventually deprived the Presidency of its right to impound in this fashion ever; all this for a short-run show of success. Power? Not in prospective terms!"[57]

If Neustadt is right, the critical incentive driving presidents is the conservation and effective use of power. Few have explored the incentives that drive presidents, and very few indeed have looked at the incentives that drive most if not all presidents with any of the detail of similar studies focusing on the incentives driving legislators. In large part this probably is the result of the available data. Each member of the House of Representatives faces election every other year; and every two years one-third of the Senate faces the voters. Furthermore, since representatives and senators are not constrained by term limits, it is fair to examine re-election as a fundamental incentive motivating their behavior throughout most of their career in Washington. For two-term presidents, personal re-election is a direct incentive for only half of their time in office.[58] Finally, there are hundreds of legislators—lots of data points—all simultaneously running for office, facing identical historical context and constraints. The presidency is another story. With only one president at a time, there is little in the way of comparative data.[59] Any presidential comparisons have to cross different historical periods. Unlike Congress, where hundreds of representatives cast hundreds of votes each year on identical measures, each president faces unique circumstances, and makes decisions which, though similar to those made by predecessors, certainly are not identical—making analysis difficult to say the least.

Though difficult, it is no less important to understand the motivations driving presidential behavior than it is to understand what motivates legislative behavior. Because the presidency is harder to study quantitatively, some have turned to more psychological approaches, but this too misses the point. If we are to understand how the institution of the presidency works, we need to explore common motivations and incentives, rather than focus exclusively on personal idiosyncracies. And though some psychological approaches have contributed to more general statements about the presidency, they have tended to focus on questions of success and failure (*how* presidents have used their power) rather than on the question of *why* presidents, in general, choose to use their power in particular ways.[60]

We know that presidents have gravitated toward foreign policy rather than domestic affairs (at least since the Second World War) in part because of greater constitutional latitude; in part because of greater public expectations, and in part because of a more compliant and cooperative Congress in this realm.[61] If this observation is largely (if not always) true, it is reasonable to ask whether this bias has achieved the objectives presidents in general seem to believe it will achieve.[62] Similarly, it is reasonable to ask *why* presidents since the Second World War have asserted, and then acted, under a prerogative interpretation in foreign policy. Again, one could hypothesize that presidents do this because prerogative powers allow them to achieve the ends they seek (whether they are policy objectives, public admiration, a place in history, re-election, support for the president's political party, or even in the hope of a spill-over in power from foreign to domestic policy). But if these are the motivations, it makes sense to ask two questions: 1) Does the strategy (the exercise of prerogative power) actually deliver the objective sought? and 2) If the strategy does *not* deliver the objective, is there another strategy that might?

If there is an alternative strategy that would be more likely to achieve the objective sought, it would be fair to assume that a rational person in the White House might be persuaded to opt for it. In this case, the counterintuitive strategy would be to share power, rather than assert exclusive authority. This is counterintuitive since most people likely assume that if a president seeks power, the rational strategy should be to assert or take as much power at each opportunity as is possible. But in fact, as both Neustadt and much research in the area of game strategy have shown, there are situations where a strategic retreat in the short term will produce gains in the long term, whereas a battlefield win at one moment will in fact powerfully sap the president's future resources and a short term power gain will translate into a permanent long term power loss.

If repeated re-election cannot serve as the key motivation (as many argue it does for legislators), what can be identified as a substitute? Whether it is specific policy objectives, ideological objectives, party objectives, or personal objectives such as a place in history, each choice a president makes will help determine whether or not these objectives are met.

The congressional literature argues that re-election is the key motivation since it is the necessary precondition to any and all other objectives whether they are policy-oriented or oriented toward personal power, institutional power, fame, or even personal gain (wealth).[63] Is there an equivalent precondition for presidents? Arguably there is, though it is far harder to identify and harder still to measure with any real precision. As Neustadt phrases it, the common precondition to the accomplishment of any viable objectives for all presidents is the development and maintenance of "effective influence." A president's "own prospects for effective influence are regulated (insofar as he controls them) by his choices of objectives, and of timing, and of instruments, and by his choice of choices to avoid."[64] One source of influence is the power of popularity. Even if the president is not interested in re-election, representatives and senators are, and a popular president can help or hurt their electoral chances. In this regard, Theodore Lowi argues that the emphasis on foreign policy has a fairly clear electoral connection.[65] Domestic policy is a losing proposition: Someone or some group will always be hurt, and ultimately a focus on domestic policy is a sure way to diminish popular support. Domestic policy is nearly always a zero-sum game where popularity with one group is always countered by the anger of another. This can come in hot-button issues such as abortion, civil rights, and affirmative action, and it can come in far less inflammatory areas such as agricultural price supports, environmental regulation, or school funding.

Foreign policy is a bit different. Foreign policy seems appealing since both success and failure actually can improve a president's standing. Success in foreign policy, particularly in national security areas, holds obvious appeal for any president. But failure? Well, not all failures. A president who promises what cannot be delivered may ultimately be made to pay for such folly in significant popularity losses. Disaster, however, can have the effect of causing the public as well as Congress to rally-round-the-flag,[66] and with the president as the national symbol, to rally-round-the-president.[67] In this case "a disaster can rally the American people just as effectively as a triumph."[68]

There is a problem with turning to foreign policy for a quick surge of popularity. Foreign policy is complicated, and a president can easily be bogged down in the long-term consequences of quick strikes. Furthermore, the rallying effect, though appealing, likely will fade as public attention returns to problems at home, rather than distant successes or failures.[69] Finally, the president has a surprisingly narrow window of opportunity to be effective in foreign policy. Discussing the electoral cycle, and the need to develop expertise as well as a reputation abroad,

William Quandt argues that "Presidents have little time during their incumbency when they have both the experience and the power needed for sensible and effective conduct of foreign policy."[70] While this cycle might well influence a president to turn to foreign policy when the rallying effect will have its greatest impact, it doesn't explain a president who focuses undue and consistent attention on foreign policy, nor does it explain why a president should try to assume sole responsibility for foreign policy through the assertion of prerogative powers.[71]

To understand the consistent focus on foreign policy, and the choice to assert prerogative power in foreign policy, it is useful to return to Neustadt, who argues that effective influence is the function of three factors: formal executive powers, reputation within the Washington community, and public prestige. As Neustadt puts it, effective influence stems from three related sources: a president's ability to persuade others that what the president wants is what they ought to do; second, that others believe the president can and will use power to achieve those objectives; and finally, that the president's public support is such that opposition to the president will be costly to the legislator's own goals and objectives including re-election, political influence, and good policy.[72]

If prerogative claims and the exercise of prerogative power enhance a president's reputation and public prestige, it is plausible to argue that the assertion of prerogative power is a reasonable strategy for a president to pursue. If, on the other hand, the assertion of prerogative power diminishes these tools of influence, then one might be tempted to search for an alternative strategy to achieve the president's objectives.

Evaluating the effect of the assertion of prerogative power on the president's professional reputation and popular prestige is a difficult proposition, made all the more difficult by the underlying assumption that this assertion of power came as an act of free will on the part of the president. Ultimately, Neustadt's argument hinges on choice—his prescription is that presidents "ought to think about their prospects for effectiveness as they make current choices—deriving either cautions for the future or guidance for the present. The better they think about power in prospective terms, the likelier they are to buttress future influence and also chosen policies."[73]

What choice does the president have, and what are the external constraints on that choice? From 1945 to the early 1990s, there were two sets of external constraints: 1) What had been delegated to the president, including the power to control America's nuclear arsenal and the responsibility to make the final decision on nuclear retaliation; and 2) the general atmosphere dictated by a constant perceived state of emergency where even presidents reluctant to focus on foreign policy were unable to avoid it, and similarly unable to resist the pressure to take sole responsibility for it. A clear example of the latter was Lyndon Johnson, whose Great Society program ultimately was undermined by the foreign policy choices and responsibilities Johnson seemed unable to escape.[74]

Just Say No?

When we think about claims of executive prerogative, we think of presidential usurpation, but that is only half the story. While presidents since Truman have claimed ever more power, Congress has thrust power upon them and the courts have sanctioned these delegations. A president who sought to maximize his or her influence would need to reconsider both the attempt to assert power as well as the effort in Congress to delegate power (and, therefore, responsibility).

By asserting prerogative power under a new interpretation of the Constitution, presidents since Truman have inadvertently added yet another dimension of power and responsibility to the presidency—the power and responsibility for interpreting the Constitution. Surely this always was a part of the president's job, but by explicitly asserting constitutional powers, the president has removed a layer of protection. Where once a president might have used constitutional disputes as a face-saving way to accede to the demands of Congress, the Court, or even strong interest groups, now presidents have placed themselves in the potentially uncomfortable position of *independent* interpreters of the Constitution, making it hard to back down from their own interpretation or earlier executive precedents. After all, if the president feels free to interpret the Constitution (and act on that interpretation), then it is hard to see how he or she can simply bow to a different constitutional interpretation offered by one of the other branches of government.

In the steel seizure case, Truman claimed that he could and would act under his own authority in accord with his interpretation of the Constitution, but in the end, he reluctantly accepted the Court's ruling that ordered him to reverse his decision.[75] Truman had argued that the executive's seizure power in a time of emergency was "inherent in the Constitution of the United States,"[76] and that "nobody can take it away from the President, because he is the Chief Executive of the Nation, and he has to be in a position to see that the welfare of the people is met."[77] Despite this strong statement of prerogative power, Truman was willing to abide by (if not agree to) the Court's interpretation of the Constitution and follow his pledge that if the Court ordered it, he would "turn the steel industry back to the companies, and see what happens."[78] Though he maintained that his was the more accurate reading of the Constitution, he abided by the reading ordered by the Court.

Since Truman, a number of presidents have argued that they have a constitutional right to prerogative powers in foreign policy cases. Among other devices that contributed to this turn of events was the increasing reliance on what is often called a signing statement. The tradition of signing legislation (making it law), but attaching an executive interpretation, or understanding, to that law, seems to have started with Truman. In 1946 and 1947 Truman attached his own interpretation to two labor laws. As Arthur Krock noted, Truman had "twice expanded in unusual fashion his part in the legislative process."[79] The objective was to establish an alternative understanding of the law should the law ultimately wind up in litigation. This approach has become a staple of presidential action, and it was particularly common in the 1970s as presidents consistently signed (and followed) laws that were predicated on legislative vetoes. Just as consistently, they attached signing statements disputing the constitutionality of the restriction.[80] As President Ford noted in signing the National Emergencies Act in 1976, "I support the purposes of the enrolled bill. One of its provisions, however, would purport to permit the Congress to terminate a national emergency by a concurrent resolution. This feature of the bill is unconstitutional." But, Ford added, he considered the veto provision "as separable from the rest of the bill, and would therefore expect the other provisions relating to emergency powers to remain in force."[81] Though the Court has fairly consistently maintained that signing statements in no way release the executive from executing the laws as written,[82] later cases indicate that the Court is willing to grant the president a great deal of latitude in the interpretation of statutes, barring the most explicit language from Congress.[83]

The proliferation of signing statements suggest that presidents are willing to increase their responsibility for the interpretation as well as the execution of laws—and with that, responsibility for often less than optimal results. These statements seem to contribute to the notion that the president not only is free to interpret the Constitution (as are all three branches) but, perhaps, is free to follow the executive interpretation, even when that flies in the face of the interpretation insisted upon by the other branches. If this comes to be seen as more than a simple tool of presidential power, but rather as a presidential *responsibility*, it seems likely to further constrain a president's flexibility and erode a president's potential for effective influence across the board in foreign and domestic policy.

This raises the argument that presidents would be wise to reduce their broad claims to power in the interest of securing and advancing their own interests, and in the interest of increasing their effective influence. There is also a second half to the story—not only should presidents be more cautious in their assertion of powers that carry undue responsibility with them, but they should be very suspicious of a Congress that willingly and even eagerly hands over its most precious commodity—power.

If Madison was right, the fear was that legislators would grab too much power, not that they would give it away. "In republican government, the legislative authority necessarily predominates." After dividing the legislative branch in half, to dissipate some of its power, Madison suggested that it "may even be necessary to guard against dangerous encroachments" by Congress against the other branches of government "by still further precautions."[84]

Madison's concerns were legitimate. He was right to believe that each legislator would seek to maximize his or her political interests, and that legislators likely would encroach on the powers of the other branches to do so. The irony is that by delegating power and discretion in foreign policy to the president, legislators were following a perfectly logical path to the increase of their effective influence in policy areas that mattered to them, and to the institution of Congress. The president, by accepting that power, discretion and *sole* responsibility, may well have been the one who failed to struggle for his own interests, and for the institutional interests of the executive branch.

To jettison power may seem incompatible with this concern, but it is not, if jettisoning symbolic and costly power in foreign policy ultimately weakens or distracts the other branch, and opens opportunities to influence or control power where it really counts (from the perspective of the legislator). The gift of power, in that case, is little different than the gift of a Trojan horse.

Could it be in the president's best interest to reject the huge delegations of sole responsibility that come with both the assertion of prerogative power by the president and the delegation of power and discretion from Congress? Theodore Lowi argues that "at a minimum, a rational President would veto congressional enactments delegating powers so broad and so vague that expectations cannot be met."[85] Would this have made sense over the past 45 years? The answer might be a qualified yes, a yes qualified by the pressure of the emergency environment within which both elected branches and the Court operated. But if it was a qualified yes before, now, in the wake of the end of the Cold War, it seems more convincing.

VI

Conclusion

10

Conclusion

The early chapters of this book argued that the executive prerogative interpretation was a radical departure from the founders' constitutional understanding and generally shared by most elected officials up to the world wars. This is not to say that constitutional interpretation was stagnant in that period, far from it. But there was a shared sense that the Constitution established certain parameters and divided power among the branches in such a way that the government was capable of energetic action, and yet unable to obliterate liberty. As Madison argued in *Federalist* 37, one of the hardest tasks facing the founders was their need to combine "the requisite stability and energy in government with the inviolable attention due to liberty and to the republican form."[1] This delicate balance was achieved in part by a complicated set of checks and balances, as well as by explicit limitations on each branch of government. This same delicate balance, which Woodrow Wilson referred to as the founders' mechanical theory of government,[2] was more than a simple set of procedures. The Constitution's mechanical process facilitated substantive objectives, imposing explicit as well as implicit limits and constraints. While the Constitution had to be interpreted and adapted to times and circumstances, there was a general understanding that those limits and substantive commitments did matter. When Jefferson reluctantly agreed to proceed with the Louisiana purchase despite his conviction that the national government lacked the constitutional authority to do so without an Amendment, he refused to adjust the Constitution through interpretation. He went ahead and made an exception, but made no effort to stretch the Constitution to fit his objective. Jefferson argued that the exception might be seen as just that, while a fundamental reinterpretation of the Constitution would have far more profound ramifications. "Our peculiar security is in the possession of a written Constitution. Let us not make it a blank paper by construction."[3] Though Jefferson may have erred in believing that his action would not be used as a precedent for the expansion of executive and national power,[4] he was quite right about the importance of constitutional interpretation.

One great difference between the various presidents before and after the 1940s has been their readiness to reinterpret the Constitution. Before the world wars presidents made exceptions to the Constitution, and certainly stretched it. After the wars, presidents articulated a new executive prerogative interpretation of the Constitution, significant because it increasingly has been accepted by Congress and the Supreme Court. That reinterpretation has been adopted in law and enshrined in precedent. The exception has become the rule. Any effort to move away from this will require more than a mere adjustment or evolution—it will require a whole new interpretation to emerge, rather than the more elastic adjustment to time and circumstance envisioned by the founders.

The Judicial Role in the Imbalance of Powers

The Constitution is a short document. "Its nature," Chief Justice Marshall wrote, "requires that only its great outlines should be marked, its important objects designated, and the minor ingredients which compose those objects, to be deduced from the nature of the objects themselves."[5] The Constitution shapes and constrains American foreign policy in direct and indirect ways. It has a direct impact in those clauses where it specifically delegates particular powers to particular branches. Indirectly, but no less profoundly, the Constitution shapes American foreign policy by establishing the institutions and methods of government that are built on the constitutional model. The Constitution creates a way of achieving policy objectives that limits and shapes those objectives. The Supreme Court, whose job it is "to say what the law is,"[6] considers both the constitutional process through which a bill is made law and the process by which that law subsequently is executed. And the Court also must judge whether the law violates the substantive guarantees written into the Constitution or its amendments.

The Court has developed a fairly consistent and coherent doctrine in foreign policy cases. The first consideration is whether the law in question violates any specific constitutional guarantees. Does the government have the constitutional authority to act as it has? If the answer to this question is yes, the Court must then decide whether the law was enacted and executed properly. While the government as a whole may well have the authority to act as it has, that does not necessarily mean that the president acting alone, or against the wishes of a majority of legislators in Congress, has the constitutional authority to act as he has. A review of the Court's experience in foreign policy cases reveals that the Court will intervene to police the process and to protect certain individual liberties guaranteed by the Constitution.

Over the past 200 years, the justices have come to accept the idea that the Constitution can be read somewhat differently when a case deals with foreign policy than when it deals with domestic affairs. This interpretation has no solid textual roots, for the Constitution clearly is a unitary document, designed to apply at home and abroad equally. But world events pushed the justices into seeing the Constitution somewhat differently in these policy spheres. In very recent cases the Court has made it clear that while the Constitution continues to apply to foreign policy much as it always has, the emphasis in interpretation is shifting. The judiciary in recent years has tended to read statutory restrictions on the executive very narrowly in foreign and domestic policy alike.[7] Unless the law explicitly forbids the executive from doing something, the Court is likely to give the executive broad latitude in the interpretation and execution of the law. At the same time, the Court has indicated as well that it will read the Constitution broadly when the president's actions are not covered by statute. The same justices, when domestic issues arise, are quite willing to read the Constitution narrowly. While this certainly seems incongruous, it has happened, and one must realistically consider that record in any effort to address a perceived imbalance between the branches in foreign policy.

Three recent cases illustrate the problem. In two immigration cases dealing with Haitian refugees and in a case dealing with the North American Free Trade Agreement, the judicial branch has reiterated its doctrine. One of the immigration cases found the Supreme Court justices engaging in a tortured decision, struggling to find a constitutional way to support the executive's policy of intercepting refugees at sea and returning them to Haiti; the second case overturned the government's processing system for refugees who had been detained at the U.S. military base at Guantanamo, Cuba. Both of those cases tried to maintain a clear distinction between foreign and domestic policy. The inability to maintain a clear foreign/domestic distinction was made clear in a third recent case concerning the North American Free Trade Agreement.

The two Haitian cases are most easily understood neither as immigration cases nor as questions of executive power in foreign affairs. Rather, they are best understood if we return to the Court's traditional approach to foreign policy. Recall that the Court tends to be least interventionist where the president and Congress act together—but that even where they do act together, the Court will intervene in foreign policy cases when individual rights are at stake. In the Guantanamo case, *Haitian Centers Council v. Immigration and Naturalization Service* (1993), the District Court for the Eastern District of New York ruled against the administration, holding that the government failed to provide due process to the detainees; that the detainees had been denied access to lawyers and other interested American citizens, violating the Americans of their First Amendment rights; and holding that the Attorney General was violating her discretionary authority under immigration law. By contrast, the Supreme

Court's ruling in a second Haitian case, *INS v Haitian Centers Council* (1993), upheld the administration's order to intercept boats of Haitian refugees and return them to Haiti. Here, despite claims of violations of American treaty obligations, U.N. resolutions, and the Refugee Act of 1980,[8] the Court held that the administration was free to enforce the executive order that directed the Coast Guard to intercept the Haitians at sea and return them to Haiti. Since the Haitians were intercepted in international waters, they were not entitled to individual rights protection or guarantees of due process that would be available had they landed on American soil. In a stinging dissent, Justice Blackmun admonished his colleagues for upholding what he saw as a clear violation of a U.N. treaty protocol[9] as well as the 1980 refugee statute, which reflected the protocol's commitment not to return a refugee to a country where he or she would face political persecution. In this second immigration case, the Court found a way to support the executive action largely through a tortured review of the language of the U.N. protocol, including an extensive discussion of the proper translation of the French verb *refouler*, which usually translates as "to return." The Court dispensed with the debate over the original intent of the signatories to the protocol through its discussion of French translation. The question of domestic legislation was far trickier, again suggesting the degree to which the executive prerogative interpretation has now become ingrained in American law.

In 1980 Congress amended the Refugee Act. This statutory change was directed at removing a great deal of the Attorney General's discretion to overrule deportation orders. The executive order governing the return of the Haitians on the high seas included a provision giving the Attorney General the authority, the "unreviewable discretion," to allow an alien to remain. While this would seem to fly in the face of the congressional statute, the Supreme Court majority maintained that legislators were only thinking about aliens who were already in the territorial United States. The Court then argued that a long-standing doctrine held that the Court will assume that "Acts of Congress normally do not have extraterritorial application unless such an intent is clearly manifested." Therefore it would be reasonable to hold the statute nonapplicable in international waters. The Court then held that this common interpretive presumption had "special force" when the Court construed "statutory provisions that may involve foreign and military affairs for which the president has unique responsibility."[10] This interpretation was too much for Justice Blackmun, who pointed out that "the presumption that Congress did not intend to legislate extraterritorially has less force—perhaps, indeed, no force at all—when a statute on its face relates to foreign affairs." Blackmun also rejected the notion that the president had sole authority here under his powers as commander in chief. "The suggestion that the President somehow is acting in his capacity as Commander-in-Chief is thwarted by the fact that nowhere among [the Executive Order's] numerous references to the immigration laws is that authority even once invoked."[11] The powerful message here is the Court's readiness to defend executive action as flowing from the powers of the commander in chief, when the president's own attorneys never even made that argument.[12] Here, in 1993, in a case with no military-security issues at stake, the Court found prerogative power where none was claimed.

The third case, also handed down in 1993, threw a temporary judicial wrench in the North American Free Trade Agreement. In the NAFTA case, *Public Citizen, Sierra Club and Friends of the Earth v. Office of the U.S. Trade Representative*, the District Court for the District of Columbia ruled that under provisions of the Trade Act of 1974, an environmental impact statement on the NAFTA agreement had to be submitted before the president could present the treaty to Congress. Here the District Court opened the door to congressional prerogatives in foreign policy. While the court conceded that it was the president's duty and power to negotiate foreign agreements, at the same time it held that "the power to regulate commerce with foreign nations is given to the Congress under the Constitution." The answer was that while it might be a violation of the separation of powers to order an environmental impact statement before the treaty was negotiated, once it was "a completed document, which has been signed and agreed to by the three heads of state," then to order the impact statement would not interfere in foreign affairs. Once the agreement was complete, the court ruled, the impact statement requirement would be seen as "a domestic issue, where an agency must inform the relevant decision maker, in this case the Congress, of the environmental consequence of a proposal for legislation."[13] Does NAFTA fall under domestic or foreign policy? Can we really say that once submitted to Congress, a foreign policy question becomes a domestic policy question?

At least two lessons may be drawn from the NAFTA case: 1) the Court increasingly will have to confront the overlap of foreign and domestic policy—a doctrine based on an artificial distinction between the two simply will not be able to stand as these areas become increasingly interwoven, 2) where Congress has the proper constitutional means at its disposal and the political tools needed to accomplish its ends and, most importantly, the proper incentives to act, the courts can and will support congressional prerogatives. But, as in the Haitian refugee case, in the absence of congressional action, or in the face of less than precise legislative language, the courts still will strain to give the president extraordinary latitude. The judicial branch is not about to save Congress, but should legislators attempt to assert their prerogatives, or should the president insist on congressional participation in foreign policy (and therefore on shared responsibility for foreign policy and for its domestic policy implications), the courts likely will be willing and able to adjust to this re-interpretation of constitutional powers in foreign policy.

Incentives to Rebalance Power

Whereas the Court reluctantly arrived at the idea that foreign affairs could be viewed somewhat differently than domestic policy, legislators have embraced that idea with enthusiasm. But why would legislators surrender power? Were the framers of the Constitution wrong about human nature?

The founders weren't wrong about Congress—actually, one could argue that they were far too prescient. Legislators very predictably continue to calculate their own interests and pursue power where their interests lead them. As a host of literature on the Congress has argued,[14] legislators understand their own electoral interests, and those interests largely, though not exclusively, drive their political behavior. Foreign policy is certainly of electoral importance in some districts, particularly those with large immigrant populations. But for most representatives, the gains to be had from a high profile in foreign policy issues is more than offset by the political price to be paid for opposing the president on questions of national security. As foreign and domestic policy become more interwoven, many legislators have discovered that they can gain electoral benefits by influencing foreign policy, without incurring the electoral costs that might come with control (and responsibility for that control) of foreign policy. With this rational calculus in mind, legislators often have been far more willing to delegate power or simply acquiesce in the president's exercise of power in foreign policy.

In the 1970s, the deference to the executive in foreign policy came home for two reasons: the electoral salience of American policy in Vietnam and the expansion of executive prerogative at home built on national security arguments. The war in Vietnam became one of the most dominant political questions, and at the same time, President Nixon began to expand the broad claims for prerogative in foreign policy that had been advanced by earlier chief executives, and to use those as justification for the exercise of prerogative power at home. As outlined in Chapter 4, Nixon argued that *since* the Constitution authorized broad prerogative powers abroad, the president logically should be governed by those same rules when he was attempting to achieve foreign policy objectives at home. Anything that threatened to destabilize domestic politics was, the president argued, a threat to national security, and thus should be governed by the constitutional interpretation that applied to foreign policy. The president's exercise of prerogative powers at home, combined with the growing outcry for an end to the war in Vietnam, led legislators to review the state of delegated powers in foreign policy. The first thing they did was to draft and pass a War Powers Resolution that was meant to restore a role for Congress in the decision to go to war or to place troops in situations where war was likely. In its original form, this bill narrowly and clearly defined those instances when the president might act without Congress. In those rare cases where the president actually was authorized to act on his own, Congress used the constitutionally suspect legislative veto as a device to reverse the traditional political burden. The new approach was that the president would be forced to withdraw troops unless Congress explicitly voted to extend their deployment. But the bill was compromised with the House to achieve the super-majority needed to override a likely veto from President Nixon. The final version removed the narrow definitions and limits on the president's use of force; it authorized a longer period of time for the president to act alone, and it included a severability clause that was designed to preserve the bill even if the legislative veto on which it hinged was ruled unconstitutional.

In the immediate aftermath of Watergate, Congress was infused with a large number of reform-minded legislators. They revised the seniority system of Congress, and with it the committee structure. They wrote a number of foreign policy laws, modeled after the War Powers Resolution, that strove to regain authority for Congress. These measures had varying degrees of success. But even in the most successful cases, they all followed the pattern of the War Powers Resolution by starting out as fairly rigorous, narrowly defined efforts that ultimately were compromised to achieve majority support. In the end, these bills delegated authority to the president in areas that had always been gray in the past. Where before a president had to act with care in these areas, cautiously laying out constitutional justifications for his actions, or appealing to Congress for specific authority or *post hoc* approval, now Congress explicitly delegated power to the president in exchange for monitoring provisions that often were tied to legislative vetoes.

Why these compromises came about is no great mystery. Unlike the executive branch, different factions in Congress must compromise to put together legislative majorities. These compromises are even more critical in cases where a presidential veto is likely, and Congress must be able to muster a two-thirds majority to override. But is compromised legislation the only answer? Even in the face of a truly divided government, with the Republicans taking control of both houses of Congress in 1994 while the Democrats held tenuously to the White House, the new majority in Congress was eager to pass constitutional amendments to provide the president with a line-item veto and to limit their own discretion by mandating a balanced budget.[15] And, in foreign policy, we found the new Speaker of the House and the new Senate Majority Leader eager to repeal the War Powers Resolution of 1973 to "untie the President's hands in using American forces to defend American interests."[16]

If the Congress does develop a sudden interest in reasserting legislative prerogatives in foreign policy, the most plausible routes are either the passage of constitutional amendments or the revival of congressional power through informal confrontation and negotiation with the executive. There is little reason to believe that legislators suddenly will develop a taste for the reassertion of formal authority through the enactment of veto-proof, narrow, explicit legislation, though this obviously would be the most effective option.

Constitutional amendment has its appeal,[17] but it was designed to be a difficult process, and so far the United States has seen only 26 Amendments ratified into law in more than 200 years. While it is conceivable that a crisis of sufficient magnitude in foreign policy could temporarily coalesce an overwhelming majority in the nation to press for and support an amendment that would clearly repudiate the notion of executive prerogative in foreign policy, it is highly unlikely. A slightly more likely amendment might revive the legislative veto. If legislators, as many do, believe that the president must be delegated broad powers in foreign affairs—be it in trade negotiations, troop deployments, or intelligence—legislators must find a way to delegate that discretion without eliminating a checking role for Congress. The method that was extensively exercised in the legislation discussed in previous chapters was the legislative veto. But that device, which had always been under a constitutional cloud, was ruled invalid in large part by the Supreme Court's 1983 ruling in *INS. v. Chadha.*[18] That ruling jeopardized the use of the legislative veto in an enormous number of laws in both foreign and domestic policy, crippling a useful and practical means that the executive had come to accept in exchange for the flexibility and discretion Congress had been willing to delegate. While there is no great swell of support for a constitutional amendment that would authorize the use of this or a similar device, it does have the added attraction of restoring a measure of congressional power in domestic as well as foreign policy, and thus perhaps the potential of attracting greater congressional support than would an amendment dealing exclusively with the balance of power between the two branches in foreign policy. Again, the most likely way to garner the needed support would be through a significant foreign policy crisis. However, given that neither the war in Vietnam nor the Iran-Contra scandal were able to generate constitutional amendments, it is improbable that such an amendment will be proposed, never mind approved and ratified.[19]

Even discussing an amendment to the Constitution presumes that there is a clear demand within Congress for a rebalance of powers in foreign policy. Such a demand is far from clear. Despite the Republican resurgence of the midterm elections in 1994, there is little reason to expect legislators to exchange short-term calculations of their political interests for long-term considerations of the balance of power. Senate Majority Leader Robert Dole announced at the opening of the 104th Congress in January 1995 that the Republican leadership in the Senate was determined to "take a close look" at a number of foreign policy issues, "in a manner consistent with our constitutional role to appropriate funds and to advise and consent on matters of foreign policy."[20] But this commitment, combined with the effort to repeal the War Powers Resolution, seems to confirm that the interest among legislators is in achieving a measure of influence in day-to-day policy results, and far less interest in reclaiming constitutional power (and responsibility) for setting American foreign policy.

A number of scholars have shown that legislators have found ways other than confrontational legislation to gain influence in foreign policy areas of concern to them and to their constituents. That influence does nothing to countermand the evolution and legitimacy of the executive prerogative interpretation, and the growing legitimacy of that interpretation has consequences not only for future confrontations over foreign policy, but for future confrontations in domestic policy as well.

The most likely scenario is the continued development of alternative avenues of influence combined with a stream of compromised legislation, legislation that emerges as a compromise between those who favor executive prerogative in foreign affairs and those who would like to eliminate as much executive discretion in foreign affairs as they possibly can. The argument favoring the passage of compromised legislation is that Congress must act, it must make a statement, even if that statement is a weak one. The idea is that any legislation is better than no legislation.[21] This book has tried to demonstrate that in many cases *any* legislation often is worse than no legislation, the reason having to do with the precedents set by compromised legislation and the role they later play in the development of the judicial doctrine in foreign policy. Compromised legislation contributes to compromised constitutional interpretation, and compromised constitutional interpretation can be and is set into law by judges interpreting the laws passed by Congress and executed by the president. When Congress delegates power to the president, it reinforces the prerogative interpretation. The expectation that the courts ultimately will interpret the law to favor a congressional interpretation is false and misleading. Members of Congress might achieve their objectives through narrow and tightly worded legislation, but the political incentives to generate that effort do not exist. If anything, the incentives that do exist seem to encourage the opposite strategy of compromised legislation tied to day-to-day policy concessions.

Presidential Incentives to Share Power

There is an imbalance of powers in the making of American foreign policy instigated by presidents of both parties, acquiesced to by legislators of both parties, and influenced and legitimated by a series of court decisions over the years since the world wars. If legislators have no clear incentive to reclaim their authority, and if we have no reason to believe that the justices of the Supreme Court are likely to re-craft constitutional interpretation in this area, then perhaps we should consider re-examining the executive branch.

The framers never suggested that individuals would seek to grab all power, but that they would seek to protect and extend the power of their offices. It may be that Congress has followed the blueprint rather well, and that it is the executive who may be in error. We need to consider the counterintuitive conclusion that it may be in the president's own best political interests to bring Congress back in—to rebalance power as well as responsibility.

The Court may be the final arbiter of what the law is, but it is not the only branch involved in constitutional interpretation. The Congress passes laws, and the president executes them. If a president chose to defer to

Congress in foreign policy, nothing in the Constitution would prevent this from happening. The founders, however, were confident that it would not happen. To make the American system work, Madison wrote, "The interest of the man must be connected with the constitutional rights of the place."[22] The president wasn't only expected to protect and expand the powers of the office of chief executive, he *had* to make that effort if the system were to work. The natural conclusion is that the evolution, articulation, and defense of the prerogative interpretation in foreign policy is a logical one that should be expected and even applauded. And yet one is forced to pause when one considers that this interpretation wasn't articulated in full until the 1940s, about 150 years after the Constitution was signed. American presidents functioned under a broad, traditional interpretation prior to the Second World War. While some of these executives exercised extraordinary powers in this period, these exercises of power were acknowledged by them to be extraordinary. Often they appealed to Congress for *post hoc* approval. But they never asserted that these were fully legitimate, prerogative powers delegated to the executive by the Constitution. The historical context of the Second World War and the emergence of the Cold War had a great deal to do with the appearance of the prerogative interpretation. But it is hard to imagine that any of the actions taken by the post–Second World War presidents couldn't have been taken under a more traditional interpretation. The switch was logical, though not inevitable. In part, these executives moved to a new view because of the context; in part because it facilitated their own flexibility, and in part because Congress acquiesced and even encouraged this view. With the Cold War over, one is tempted to ask whether presidents now will revert to the traditional interpretation. There are many good reasons why they should. The traditional approach forces the president to ensure broad public approval and, ultimately, congressional approval, both of which clearly add legitimacy to any executive act, and both of which can depersonalize policy and spread the ultimate responsibility and even blame for failed initiatives. But Madison and his colleagues in Philadelphia were surprisingly skilled at building a system that would encourage presidents not to share power, but to strive for it. The founders had a realistic, though ultimately positive, view of human nature. Ambition could not be eliminated, but it could be harnessed for positive results. "Ambition," Madison wrote, "must be made to counteract ambition."[23] Can presidents be persuaded that real power is more complicated than a daily scorecard, that often real power may result from coopting Congress, from forcing Congress to take responsibility for risky choices?

* * *

Is the prescription that a president should avoid all discretionary power, reject delegations of authority, and give away responsibility at every opportunity? Absolutely not. The prescription is an application of Richard Neustadt's advice. Presidents must consider their "prospects for effectiveness as they make current choices . . . The better they think about power in *prospective* terms, the likelier they are to buttress future influence and also chosen policies."[24] Before blindly asserting prerogative power or accepting the delegation of discretion (and with it responsibility for policies the legislators are happy to be rid of), each president should give serious attention to the costs these assertions and delegations entail. Will they ultimately advance the president's agenda, and improve the president's effectiveness in both domestic and foreign policy? Is there a better way to accomplish the same ends without the high costs that prerogative power and sole responsibility may entail? Where can presidents look for some guidance?

The easiest, most obvious, and least examined area is the past. It is vital to remember that the prerogative interpretation is less than 50 years old, and that there are other models for presidents to consider. Just as Woodrow Wilson reinterpreted the Constitution for his time and place, so too have the prerogative-power presidents and legislators done so for the past 50 years.[25] But Wilson's choices were just that—choices. They were not foreordained, and the evolution of a prerogative interpretation certainly does not mean that this is the only evolutionary direction constitutional interpretation in foreign policy might have taken. Now that the context within which the prerogative interpretation blossomed has fundamentally changed, it may be both useful, and politically possible, to return to the point at which these interpretative choices were made, and ask if a different evolutionary path—built on the same, shared, historical past—might be a wiser choice.

Building a new interpretation of constitutional power in foreign policy upon a *reinterpretation* of the traditional approach makes sense for the president for two broad reasons: 1) The world has changed profoundly in the past five years, and the end of the Cold War (and the impact that has had on nuclear strategy) is a sufficiently profound event that all three branches should reconsider their approach to foreign and domestic policy and the power that is needed to govern; and 2) even without the end of the Cold War, the prerogative interpretation along with the broad delegations of power, responsibility, and discretion to the Executive simply aren't working to the president's—or the nation's—advantage.

The prerogative interpretation represents a significant change in constitutional interpretation; it created and accepted an artificial distinction between foreign and domestic policy powers that has no clear basis in the Constitution itself, and it has the potential fundamentally to undermine the whole structure of government. For better or worse, American political institutions are predicated on competition. As Neustadt put it, "our Madisonian government is energized by productive tension among its working parts."[26] To collapse that structure—to delegate foreign-policy control to the executive while hoarding domestic-policy control in Congress—is to fundamentally revise the Constitution without discussion or debate.

If the system doesn't work, it ought to be changed, but it ought to be changed formally, thoughtfully, and thoroughly—not informally adjusted to the interests of particular people at one point in time. As long as we retain our political system and its institutions, all of which were built on Madisonian assumptions about the advantages of inefficiency and productive tension, then we must craft a constitutional interpretation of foreign policy that is consistent with, and able most productively to exploit, that system and those institutions.

* * *

There are two routes to effective foreign policy: prerogative power built on a highly centralized, efficient foreign policy mechanism; or a reinterpretation of the traditional approach to the balance of powers in foreign as well as domestic policy. Though the prerogative power approach might produce effective foreign policy, it fundamentally undermines the American political system. Just as the Constitution makes no formal distinction between foreign and domestic policy, the American political system as currently constituted is incapable of isolating foreign policy objectives from the underlying, fundamental objectives of the American political system. As Madison put it in 1792, "every word" in a constitution "decides a question between power and liberty."[27] Balancing those often conflicting yet interdependent objectives is the core function of the Constitution. If the commitment to balancing power and liberty no longer lies at the heart of the American political system, then the charter that governs, directs, and constrains that system should be openly and formally changed. If, on the other hand, the American political system still rests on similar commitments, then it is time to return to that charter and adjust our institutions and political practices so that they continue to serve that goal. To build an effective government, to achieve a *successful* foreign policy that reflects this overarching objective, requires that we strive to reduce the imbalance of powers in the national government, and recognize the degree to which constitutional interpretation shapes American foreign policy—and the degree to which foreign policy shapes American constitutional interpretation.

Notes

Introduction

1. A concept developed by Arthur M. Schlesinger Jr., (Schlesinger 1973, 1989).

2. Glennon 1990; Koh 1990; Henkin 1990; Henkin, Glennon, and Rogers 1990; and Henkin 1975 are among the very few books that have focused on judicial doctrine in American foreign policy.

3. *Washington Post*, 5 January 1995, A 10. This proposal echoed an earlier debate in Congress over the Bricker Amendment, a 1953 effort to regulate executive agreements with international organizations and, at the same time, to limit the treaty power, mandating that no law passed in pursuance of a treaty would be held constitutional if that law would not have passed constitutional scrutiny in the absence of the treaty. This episode is considered in Chapter 3, and is carefully analyzed in Tananbaum 1988.

4. The proposed amendment was attached to H.R. 1561, Fiscal 1996–97 Foreign Aid and State Department Authorization.

5. Gingrich, *Congressional Record*, House, 7 June 1995, H 5672.

6. The Bosnian debate in the summer of 1995 is particularly remarkable for the absence of argument over constitutional powers and constitutional interpretation—the focus of much passion in the debate over the repeal of the War Powers Resolution. See the *Congressional Record* for 26 July 1995 in the Senate, and for 1 August 1995 in the House.

7. Nunn, *Congressional Record*, Senate, 13 December 1995, S18494.

8. Cohen, *Congressional Record*, Senate, 12 December 1995, S18428, S18431.

9. This conclusion, that political problems require political solutions, contrasts with that of some legal scholars that the failure was poorly written statutes, and that the answer lies in better laws.

10. This case is discussed in detail in Chapter 2. See also Adams 1986 and DeConde 1976.

11. Abraham Lincoln, Special Message to Congress, 4 July 1861, printed in Basler 1953, 440.

12. T. Roosevelt 1914, 371–372.

13. Schlesinger 1973, 1989.

14. In the Pentagon papers case—*New York Times Co. v. United States*, 403 U.S. 713 (1971)—the Supreme Court refused to impose a prior restraint on the *New York Times*, and allowed the newspaper to publish what the Nixon administration claimed would be highly damaging documents about the history of the conduct of the war in Vietnam.

15. *Youngstown Sheet & Tube Co. v. Sawyer*, 343 U.S. 579, 637 (1952).

16. *Dames & Moore v. Regan*, 453 U.S. 654, 669 (1980).

17. Madison, *Federalist* 51 quoted in Rossiter 1961, 321.

18. *Immigration and Naturalization Service v. Chadha*, 462 U.S. 919 (1982).

19. Ripley and Lindsay 1993b.

20. Lindsay 1993.

21. Burgin 1993.

22. O'Halloran 1993, 284, 303.

23. See Silverstein 1994b.

24. Most recently in cases concerning the North American Free Trade Agreement and the status of Haitian refugees—see *Public Citizen v. Office of the U.S. Trade Representative*, 822 F.Supp 21 (1993); *Haitian Centers Council v. INS*, 823 F.Supp 1028 (1993); and *Chris Sale, Acting Commissioner, INS v. Haitian Centers Council*, 113 S.Ct. 2549 (1993). But the change in the Court's default doctrine has not been limited to foreign policy—in strictly domestic cases concerning administrative interpretation of statutes, the Court has shifted its default presumption decidedly in the favor of deference to the executive branch. See *Chevron v. Natural Resource Defense Council*, 467 U.S. 837 (1984).

25. Madison, *Federalist* 51 quoted in Rossiter 1961.

26. Lindsay 1994a; Burgin 1993; Ripley and Lindsay 1993; Lindsay 1993a. A thorough literature review on the subject can be found in Ripley and Lindsay 1992.

27. As discussed above, this tendency was evident even as the Republicans regained control of Congress in 1995 and immediately promised swift passage of a constitutional amendment to delegate line-item veto power to the president as well as a balanced-budget amendment and legislation to repeal the War Powers Resolution of 1973.

28. A powerful argument along these lines is offered in Eastland 1992. See also Cheney 1990; Crovitz and Rabkin 1989; Jones and Marini 1988; Tower 1981/82.

29. See Neustadt 1990.

30. Lowi 1985, 210.

31. Jefferson, in fact, advocated in one letter that the Constitution should expire with every generation, since it was his view that one generation had no right to bind a future generation. Jefferson wrote that he took it as "self-evident" that "the earth belongs in usufruct to the living," and "that the dead have neither powers nor rights over it." One can only speculate at his reaction to learning that the Constitution has survived to the end of the twentieth century with

just 26 amendments. See Thomas Jefferson's letter to James Madison, 6 September 1789, printed in Peterson 1975, 444.

Chapter 1

The quotation by Chief Justice John Marshall that begins this chapter is from *Marbury v. Madison*, 5 U.S. (1 Cranch) 137, 177–178 (1803).

1. *Youngstown Sheet & Tube Co. v. Sawyer*, 343 U.S. 579, 613 (1952), also known as the steel seizure case.
2. Madison, *Federalist* 51, quoted in Rossiter 1961, 323.
3. *Perez v. Brownell*, 356 U.S. 44, 58 (1958).
4. *Kennedy v. Mendoza-Martinez*, 372 U.S. 144, 160 (1963).
5. *United States v. Robel*, 389 U.S. 258, 264 (1967).
6. *Korematsu v. United States*, 323 U.S. 214, 246 (1944), Justice Jackson dissenting.
7. Madison, *Federalist* 78, quoted in Rossiter 1961, 465.
8. Madison, *Federalist* 37, quoted in Rossiter 1961, 226.
9. As Hamilton put it in *Federalist* 70 (quoted in Rossiter 1961, 423), "Energy in the executive is a leading character in the definition of good government. It is essential to the protection of the community against foreign attacks; it is not less essential to the steady administration of the laws. . . ."
10. Madison, *Federalist* 51, quoted in Rossiter 1961, 323.
11. *United States v. Curtiss-Wright Export Corp.*, 299 U.S. 304 (1936).
12. *Curtiss-Wright* was the subject of national debate in as recent, and as prominent, a forum as the 1987 House and Senate Hearings on the Iran-Contra affair, where Lt. Col. Oliver North argued that Justice Sutherland's decision offered legal support to his contention that the executive branch was acting constitutionally in the Iran-Contra affair. In a heated exchange, committee member George Mitchell rejected North's assertion. See: Testimony at Joint Hearings before the House Select Committee to Investigate Covert Arms Transactions with Iran and the Senate Select Committee on Secret Military Assistance to the Nicaraguan Opposition, 100th Cong., 1st Sess., 1987, Vol. 100–7, part II, 37–38.
13. *New York Times Co. v. United States* (the Pentagon papers case), 403 U.S. 713, 731 (1971).
14. *Marbury v. Madison*, 5 U.S. (1 Cranch) 137 (1803).
15. A full discussion of the case is presented in Glennon 1990.
16. *Little v. Barreme*, 6 U.S. (2 Cranch) 170, 171 (1804).
17. Ibid., 176
18. Ibid., 179.
19. Marshall's argument here foreshadows many of the arguments of the justices in the majority in the steel seizure case, discussed below.
20. Congress had authorized the seizure of vessels bound *to* French ports. Marshall acknowledged that such a law was easily skirted, and that the president's instruction to seize ships bound *to* or *from* French ports was far more likely to interdict the trade Congress sought to block. Although the executive's construction of this law was, Marshall wrote, "much better calculated to give it effect," the executive was, nonetheless, bound to follow the will and explicit instructions of Congress (*Little v. Barreme*, 178).
21. Ibid., 179.
22. In the 1882 case of *United States v. Lee*, 106 U.S. 196 (1882), the

Supreme Court unequivocally said that "No man in this country is so high that he is above the law," adding that "all the officers of the government, from the highest to the lowest, are creatures of the law, and are bound to obey it." Nearly 100 years later, in the case of *Nixon v. Sirica*, 487 F.2d 700 (1973), the United States Court of Appeals in Washington D.C. ruled that even the president "is not above the law's commands."

23. *McCulloch v. Maryland*, 17 U.S. (4 Wheat) 316, 423 (1819).

24. U.S. Constitution, article 2, section 2, paragraph 1; article 1, section 8, paragraphs 12, 13, and 11; article 2, section 2, paragraph 2; article 1, section 8, paragraph 18, article 2, section 1, paragraph 1.

25. *McCulloch v. Maryland*, 316.

26. Ibid., 316.

27. Ibid., 408.

28. Ibid., 408.

29. Corwin 1913, 58.

30. See *Worcester v. State of Georgia*, 31 U.S. (6 Pet.) 515 (1832). In *Worcester*, a Georgia law required those living on Indian lands to be licensed by the state. In an opinion by Chief Justice Marshall, the Court ruled this state law unconstitutional, leading to the famous rumor that President Jackson, having learned of Marshall's decision, said: "John Marshall has made his decision, now let him enforce it." Indeed, it never was enforced.

31. *Worcester v. State of Georgia*, 559–562.

32. *McCulloch v. Maryland*, 421.

37. Two lower courts ruled that the law was unconstitutional because it was not within any enumerated power delegated to Congress: *United States v. Shauver*, 214 F. 154 (E.D. Ark. 1914); and *United States v. McCullagh*, 221 F. 288 (D.C.Kan. 1915).

34. *Missouri v. Holland*, 252 U.S. 416 (1920). This was not the first time the Supreme Court had ruled that treaties might override state laws. Before John Marshall's time, the Court had ruled that a national treaty invalidated a Virginia confiscation law. And in *Hauenstein v. Lynham*, 100 U.S. 483 (1880) a Virginia law that allowed the state to take the estate of aliens dying intestate was struck down as conflicting with a treaty. See also *Martin v. Hunter's Lessee* 14 U.S. (1 Wheat) 304 (1816). See generally Tribe 1988, 266, n. 7.

35. *Missouri v. Holland*, 434. The Tenth Amendment reads: "The powers not delegated to the United States by the Constitution, nor prohibited by it to the States, are reserved to the States respectively, or to the people."

36. *Missouri v. Holland*, 434.

37. Ibid., 431.

38. This was far easier to imagine, no doubt, in an era before the term *interdependence* evolved.

39. See the discussion of *Little v. Barreme* above.

40. *Durand v. Hollins*, 8 Fed. Cas. 111–112 (case no. 4186) (Cir.Ct. S.D.N.Y., 1860).

41. Glennon, 1990, 75.

42. While Nelson assumed and argued that the president's orders concerned protection for American citizens abroad, Francis D. Wormuth and Edwin B. Firmage have argued that "What occurred was not what Nelson justified—interposition to protect citizens or their property from impending harm; it was reprisal for past injury, punitive rather than preventive" (Wormuth and Firmage 1989, 41).

43. *Legal Tender Cases*, 79 U.S. (12 Wall.) 531 (1870) (emphasis added).
44. Ibid., 533
45. Ibid., 554, 555.
46. Ibid., 582.
47. Ibid., 647.
48. Ibid., 664.
49. Ibid., 648.
50. Ibid., 604.
51. *Chae Chan Ping v. United States* (Chinese exclusion case) 130 U.S. 604 (1889).
52. Henkin 1976, 599.
53. *Oetjen v. Central Leather Co.*, 246 U.S. 297, 302 (1917).
54. See *Korematsu v. United States*, 323 U.S. 214 (1944).
55. *U.S. v. Curtiss-Wright Export Corp.*, 299 U.S. 304 (1936).
56. LaFeber 1987, 51.
57. Quoted from *Carter v. Carter Coal Co.*, 298 U.S. (1936), in Henkin 1975, 25.
58. Sutherland 1919, 20.
59. Ibid., 11.
60. Ibid., 21.
61. Ibid., 20–21.
62. *Curtiss-Wright*, 316.
63. While it is true that Sutherland did not make this claim explicit in his opinion in *Curtiss-Wright*, he did so in his 1919 book, where he wrote that "legislation may be in a sense *extra*-constitutional without being *un*constitutional." His argument in the Court opinion clearly depends upon such a reading. See Sutherland 1919, 55 (emphasis added).
64. Sutherland 1919, 46. Sutherland repeated this argument in *Curtiss-Wright* where he wrote: "The two classes of powers are different, both in respect of their origin and their nature. The broad statement that the federal government can exercise no powers except those specifically enumerated in the Constitution, and such implied powers as are necessary and proper to carry into effect the enumerated powers, is categorically true only in respect of our internal affairs." *Curtiss-Wright*, 315–316.
65. Henkin 1975, 25–26.
66. *Curtiss-Wright* served as an important foundation for the Court's rulings in challenges to foreign policy executed via executive agreements rather than by treaty in, among other cases, *United States v. Belmont*, 301 U.S. 324 (1937) and *United States v. Pink*, 315 U.S. 203 (1942), both of which concerned the Litvinov Agreement between the United States and the Soviet Union dealing with outstanding property claims on both sides.

Sutherland's conception of a government of limited powers at home and a government of limited restraints abroad seems to grow out of an earlier distinction between state and federal authority. As Laurence Tribe has written, in granting Congress domestic power, the Constitution "simultaneously limits it: An act of Congress is invalid unless it is affirmatively authorized under the Constitution. State actions, in contrast, are valid as a matter of federal constitutional law unless *prohibited*, explicitly or implicitly, by the Constitution" (Tribe 1988, 298).

67. The Court's distinction among cases where the president acts alone, acts with Congress, or acts against Congress was most clearly drawn by Justice Jack-

son in his concurrence in the steel seizure case, *Youngstown Sheet & Tube Co. v. Sawyer.*

68. LaFeber 1987, 54.

Chapter 2

1. T. Roosevelt 1914, 372.

2. Taft 1916, 139.

3. Among many examples, consider Theodore Roosevelt's response to the charge that his taking of the Panama Canal was unconstitutional: "There was much accusation about my having acted in an 'unconstitutional' manner—a position which can be upheld only if Jefferson's action in acquiring Louisiana be also treated as unconstitutional" (T. Roosevelt 1914, 526).

4. Thomas Jefferson, First Annual Message to Congress, 8 December 1801, quoted in from: Bergh 1907, 3:329.

5. This wasn't exactly what had happened. In fact, the ships had acted under orders from the Secretary of the Navy that should the Commodore on the scene judge that "the Barbary powers have declared war against the United States," then he was to distribute his forces "so as best to protect our commerce and chastise their insolence—by sinking, burning, or destroying their ships and vessels wherever you shall find them" (Goldsmith 1974, 1:376).

6. See Ellis and Wildavsky 1989, 72.

7. Jefferson letter to William Dunbar, 17 July 1803, quoted in DeConde 1976, 181.

8. Jefferson to Thomas Paine, 18 August 1803, quoted in Ford 1905, 10:8.

9. Albert Gallatin to Thomas Jefferson, 13 January 1803, quoted in Adams 1879, 1:113. This rationale was revived by Justice Sutherland in *United States v. Curtiss-Wright*, one of the seminal foreign policy cases before the Supreme Court. See the extensive discussion of this case in Chapter 1.

10. Albert Gallatin to Thomas Jefferson, 13 January 1803, quoted in Adams 1879, 1:114. Gallatin would go on to lead the attack against President Polk's exercise of executive power in the Mexican-American War. See Gallatin 1847.

11. Jefferson to Senator William C. Nicholas, 7 September 1803, quoted in Goldsmith 1974, 1:445–446.

12. Jefferson to John Breckinridge, 12 August 1803, quoted in Bergh 1907, 10:420.

13. Adams 1986, 363.

14. See *Gilchrist et al v. Collector of Charleston*, 10 Fed. Cas. 355; 5 Hughes 1 (case no. 5,420), 28 May 1808, and *United States v. Hoxie*, 26 Fed. Cas. 397; 1 Paine 265 (case no. 15,407), Oct. 1808.

15. Casper 1995, 496.

16. In an 1837 letter to Andrew Jackson, Polk praised President Van Buren for his strict construction of the Constitution. The president, Polk wrote, "possesses no discretion; he cannot alter or change a law of Congress, but is bound to see it faithfully executed as he finds it" James K. Polk to Andrew Jackson, 14 June 1837, quoted in Weaver 1977, 4 (1837–1838): 143.

17. John Tyler to the House of Representatives, 19 June 1844, quoted in Richardson 1908, 4:323.

18. McCoy 1960, 87–88.

19. Nevins 1929, 83 n.

20. Ibid., 87 n.

21. Herndon wrote that should Congress be silent, it was the president's duty as commander in chief to meet any necessity and to protect the country, even if to do so required that he send the Army "into the very heart of Mexico" to prevent the invasion. (Letter from William Herndon to Abraham Lincoln reprinted in Goldsmith 1974, 2:875).

22. Abraham Lincoln to William Herndon, 15 February 1848, quoted in Basler 1953, 451.

23. James K. Polk, Special Message to Congress, 11 May 1846, quoted in Richardson 1908, 4:443.

24. See: *The Prize Cases*, 67 U.S. (2 Black) 635, 638 (1863), discussed in Chapter 1.

25. One other oft-cited, and misunderstood, precedent was John Adams and his role in the "Quasi-War of 1798." As Dean Alfange (1994) well explains, Adams' approach and actions fit well within the broad contours of the traditional interpretation laid out in this chapter.

26. Message to Congress in special session, 4 July 1861, quoted in Basler 1953, 4:428.

27. Ibid., 430.

28. Ibid., 430.

29. Ibid., 431.

30. Ibid., 429.

31. Letter to Governor Horatio Seymour, 7 August 1863, responding to the governor's complaint that some New York districts were unfairly burdened by the draft, quoted in Basler 1953, 6:370.

32. Letter on emancipation to Salmon P. Chase, 2 Sept. 1863, quoted in Basler 1953, 6:429.

33. Schlesinger 1989, 458.

34. Rossiter 1948, 231.

35. Taft 1916, 147.

36. Ibid., 148.

37. T. Roosevelt 1914, 372.

38. Ibid., 372.

39. Before the Constitution was enacted, Wilson argued that "The United States have general rights, general powers, and general obligations, not derived from any particular States, nor from all the particular States taken separately; but resulting from the union of the whole" (quoted in Willoughby 1929, 1:80).

40. Ibid., 81.

41. Ibid., 80.

42. T. Roosevelt 1914, 373.

43. Ibid., 524.

44. Ibid., 524.

45. Quoted in Goldsmith 1974, 2:1239.

46. In his autobiography, Roosevelt contrasted his own views of the presidency—which he labeled the Lincoln-Jackson school—with those presidents, like Taft, who "took the opposite . . . narrowly legalistic view that the President is the servant of Congress rather than that of the people, and can do nothing, no mat-

ter how necessary it be to act, unless the Constitution explicitly commands the action" (T. Roosevelt 1914, 378).

47. Taft 1916, 78.

48. "[H]e shall take care that the laws be faithfully executed"—U.S. Constitution, article 2, section 3.

49. Taft 1916, 88.

50. Ibid., 139.

51. Ibid., 145 (emphasis added).

52. Woodrow Wilson address at the Woman Suffrage Convention, Atlantic City, 8 September 1916, printed in Baker and Dodd 1925–1927, 2:298.

53. W. Wilson 1908, 56.

54. Ibid., 70.

55. Ibid., 71.

56. Opinion of the attorney general, cited in Small 1932, 61.

57. Woodrow Wilson address to Congress, 26 February 1917. Printed in Baker and Dodd, 1925–1927, 2:431. Among the many statutes delegating extraordinary power to the president were the Lever Act and the Overman Act.

58. As he put it in an address in 1912, "[T]he place where the strongest will is present will be the seat of sovereignty. If the strongest will is present in Congress, then Congress will dominate the Government; if the strongest guiding will is in the Presidency, the President will dominate the government; if a leading and conceiving mind like Marshall's presides over the Supreme Court of the United States, he will frame the Government, as he did" (Woodrow Wilson, address to Economic Club of New York, 23 May 1912, printed in Link 1966, 416–417).

59. Franklin D. Roosevelt, remarks at the opening of the New York World's Fair, 30 April 1939, printed in F.D. Roosevelt 1938–1950, 1939:298.

60. Franklin D. Roosevelt, in a press conference, 8 August 1939. From F.D. Roosevelt 1938–1950, 1939:428–429 (emphasis added).

61. Ibid., 520.

62. Edward Corwin argues that the destroyer deal was a conspicuous exception to FDR's fidelity to a more traditional interpretation of executive powers in foreign affairs that he had exercised prior to the enactment of the Lend-Lease legislation in 1941. See Corwin 1947, 33.

63. *Opinions of the Attorneys General*, 39 Op.A.G. 484, 488 (27 August 1940).

64. Rossiter 1948, 270.

65. Corwin 1947, 29.

66. The Court might have been expected to treat Lend-Lease much as it treated the extraordinary delegation of authority in the National Industrial Recovery Act—where Justice Cardozo argued that Congress had exceeded its constitutional authority to delegate its own power. See *Schechter Poultry Corp. v. United States*, 295 U.S. 495 (1935). But, as argued in the previous chapter, the Court is particularly generous in its acceptance of the delegation of power in foreign affairs when Congress and the president act together and no individual liberties are directly infringed.

67. Franklin D. Roosevelt, radio address, 11 September 1941. Printed in F.D. Roosevelt 1938–1950, 1941:390.

68. Ibid., 391 (emphasis added).

69. Ibid., 391.

70. Franklin D. Roosevelt, message to Congress, 7 September 1942, printed in F.D. Roosevelt, 1938–1950, 1942:357.

71. Ibid., 364.

Chapter 3

1. Harry S Truman, news conference, 2 March 1950, published in *Public Papers of the Presidents of the United States: Harry S Truman,* 1 vol., (Washington, D.C.: GPO, 1965), 183.

2. Harry S Truman, address to joint session of the United States Congress, *Congressional Record*, House, 25 May 1946, H 5753.

3. New Jersey Representative Eaton reflected a common theme when he took the floor moments after Truman's speech to say that "I stood by the President of the United States in time of war, as was my duty as a citizen, and I am going to stand by the President of the United States in this time of civil war, which this situation amounts to"—*Congressional Record*, House, 25 May 1946, H 5756.

4. Senator Robert LaFollette of Wisconsin, *Congressional Record*, Senate, 29 May, 1946, S 5900.

5. Ibid., 5899.

6. *Congressional Record*, House, 25 May 1946, H 5752.

7. For a full list of amendments offered and their disposition, see the narrative provided in *Congressional Quarterly* 2, No. 2: April–June 1946 (Washington, D.C.: Press Research Inc., 1946) 298–307.

8. *Congressional Record*, Senate, 27 June 1950, S 9228.

9. "Authority of the President to Repel the Attack in Korea", Department of State Memorandum of 3 July 1950; *Department of State Bulletin*, 31 July 1950, 173.

10. Ibid., 176.

11. See Fisher 1995a.

12. Quoted by Senator Robert Taft, *Congressional Record*, Senate, 5 January 1951, S 57.

13. "Although I should be willing to vote to approve the President's new policy as a policy, and give support to our forces in Korea, I think it is proper and essential that we discuss at this time the right and power of the President to do what he has done" (Senator Robert Taft, *Congressional Record*, Senate, 28 June 1950, S 9322).

14. Senator Paul H. Douglas, Congressional Record, Senate, 5 January 1951, S 61.

15. Senator Scott Lucas, *Congressional Record*, Senate, 28 June 1950, S 9328.

16. Senator Wayne Morse, *Congressional Record*, Senate, 27 June 1950, S 9231. Morse was one of only two votes in both houses of Congress against the Tonkin Gulf Resolution.

17. Paige 1968, 149.

18. President Truman, in a news conference, 11 January 1951, published in *Public Papers of the Presidents*, Harry S Truman, 1951, 19.

19. "Powers of the President to Send Armed Forces Outside the United States," a report for the Senate Joint Committee of the Committee on Foreign

Relations and the Committee on Armed Services. 82d Congress, 1st Session, 28 February 1951, 3.

20. *Public Papers of the Presidents*: Harry S Truman, 1951. Press conference, 11 January 1951, 22.

21. For a fine review of these options, see Marcus 1977, particularly pages 58–83.

22. Truman 1956, 472–473.

23. Reporter: "You said on a previous occasion on the same subject, that you would abide by whatever . . . decision the Supreme Court handed down." President Truman: "That is exactly what I expect to do" (*Public Papers of the Presidents*, Harry S Truman, 1952, 363).

24. Ibid., 413.

25. Truman 1956, 478.

26. *The Public Papers and Messages of Franklin D. Roosevelt*, (New York: Harper & Bros., 1950) 1942:357. For a discussion of Roosevelt's speech, see Chapter 2.

27. "Remarks at a Meeting of an Orientation Course Conducted by the CIA," *Public Papers of the Presidents*, Harry S Truman, 21 November 1952, 1061.

28. Truman, "State of the Union Address," 7 January 1953, printed in *New York Times*, 8 January 1953, 10.

29. *Congressional Record*, Senate, 5 January 1951, 55.

30. Dwight D. Eisenhower, press conference, 10 March 1954 in *Public Papers of the Presidents of the United States: Dwight D. Eisenhower*, 1 vol. (Washington, D.C.: GPO, 1960), 306.

31. See Tananbaum 1988, 200.

32. News conference, 17 March 1954, Dwight D. Eisenhower, *Public Papers of the Presidents*, 1954: 324.

33. Eagleton 1974, 87. How the Eisenhower administration developed and tested various policy options in Indochina is exhaustively studied in Billings-Yun 1988 and in Burke and Greenstein 1989.

34. *Missouri v. Holland*, 252 U.S. 416, 434–435 (1919).

35. An excellent analysis of the Bricker Amendment is offered in Tananbaum 1988.

36. Senate Joint Resolution 1, as reported by the Senate Judiciary Committee on 15 June 1953. Printed in Tananbaum, 1988, appendix F, 224.

37. In a news conference in 1954, Eisenhower said "I suppose if you were going to class me as anything else, you would class me as a States' Rights [advocate]" (news conference, 13 January 1954 published in Dwight D. Eisenhower, *Public Papers of the Presidents*, 1954:52.

38. News conference, 3 February 1954, Eisenhower, *Public Papers of the Presidents*, 1954:225.

39. The Middle East Resolution said that "the United States regards as vital to the national interest and world peace the preservation of the independence and integrity of the nations of the Middle East. To this end, if the President determines the necessity thereof, the United States is prepared to use armed forces to assist any nation . . . requesting assistance against armed aggression. . . .The President is hereby authorized to use . . . up to $200 million from any appropriation now available for carrying out the provisions of the Mutual Security Act of 1954." (*Congressional Record*, Senate, 19 February 1957, S 2231).

40. Senate, Committee on Foreign Relations, *Hearings on the President's Proposal on the Middle East*, 85th Cong, 1st Sess. January and February 1957, 326.

41. See exchange in the *Congressional Record*, Senate, 27 January 1955, S 819.

42. J. William Fulbright, Senate speech, 24 January 1957, printed in Branyan and Larsen 1971, 716.

43. *Senate hearings on the president's proposal in the Middle East*, 326.

44. *Congressional Record*, Senate, 27 January 1955, S 842.

45. The important role statutory language has played in constitutional interpretation in the courts is examined in Chapter 8.

46. *Congressional Record*, House, 25 January 1955, H 667.

47. *Congressional Record*, Senate, 25 February 1957, S 2518.

48. Senator Lyndon B. Johnson, *Congressional Record*, Senate, 19 February 1957, S 2241.

49. Representative Chet Holifield, *Congressional Record*, House, 25 January 1955, H 674.

50. Request by President John F. Kennedy to Congress for standby authority to call up reserves, 7 September 1962, reprinted in Larson 1986, 20.

51. Senate, Joint Hearing by the Committee on Foreign Relations and the Committee on Armed Services on *The Situation in Cuba*, Monday, 17 September 1962 (Washington, D.C.: GPO, 1962) 35.

52. *Situation in Cuba*, 36.

53. News conference, 13 September 1962 printed in *Public Papers of the Presidents of the United States: John F. Kennedy* (Washington, D.C.: GPO, 1963) 1962:679. In *The Imperial Presidency*, Schlesinger notes that "Kennedy attached no great importance to the exercise [the passage of the Cuba resolution] and did not refer to the resolution when it came time to act" (Schlesinger 1989, 175).

54. Address to a meeting of the American Foreign Service Association, 2 July 1962, printed in *Public Papers of the Presidents*, John F. Kennedy, 1962:532.

55. Sorensen 1965, 702.

56. Senator John F. Kennedy, "The Challenges of the Modern Presidency," address to the National Press Club, 14 January 1960, printed in Goldsmith 1974, 1621.

57. Kennedy speech to National Press Club, 14 January 1960, printed in Goldsmith 1974, 1623 (emphasis added).

58. John F. Kennedy, address to the nation, 22 October 1962, printed in Larson 1986, 61.

59. Schlesinger 1989, 176 (emphasis in original).

60. For a discussion of the use and misuse of historical lessons in political decision-making, see Neustadt and May 1986.

61. Schlesinger 1989, 176.

Chapter 4

1. The Tonkin Gulf Resolution, printed in *Congressional Record*, Senate, 7 August 1964, S 18471.

2. *Congressional Record*, House, 7 August 1964, H 18452.

3. Ibid., p 18457.

4. Lyndon B. Johnson, news conference, 26 February 1966; printed in *Pub-*

lic Papers of the Presidents of the United States: Lyndon B. Johnson, 2 vols. (Washington, D.C.: GPO, 1967), 1966:222.

5. Quoted in Lofgren 1986, 221.

6. News conference, 18 August 1967: *Public Papers of the Presidents*, Lyndon B. Johnson, 1967:794.

7. *Congressional Record*, Senate, 6 August 1964, S 18403.

8. Senate, Committee on Foreign Relations, *Hearing on U.S. Commitments to Foreign Powers*, 90th Cong. 1st sess., August and September 1967, 139.

9. Ibid., 153.

10. Special Message to Congress on U.S. Policy in Southeast Asia, 5 August 1964, printed in Lyndon B. Johnson, *Public Papers of the Presidents*, 1963–64: 91 (emphasis added).

11. News conference, 18 August 1967, printed in Lyndon B. Johnson, *Public Papers of the Presidents*, 1967:794.

12. Senate *Hearing on U.S. Commitments to Foreign Powers*, 140–141.

13. Representative H. R. Gross, *Congressional Record*, House, 7 August 1964, H 18546.

14. *Congressional Record*, Senate, 7 August 1964, S 18433.

15. *Congressional Record*, Senate, 26 February 1957, S 2595.

16. U.S. Congress, Senate, Committee on Foreign Relations and Committee on Armed Services, *Joint Hearing on the Southeast Asia Resolution*, 88th Cong., 2nd sess., 6 August 1964, 3.

17. Congressman Dante Fascell, *Congressional Record*, House, 7 August 1964, H 18549.

18. Senate, *Hearings on U.S. Commitments to Foreign Powers*, 1967, 170.

19. *Congressional Record*, Senate, 7 August 1964, S 18445.

20. *New York Times* editorial, reprinted in the *Congressional Record*, Senate, 14 May 1965, S 10578.

21. The role of electoral and political incentives in constitutional interpretation in foreign policy will be discussed in Chapter 9.

22. Senate, Committee on Foreign Relations, *Report on National Commitments to Accompany S.Res. 85*, 91st Cong., 1st sess., 16 April 1969, 7–8.

23. For a detailed account of the legislative pattern, please see Chapters 6 and 7.

24. The 19 September 1968 speech by Nixon is quoted in Kutler 1990, 130–131.

25. While Nixon wasn't the first president to order such wiretaps (every president from FDR to Nixon had ordered some), he was the only one who went to court to argue for the president's right to do so.

26. Senator McGee, *Congressional Record*, Senate, 20 June 1969, S 16756.

27. Senate, *Report on National Commitments*, minority report, 42.

28. *Congressional Record*, Senate, 25 June 1969, S 17215.

29. *Congressional Record*, Senate, 20 June 1969, S 16748.

30. Ibid., 16779.

31. Letter to Senator Fulbright from William B. Macomber, Jr., Assistant Secretary of State for Congressional Relations, 10 March 1969. Printed as an appendix to the Senate *Report on National Commitments*, 37.

32. Nixon 1978, 382.

33. Richard Nixon, quoted in Schlesinger 1989, 187.

34. Schlesinger 1989, 194.

35. Rehnquist 1970, 628.

36. Ibid., 632.

37. Ibid., 636–637.

38. Nixon quoted in Schlesinger 1989, 194.

39. Nixon 1978, 468.

40. *New York Times*, "Challenge to Nixon on Power to Make War," 17 May 1970, 1.

41. Presidential address on the Watergate investigation, 15 August 1973, printed in Boyan 1976, 4:43.

42. *United States v. Smith*, 321 F.Supp. 424, 426 (1971), emphasis added.

43. Wire Interception and Interception of Oral Communications, 18 U.S.C. sections 2510–2520, 90th Congress, 2d sess., 19 June 1968.

44. Omnibus Crime Control and Safe Streets Act of 1968, printed in Boyan 1976, 4:11.

45. *United States v. United States District Court*, 407 U.S. 297, 303 (1971), emphasis added.

46. The Nixon administration had turned the language around. Traditionally we speak of government powers, and the rights of individual citizens. "However, the officers of the Nixon administration had fallen into the habit of defending their 'right' to take this or that government action. . . . The President referred, for example, to his 'right' to appoint Supreme Court Justices. . . . At the same time, the President had become worried about the 'powers' of the citizens and of the press" (Shell 1976, 157).

47. Congress "shall have Power to lay and collect taxes, duties, imposts and excises, to pay the debts and provide for the common defense and general welfare. . . . To borrow money on the credit of the United States. . . . to regulate commerce. . . . [and] No money shall be drawn from the Treasury, but in consequence of appropriations made by law," U.S. Constitution, article 1, sections 8 and 9.

48. Richard M. Nixon, press conference, 31 January 1973. Printed in G. W. Johnson, 1978, 309.

49. Attorney General Ramsey Clark, 42 Op.At.Gen. 347, 350–351 (25 Feb. 1967).

50. Kutler 1990, 134. See as well Sundquist 1981.

51. Richard M. Nixon, press conference, 31 January 1973. Printed in G. W. Johnson 1978, 309.

52. Kutler 1990, 133.

53. Ibid., 135.

54. Richard M. Nixon, press conference, 4 March 1971. Printed in G. W. Johnson 1978, 157. Stephen E. Ambrose notes that in preparing for this press conference, Nixon asked John Dean to "work up a defense of the doctrine." In the end, though "Dean had to admit that the doctrine could only be derived by 'implication' from the Constitution, the precedent was clear: 'The President and his immediate advisers are absolutely immune from testimonial compulsion by a Congressional committee." See Ambrose 1989, 426–427.

55. Brief for the respondent, cross-petitioner Richard M. Nixon, in *U.S. v. Nixon*, printed in Friedman 1974, 350.

56. Testimony of Assistant Attorney General, Criminal Division, Henry E. Peterson, before the Subcommittee on Courts, Civil Liberties, and the Administration of Justice of the House Judiciary Committee, Hearings on House Resolution 1597, 93d Con., 2d sess., 1974. Printed in Boyan 1976, 4:287.

57. *United States v. Nixon*, 418 U.S. 683, 711 (1973).

Chapter 5

1. Bickel 1961, 75.

2. *Oetjen v. Central Leather Co.*, 246 U.S. 297 (1918). See Chapter 1 for a discussion of this case.

3. *Baker v. Carr*, 369 U.S. 186, 211 (1962).

4. Neustadt 1976, 12.

5. Madison, *Federalist* 51, quoted in Rossiter 1961, 322.

6. *Myers v. United States*, 272 U.S. 52, 293 (1926).

7. As Justice Brennan noted in *Baker v. Carr* at 211–212, the resolution of foreign policy cases often turns "on standards that defy judicial application, or involve the exercise of a discretion demonstrably committed to the executive or legislature." Brennan argued that foreign policy cases could and should be decided by the Court, but that they do require "a discriminating analysis of the particular question posed . . . of its susceptibility to judicial handling in the light of its nature and posture in the specific case, and of the possible consequences of judicial action."

8. U.S. Constitution, article 2, section 2, paragraph 1; article 1, section 8, paragraphs 12, 13, and 11; article 2, section 2, paragraph 2; article 1, section 8, paragraph 18; article 2, section 1, paragraph 1.

9. One of the best structural arguments about constitutional interpretation can be found in Black 1960.

10. *Goldwater v. Carter*, 444 U.S. 996, 1007 (1979). This case is discussed in detail in Chapter 8.

11. *Youngstown*, 652.

12. *Youngstown*, 637.

13. One example would be cases where both branches act in concert and the allegation is that they have, together, exceeded the constitutional authority of the national government; a second type would be cases where it is alleged that Congress has unconstitutionally delegated its legitimate authority to the executive. *Curtiss-Wright* would be an example of the latter.

14. *Youngstown*, 604.

15. Ibid., 602.

16. Ibid., 662.

17. Ibid., 640.

18. Ibid., 637.

19. Ibid., 635, 636.

20. Ibid., 636, 637.

21. *United States v. Robel*, 389 U.S. 258, 264 (1967). This case arose when a man was fired from his shipyard job because he belonged to a Communist organization. The Court ruled that while association is potentially disqualifying, mere association is not enough. To be valid, the law would have to provide adequate due process.

22. Ibid., 264.

23. *Korematsu v. United States*, 323 U.S. 214, 246 (1944), Justice Jackson dissenting.

24. Ibid., 246.

25. For a clear argument about the political question doctrine, see Henkin 1976, 612 (discussed below).

26. *Korematsu*, 235, 240, 242.

27. *Home Building & Loan Assn. v. Blaisdell*, 290 U.S. 398, 426 (1934).

28. As Frankfurter put it in *Perez v. Brownwell*, 356 U.S. 44, 58 (1958), "Broad as the power in the National Government to regulate foreign affairs must necessarily be, it is not without limitation. The restrictions confining Congress in the exercise of any of the powers expressly delegated to it in the Constitution apply with equal vigor when that body seeks to regulate our relations with other nations."

29. Ibid., 63.

30. Ibid., 65.

31. Ibid., 64.

32. Ibid., 65.

33. Ibid., 78.

34. Ibid., 79.

35. Ibid., 82.

36. *Trop v. Dulles*, 356 U.S. 86 (1958).

37. *Afroyim v. Rusk*, 387 U.S. 253, 257 (1967).

38. Ibid., 268.

39. *Kennedy v. Mendoza-Martinez*, 372 U.S. 144, 164 (1963). The quote is from the majority opinion written by Justice Goldberg.

40. *Kennedy v. Mendoza-Martinez*, 187. Justices Black and Douglas both maintained their earlier position that the government cannot strip a native-born citizen of his citizenship, period.

41. *United States v. Robel*, 389 U.S. 258, 265 (1967).

42. Ibid., 262.

43. Ibid., 263.

44. The Japanese-American internment case discussed above.

45. Both Justice Sutherland and Chief Justice Marshall offered powerful statements to the effect that there are things the United States government simply cannot do, regardless of the justification. In *McCulloch v. Maryland*, 17 U.S. (4 Wheat.) 316, 422 (1819), Marshall wrote: "Should Congress, in the execution of its powers, adopt measures which are prohibited by the Constitution; or should Congress, under the pretext of executing its powers, pass laws for the accomplishment of objects not entrusted to the government; it would become the painful duty of this tribunal . . . to say that such an act was not the law of the land." It is worth remembering that in *Curtiss-Wright*, Sutherland repeated what he had spelled out in greater depth in his 1919 book, the fact that by his doctrine, every "governmental power, must be exercised in subordination to the applicable provisions of the Constitution," *United States v. Curtiss-Wright Export Corp.*, 299 U.S. 304, 320 (1936).

46. *Valentine v. U.S. ex rel Neidecker*, 266 U.S. 5, 8 (1936).

47. Ibid., 9.

48. *Duncan v. Kahanamoku*, 327 U.S. 304, 315–324 (1946).

49. *U.S. v. Robel*, 275, Brennan concurring in the result.

50. See *Trop v. Dulles*, 356 U.S. 86 (1958); *Kent v. Dulles*, 357 U.S. 116 (1958); *Aptheker v. Secretary of State*, 378 U.S. 500 (1964); *Afroyim v. Rusk*, *U.S. v. Robel*, and *U.S. v. Bishop*, 555 F.2d 771 (10th.Cir. 1977).

51. *New York Times Co. v. United States*, 403 U.S. 713 (1971), also known as the Pentagon papers case.

52. Ibid., 719.
53. Ibid., 726, 727.
54. Ibid., 747.
55. Ibid., 747.
56. Ibid., 720.
57. Ibid., 722.
58. Generally, this carries the caveat that the policy not contradict an explicit prohibition. In the case of the *Progressive*, Justice Black almost undoubtedly would have argued that there was such an explicit prohibition in the First Amendment. As we have seen, however, this was a unique position among the vast majority of judges and justices in this country.
59. Hamilton, *Federalist* 78, quoted in Rossiter 1961, 470.
60. *Washington Post*, 27 July 1991, "Covert Acts Restricted Under Pact," 1.

Chapter 6

1. Clark Clifford, one of the authors of the 1947 National Security Act, quoted in Smist 1990, 5.
2. Johnson 1989 and 1991; Crabb and Holt 1989; Sundquist 1981.
3. Mann 1990; Jones and Marini 1988; Fisher 1991a; Franck and Weisband 1979.
4. Huntington 1961; Ripley and Lindsay 1993b.
5. Neustadt 1990, p 321. Neustadt's 1990 volume, *Presidential Power and the Modern Presidents* is an updated and expanded revision of his earlier *Presidential Power* (1960).
6. L. K. Johnson 1994; Kaiser 1992; Treverton 1990; Oseth 1985; Smist 1990.
7. Destler 1994; Nivola 1993; O'Halloran 1993.
8. Platt and Weiler 1978; Frye 1994; Blechman 1990a, 1990b.
9. Burgin 1993.
10. Schoenbrod 1993; Hinckley 1994.
11. An excellent review of the history of the battle over war powers can be found in Fisher 1995b and Wormuth and Firmage 1989.
12. Testimony of Senator Thomas Eagleton, "The War Power After 200 Years: Congress and the President at a Constitutional Impasse," hearings before the Special Subcommittee on War Powers of the Senate Committee on Foreign Relations. 100th Cong., 1st sess., 13 July 1988, 365.
13. Robert Turner (1991) argues strenuously that the resolution has had a significant detrimental effect; former Senator John Tower argues that the War Powers Act unconstitutionally and unwisely shifted power from the president to Congress. Congress, Tower argues, "institutionalized its differences with the President by legislating permanent solutions to a temporary problem" (Senate Hearings, "The War Powers After 200 Years," 1988, 66–67).
14. Ely 1993; Glennon 1990; Koh 1990. Though Ely, Glennon, and Koh disagree on important points, all three argue that an effective law is possible.
15. A thorough review of the role of the appropriations power in national security law can be found in Banks and Raven-Hansen 1994.
16. Hinckley 1994.

17. A review of these is available in a report for the House Committee on Foreign Affairs: *The War Powers Resolution: A Special Study of the Committee on Foreign Affairs*, 97th Cong., 2d sess., 15 April 1982. Also see Fisher 1995b.

18. As recently as September 1994, in his speech to the nation to explain the need to use force in Haiti, President Bill Clinton never mentioned the Constitution or the War Powers Resolution, nor did he suggest that there was any legitimate role for Congress in the decision-making process.

19. Testimony of Nicholas Katzenbach. *Congress, the President, and the War Powers.* Hearings before the Subcommittee on National Security Policy and Scientific Developments of the Committee on Foreign Affairs, House of Representatives, 91st Cong., 2nd sess., 28 July 1970, 303.

20. Ibid., 303.

21. Eagleton, *Congressional Record*, Senate, 7 November 1973 S 36177.

22. Senator Goldwater, quoted in Eagleton 1974, 207.

23. See Kutler 1990.

24. DuPont, *Congressional Record*, House, 12 October 1973, H 33862.

25. *The War Powers After 200 Years*, Senate hearings, testimony of Senator Thomas Eagleton, 13 July 1988, 16. See also Eagleton 1974, 220.

26. Dellums, *Congressional Record*, House, 7 November 1973, H 36220.

27. Abzug, *Congressional Record*, House, 7 November 1973, H 36221.

28. See Chapter 3.

29. *Washington Post*, 5 Jan. 1995, A10.

30. The vote was on H.R. 1561, Fiscal 1996–97 Foreign Aid and State Department Authorization.

31. Gingrich, *Congressional Record*, House, 7 June 1995, H 5672.

32. Ibid., H 5673.

33. Hyde, *Congressional Record*, House, 7 June 1995, H 5667.

34. DeFazio, *Congressional Record*, House 7 June 1995, H 5663.

35. Hamilton, *Congressional Record*, House, 7 June 1995, H 5665.

36. Portman, *Congressional Record*, House, 7 June 1995, H 5657.

37. Funderburk, *Congressional Record*, House, 7 June 1995, H 5662.

38. Hamilton, *Congressional Record*, House, 7 June 1995, H 5672.

39. Dellums was one of the few liberal Democrats who voted against the original War Powers Resolution and supported Nixon's veto on the ground that the resolution as written actually ceded to the president powers delegated to Congress by the Constitution.

40. In the 1995 debate, Representative DeFazio pointed to this as one of the most critical flaws of the resolution: "Prior restraint was in the Senate version of the War Powers Act . . . [H]ad we adopted the Senate version instead of the more watered-down House version, we would have an effective War Powers Act" (*Congressional Record*, House, 7 June 1995, H 5663).

41. *The War Powers After 200 Years*, Senate hearings, testimony of Senator Eagleton, 1988, 366.

42. Ibid.

43. A strong case can be made that the law provides Congress with the best of both worlds: the rhetoric of power and control, and yet the ability to let the president take responsibility for troop deployments. See Doherty 1990.

44. Hatfield, *Congressional Record*, Senate, 13 December 1995, S 18488.

45. House Committee on Foreign Affairs, *The War Powers Resolution*, 1982, 281.

46. Testimony of Alexander Bickel, Senate Committee on Foreign Relations, *War Powers Legislation*, 92d Cong., 1st sess., 26 July 1971, 567.

47. Leggett, *Congressional Record*, House, 7 Nov. 1973, H 36215.

48. Cohen, *Congressional Record*, daily edition, Senate, 5 Oct. 1990, S 14622.

49. Bush letter to Speaker Tom Foley, 9 Aug. 1990, printed in *Congressional Record*, daily edition, House, 1 Oct. 1990, H 8446.

50. Bush letter to Speaker Tom Foley, 16 Nov. 1990, printed in *Congressional Record*, daily edition, 12 January 1991, H 447.

51. Ibid., H 447.

52. Senate Joint Resolution 376, printed in *Congressional Record*, daily edition, Senate, 5 October 1990, S 14618.

53. House Joint Resolution 658, printed in *Congressional Record*, daily edition, House, 1 October 1990, H 8441.

54. *Congressional Record*, daily edition, Senate, 5 October 1990, S 14618.

55. Ibid., S 14620.

56. Ibid., S 14620–14621.

57. *Congressional Record*, daily edition, House, 1 October 1990, H 8444.

58. Ibid., H 8450.

59. Ibid., H 8448–8449.

60. House Concurrent Resolution 399 provided that "The Speaker of the House and the Majority Leader of the Senate, acting jointly after consultation with the Minority Leader of the House and the Minority Leader of the Senate, shall notify Members of the House and Senate, respectively, to reassemble whenever, in their opinion, the public interest shall warrant it." *Congressional Record*, daily edition, House, 27 October 1990, H 12370.

61. *Congressional Record*, daily edition, Senate, 4 January 1991, S 47.

62. *Congressional Record*, daily edition, Senate 12 January 1991, S 393.

63. *Congressional Record*, daily edition, Senate, 12 January 1991, S 374.

64.. *Congressional Record*, daily edition, House, 12 January 1991, H 395.

65. House, House Committee on Foreign Affairs, *The War Powers Resolution of 1973*, 93d Cong., 1st Sess., House Report 93-287, 18.

Chapter 7

1. Neustadt 1990, 321; see discussion in Chapter 6.
2. Ripley and Lindsay 1993b.
3. Ripley and Lindsay 1993a, 19.
4. Lindsay 1994; Burgin 1993; Ripley and Lindsay 1993a, b, and c; O'Halloran 1993.
5. Banks and Raven-Hansen 1994.
6. Lindsay 1993a.
7. Burgin 1993.
8. Ripley and Lindsay 1993b, 19.
9. Lindsay 1993a, 607.
10. O'Halloran 1993, 284, 303.
11. Treverton 1990, 70.
12. Ransom 1988, 66.

13. Treverton 1990, 106.

14. Kaiser 1992, 296, 300. See also, Aberbach 1990.

15. L. K. Johnson 1989, 247; L. K. Johnson 1994, 69.

16. Smist 1990, 275.

17. The Church Committee's operations are carefully presented and analyzed in L. K. Johnson 1988.

18. Cited in Oseth 1985, 89.

19. This problem largely was ameliorated when Congress established permanent intelligence committees, cutting down to two the number of committees that had to be informed about covert action. See L. K. Johnson 1989 and 1985; Smist 1994 and 1990; and Oseth 1985.

20. The key phrase directed the CIA to "perform such other functions and duties related to intelligence affecting the national security as the National Security Council may from time to time direct." Quoted in Oseth 1985, 36.

21. Senate Select Committee to Study Governmental Operations with Respect to Intelligence Activities, *Foreign and Military Intelligence*, Final Report, 94th Congr., 2d sess., 26 April 1976, Book I, 505.

22. Ibid., Additional Views of Senator Philip A. Hart, Book II, 362.

23. Tower 1981/82, 242.

24. Oseth 1985, 146.

25. Weiss, *Congressional Record*, House, 30 September 1980, H 28395.

26. L. K. Johnson 1980.

27. S. 2284, the Intelligence Oversight Act of 1980, printed in *Congressional Record*, Senate, 15 May 1980, S 11427–11428.

28. Ibid., 11427.

29. Huddleston, *Congressional Record*, Senate, 3 June 1980, S 13096.

30. Kaiser 1992; L. K. Johnson 1989.

31. Weiss, *Congressional Record*, House, 30 September 1980, H 28395.

32. See Draper 1991.

33. Memorandum of the Office of Legislative Counsel, Department of Justice, 17 January 1962, printed in Church Committee, Final Report, Book I, 36.

34. Ibid., 36 (emphasis added).

35. Senator Huddleston noted that "Both the bill and its accompanying report are fully supported by the executive branch. The administration is to be commended for recognizing that intelligence activities are the joint responsibility of Congress and the executive branch" (*Congressional Record*, Senate, 15 May 1980, S 11427).

36. Executive Order 11905, 18 February 1976, printed in the *Federal Register*, vol. 41, no. 34, 19 February 1976, 7703; replaced by Executive Order 12036, 24 January 1978, printed in the *Federal Register*, vol. 43, no. 18, 26 January 1978, 3674.

37. Executive orders 12333 and 12334, *Weekly Compilation of Presidential Documents*, vol. 17, no. 49, 7 December 1981, 1335 and 1348.

38. Reagan executive order 12333, quoted in Oseth 1985, 154 (emphasis added). Regarding possible violations of individual rights, the Reagan order instructed the intelligence community to act "with full consideration of the rights of United States persons," and it is worth noting that full consideration is quite different from a prohibition on the violation of those rights.

39. Koh 1990, 52.

40. See Reisman and Baker 1992; Koh 1990; and Treverton 1990.

41. North 1987, 523.

42. Ibid., 525.

43. Church Committee, Final Report, Book 1, 425.

44. Morton Halperin of the Center for National Security Studies argued in 1978 that "covert action operations were useless, counterproductive, difficult to control, and ought to be abolished." Halperin testimony cited in Oseth 1985, 130.

45. Quoted in Brinkley 1988, 406.

46. Banks and Raven-Hansen 1994.

47. *Congressional Record*, Daily Edition, Senate, 17 July 1989, S 8035.

48. Letter from Lawrence Eagleburger, Deputy Secretary of State, printed in *Congressional Record*, daily edition, Senate, 17 July 1989, S 8033.

49. Senator Helms, *Congressional Record*, daily edition, Senate, 17 July 1989, S 8033.

50. Block and Rivkin 1990, 50. Block was the Senior Attorney-Advisor, Office of Policy Development in the Department of Justice, Rivkin was the legal advisor to the counsel to the president.

51. House Conference Committee, *Intelligence Authorization Act for Fiscal Year 1991*, House Report 101-928, 101st Cong., 2d sess., 23 October 1990, 14.

52. Ibid., 16.

53. Letter from George Bush, 20 August 1990, printed in *Conference Report on Intelligence Authorization Act for Fiscal Year 1991*, 27.

54. "Covert Acts Restricted Under Pact," *Washington Post*, 27 July 1991, 1.

55. Aspin, *Congressional Record*, House, 30 September 1980, H 28395.

56. "Covert Acts Restricted Under Pact," *Washington Post*, 27 July 1991, A13.

57. See Destler 1994, 1992; Nivola 1993; O'Halloran 1993; Porter 1988.

58. A similar pattern in domestic policy is well articulated and documented in Schoenbrod 1993.

59. L. K. Johnson 1991; Crabb and Holt 1989; Polsby 1986.

60. Fisher 1993b; Spitzer 1993.

61. Senate, Special Committee on the Termination of the National Emergency, *National Emergency*, 93d Cong. 1st sess., 24 July 1973, 509.

62. Senate, Special Committee on the Termination of the National Emergency, 93d Cong., 1st Sess., 1973, 504.

63. An effort that took more than three years, and resulted in the National Emergencies Act, Public Law 94-412, signed by President Ford, 14 September 1976.

64. Senate, Committee on Government Operations and the Special Committee on National Emergencies and Delegated Emergency Powers, *Source Book and Legislative History of "The National Emergencies Act,"* 94th Cong., 2d sess., November 1976, vii.

65. On legislative vetoes see Greene 1994; Hinkley 1994; Fisher 1993a; Gibson 1992; Korn 1996, 1992a, 1992b; and Craig 1983.

66. The five were Representatives John Conyers, Ron Dellums, Robert Drinan, Elizabeth Holtzman, and John Moss. Drinan and Holtzman provided critical votes to override Nixon's veto of the War Powers Resolution in November 1973.

67. Holtzman, *Congressional Record*, House, 4 September 1975, H 27645.

68. See the *Foreign Relations Authorization Act*, Public Law 99–93, 99th Cong., 1st sess., 16 August 1985, and the discussion in Fisher 1993a.

69. Fisher 1993a, 286.

70. Franklin 1991.

71. Koh 1990.

72. House, Committee on International Relations, *Trading with the Enemy Act Reform Legislation*, 95th Cong., 1st sess., Report H 95-459, June 1977, 10.

73. In fact, the Court did just that in *Regan v. Wald* and in *Dames & Moore v. Reagan*. These cases and the Court's interpretation of IEEPA and the National Emergencies Act will be discussed in the next chapter.

74. Bingham, *Congressional Record*, House, 12 July 1977, H 22475.

75. House, Committee on Foreign Affairs, *Hearing on Emergency Economic Powers: Iran*, 97th Cong., 1st sess., 5 March 1981. Prepared statement of Lloyd Cutler, Robert Carswell and Robert Owen, 2.

76. Ibid., 2.

77. Ibid., 3.

78. Ibid., 4. Statement of Robert Carswell, former Deputy Secretary of the Treasury.

79. Ibid., 4.

80. The IEEPA was challenged in court in 1981 in *American International Group v. Islamic Republic of Iran*, 657 F2d 430 (1981) and in *Dames & Moore v. Reagan*, 453 U.S. 654 (1981). It was also the subject of litigation in *Reagan v. Wald*, 468 U.S. 222 (1983) and in *Beacon Products Corp. v. Reagan*, 633 F.Supp. 1191 (1986), affirmed on appeal, 814 F2d 1 (1987).

81. This is not to suggest that Carter's actions were inappropriate. In fact, the complicated negotiations that led to the release of the hostages without armed attack was a great, though prolonged, success.

82. Greene 1994; Gibson 1992; Koh 1990.

83. On defense and arms control see: R. Carter 1994; Frye 1994, 1975; Blechman 1990a, 1990b; Platt and Weiler 1978; and Warburg 1989. On trade, see: Destler 1994, 1992, 1985; Nivola 1993; O'Halloran 1993; and Porter 1988.

84. Lindsay 1994 and 1993a; Burgin 1993; O'Halloran 1993; Ripley and Lindsay 1993b.

85. Neustadt 1990, 321, discussed above.

86. Banks and Raven-Hansen 1994.

87. Lindsay 1993b; Ferrell 1988.

88. Senate. Committee on Foreign Relations, *Report on S. 2662, International Security Assistance and Arms Export Control Act of 1976*, (S. Rept. 94-605) 94th Cong., 2d sess., 30 January 1976, 5.

89. Ibid., 5.

90. President Gerald Ford, veto message on S. 2662, printed in the *Congressional Record*, Senate, 10 May 1976, S 13053.

91. Ibid., 13054.

92. Banks and Raven-Hansen 1994.

93. *Congressional Record*, Senate, 18 February 1976, S 3625.

94. Blechman 1990a, 133.

95. Burgin 1991.

96. Fiorina 1981.

97. Arnold 1990.

98. The president "shall have power, by and with the advice and consent

of the Senate, to make treaties, provided two-thirds of the Senators present concur." (U.S. Constitution, article 2, section 2, paragraph 2).

99. Frye 1994; Garthoff 1987.

100. Senate, Committee on Foreign Relations and the Committee on the Judiciary, *Joint Hearings* on *the ABM Treaty and the Constitution*, 100th Cong. 1st sess. 1987.

101. Sofaer 1989, 1986.

102. Senate hearings, *The ABM Treaty and the Constitution*, 61.

103. Ibid., 62.

104. Senator Pete Wilson, address to the Senate on 14 May 1987, reprinted in *Congressional Digest*, 66, No. 11 (November 1987), 283.

105. Senator Dan Quayle, in an address to the Senate, 13 May 1987, printed in *Congressional Digest*, 66, No. 11 (November 1987), 273.

106. Senator John Warner, in an address to the Senate, 13 May 1987, printed in *Congressional Digest*, 66., No. 11 (November 1987), 267.

107. Senator Sam Nunn, in an address to the Senate, 13 May 1987, printed in *Congressional Digest*, 66., No. 11 (November 1987), 274.

108. *Congressional Quarterly*, Weekly edition, 3 October 1987, 2359.

109. *Congressional Quarterly*, Weekly edition, 14 November 1987, 2795.

110. *Congressional Quarterly*, Weekly edition, 21 November 1987, 2865.

111. Rourke 1983, 259.

112. Franck and Weisband 1979, 144.

113. United States Constitution, article 1, section 8, paragraph 1.

114. O'Halloran 1993, 284.

115. Destler 1994, 244.

116. Ibid., 245.

117. Ullman, *Congressional Record*, House, 10 December 1973, H 40501–40502.

118. House, Committee on Ways and Means, *Report on Trade Reform Act of 1973, (H. Rept. 93-571)*, 93d Cong., 1st sess., 1973, 1 (emphasis added).

119. Whalen, *Congressional Record*, House, 11 December 1973, H 40775.

120. Representative James A. Burke, *Congressional Record*, House, 10 December 1973, H 40533.

121. House, *Report on the Trade Reform Act of 1973*, dissenting views of Representative James A. Burke, 199.

122. Ibid., 3–4.

123. Ullman, *Congressional Record*, House, 10 December 1973, H 40502.

124. Report to the House on "Trade Reform Act of 1973," dissenting views of Representative James A. Burke, 200.

125. Bingham, *Congressional Record*, House, 11 December 1973, H 40786.

126. Statement by the president on signing H.R. 3884 into law, 14 September 1976. Printed in National Emergencies Source Book: Legislative History, Texts, and other Documents, Senate Committee on Government Operations and the Special Committee on National Emergencies and Delegated Emergency Powers. 94th Cong., 2d Sess., November 1976, 343.

127. The tradition of attaching constitutional objections to legislation seems to go back to President Truman. In 1946 and 1947 Truman attached his own interpretation to two labor laws. As Arthur Krock noted, Truman had "twice expanded in unusual fashion his part in the legislative process" (Arthur Krock, "In the Nation," *New York Times*, 16 May 1947).

128. In *Lear Siegler Inc. v. Lehman* 842 F.2d 1102, 1121 (9th Cir., 1988), the court ruled that the president has no authority to determine which part of the law to "faithfully execute."

129. *Washington Post,* "Covert Acts Restricted Under Pact," 27 July 1991, 1.

130. See detailed discussion in the next chapter of: *United States v. Yoshida International,* 378 F.Supp. 1155 (1974), rev'd 526 F.2d 560 (1975); *American International Group v. Islamic Republic of Iran,* 657 F.2d 430 (1981); *Regan v. Wald,* 486 U.S. 222 (1983); *Japan Whaling Assoc. v. American Cetacean Society,* 478 U.S. 221 (1985); *Beacon Products Corp. v. Reagan,* 633 F.Supp. 1191 (1986), affirmed on appeal, 814, F.2d 1 (1987).

131. See Silverstein 1994b.

Chapter 8

1. Letter from George Bush, 20 August 1990, printed in *Conference Report on Intelligence Authorization Act for Fiscal Year 1991,* 101st Cong., 2d sess., 23 October 1990, House Report 101-928, 27.

2. *Washington Post,* "Covert Acts Restricted Under Pact," 27 July 1991, 1.

3. See Silverstein 1994b.

4. Most recently in cases concerning the North American Free Trade Agreement and the status of Haitian refugees. See *Public Citizen v. Office of the U.S. Trade Representative,* 822 F.Supp 21 (D.D.C. 1993); *Haitian Centers Council v. INS,* 823 F.Supp 1028 (E.D.N.Y.1993); and *Chris Sale, Acting Commissioner, INS v. Haitian Centers Council,* 113 S.Ct. 2549 (1993). But this change has not been limited to foreign policy—in strictly domestic cases concerning administrative interpretation of statutes, the Court has shifted its default presumption decidedly in the favor of deference to the executive branch. See *Chevron v. Natural Resource Defense Council,* 467 U.S. 837 (1984).

5. See also the more extensive discussion in the lower court consideration of this case, *Goldwater v. Carter,* 617 F.2d 697 (1979).

6. *Goldwater v. Carter* 444 U.S. 996, 1002 (1979).

7. Ibid., 1007.

8. Ibid., 998.

9. *Ramirez de Arellano v. Weinberger,* 724 F.2d 143, 147 (U.S. App. D.C. 1983).

10. Here, Scalia quoted Baker v. Carr, 369 U.S. 186, 217 (1962) in which Justice William Brennan wrote: "the doctrine . . . is one of 'political questions,' not one of 'political cases.' "

11. *Ramirez de Arellano v. Weinberger,* 745 F.2d 1500, 1515 (D.C. Cir. 1984) (rehearing *en banc*). This of course echoes Justice Holmes' argument that the United States could accomplish some objectives through a treaty that it could not otherwise accomplish through simple statutory law, provided "the treaty in question does not contravene any prohibitory words to be found in the Constitution" (*Missouri v. Holland,* 252 U.S. 416, 431 (1920)).

12. *Ramirez,* 1515.

13. Franck (1992) actually cites three areas: property rights, civil liberties, and separation of powers cases.

14. *Goldwater* at 997.

15. *Dames & Moore v. Regan,* 453 U.S. 654, 669 (1981). Justice Rehnquist

noted, however, that "we have in the past found and do today find Justice Jackson's classification of executive actions into three general categories analytically useful" *Dames & Moore* 669.

16. *Goldwater* 997.

17. Ibid., at 1001. Justice Powell was quoting *United States v. Nixon*, 418 U.S. 633, at 703 which, in turn, was quoting *Marbury v. Madison*, 5 U.S. (1 Cranch) 137, 177. This argument was most recently revived in *Dellums v. Bush*, 752 F. Supp. 1141 (D.D.C. 1990), when 53 members of Congress challenged President Bush's authority to engage American troops in combat in Iraq and Saudi Arabia.

18. "Before he enter on the Execution of his Office, he shall take the following Oath or Affirmation:—'I do solemnly swear (or affirm) that I will faithfully execute the Office of President of the United States' " (U.S. Constitution, article 2, section 1, paragraph 8). Also, "he shall take care that the laws be faithfully executed"—(article 2, section 3, paragraph 1).

19. *Lear Siegler Inc. v. Lehman, Secretary of the Navy*, 842 F.2d 1121 (9th Cir. 1988).

20. Ibid., 1124.

21. Attorney General William French Smith argued in 1981 that "in the case of laws that are clearly and indefensibly unconstitutional, the executive can refuse to enforce them and urge invalidation by the courts" (*New York Times*, 30 Oct. 1981, A22, col. 1). He must not have read Assistant Attorney General William Rehnquist, who said in 1969 that "it seems an anomalous proposition that because the Executive Branch is bound to execute the laws, it is free to decline to execute them" (quoted in *Lear Siegler* at 1124). As a Supreme Court Justice, Rehnquist has indicated no change of mind. Among others, see *Dames & Moore*, 688.

22. Koh 1990.

23. *American International Group, Inc. v. Islamic Republic of Iran*, 657 F.2d 430, 444 (D.C. Cir. 1981).

24. Ibid., 444: "The President has entered into binding settlements with foreign nations compromising the claims of U.S. nationals at least 10 times since 1952 without seeking the advice and consent of the Senate."

25. Ibid., 445 (emphasis added).

26. *Dames & Moore*, 678.

27. Ibid., 680 (emphasis added). Though Rehnquist argued for broad executive discretion, he explicitly rejected the notion that there was an executive prerogative: "We do not decide that the President possesses plenary power to settle claims, even as against foreign governmental entities" (*Dames & Moore*, 688). Similarly, the Appeals Court in *American International* held that "to the extent that denominating the President as the 'sole organ' of the United States in international affairs constitutes a blanket endorsement of plenary Presidential power over any matter extending beyond the borders of this country, we reject that characterization" (*American International*, 438, n 6).

28. *Regan v. Wald*, 468 U.S. 222, 262 (1984).

29. *Japan Whaling Association v. American Cetacean Society*, 478 U.S. 221, 243–244 (1986).

30. Ibid., 246.

31. Ibid., 241, 242.

32. *Yoshida International Inc. v. United States*, 526 F.2d 560, 577, 583–584 (C.C.P.A.1975).

33. For a critique of the search for legislative intent, see Shepsle 1992. A response can be found in Silverstein 1994b.

34. For example, a case concerning military base closing, *Specter v. Secretary of the Navy* 971 F.2d 936 (3rd.Cir.1992); an environmental protection case, *Bethlehem Steel v. Bush* 918 F.2d 1323 (7th.Cir.1990); and *County of Seneca v. Richard Cheney, Secretary of Defense*, 806 F.Supp. 387 (W.D.N.Y.1992), all cited *Japan Whaling Association v. American Cetacean Society*, 478 U.S. 221 (1986) in various arguments about executive discretion in statutory interpretation.

35. Schoenbrod 1993.

36. *Chevron v. Natural Resources Defense Council*, 467 U.S. 842 (1984).

37. Ibid., 844.

38. Scalia 1989, 516.

39. Ibid., 520.

40. *Youngstown Sheet & Tube Co. v. Sawyer*, 343 U.S. 579, 635–637 (1952).

41. In foreign affairs, again please consider *Regan v. Wald* and *Japan Whaling Association v. American Cetacean Society*, both discussed in Chapter 5.

42. *Field v. Clark*, 143 U.S. 649, 692 (1892).

43. Ibid., 692.

44. There have been objections. In *Field v. Clark* itself there were two dissenting voices. Though they concurred in the overall decision, Justice Lamar and Chief Justice Fuller unequivocally denounced the delegation, calling it patently unconstitutional.—*Field v. Clark*, 699–700.

45. *J.W. Hampton Jr. & Co. v. United States*, 276 U.S. 394 (1928) at 409.

46. Ibid., 406.

47. *Panama Refining Co. v. Ryan*, 293 U.S. 388 443–444 (1935).

48. Ibid., 421.

49. *Buckley v. Valeo*, 424 U.S. 1, 121 (1976).

50. See *National Labor Relations Board v. Jones & Laughlin Steel Corp.*, 301 U.S. 1 (1937). The new doctrine was fleshed out a bit in *U.S. v. Carolene Products Co.*, 304 U.S. 144 (1938), where the majority held that all that was required was a rational connection between the economic need and the economic regulation.

51. See Gilman 1993.

52. *Industrial Union Department, AFL-CIO v. American Petroleum Institute*, 448 U.S. 607, 673–674 (1980).

53. Ibid., 686, Justice Rehnquist quoting John Hart Ely.

54. Ibid., 686.

55. For a full discussion of the legislative veto and the *Chadha* case see: Fisher 1993a; Gibson 1992; Korn 1996, 1992a and 1992b and Craig 1988 and 1983.

56. *Immigration and Naturalization Service v. Chadha*, 462 U.S. 919, 948 (1983).

57. Ibid., 986.

58. Ibid., 968.

59. *Youngstown* was cited, among other places, in *Buckley v. Valeo* at 122 and in *INS v. Chadha* at 959, 963, and 968.

60. *INS v. Chadha*, 959.

61. Ibid., 969.

62. Ibid., 978, quoting Justice Jackson's concurrence in *Youngstown.*

63. Ibid., 987.

64. *Synar v. United States*, 626 F.Supp. 1374, 1384 (D.D.C. 1986).

65. *Bowsher v. Synar*, 478 U.S. 714, 759 (1986).

66. Recall the discussion of *Regan v. Wald* and *Dames & Moore v. Regan*, among others.

Chapter 9

1. Lindsay 1994a; Burgin 1993; Ripley and Lindsay 1993b; Lindsay 1993a. A thorough literature review on the subject can be found in Ripley and Lindsay 1992.

2. This pattern has been described in domestic policy (Schoenbrod 1993 and Weaver 1986) as well as in foreign policy (Weissman 1995).

3. J. Q. Wilson 1989, 6.

4. Russell 1986, 19.

5. In trying to gauge the "explanatory and predictive usefulness of power," Nagel concludes, we are far from an "adequately complex theory. Indeed, no one theory is likely to suffice. There are simply too many processes by which preferences can cause outcomes" (Nagel 1975, 179).

6. Dowding 1991, 1.

7. See Arrow 1963. As Kenneth Shepsle (1992, 241–242) explains, "the final outcome may be arbitrary (for example, a function of group fatigue) or determined by specific institutional features of decision-making (for example, rules governing the order of voting on measures).

8. Neustadt 1990, 321. Neustadt's 1990 volume, *Presidential Power and the Modern Presidents* is an updated and expanded revision of his earlier *Presidential Power* (1960).

9. Lindsay 1994a; Burgin 1993; Ripley and Lindsay 1993b; Lindsay 1993a. A thorough literature review on the subject can be found in Ripley and Lindsay 1992.

10. Lindsay, 1994a, 138

11. Ripley and Lindsay 1993a, 1993c.

12. See Fisher 1991a and Silverstein 1994b.

13. Sinclair 1993.

14. Arnold 1993, 1990; Burgin 1991; Kingdon 1981.

15. Hilsman and Weitsman 1993; Schneier and Gross 1993; Spanier and Uslaner 1989; Schlozman and Tierney 1986.

16. Tierney 1993.

17. Fiorina 1981.

18. Mayhew 1974; but see Lindsay 1994a for a discussion of the applicability of these assumptions in congressional foreign policy–making.

19. Fenno 1973, 1.

20. Madison, *Federalist* 57, quoted in Rossiter 1961, 352.

21. See Maass 1983.

22. This anomaly is largely due to the high number of incumbents who declined to run for re-election in 1994.

23. Weaver 1986, 371.

24. Burgin 1993; O'Halloran 1993; Kiewiet and McCubbins 1991; Mezey 1991.

25. LaFeber 1987, 54.

26. See Stoll 1987.

27. Schoenbrod 1993 and Weissman 1995 focus on the incentives and implications of legislative delegation and deference to the executive.

28. Weaver 1986, 372.

29. Fisher 1995a, 1995b.

30. Spitzer 1993; Wormuth and Firmage 1989; Henkin 1975; Eagleton 1974; Javits 1973.

31. *Congressional Record*, daily edition, Senate, 12 January 1991, S 374.

32. Naturally, there are exceptions in particular districts. Legislators from districts with a high percentage of people from particular national backgrounds will have a far more significant electoral stake in some foreign policy issues, whether it is a representative with a large Korean-American population in Los Angeles, or a district with a large Vietnamese population in Texas. Similarly, those representatives with districts heavily dependent on foreign trade will take a particularly high interest in some trade bills.

33. Mayhew 1974, 73.

34. Maass 1983.

35. Mezey (1991) argues that legislators can be more effective when they play a "representation" role rather than as activist policymakers.

36. Kiewiet and McCubbins 1991, 3.

37. Ibid., 19.

38. Banks and Raven-Hansen 1994.

39. Hamilton, *Congressional Record*, House, 7 June 1995, H 5672. A clear demonstration of this difficulty was spelled out in the debate over a bid to cut off funds for the deployment of American troops to Bosnia in December 1995. A narrow majority in the House and a far wider majority in the Senate ultimately accepted amendments that would support the troops, while trying to distance themselves from the decision to send the troops. As New York Republican Susan Molinari argued, "I think we have an obligation. Tonight we are not only reiterating our opposition to that flawed policy that brought us here; we are also saying to our troops, Godspeed with your mission. It is a terrible policy, but it is a noble mission that may bring peace to a region that has not known peace. . . . [S]ince there is nothing Congress can do to change the president's course, I think we have an obligation to make sure that our troops are not caught in the middle of two wars, one in Bosnia and one in Washington." (Molinari, *Congressional Record*, House, 13 December 1995, H 14851.)

40. O'Halloran 1993; Destler 1992, 1985.

41. Destler 1994.

42. Nivola 1993; Ripley and Lindsay 1993b.

43. Rourke 1983, 267.

44. Destler 1994.

45. Weaver 1986.

46. A powerful argument along these lines is offered in Eastland 1992. Also see Cheney 1990; Crovitz and Rabkin 1989; Jones and Marini 1988; Tower 1981/82.

47. Neustadt 1990, 29.

48. Madison, *Federalist* 51, quoted in Rossiter 1961, 321.

49. See the previous chapter for a fuller exploration of this argument.

50. Levinson 1995 provides an excellent overview of the issues involved in constitutional amendment.

51. "The argument may serve as a smoke-screen for critics unhappy with the constitutional structure because it allows a Democratic Congress to oppose or check a Republican president and hinder the "national interest" (Burgin 1993, 350).

52. Pastor 1991, 103.

53. P. Peterson 1994; Neustadt 1990.

54. Drapper 1991; Cohen and Mitchell 1988; Moyers 1988.

55. Richard Neustadt's book on presidential power, originally written in 1960, has been updated and revised a number of times, most recently in 1990. Two other scholars recently added to this literature—Skowronek 1993 and Jones 1994.

56. Neustadt 1990, 321.

57. Neustadt 1990, xi–xii.

58. This limit only dates from the passage of the 22nd Amendment, but prior to Franklin Roosevelt no president served more than two terms, following a tradition set by George Washington, who imposed a two-term limit on himself.

59. A recent exception is King and Ragsdale (1988), where the authors drew together a wealth of statistical information about different presidents and administrations in an effort to discover, as the book's subtitle puts it, "statistical patterns in the presidency."

60. J. D. Barber 1972.

61. Wildavsky 1966; but see also Shull 1991.

62. A debate that is taken up by a number of scholars in Shull 1991.

63. Fenno notes that there are five goals: re-election, influence within the House, good public policy, a career beyond the House, and private gain. He closely examines the first three, considers the fourth, and does not examine the fifth (Fenno 1973, 1).

64. Neustadt, 1990, 90.

65. Lowi 1985.

66. Stoll 1987.

67. Mueller 1973, 1994.

68. Lowi 1985, 17.

69. Consider how quickly President Bush's popularity faded between the war against Iraq and the election defeat of 1992.

70. Quandt 1986, 825.

71. As Lowi puts it, [T]he effects of the rallying event tend to be brief. In a short time, approval ratings return to their downward tendency until there is another foreign policy fix, or until [a national election]. . . . For each president, voters tend to suspend judgment about presidential performance as the presidential election approaches." Lowi 1985, 19.

72. Neustadt 1990, 24. It should be noted that to be effective in foreign policy a president would have to consider the foreign version of these three categories—the president's formal power abroad (acting alone, or with United Nations' authorization); the president's professional reputation in foreign affairs; and the president's international prestige and general popularity, as well as the prestige and popularity of the United States in different countries and different foreign policy areas.

73. Neustadt 1990, xi. See also Neustadt and May 1986.

74. Herring 1994; Burke and Greenstein 1989; Turner 1991; Miller 1980; Goodwin 1976; Johnson 1971; Wicker 1968.

75. Westin 1958.

76. News conference, 22 May 1952 in *Public Papers of the Presidents of the United States, Harry S. Truman*, 1 vol., (Washington D.C.: U.S. Government Printing Office, 1965) 1952:363.

77. Ibid., 362. Incredulous reporters at the news conference asked Truman a number of times to repeat his position, asking whether "The President would have that as statutory power in reserve, or would you have him go to Congress at each emergency?"; asking for clarification—"but you see, as it stands now, it appears that you have said the Court can't take the power away."; and in asking Truman to repeat his answers, one reporter pleaded that he was being persistent because he "was just uneasy about my desk [editors] wanting an explanation!"

78. Ibid., 363.

79. Arthur Krock, "In the Nation," *New York Times*, 16 May 1947.

80. Here is another example of the pattern described in earlier chapters of the executive (along with the Court) accepting the delegation of power by Congress as fully constitutional, but disputing the constitutionality of any restraints Congress tried to impose on that delegation.

81. Statement by the president on Signing H.R. 3884 into Law, 14 September 1976: Printed in National Emergencies Act Source Book: Legislative History, Texts, and other Documents, Senate Committee on Government Operations and the Special Subcommittee on National Emergencies and Delegated Emergency Powers. 94th Cong., 2d sess., November 1976, 343.

82. In *Lear Siegler Inc. v. Lehman* and *U.S. Senate v. Lehman*, 842 F.2d 1102 (9th Cir., 1988), the court ruled that the President has no authority to determine which part of the law to "faithfully execute."

83. See the discussion of this case in Chapter 5, particularly about *Japan Whaling Association v. American Cetacean Society*, 478 U.S. 221 (1985).

84. Madison, *Federalist* 51, quoted in Rossiter, 1961, 322.

85. Lowi 1985, 210, emphasis added.

Conclusion

1. Madison, *Federalist* 37 quoted in Rossiter 1961, 226.

2. W. Wilson 1908, 54.

3. Thomas Jefferson to John Breckinridge, 12 August 1803, printed in Bergh 1907, 10:419.

4. As Henry Adams noted, the evils Jefferson foresaw as a possible outcome of his decision on Louisiana were but remote possibilities; Jefferson believed that "in the hands of true Republicans the Constitution, even though violated, was on the whole safe; the precedent, though alarming, was exceptional" and would not serve to expand power (Adams 1986, 363).

5. *McCulloch v. Maryland*, 17 U.S. (4 Wheat) 316, 408 (1819).

6. *Marbury v. Madison*, 5 U.S. (1 Cranch) 137, 177 (1803).

7. See Silverstein 1994b and Lindsay 1994b.

8. *The Refugee Act of 1980*, Public Law 96-212, 96th Cong., 2d sess., 17 March 1980.

9. United Nations Protocol Relating to the Status of Refugees, 31 Jan 1967, [1968] 19 U.S.T. 6223, TIAS 6577.

10. *INS v. Haitian Centers Council*, 125 L.Ed 128, 155 (1993).

11. Ibid., 167.

12. This approach, where the Court finds and articulates a constitutional justification for executive action, is reminiscent of *Durand v. Hollins*, where the justice riding Circuit creates a justification for the president's orders to bomb the town of Greytown, Nicaragua. See Chapter 1.

13. *Public Citizen v. Office of U.S.T.R.*, 822 F.Supp 21, 27 (1993).

14. Among many others, see Miller and Stokes 1963; Fiorina 1974; and Maisel and Cooper 1977.

15. There were a range of different versions of these proposals—some limiting discretion in word only. But this book has tried to argue that language matters, particularly when ambiguous legislative measures are interpreted by the courts.

16. As noted above, Senator Dole's proposal would also attempt to restrict the president's discretion to use troops *only* when those troops would be involved in United Nations missions, or when those troops might be placed under foreign command (*Washington Post*, 5 Jan. 1995, A10).

17. Immediately after the 1994 midterm elections, Republican leaders were publicly endorsing amendments such as a line-item veto amendment, a balanced budget amendment, an amendment to limit benefits and social services offered to illegal immigrants, and an amendment to allow prayer in school.

18. See Gibson 1992; Korn 1996, 1992a, 1992b.

19. See Levinson 1995.

20. *Washington Post*, 5 January 1995, A10.

21. Harold Hongju Koh's book (1990) is one of the best articulations of the argument that the failure lies in bad drafting of legislation, rather than in a flawed strategy of turning to any legislation at all. See also Ely 1993; Franck 1992; and Glennon 1990.

22. Madison, *Federalist* 51, quoted in Rossiter 1961, 322.

23. Ibid., 322.

24. Neustadt 1990, xi, emphasis added.

25. For a clear argument about Wilson's choices and their impact, see Tulis 1987. See also Stid 1993.

26. Neustadt 1990, xviii.

27. Madison quoted in LaFeber 1988, 35.

References and Bibliography

Aberbach, Joel. 1990. *Keeping a Watchful Eye: The Politics of Congressional oversight.* Washington, DC: The Brookings Institution.

Abshire, David M. 1979. *Foreign Policy Makers: President vs. Congress.* Beverly Hills, Calif.: Sage Publications.

Adams, Henry. 1986. *History of the United States of America During the Administrations of Thomas Jefferson.* New York: The Library of America.

Adams, Henry, ed. 1879. *The Writings of Albert Gallatin.* Philadelphia: Lippincott & Co.

Alfange, Dean. 1994. "The Quasi-War and Presidential Warmaking." Paper delivered at the 1994 Annual Meeting of the American Political Science Association, in New York City.

Almond, Gabriel. 1950. *The American People and Foreign Policy.* New York: Harcourt, Brace.

Ambrose, Stephen E. 1989. *Nixon: The Triumph of a Politician 1962–1972.* New York: Simon & Schuster.

Ambrose, Stephen E. 1984. *Eisenhower: Volume Two, The President.* New York: Simon & Schuster.

Ambrose, Stephen E. 1971. *Rise to Globalism: American Foreign Policy Since 1938.* London: Penguin Press.

Anderson, Donald. 1973. *William Howard Taft: A Conservative's Conception of the Presidency.* Ithaca, N.Y.: Cornell University Press.

Arkes, Hadley. 1972. *Bureaucracy, the Marshall Plan and the National Interest.* Princeton, N.J.: Princeton University Press.

Arnold, R. Douglas. 1993. "Can Inattentive Citizens Control Their Elected Representatives?" in Lawrence Dodd and Bruce Oppenheimer, eds. *Congress Reconsidered.* 5th ed. Washington, DC: CQ Press.

Arnold, R. Douglas. 1990. *The Logic of Congressional Action.* New Haven, Conn.: Yale University Press, 1990.

Arrow, Kenneth. 1963. *Social Choice and Individual Values.* New York: Wiley.

Baker, Ray and Dodd, William, eds. 1925–1927. *The Public Papers of Woodrow Wilson—The New Democracy (1913–1917).* Vols 1–6. New York: Harper and Bros.

Ball, Howard. 1990. *"We Have a Duty": The Supreme Court and the Watergate Tapes Litigation.* New York: Greenwood Press.

Banks, William and Raven-Hansen, Peter. 1994. *National Security Law and the Power of the Purse.* New York: Oxford University Press.

Barber, James David. 1972. *The Presidential Character: Predicting Performance in the White House.* Englewood Cliffs, N.J.: Prentice Hall.

Barber, Sotirios. 1975. *The Constitution and the Delegation of Congressional Power.* Chicago: The University of Chicago Press.

Barnet, Richard J. 1990. *The Rockets' Red Glare: When America Goes to War.* New York: Simon & Schuster.

Barnet, Richard J. 1973. *Roots of War: The Men and Institutions Behind U.S. Foreign Policy.* Baltimore, Md.: Penguin.

Basler, Roy, ed. 1953. *The Collected Works of Abraham Lincoln.* New Brunswick, N.J.: Rutgers University Press.

Berdahl, Clarence A. 1921. *War Powers of the Executive in the United States.* PhD Dissertation. University of Illinois.

Bergh, Albert, ed. 1907. *The Writings of Thomas Jefferson.* Volume 3. Washington, D.C.: The Thomas Jefferson Memorial Association.

Bessette, Joseph M. and Tulis, Jeffrey. 1981. *The Presidency in the Constitutional Order.* Baton Rouge, La: Louisiana State University Press.

Bickel, Alexander. 1986. *The Least Dangerous Branch.* 2d ed. New Haven: Yale University Press.

Bickel, Alexander. 1961. "The Supreme Court, 1960 Term—Foreword: The Passive Virtues." *Harvard Law Review* 75:40.

Bigel, Alan. 1986. *The Supreme Court on Emergency Powers, Foreign Affairs and Protection of Civil Liberties 1935–1975.* Lanham, Md: University Press of America.

Billings-Yun, Melanie. 1988. *Decision Against War: Eisenhower and Dien Bien Phu, 1954.* New York: Columbia University Press.

Binkley, Wilfred E. 1937. *The Powers of the President: Problems of American Democracy.* Garden City, N.Y.: Doubleday.

Bishop, Donald. 1965. *The Roosevelt-Litvinov Agreements.* Syracuse, N.Y.: Syracuse University Press.

Black, Charles. 1960. *The People and the Court.* New York: Macmillan.

Blechman, Barry M. 1990a. *The Politics of National Security: Congress and U.S. Defense Policy.* New York: Oxford University Press.

Blechman, Barry M. 1990b. "The New Congressional Role in Arms Control," in Thomas Mann, ed., *A Question of Balance: The President, Congress and Foreign Policy.* Washington, DC: The Brookings Institution.

Block, Lawrence and Rivkin, David B., Jr. 1990. "The Constitution in Danger: An Exchange. *The New York Review of Books.* 17 May, 50.

Blum, John M. 1980. *The Progressive Presidents: Roosevelt, Wilson, Roosevelt and Johnson.* New York: Norton.

Bohlen, Charles. 1969. *The Transformation of American Foreign Policy.* New York: Norton.

Bond, Jon and Fleisher, Richard. 1990. *The President in the Legislative Arena.* Chicago: The University of Chicago Press.

Boston University Law Review. 1970. "History and Structure: Limitations on Congressional Abilities to Make Foreign Policy." *Boston University Law Review* 50:64.

Boyan, A. Stephen, Jr. 1976. *Constitutional Aspects of Watergate: Documents and Materials.* 6 vols. Dobbs Ferry, N.Y.: Oceana Publications.

Branyan, Robert L. and Larsen, Lawrence H., eds. 1971. *The Eisenhower Administration 1953–1961: A Documentary History.* New York: Random House.

Briggs, Philip. 1991. *Making American Foreign Policy: President-Congress Relations from the Second World War to Vietnam.* Lanham, Md: University Press of America.

Brinkley, Joel. ed. 1988. *Report of the Congressional Committees Investigating the Iran-Contra Affair With the Minority Views.* Abridged ed. New York: Random House.

Brown, Everett Somerville. 1920. *The Constitutional History of the Louisiana Purchase 1803–1812.* Berkeley, Calif.: The University of California Press.

Brown, Roger H. 1971. *The Republic in Peril: 1812.* New York: Norton.

Bryce, James. 1888. *The American Commonwealth.* London: Macmillan.

Burgess, Susan. 1992. *Contest for Constitutional Authority: The Abortion and War Powers Debates.* Lawrence, Kans.: Kansas University Press.

Burgin, Eileen. 1993. "Congress and Foreign Policy: The Misperceptions," in Lawrence Dodd and Bruce Oppenheimer, *Congress Reconsidered.* 5th ed. Washington, DC: CQ Press.

Burgin, Eileen. 1991. "Representatives' Decisions on Participation in Foreign Policy Issues." *Legislative Studies Quarterly,* 16, No. 4:521.

Burke, John and Greenstein, Fred. 1989. *How Presidents Test Reality.* New York: Russell Sage Foundation.

Burns, James MacGregor. 1984. *The Power to Lead: The Crisis of the American Presidency.* New York: Simon & Schuster.

Cain, Bruce; Ferejohn, John and Fiorina, Morris. 1987. *The Personal Vote: Constituency Service and Electoral Independence.* Cambridge, Mass.: Harvard University Press.

Campbell, Karlyn Kohrs and Jamieson, Kathleen Hall. 1990. *Deeds Done in Words: Presidential Rhetoric and the Genres of Governance.* Chicago: University of Chicago Press.

Caraley, Demetrios. 1987. *The President's War Powers from the Federalists to Reagan.* New York: Academy of Political Science.

Carter, Paul. 1989. *Revolt Against Destiny: An Intellectual History of the United States.* New York: Columbia University Press.

Carter, Ralph. 1994. "Budgeting for Defense," in Paul Peterson, ed. *The President, The Congress and the Making of Foreign Policy.* Norman, Okla.: University of Oklahoma Press.

Casper, Gerald. 1976. "Constitutional Constraints on the Conduct of Foreign and Defense Policy: A Non-judicial Model." *University of Chicago Law Review* 43:463–498.

Casper, Gerhard. 1995. "Executive-Congressional Separation of Power During the Presidency of Thomas Jefferson." *Stanford Law Review* 47:473–497.

Cheever, D.S. and Haviland, H.F. 1952. *American Foreign Policy and Separation of Powers.* Cambridge, Mass.: Harvard University Press.

Cheney, Richard. 1990. "Congressional Overreaching in Foreign Policy," in Robert Goldwin and Robert Licht eds., *Foreign Policy and the Constitution*. Washington, DC: American Enterprise Institute.

Clark, Robert D., Egeland, Andrew M. Jr., and Sanford, David B. 1985. *The War Powers Resolution: Balance of War Powers in the Eighties*. Washington, D.C.: National Defense University Press.

Cochran, Bert. 1973. *Harry Truman and the Crisis Presidency*. New York: Funk & Wagnalls.

Cohen, William S. and Mitchell, George J. 1988. *Men of Zeal: A Candid Inside Story of the Iran-Contra Hearings*. New York: Viking.

Commager, Henry Steele. 1974. *The Defeat of America*. New York: Simon & Schuster.

Cooper, John M., Jr. 1983. *The Warrior and the Priest: Woodrow Wilson and Theodore Roosevelt*. Cambridge, Mass.: Harvard University Press.

Corwin, Edward S. 1984. *The President, Office and Powers, 1787–1984*. 5th rev. ed. New York: New York University Press.

Corwin, Edward S. 1978. *Edward S. Corwin's The Constitution and What it Means Today*. 14th ed., revised by Harold Chase and Craig Ducat. Princeton, N.J.: Princeton University Press.

Corwin, Edward S. 1970. *The President's Control of Foreign Relations*. New York: Johnson Reprint.

Corwin, Edward S. 1947. *Total War and the Constitution*. New York: Knopf.

Corwin, Edward S. 1913. *National Supremacy: Treaty Power vs. State Power*. New York: Henry Holt & Co.

Cox, Henry Bartholomew. 1984. *War, Foreign affairs, and Constitutional Power: 1829–1901*. Cambridge, Mass.: Ballinger.

Craig, Barbara. 1988. *Chadha: The Story of an Epic Constitutional Struggle*. New York: Oxford University Press.

Craig, Barbara. 1983. *The Legislative Veto: Congressional Control of Regulation*. Boulder, Colo.: Westview Press.

Crabb, Cecil V., Jr. 1982. *The Doctrines of American Foreign Policy, Their Meaning, Role and Future*. Baton Rouge, La: Louisiana State University Press.

Crabb, Cecil V., Jr. and Holt, Pat M. 1989. *Invitation to Struggle: Congress, the President and Foreign Policy*. 3d ed. Washington, D.C.: CQ Press.

Crovitz, L. Gordon and Rabkin, Jeremy A., eds. 1989. *The Fettered Presidency: Legal Constraints on the Executive Branch*. Washington, D.C.: American Enterprise Institute.

Curtis, Thomas and Westerfield, Donald. 1992. *Congressional Intent*. Westport, Conn.: Praeger.

Dahl, Robert A. 1950. *Congress and Foreign Policy*. New York: Norton.

Dallek, Robert. 1983. *The American Style of Foreign Policy: Cultural Politics and Foreign Affairs*. New York: Oxford University Press.

Davidson, Roger and Oleszek, Walter, eds. 1994. *Congress and Its Members*. 4th ed. Washington, DC: CQ Press.

DeConde, Alexander. 1976. *This Affair of Louisiana*. New York: Scribners.

Deese, David. 1994. *The New Politics of American Foreign Policy*. New York: St. Martin's Press.

Destler, I. M. 1994. "Delegating Trade Policy," in Paul Peterson ed. *The President, The Congress and the Making of Foreign Policy*. Norman, Okla.: The University of Oklahoma Press.

Destler, I. M. 1992. *American Trade Politics*, 2nd ed. Washington, D.C.: Institute for International Economics.

Destler, I. M. 1985. "Executive-Congressional Conflict in Foreign Policy," in Lawrence Dodd and Bruce Oppenheimer eds. *Congress Reconsidered*. 3d ed. Washington, DC: CQ Press.

Diggins, John P. 1984. *The Lost Soul of American Politics: Virtue, Self-Interest and the Foundations of Liberalism*. New York: Basic Books.

Divine, Robert. 1974. *Foreign Policy and U.S. Presidential Elections*. New York, Franklin Watts.

Dodd, Lawrence. 1991. "Congress, the Presidency and the American Experience: A Transformational Perspective," in James Thurber, ed. *Divided Democracy: Cooperation and Conflict Between the President and Congress*. Washington, DC: CQ Press.

Dodd, Lawrence and Jillson, Calvin, eds. 1994. *New Perspectives on American Politics*. Washington, DC: CQ Press.

Dodd, Lawrence and Oppenheimer, Bruce, eds. 1993. *Congress Reconsidered*, 5th ed. Washington, DC: CQ Press.

Doherty, Sean M. 1990. *Hiding Behind the Law: Congressional Deference and the War Powers Resolution of 1973*. Senior Honors Thesis, Harvard University Archives.

Dowding, Keith. 1991. *Rational Choice and Political Power*. London: Edward Elgar.

Draper, Theodore. 1991. *A Very Thin Line: The Iran-Contra Affairs*. New York: Hill and Wang.

Eagleton, Thomas F. 1974. *War and Presidential Power: A Chronicle of Congressional Surrender*. New York: Liveright.

Eastland, Terry. 1992. *Energy in the Executive: The Case for the Strong Presidency*. New York: The Free Press.

Edwards, George and Walker, Wallace, eds. 1988. *National Security and the U.S. Constitution: The Impact of the Political System*. Baltimore, Md.: The Johns Hopkins University Press.

Eisenhower, Dwight David. 1958–1961. *Public Papers of the Presidents of the United States: Dwight David Eisenhower*. Washington, D.C.: Government Printing Office.

Ellis, Richard E. 1971. *The Jeffersonian Crisis: Courts and Politics in the Young Republic*. New York: Norton.

Ellis, Richard and Wildavsky, Aaron. 1989. *Dilemmas of Presidential Leadership from Washington through Lincoln*. New Brunswick, N.J.: Transaction Press.

Ely, John Hart. 1993. *War and Responsibility: Constitutional Lessons of Vietnam and its Aftermath*. Princeton, N.J.: Princeton University Press.

Ely, John Hart. 1980. *Democracy and Distrust: A Theory of Judicial Review*. Cambridge, Mass.: Harvard University Press.

Epstein, David F. 1984. *The Political Theory of The Federalist*. Chicago: The University of Chicago Press.

Fausold, Martin and Shank, Alan. 1991. *The Constitution and the American Presidency*. Albany, N.Y.: SUNY Press.

The Federalist Papers. *The Federalist Papers: Alexander Hamilton, James Madison, John Jay*. Clinton Rossiter, ed. New York: New American Library-Mentor.

Feis, Herbert. 1960. *Between War and Peace: The Potsdam Conference*. Princeton, N.J.: Princeton University Press.

Fenno, Richard. 1978. *Home Style: House Members in their Districts.* Boston: Little, Brown.

Fenno, Richard. 1973. *Congressmen in Committees.* Boston: Little, Brown.

Ferrell, Robert. 1988. "Conducting Diplomacy," in George Edwards and Wallace Walker, eds. *National Security and the U.S. Constitution: The Impact of the Political System.* Baltimore, Md.: Johns Hopkins University Press.

Ferrell, Robert. 1983. *Harry S Truman and the Modern American Presidency.* Boston: Little, Brown.

Filler, Louis. 1983. *The Presidency in the 20th Century.* Englewood, N.J.: J. S. Ozer.

Fiorina, Morris. 1981. *Retrospective Voting in American National Elections.* New Haven, Conn.: Yale University Press.

Fiorina, Morris. 1974. *Representatives, Roll Calls, and Constituencies.* Lexington, Mass.: Heath.

Fiorina, Morris and Rohde, David, eds. 1989. *Home Style and Washington Work: Studies of Congressional Politics.* Ann Arbor, Mich.: University of Michigan Press.

Firestone, Bernard and Vogt, Robert. 1988. *Lyndon Baines Johnson and the Uses of Power.* New York: Greenwood Press.

Fisher, Louis. 1995a. "The Korean War: On What Legal Basis Did Truman Act?" *The American Journal of International Law* 89 No. 1:21–39.

Fisher, Louis. 1995b. *Presidential War Power.* Lawrence, Kans.: The University of Kansas Press.

Fisher, Louis. 1993a. "The Legislative Veto: Invalidated, it Survives." *Law and Contemporary Problems* 56:4.

Fisher, Louis. 1993b. *The Politics of Shared Power: Congress and the Executive.* 2nd ed. Washington, DC: CQ Press.

Fisher, Louis. 1991a. *Constitutional Conflicts Between Congress and the President.* 3d ed. Lawrence, Kans.: University Press of Kansas.

Fisher, Louis. 1991b. "The Constitution and Presidential Budget Powers: The Modern Era," in Martin Fausold and Alan Shank, eds. *The Constitution and the American Presidency.* Albany, N.Y.: SUNY Press.

Fisher, Louis. 1985. *Constitutional Conflicts Between Congress and the President.* Princeton, N.J.: Princeton University Press.

Fisher, Louis. 1975. *Presidential Spending Power.* Princeton, N.J.: Princeton University Press.

Ford, Paul, ed. 1905. *The Works of Thomas Jefferson.* New York: G.P. Putnam's Sons.

Franck, Thomas M. 1992. *Political Questions, Judicial Answers.* Princeton, N.J.: Princeton University Press.

Franck, Thomas M., ed. 1981. *The Tethered Presidency: Congressional Restraints on Executive Power.* New York: NYU Press.

Franck, Thomas M., and Weisband, Edward. 1979. *Foreign Policy by Congress.* New York: Oxford University Press.

Franklin, Daniel. 1991. *Extraordinary Measures: The Exercise of Prerogative Powers in the United States.* Pittsburgh, Pa.: The University of Pittsburgh Press.

Freeland, Richard M. 1972. *The Truman Doctrine and the Origins of McCarthyism.* New York: Knopf.

Friedman, Leon, ed. 1974. *United States v. Nixon: The President Before the Supreme Court.* New York: Chelsea House.

Frost, David. 1978. *"I Gave them a Sword": Behind the Scenes of the Nixon Interviews.* New York: William Morrow & Co.

Frye, Alton. 1994. "Searching for Arms Control," in Paul Peterson, ed. *The President, The Congress and the Making of Foreign Policy.* Norman, Okla.: University of Oklahoma Press.

Frye, Alton. 1975. *A Responsible Congress: The Politics of National Security.* New York: McGraw Hill.

Fulbright, J. William. 1989. *The Price of Empire.* New York: Pantheon.

Gallatin, Albert. 1847. *Peace with Mexico.* New York: Barlett & Welford.

Garthoff, Raymond. 1987. *Policy versus the Law: The Reinterpretation of the ABM Treaty.* Washington, DC: The Brookings Institution.

Genovese, Michael A. 1980. *The Supreme Court, The Constitution and Presidential Power.* Lanham, Md: University Press of America.

Gibson, Martha. 1992. *Weapons of Influence: The Legislative Veto, American Foreign Policy, and the Irony of Reform.* Boulder, Colo.: Westview Press.

Gilman, Howard. 1993. *The Constitution Besieged: The Rise and Demise of Lochner Era Police Powers Jurisprudence.* Durham, N.C.: Duke University Press.

Glennon, Michael J. 1990. *Constitutional Diplomacy.* Princeton, N.J.: Princeton University Press.

Glennon, Michael J.; Franck, Thomas M.; Cassidy, Robert C., Jr., eds. 1984. *United States Foreign Relations Law: Documents and Sources.* Vol 5. New York: Oceana Publications.

Goldman, Robert and Licht, Robert, eds. 1990. *Foreign Policy and the Constitution.* Washington, DC: American Enterprise Institute.

Goldsmith, William. 1983. *The Growth of Presidential Power.* New York: Chelsea House.

Goldsmith, William. 1974. *The Growth of Presidential Power.* New York: Chelsea House.

Gosnell, Harold F. 1980. *Truman's Crises: A Political Biography of Harry S Truman.* Westport, Conn.: Greenwood Press.

Graebner, Norman A. 1964. *Ideas and Diplomacy: Readings in the Intellectual Tradition of American Foreign Policy.* New York: Oxford University Press.

Green, David. 1987. *Shaping Political Consciousness: The Language of Politics in America from McKinley to Reagan.* Ithaca, N.Y.: Cornell University Press.

Greene, Abner. 1994. "Checks and Balances in an Era of Presidential Lawmaking." *University of Chicago Law Review* 61:1.

Hartz, Louis. 1955. *The Liberal Tradition in America.* New York: Harcourt Brace Jovanovich.

Harvard Law Review, 1983. "The International Emergency Economic Powers Act: A Congressional Attempt to Control Presidential Emergency Power," Harvard Law Review 96:1102.

Henkin, Louis. 1990. *Constitutionalism, Democracy and Foreign Affairs.* New York: Columbia University Press.

Henkin, Louis. 1976. "Is There a 'Political Question' Doctrine?" *Yale Law Journal* 85:597.

Henkin, Louis. 1975. *Foreign Affairs and the Constitution.* New York: Norton.

Henkin, Louis, Glennon, Michael, and Rogers, William. 1990. *Foreign Affairs and the United States Constitution.* Ardsley-on-Hudson, N.Y.: Transnational Publishers.

Henry, J. Buchanan, ed. 1888. *The Messages of President Buchanan.* New York: J. Buchanan Henry.

Herring, George. 1994. *LBJ and Vietnam: A Different Kind of War.* Austin, Tex.: University of Texas Press.

Hilsman, Roger with Gaughran, Laura, and Weitsman, Patricia. 1993. *The Politics of Policy Making in Defense and Foreign Affairs.* Englewood Cliffs, N.J.: Prentice Hall.

Hinckley, Barbara. 1994. *Less than Meets the Eye: Foreign Policy Making and the Myth of the Assertive Congress.* Chicago: University of Chicago Press.

Hofstadter, Richard. 1973. *The American Political Tradition and the Men Who Made It.* New York: Vintage Books.

Hunt, Michael H. 1987. *Ideology and U.S. Foreign Policy.* New Haven, Conn.: Yale University Press.

Huntington, Samuel P. 1981. *American Politics: The Promise of Disharmony.* Cambridge, Mass.: Harvard University Press.

Huntington, Samuel P. 1961. *The Common Defense: Strategic Programs in National Politics.* New York: Columbia University Press.

Jackson, Robert H. 1941. *The Struggle for Judicial Supremacy: A Study of a Crisis in American Power Politics.* New York: Random House.

Javits, Jacob K. 1973. *Who Makes War: The President Versus Congress.* New York: William Morrow.

Johnson, George W., ed. 1978. *The Nixon Presidential Press Conferences.* New York: Earl M. Coleman.

Johnson, Loch K. 1994. "Playing Hardball With the CIA," in Paul Peterson, ed. *The President, The Congress and the Making of Foreign Policy.* Norman, Okla.: University of Oklahoma Press.

Johnson, Loch K. 1991. *America as a World Power: Foreign Policy in a Constitutional Framework.* New York: McGraw Hill.

Johnson, Loch K. 1989. *America's Secret Power: The CIA in a Democratic Society.* New York: Oxford University Press.

Johnson, Loch K. 1985. *A Season of Inquiry: The Senate Intelligence Investigation.* Lexington, Ky.: The University Press of Kentucky.

Johnson, Loch K. 1984. *The Making of International Agreements: Congress Confronts the Executive.* New York: New York University Press.

Johnson, Loch K. 1980. "The U.S. Congress and the CIA: Monitoring the Dark Side of the Government." in *Legislative Studies Quarterly*, 5:477.

Johnson, Lyndon B. 1965–1970. *The Public Papers of the Presidents of the United States: Lyndon Baines Johnson.* 2 vols. Washington, D.C.: Government Printing Office.

Jones, Charles. 1994. *The Presidency in a Separated System.* Washington, DC: The Brookings Institution.

Jones, Gordon and Marini, John. 1988. *The Imperial Congress: Crisis in the Separation of Powers.* New York: Pharos Books.

Kaiser, Frederick. 1992. "Congress and the the Intelligence Community," in Roger Davidson, ed. *The Postreform Congress.* New York: St. Martin's Press.

Kamath, P.M. 1982. *Executive Privilege versus Democratic Accountability: The Special Assistant to the President for National Security Affairs, 1961–1969*, Atlantic Highlands, N.J.: Humanities Press.

Kammen, Michael, ed. 1971. *The Contrapuntal Civilization.* New York: Thomas Y. Crowell.

Kennedy, John F. 1962–1964. *The Public Papers of the Presidents of the United States: John F. Kennedy.* 2 vols. Washington, D.C.: Government Printing Office.

Kernell, Samuel. 1986. *Going Public: New Strategies of Presidential Leadership.* Washington, DC: CQ Press.

Keynes, Edward. 1982. *Undeclared War: Twilight Zone of Constitutional Power.* University Park, Pa: The Pennsylvannia State University Press.

Kiewiet, D. Roderick and McCubbins, Mathew. 1991. *The Logic of Delegation: Congressional Parties and the Appropriations Process.* Chicago: The University of Chicago Press.

King, Gary and Ragsdale, Lyn. 1988. *The Elusive Executive: Discovering Statistical Patterns in the Presidency.* Washington, DC: CQ Press.

Kingdon, John. 1984. *Agendas, Alternatives, and Public Policies.* Boston: Little, Brown.

Kingdon, John. 1981. *Congressmen's Voting Decisions.* 2d ed. New York: Harper & Row.

Koenig, Louis. 1991. "The Modern Presidency and the Constitution: Foreign Policy," in Martin Fausold and Alan Shank, eds. *The Constitution and the American Presidency.* Albany, N.Y.: SUNY Press.

Koenig, Louis. 1944. *The Presidency and the Crisis: From Poland to Pearl Harbor.* New York: King's Crown Press.

Koh, Harold Hongju. 1990. *The National Security Constitution: Sharing Power After the Iran-Contra Affair.* New Haven, Conn.: Yale University Press.

Korn, Jessica. 1996. *The Power of Separation: American Constitutionalism and the Myth of the Legislative Veto.* Princeton, N.J.: Princeton University Press.

Korn, Jessica. 1992a. "Institutional Reforms that Don't Matter: Chadha and the Legislative Veto in Jackson-Vankik." *The Harvard Journal of Legislation* 29:2.

Korn, Jessica. 1992b. "The Separation of Powers in Practice: The Limits of the Legislative Veto and the Impact of Chadha." Ph.D. Dissertation. Harvard University Archives.

Kraft, Victoria Marie. 1991. *The U.S. Constitution and Foreign Policy: Terminating the Taiwan Treaty.* Westport, Conn.: Greenwood Press.

Krinsky, Fred. 1988. *Crisis and Innovation: Constitutional Democracy in America.* New York: Basil Blackwell.

Kutler, Stanley. 1990. *The Wars of Watergate.* New York: Knopf.

LaFeber, Walter. 1989. *The American Age: United States Foreign Policy at Home and Abroad Since 1750.* New York: Norton.

LaFeber, Walter. 1988. "The Constitution and United States Foreign Policy," in David Thelen, ed., *The Constitution and American Life.* Ithaca, N.Y.: Cornell University Press.

Larson, David. 1986. *The "Cuban Crisis" of 1962: Selected Documents, Chronology and Bibliography.* Lanham, Md: University Press of America.

LeLoup, Lance and Shull, Steven. 1993. *Congress and the President: The Policy Connection.* Belmont, Calif.: Wadsworth.

Levinson, Sanford. 1995. *Responding to Imperfection: The Theory and Practice of Constitutional Amendment.* Princeton, N.J.: Princeton University Press.

Levinson, Sanford. 1988. *Constitutional Faith.* Princeton, N.J.: Princeton University Press.

Levy, Leonard W. 1988. *Original Intent and the Framers' Constitution.* New York: Macmillan.

Lindsay, James. 1994a. *Congress and the Politics of U.S. Foreign Policy.* Baltimore, Md.: Johns Hopkins University Press.

Lindsay, James. 1994b. "Congress, Foreign Policy, and the New Institutionalism." *International Studies Quarterly,* 38:281.

Lindsay, James. 1993a. "Congress and Foreign Policy: Why the Hill Matters." *Political Science Quarterly* 107, No. 4:607.

Lindsay, James. 1993b. "Congress and Diplomacy," in Randall Ripley and James Lindsay, *Congress Resurgent: Foreign and Defense Policy on Capitol Hill.* Ann Arbor: University of Michigan Press.

Link, Arthur S. ed. 1966. *The Papers of Woodrow Wilson.* Princeton, N.J.: Princeton University Press.

Lippmann, Walter. 1943. *U.S. Foreign Policy: Shield of the Republic.* Boston: Little, Brown.

Lipset, Seymour Martin. 1979. *The First New Nation: The United States in Historical and Comparative Perspective.* New York: Norton.

Loewenberg, Gerhard, Patterson, Samuel, and Jewell, Malcom, eds. 1985. *Handbook of Legislative Research.* Cambridge, Mass.: Harvard University Press.

Lofgren, Charles. 1986. *"Government From Reflection and Choice": Constitutional Essays on War, Foreign Relations and Federalism.* New York: Oxford University Press.

Lowi, Theodore J. 1985. *The Personal President: Power Invested, Promise Unfulfilled.* Ithaca, N.Y.: Cornell University Press.

Maass, Arthur. 1983. *Congress and the Common Good.* New York: Basic Books.

Maisel, Louis and Cooper, Joseph. 1977. *The Impact of the Electoral Process.* Beverly Hills, Calif.: Sage Publications.

Mann, Thomas. 1990. *A Question of Balance: The President, the Congress and Foreign Policy.* Washington, DC: The Brookings Institution.

Mansfield, Harvey C., Jr. 1989. *Taming the Prince: The Ambivalence of Modern Executive Power.* New York: The Free Press.

Marcus, Maeva. 1977. *Truman and the Steel Seizure Case: The Limits of Presidential Power.* New York: Columbia University Press.

Marks, Frederick W. 1986. *Independence on Trial: Foreign Affairs and the Making of the Constitution.* Wilmington, Del.: Scholarly Resources.

Marshall, Burke, ed. 1987. *A Workable Government?: The Constitution After 200 Years.* New York: Norton.

Martin, Fenton. 1987. *The American Presidency: A Bibliography.* Washington, DC: CQ Press.

May, Christopher N. 1989. *In the Name of War: Judicial Review and the War Powers Since 1918.* Cambridge, Mass.: Harvard University Press.

May, Ernest R. 1960. *The Ultimate Decision: The President as Commander in Chief.* New York: Braziller.

Mayhew, David. 1974. *Congress: The Electoral Connection.* New Haven, Conn.: Yale University Press.

McClosky, Herbert and Zaller, John. 1984. *The American Ethos: Public Attitudes Toward Capitalism and Democracy.* Cambridge, Mass.: Harvard University Press.

McClure, Arthur F. 1969. *The Truman Administration and the Problems of Postwar Labor, 1945–1948.* Rutherford, N.J.: Fairleigh Dickinson University Press.

McCormick, James. 1993. "Decision Making in the Foreign Affairs and Foreign

Relations Committees," in Randall Ripley and James Lindsay, eds. *Congress Resurgent: Foreign and Defense Policy on Capitol Hill.* Ann Arbor, Mich.: University of Michigan Press.

McCoy, Charles. 1960. *Polk and the Presidency.* Austin, Tex.: University of Texas Press.

McCubbins, Mathew and Page, Talbot. 1987. "A Theory of Congressional Delegation," in Mathew McCubbins and Terry Sullivan, eds. *Congress: Structure and Policy.* Cambridge: Cambridge University Press.

McDonald, Forrest. 1994. *The American Presidency: An Intellectual History.* Lawrence Kans.: University Press of Kansas.

Melnick, R. Shep. 1983. *Regulation and the Courts: The Case of the Clean Air Act.* Washington, D.C.: The Brookings Institution.

Merli, F.J., ed. 1974. *Makers of American Diplomacy: From Benjamin Franklin to Henry Kissinger.* New York: Scribners.

Mezey, Michael. 1991. "The Legislature, the Executive, and Public Policy: The Futile Quest for Congressional Power," in James Thurber, ed. *Divided Democracy: Cooperation and Conflict Between the President and Congress.* Washington, DC: CQ Press.

Milkis, Sidney and Nelson, Michael. 1994. *The American Presidency: Origins and Development.* Second edition. Washington, DC: CQ Press.

Miller, Warren and Stokes, Donald. 1963. "Constituency Influence in Congress." *American Political Science Review* 57:45–56.

Morgan, Donald G. 1966. *Congress and the Constitution: A Study of Responsibility.* Cambridge, Mass.: Harvard University Press.

Morgenthau, Hans J. 1951. *In Defense of the National Interest.* New York: Knopf.

Moyers, Bill. 1988. *The Secret Government: The Constitution in Crisis.* Washington, DC: Seven Locks Press.

Mueller, John E. 1994. *Public Opinion in the Gulf War.* Chicago: The University of Chicago Press.

Mueller, John E. 1973. *War, Presidents and Public Opinion.* New York: Wiley.

Nagel, Jack. 1975. *The Descriptive Analysis of Power.* New Haven, Conn.: Yale University Press.

Neustadt, Richard E. 1990. *Presidential Power and the Modern Presidents.* New York: Free Press.

Neustadt, Richard E. 1976. *Presidential Power: The Politics of Leadership with Reflections on Johnson and Nixon.* New York: John Wiley.

Neustadt, Richard E. 1960. *Presidential Power.* New York: John Wiley.

Neustadt, Richard E., and May, Ernest R. 1986. *Thinking in Time: The Uses of History for Decision Makers.* New York: The Free Press.

Nevins, Allan, ed. 1929. *Polk: The Diary of a President 1845–1849.* London: Longmans, Green.

Nikolaieff, George, ed. 1974. *The President and the Constitution.* New York: H. H. Wilson Co.

Nivola, Pietro. 1993. *Regulating Unfair Trade.* Washington, DC: The Brookings Institution.

Nixon, Richard M. 1978. *RN: The Memoirs of Richard Nixon.* New York: Simon & Schuster.

North, Oliver L. 1987. *Taking the Stand: The Testimony of Lieutenant Colonel Oliver L. North.* New York: Pocket Books.

O'Halloran, Sharyn. 1993. "Congress and Foreign Trade Policy," in Randall Ripley and James Lindsay eds. *Congress Resurgent: Foreign and Defense Policy on Capitol Hill.* Ann Arbor, Mich.: University of Michigan Press.

Oseth, John M. 1985. *Regulating U.S. Intelligence Operations: A Study in Definition of the National Interest.* Lexington, Ky.: The University Press of Kentucky.

Oudes, Bruce, ed. 1989. *From the President: Richard Nixon's Secret Files.* New York: Harper & Row.

Pastor, Robert. 1991. "Congress and U.S. Foreign Policy: Comparative Advantage or Disadvantage?" *The Washington Quarterly* Autumn 1991.

Pastor, Robert. 1980. *Congress and the Politics of U.S. Foreign Economic Policy.* Berkeley, Calif.: The University of California Press.

Paige, Glenn. 1968. *The Korean Decision.* New York: The Free Press.

Peterson, Mark. 1990. *Legislating Together: The White House and Capitol Hill From Eisenhower to Reagan.* Cambridge, Mass.: Harvard University Press.

Peterson, Merrill, ed. 1975. *The Portable Thomas Jefferson.* New York: Penguin.

Peterson, Paul. 1994. *The President, the Congress and the Making of Foreign Policy.* Norman, Okla.: University of Oklahoma Press.

Pfiffner, James. 1992. "The President and the Postreform Congress," in Roger Davidson, ed, *The Postreform Congress.* New York: St. Martin's Press.

Platt, Alan and Weiler, Lawrence D., eds. 1978. *Congress and Arms Control.* Boulder, Colo.: Westview Press.

Polsby, Nelson. 1986. *Congress and the Presidency.* 4th ed. Englewood Cliffs, N.J.: Prentice Hall.

Porter, Roger. 1988. "Engaging in International Trade," in George Edwards and Wallace Walker, eds. *National Security and the U.S. Constitution: The Impact of the Political System.* Baltimore, Md.: The Johns Hopkins University Press.

Quandt, William. 1986. "The Electoral Cycle and the Conduct of Foreign Policy." *Political Science Quarterly* 101:5.

Randall, J. G. 1963. *Constitutional Problems Under Lincoln.* rev. ed. Gloucester, Mass.: Peter Smith.

Ransom, Harry. 1988. "Producing Foreign Intelligence," in George Edwards and Wallace Walker, eds. *National Security and the U.S. Constitution: The Impact of the Political System.* Baltimore, Md.: The Johns Hopkins University Press.

Rehnquist, William H. 1970. "The Constitutional Issues—Administration Position." *New York University Law Review* 45 (June 1970).

Reisman, W. Michael and Baker, James E. 1992. *Regulating Covert Action.* New Haven, Conn.: Yale University Press.

Richardson, James D., ed. 1908. *A Compilation of the Messages and Papers of the Presidents: 1789–1908.* Washington, DC: Bureau of National Literature and Art.

Rieselbach, Leroy. 1994. *Congressional Reform: The Changing Modern Congress.* Washington, DC: CQ Press.

Riker, William. 1986. *The Art of Political Manipulation.* New Haven, Conn.: Yale University Press.

Ripley, Randall and Lindsay, James. eds. 1993a. *Congress Resurgent: Foreign and Defense Policy on Capitol Hill.* Ann Arbor, Mich.: University of Michigan Press.

Ripley, Randall and Lindsay, James. 1993b. "Foreign and Defense Policy in Congress: An Overview and Preview," in Randall Ripley and James Lindsay, eds. *Congress Resurgent: Foreign and Defense Policy on Capitol Hill.* Ann Arbor, Mich.: University of Michigan Press.

Ripley, Randall and Lindsay, James. 1993c. "How Congress Influences Foreign and Defense Policy," in Randall Ripley and James Lindsay, eds. *Congress Resurgent: Foreign and Defense Policy on Capitol Hill.* Ann Arbor, Mich.: University of Michigan Press.

Ripley, Randall and Lindsay, James. 1992. "Foreign and Defense Policy in Congress: A Research Agenda for the 1990s." *Legislative Studies Quarterly* 17:3.

Robinson, Donald. 1991. "The Presidency and the Future of Constitutional Government," in Martin Fausold and Alan Shank eds. *The Constitution and the American Presidency.* Albany, N.Y.: SUNY Press.

Rockman, Bert. 1994. "The New Institutionalism and the Old Institutions," in Dodd, Lawrence and Jillson, Calvin, eds. 1994. *New Perspectives on American Politics.* Washington, DC: CQ Press.

Rockman, Bert. 1985. "Legislative-Executive Relations and Legislative Oversight," in Gerhard Loewenberg, Samuel Patterson and Malcolm Jewell, eds. *Handbook of Legislative Research.* Cambridge, Mass.: Harvard University Press.

Rodgers, Daniel T. 1987. *Contested Truths: Keywords in American Politics Since Independence.* New York: Basic Books.

Roosevelt, Franklin. 1938–1950. *The Public Papers of Franklin D. Roosevelt.* New York: Macmillan.

Roosevelt, Theodore. 1914. *An Autobiography.* New York: Macmillan.

Rossiter, Clinton. 1964. *Alexander Hamilton and the Constitution.* New York: Harcourt, Brace.

Rossiter, Clinton, ed. 1961. *The Federalist Papers: Hamilton, Madison, Jay.* New York: New American Library-Mentor.

Rossiter, Clinton. 1948. *Constitutional Dictatorship: Crisis Government in the Modern Democracies.* Princeton, N.J.: Princeton University Press.

Rourke, John. 1983. *Congress and the Presidency in U.S. Foreign Policymaking: A Study of Interaction and Influence, 1945–1982.* Boulder, Colo.: Westview Press.

Russell, Bertrand. 1986. "The Forms of Power." in Steven Lukes, ed, *Power.* London: Basil Blackwell. (Reprinted from Bertrand Russell. 1938. *Power: A New Social Analysis.* London: Allen and Unwin.)

Scalia, Antonin. 1989. "Judicial Deference to Administrative Interpretations of Law." *Duke Law Journal* 1989:511.

Schlesinger, Arthur M. Jr. 1989. *The Imperial Presidency.* 2nd ed. Boston: Houghton Mifflin.

Schlesinger, Arthur M., Jr. 1986. *The Cycles of American History.* Boston: Houghton Mifflin.

Schlesinger, Arthur M. Jr. 1973. *The Imperial Presidency.* Boston: Houghton Mifflin.

Schlozman, Kay and Tierney, John. 1986. *Organized Interests and American Democracy.* New York: Harper and Row.

Schneier, Edward and Gross, Bertram. 1993. *Congress Today.* New York: St. Martin's Press.

Schoenbrod, David. 1993. *Power Without Responsibility: How Congress Abuses the People Through Delegation.* New Haven, Conn.: Yale University Press.

Schubert, Glendon A., Jr. 1957. *The Presidency in the Courts.* Minneapolis, Minn.: University of Minnesota Press.

Schurmann, Franz. 1987. *The Foreign Politics of Richard Nixon: The Grand Design.* Berkeley, Calif.: University of California Press.

Shane, Peter. 1988. *The Law of Presidential Power: Cases and Materials*. Durham, N.C.: Carolina Academic Press.

Shaw, Malcom, ed. 1987. *Roosevelt to Reagan: The Development of the Modern Presidency*. London: C. Hurst & Co.

Shell, Jonathan. 1976. *The Time of Illusion*. New York: Knopf.

Shepsle, Kenneth. 1992. "Congress is a 'They' Not an 'It': Legislative Intent as Oxymoron." *International Review of Law and Economics*, 12:239–256.

Shepsle, Kenneth. 1989. "Studying Institutions: Some Lessons from the Rational Choice Approach." *Journal of Theoretical Politics* 1:2.

Shull, Steven. 1991. *The Two Presidencies: A Quarter Century Assessment*. Chicago: Nelson-Hall.

Silbey, Joel, ed. 1991. *The First Branch of American Government: The United States Congress and its Relations to the Executive and Judiciary, 1789–1989*. Brooklyn, N.Y.: Carlson Publications.

Silverstein, Gordon. 1994a. "Judicial Enhancement of Executive Power," in Paul Peterson, ed. *The President, The Congress and the Making of Foreign Policy*. Norman, Okla.: University of Oklahoma Press.

Silverstein, Gordon. 1994b. "Statutory Interpretation and the Balance of Institutional Power." *Review of Politics* 56, No. 3 (Summer 1994).

Sinclair, Barbara. 1993. "Congressional Party Leaders and the Defense Policy Arena," in Randall Ripley and James Lindsay, eds. *Congress Resurgent: Foreign and Defense Policy on Capitol Hill*. Ann Arbor, Mich.: University of Michigan Press.

Skowronek, Stephen. 1993. *The Politics Presidents Make: Leadership from John Adams to George Bush*. Cambridge, Mass.: Harvard University Press.

Small, Norman J. 1932. *Some Presidential Interpretations of the Presidency*. Baltimore, Md.: The Johns Hopkins University Press.

Smist, Frank J., Jr. 1994. *Congress Oversees the United States Intelligence Community, 1947–1994*, 2d. ed. Knoxville, Tenn.: The University of Tennessee Press.

Smist, Frank J., Jr. 1990. *Congress Oversees the United States Intelligence Community, 1947–1989*. Knoxville, Tenn.: The University of Tennessee Press.

Smyrl, Marc. 1988. *Conflict or Codetermination?* Cambridge, Mass.: Ballinger.

Sofaer, Abraham. 1989. "Treaty Interpretation: A Comment." *University of Pennsylvannia Law Review* 137:5.

Sofaer, Abraham. 1986. "The ABM Treaty and the Strategic Defense Initiative." *Harvard Law Review* 99:8.

Sofaer, Abraham. 1976. *War, Foreign Affairs and the Constitution: The Origins*. Cambridge, Mass.: Ballinger Press.

Sorensen, Theodore. 1965. *Kennedy*. New York: Harper & Row.

Spanier, John and Uslaner, Eric. 1989. *American Foreign Policy Making and the Democratic Dilemmas*. 5th ed. Belmont, Calif.: Brooks-Cole.

Spitzer, Robert. 1993. *President and Congress: Executive Hegemony at the Crossroads of American Government*. New York: McGraw Hill.

Stebbins, Phillip. 1966. *A History of the Role of the United States Supreme Court in Foreign Policy*. Ph.D. thesis. The Ohio State University.

Stid, Daniel. 1993. *Woodrow Wilson, Responsible Government, and the Founders' Regime*. Ph.D. dissertation, Harvard University.

Stoessinger, John. 1979. *Crusaders and Pragmatists: Movers of Modern American Foreign Policy*. New York: Norton.

Stoll, Richard. 1987. "The Sound of Guns: Is There a Congressional Rally Effect After U.S. Military Action?" *American Politics Quarterly*, 15:223–237.

Strum, Phillipa. 1979. *Presidents, Power and American Democracy*. Santa Monica, Calif.; Goodyear Publishing Co.

Sundquist, James. 1981. *The Decline and Resurgence of Congress*. Washington, DC: The Brookings Institution.

Sutherland, George. 1919. *Constitutional Powers and World Affairs*. New York: Columbia University Press.

Taft, William Howard. 1916. *Our Chief Magistrate and His Powers*. New York: Columbia University Press.

Tananbaum, Duane. 1988. *The Bricker Amendment Controversy: A Test of Eisenhower's Political Leadership*. Ithaca, N.Y.: Cornell University Press.

Thelen, David ed. 1988. *The Constitution and American Life*. Ithaca, N.Y.: Cornell University Press.

Thurber, James, ed. 1991. *Divided Democracy: Cooperation and Conflict Between the President and Congress*. Washington, DC: CQ Press.

Tiefer, Charles. 1994. *The Semi-Sovereign Presidency: The Bush Administration's Strategy for Governing Without Congress*. Boulder, Colo.: Westview Press.

Tierney, John. 1993. "Interest Group Involvement in Congressional Foreign and Defense Policy," in Randall Ripley and James Linday, eds. *Congress Resurgent: Foreign and Defense Policy on Capitol Hill*. Ann Arbor, Mich.: University of Michigan Press.

Tourtellot, Arthur. 1970. *The Presidents on the Presidency*. New York: Russell & Russell.

Tower, John. 1981/82. "Congress versus the President: The Formulation and Implementation of American Foreign Policy," *Foreign Affairs*, 60, No. 2.

Treverton, Gregory. 1990. "Intelligence: Welcome to the American Government," in Thomas Mann, ed. *A Question of Balance: The President, the Congress and Foreign Policy*. Washington, DC: The Brookings Institution.

Tribe, Laurence. 1988. *American Constitutional Law*. 2d ed. Mineola, N.Y.: The Foundation Press.

Tribe, Laurence. 1985. *Constitutional Choices*. Cambridge, Mass.: Harvard University Press.

Truman, Harry S 1961–1966. *The Public Papers of the Presidents of the United States: Harry S Truman*. 1 vol. Washington, D.C.: Government Printing Office.

Truman, Harry S 1956. *Memoirs: Volume 2—Years of Trial and Hope*. Garden City, N.Y.: Doubleday.

Tugwell, Rexford. 1974. *The Presidency Reappraised*. New York: Praeger.

Tulis, Jeffrey. 1991. "The Constitutional Presidency in American Political Development," in Martin Fausold and Alan Shank, eds. *The Constitution and the American Presidency*. Albany, N.Y.: SUNY Press.

Tulis, Jeffrey. 1987. *The Rhetorical Presidency*. Princeton, N.J.: Princeton University Press.

Turner, Robert. 1991. *Repealing the War Powers Resolution: Restoring the Rule of Law in U.S. Foreign Policy*. New York: Macmillan.

United States Department of State. 1950. *Department of State Bulletin*, "Authority of the President to Repel the Attack in Korea." Department of State Memorandum of 3 July 1950

Uslaner, Eric. 1993. *The Decline of Comity in Congress.* Ann Arbor, Mich.: University of Michigan Press.

Virginia Law Review. 1975. Symposium: "Organizing the Government to Conduct Foreign Policy: The Constitutional Questions." *Virginia Law Review* 61:747.

Warburg, Gerald. 1989. *Conflict and Consensus: The Struggle Between Congress and the President Over Foreign Policymaking.* New York: Harper & Row.

Weaver, Herbert, ed. 1977. *Correspondence of James K. Polk.* Nashville, Tenn.: Vanderbilt University Press.

Weaver, R. Kent. 1986. "The Politics of Blame Avoidance." *Journal of Public Policy* 6, No. 4:371.

Weisband, Edward. 1973. *The Ideology of American Foreign Policy: A Paradigm of Lockian Liberalism.* Beverly Hills, Calif.: Sage Publications.

Weissman, Stephen. 1995. *A Culture of Deference: Congress's Failure of Leadership in Foreign Policy.* New York: Basic Books.

Westin, Alan. 1958. *The Anatomy of a Constitutional Law Case.* New York: Macmillan. (This volume was rereleased with a new introduction and conclusion by Columbia University Press in 1990).

Wilcox, F. O. 1971. *Congress, the Executive and Foreign Policy.* New York: Harper & Row.

Wildavsky, Aaron. 1966. "The Two Presidencies." *Trans-Action* 4.

Willoughby, Westel. 1929. *The Constitutional Law of the United States.* 2d ed. New York: Baker, Voorhis and Co.

Wilson, James Q. 1989. *American Government.* 4th ed. Lexington, Mass.: DC Heath.

Wilson, Woodrow. 1908. *Constitutional Government in the United States.* New York: Columbia University Press.

Wormuth, Francis D. and Firmage, Edwin B. 1989. *To Chain the Dog of War: The War Power of Congress in History and Law.* Urbana, Ill.: The University of Illinois Press.

Yergin, Daniel. 1977. *Shattered Peace: The Origins of the Cold War and the National Security State.* Boston: Houghton Mifflin.

Index